Tom Ashmore

P · O · C · K · E · T · S

ENCY C L O PEDIA

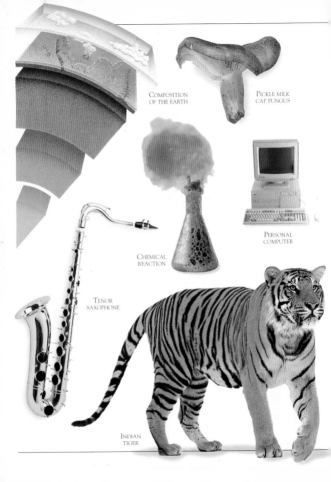

COMPOSITION
OF THE EARTH

PICKLE MILK
CAP FUNGUS

CHEMICAL
REACTION

PERSONAL
COMPUTER

TENOR
SAXOPHONE

INDIAN
TIGER

P · O · C · K · E · T · S

ENCYCLOPEDIA

Written by
JOHN FARNDON

TORNADO FIGHTER PLANE

OSCAR AWARD

VENUS FIGURINE

DK

DORLING KINDERSLEY
London • New York • Stuttgart

A DORLING KINDERSLEY BOOK

Produced for Dorling Kindersley by
PAGEOne, Cairn House, Elgiva Lane, Chesham,
Buckinghamshire HP5 2JD

Project directors	Bob Gordon, Helen Parker
Editor	Neil Kelly
Designer	Matthew Cook
DTP Designer	Chris Clark
DK team	Anna Kruger, Peter Bailey, Alastair Dougall, Sarah Crouch
Production	Ruth Cobb
Picture research	Cynthia Hole, Caroline Potts

First published in Great Britain in 1997
by Dorling Kindersley Limited
9 Henrietta Street, Covent Garden, London WC2E 8PS

A CIP catalogue record for this book is available from
the British Library.

ISBN 0 7513 5493 7

Colour reproduction by Colourscan, Singapore
Printed and bound in Italy by L.E.G.O.

CONTENTS

MANNED
MANOEUVRING
UNIT

FORMATION
OF AN
ICEBERG

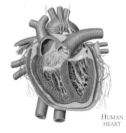

HUMAN HEART

BACTERIUM

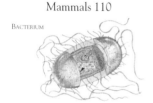

HOT-AIR
BALLOON AND
BASKET

CHEMICAL
SOLUTION

PATAGONIAN PUDU

ICE HOCKEY PLAYER

HOW TO USE THIS BOOK

These pages show you how to use the *DK Pockets Encyclopedia*. The book is divided into nine sections of photographs, cutaway artworks, fact boxes, and illustrated timelines. At the beginning of each section there is a picture page with a list of contents.

INTRODUCTION
This provides a clear overview of the subject. After reading this, you should have an idea what the pages are about.

CORNER CODING
The corners of the pages in each section are colour-coded to remind you which section you are in.

■ SPACE

■ THE EARTH

■ THE LIVING WORLD

■ THE HUMAN BODY

■ SCIENCE AND TECHNOLOGY

□ TRANSPORT

■ THE WORLD

□ PEOPLE AND SOCIETY

HISTORY

HEADING
This describes the subject of the page. This page is about crustaceans.

LABELS
For extra clarity, some pictures have labels. They may give extra information, or identify a picture when it is not obvious from the text what it is.

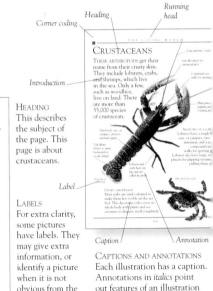

Corner coding — *Heading* — *Running head*

THE LIVING WORLD

CRUSTACEANS

THESE ARTHROPODS get their name from their crusty skin. They include lobsters, crabs, and shrimps, which live in the sea. Only a few, such as woodlice, live on land. There are more than 55,000 species of crustacean.

Introduction

Long antennae to feel

Saw-like pincers for cutting up prey

Compound eyes, stalks for spotting

Three pairs of gripping and crushing pincers

Hard body case, or carapace, protects internal organs

Tail allows lobster to swim backwards to escape danger

Lobsters and crabs have ten legs and are called decapods

ANATOMY OF A LOBSTER
Lobsters have a tough body case, or carapace, two antennae, and a pair of compound eyes on stalks for spotting prey. Lobsters also have large, muscular pincers for gripping victims and pulling them apart.

Label

CRAB CAMOUFLAGE
Most crabs are sand-coloured to make them less visible on the sea bed. This decorator crab covers its whole body with plants and sea creatures to disguise itself completely.

1 0

Caption — *Annotation*

CAPTIONS AND ANNOTATIONS
Each illustration has a caption. Annotations in *italics* point out features of an illustration and usually have leader lines.

1 2

RUNNING HEADS
These remind you
which section you
are in. The top of the
lefthand page gives
the section name.
The righthand page
gives the subject.

Country fact page

World atlas page

History timeline has a different band for each continent

Fact box

WORLD SECTION
The book includes
a countries section
with full-colour maps
of all the countries of
the world as well as
country fact pages
with essential
statistics.

VISUAL TIMELINES
Timelines on history,
space, music, art –
and many more
topics – show what
happened when.

FACT BOXES
Many pages have a fact box
containing at-a-glance
information about the subject.
This fact box gives interesting
information on crustaceans.

TWO INDEXES
There are two indexes at the back
of the book – a gazetteer index, which
lists major towns, cities, rivers, mountain
ranges, and lakes that appear on the map
pages, and an extensive subject index.

SPACE

THE UNIVERSE

FROM THE EARTH under our feet to the farthest stars, everything that exists is part of the universe. The universe is so large that it contains countless billions of stars, and it is still expanding rapidly. However, most of it consists of nothing but empty space.

LIGHT FROM A STATIONARY STAR

LIGHT FROM A MOVING STAR

LIGHT AND MOTION
If a star is moving away from Earth, its light waves are stretched out in comparison to those from other stars. The star's light becomes redder, moving towards the red end of the spectrum. This phenomenon is known as red shift.

UNIVERSE FACT

• There are an estimated 100,000 million galaxies spread throughout the universe; each of these contains approximately 1,000 million stars.

THE SCALE OF THE UNIVERSE
The universe is so vast that measurements such as kilometres and miles eventually become meaningless. A special unit called a light year is used to calculate the distances between stars and galaxies. A light year is equivalent to 9,455 billion km (5,875 billion miles), the distance that light travels in one year. The known universe spans more than 20 billion light years.

GROUND LEVEL

FLYING AT LOW ALTITUDE
1 KM
(0.6 MILES)

ORBITING AT HIGH ALTITUDE
1,000 KM
(620 MILES)

EARTH FROM SPACE
100,000 KM
(62,000 MILES)

EARTH AND MOON
1 MILLION KM
(620,000 MILES)

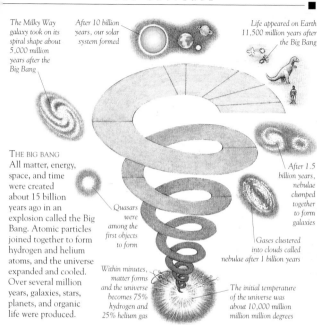

The Milky Way galaxy took on its spiral shape about 5,000 million years after the Big Bang

After 10 billion years, our solar system formed

Life appeared on Earth 11,500 million years after the Big Bang

THE BIG BANG
All matter, energy, space, and time were created about 15 billion years ago in an explosion called the Big Bang. Atomic particles joined together to form hydrogen and helium atoms, and the universe expanded and cooled. Over several million years, galaxies, stars, planets, and organic life were produced.

Quasars were among the first objects to form

After 1.5 billion years, nebulae clumped together to form galaxies

Gases clustered into clouds called nebulae after 1 billion years

Within minutes, matter forms and the universe becomes 75% hydrogen and 25% helium gas

The initial temperature of the universe was about 10,000 million million million degrees

| THE SOLAR SYSTEM 10 BILLION KM (6.2 BILLION MILES) | INTERSTELLAR SPACE 1,000 BILLION KM (620 BILLION MILES) | NEAREST STARS 100 LIGHT YEARS | MILKY WAY GALAXY 100,000 LIGHT YEARS | LOCAL GROUP OF GALAXIES 10 MILLION LIGHT YEARS | EXTENT OF THE KNOWN UNIVERSE 20 BILLION LIGHT YEARS |

GALAXIES

STARS ARE clustered together in
enormous groups called galaxies.
The galaxies were created as stars
forming from spinning clouds of
condensing gas were pulled
towards each other by gravity.
Some galaxies still rotate rapidly,
maintaining a spiral shape, while
others slow down and form ellipses
(ovals) or less regular shapes.
Large galaxies may have 1,000
billion stars, but even the smallest
contains a few hundred thousand.

DISTANT NEIGHBOUR
The Andromeda galaxy is
one of the nearest to the
Milky Way, but its light
still takes 2,200,000 years
to reach Earth. We see
the galaxy not as it is
now, but as it was
2,200,000 years ago.

FOUR TYPES OF GALAXY

ELLIPTICAL
The most common type
of galaxy, ellipticals
contain mostly old stars
and vary in shape from
ball to egg-like.

SPIRAL
These disc-shaped galaxies
are flat, with a central
nucleus of old stars.
New stars form from clouds
of gas in the spiral arms.

BARRED SPIRAL
In a third of spiral galaxies
the nucleus is elongated
into a bar. The vast spiral
arms extend from the
end of the bar.

THE MILKY WAY

The Sun is just one of 500,000 million stars in our own galaxy, the Milky Way. Ours is a spiral galaxy, with a nucleus of old stars surrounded by a halo of even older stars. All the young stars, such as the Sun, are located in the spiral arms. The galaxy is called the Milky Way because it looks like a bright, creamy band of stars stretching through space when viewed from Earth.

MILKY WAY GALAXY:
EXTERNAL SIDE VIEW

Nucleus is the brightest region of the galaxy

Galactic halo contains the oldest stars

From the side the spiral arms look like a flattened disc

MILKY WAY GALAXY:
EXTERNAL OVERHEAD VIEW

Crux–Centaurus arm

Galactic nucleus

IRREGULAR

The rarest galaxies are those that do not fit any known pattern. Some have a hint of a spiral or elliptical structure.

Location of the solar system

Orion arm (Local arm)

Sagittarius arm

STARS

A STAR is an immense globe of fiery hydrogen gas powered by nuclear reactions at its core. Stars range in size from massive supergiants to small dwarf stars. The Sun is one of billions of stars scattered throughout the universe. It is a yellow star, a typical star of average size and temperature.

Brown dwarf
1,000°C
(1,800°F)

Red dwarf
2,800°C
(5,072°F)

THE SUN

Yellow star
5,500°C
(9,900°F)

White star
10,000°C
(18,000°F)

Blue/White
star 16,000°C
(28,800°F)

Blue star
24,000°C
(43,200°F)

THE EVOLUTION OF A STAR

1 GAS CLOUD
A star begins life as material within a nebula, an enormous cloud of gas and dust. Parts of the cloud are pulled together under their own gravity, contracting into spinning balls of gas known as protostars.

2 STARBIRTH
The protostar shrinks, and its core becomes denser. Nuclear reactions begin, creating heat and light. As the star begins to shine, the leftover dust is blown away by stellar wind or forms planets around the star.

3 MAIN SEQUENCE
The major period of a star's life span is called its main sequence. During this period, the star shines steadily, radiating energy. The bigger and brighter the star, the quicker it burns hydrogen, which reduces its life span.

6 SUPERNOVA
Contraction of the star's core finally leads to a massive explosion, called a supernova. The star is as bright as a billion suns as it blows apart. The core collapses in a single second.

5 RED SUPERGIANT
The star continues to swell, swallowing up its surrounding planets. Its core fuses carbon atoms into iron but lacks energy for further contraction.

INSIDE A STAR
A star shines because of the amount of light and heat produced by the nuclear reactions taking place within it. The fusion of hydrogen atoms, creating helium, produces so much energy that the core of a star reaches millions of degrees, making the surface glow.

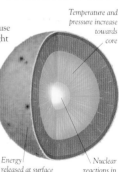

Temperature and pressure increase towards core

Energy released at surface as light and heat

Nuclear reactions in core produce energy

4 GROWING OLD
When its supply of hydrogen is exhausted, the star's core contracts, fusing helium atoms to make carbon. The star's surface gases burn, and the outer layers swell and glow red. The star is now called a red giant.

THE NORTHERN SKY

PEOPLE LIVING IN the northern hemisphere see a completely different range of stars from people in the southern hemisphere. The star pattern turns steadily through the sky as the Earth rotates, so the stars visible on any particular night depend on the latitude, time of year, and time of night.

ORION

CONSTELLATIONS

Stars viewed from Earth seem to form patterns in the sky. These patterns are known as constellations. Ancient astronomers divided the Earth's skies into 88 different constellations, each of which, such as Orion, is supposed to represent a mythological person, creature, or object.

Arcturus

PROJECTED SPHERE

This sky-map is a projection of the northern half of the celestial sphere onto a flat surface. Earth's North Pole is situated directly below the centre of the map. The stars near the centre of the sky-map are called circumpolar and can be seen throughout the year. The North Star, also known as Polaris, appears to remain directly above the North Pole.

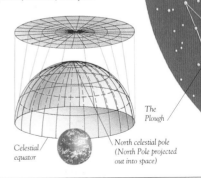

The Plough

Celestial equator

North celestial pole (North Pole projected out into space)

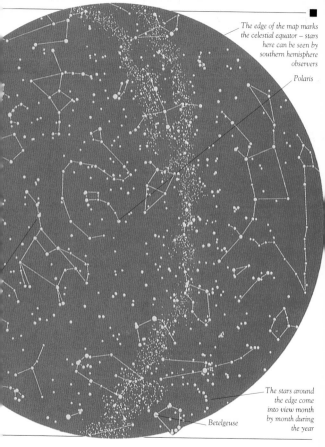

The edge of the map marks the celestial equator – stars here can be seen by southern hemisphere observers

Polaris

The stars around the edge come into view month by month during the year

Betelgeuse

2 1

THE SOUTHERN SKY

THE SOUTHERN HEMISPHERE presents a very different picture from the northern one due to the rotation of the Earth and the galaxies. The range of stars that people can see is dependent on factors such as climatic conditions, the latitude, the time of year, and the time of night.

THE CELESTIAL SPHERE

The stars viewed from Earth seem to be set on the inside of a giant sphere in the sky, called the celestial sphere. As Earth rotates on its axis and orbits around the Sun, different sections of the sphere are revealed. The motion of the planets can be plotted against the sphere.

PROJECTED SPHERE

This sky-map is a projection of the southern half of the celestial sphere onto a flat surface. The Earth's South Pole is situated directly below the centre of the map. Alpha Centauri, one of the nearest stars to the Sun, is a southern hemisphere star. The celestial equator is a projection of Earth's equator out into space.

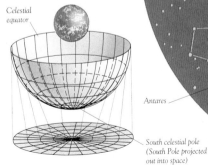

Alpha Centauri

Antares

Celestial equator

South celestial pole (South Pole projected out into space)

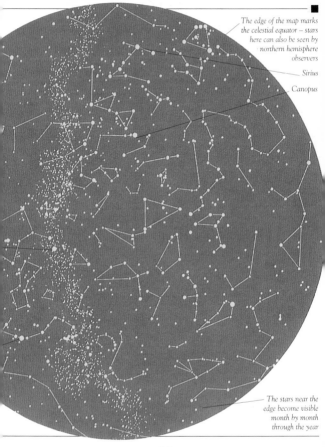

The edge of the map marks the celestial equator – stars here can also be seen by northern hemisphere observers

Sirius

Canopus

The stars near the edge become visible month by month through the year

THE SUN AND SOLAR SYSTEM

OUR SOLAR SYSTEM consists of the Sun and the many objects that orbit around it – nine planets, over 60 moons, and countless asteroids and comets. The system occupies a disc-shaped volume of space more than 12,000 million km (7,458 million miles) across. The Sun contains more than 99 per cent of the system's mass.

PLUTO

Pluto has the most eccentric orbit

NEPTUNE   URANUS

SATURN

JUPITER

The inner system (Mercury, Venus, Earth, Mars) is separated from the rest by the asteroid belt

MARS

VENUS   MERCURY

EARTH

Enlargement of the inner solar system

SPINNING IN SPACE
The whole solar system moves through space. Within the system, individual planets orbit around the rotating Sun. The planets follow elliptical paths, all moving in the same direction but at different speeds. The time taken to complete one orbit varies greatly, depending on the planet's distance from the Sun. In addition, each planet also spins on its axis.

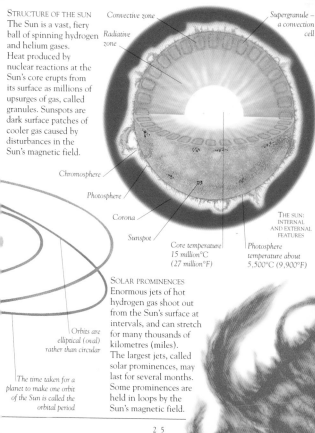

STRUCTURE OF THE SUN
The Sun is a vast, fiery
ball of spinning hydrogen
and helium gases.
Heat produced by
nuclear reactions at the
Sun's core erupts from
its surface as millions of
upsurges of gas, called
granules. Sunspots are
dark surface patches of
cooler gas caused by
disturbances in the
Sun's magnetic field.

Convective zone

Radiative
zone

Supergranule –
a convection
cell

Chromosphere

Photosphere

Corona

Sunspot

THE SUN:
INTERNAL
AND EXTERNAL
FEATURES

Core temperature
15 million°C
(27 million°F)

Photosphere
temperature about
5,500°C (9,900°F)

Orbits are
elliptical (oval)
rather than circular

The time taken for a
planet to make one orbit
of the Sun is called the
orbital period

SOLAR PROMINENCES
Enormous jets of hot
hydrogen gas shoot out
from the Sun's surface at
intervals, and can stretch
for many thousands of
kilometres (miles).
The largest jets, called
solar prominences, may
last for several months.
Some prominences are
held in loops by the
Sun's magnetic field.

2 5

THE INNER PLANETS

THE FOUR PLANETS closest to the Sun – Mercury, Venus, Earth, and Mars – are known as the inner planets. Each planet has a core of hot iron and a rocky crust, but surface conditions vary greatly.

Iron core contains 80% of the planet's mass

Silicate rock mantle

NO MOONS

MERCURY DATA

- Distance from Sun: 57.9 million km (36 million miles)

- Time taken to orbit Sun: 88 Earth days

- Diameter at equator: 4,878 km (3,031 miles)

MERCURY

A small rock world with a large, dense core, Mercury is the planet closest to the Sun. It is marked with craters, has no real atmosphere, and experiences extreme variations in surface temperature.

Daytime temperature about 430°C (806°F)

Thin rocky crust

Night temperature about –180°C (–292°F)

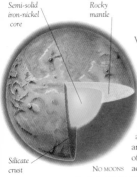

Semi-solid iron-nickel core

Rocky mantle

VENUS

The planet Venus is about the same size as Earth. Its surface is very different, however, with intense heat, crushing pressure, and unbreathable acid air. Overhead are thick clouds of sulphuric acid droplets.

Silicate crust

NO MOONS

VENUS DATA

- Distance from Sun: 108.2 million km (67.2 million miles)

- Time taken to orbit Sun: 224.7 Earth days

- Diameter at equator: 12,102 km (7,520 miles)

IMPACT CRATER FORMATION ON ROCK PLANETS

A meteorite impact blasts out a circular crater, ejecting debris.

Rock compressed by the impact forms a conical central peak.

Crater gradually filled as debris slips from walls and peak.

EARTH DATA

- Distance from Sun: 149.6 million km (93 million miles)
- Time taken to orbit Sun: 365 Earth days
- Diameter at equator: 12,756 km (7,926 miles)

1 MOON

EARTH
The third planet from the Sun, Earth, is the only planet in the solar system with liquid water and an oxygen-rich atmosphere. These two factors make it the only known planet capable of supporting life.

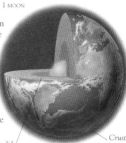

Solid rock core

Mostly solid silicate mantle

Crust of silicate rock

2 MOONS

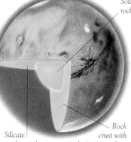

MARS
A cold, barren planet with a thin atmosphere, Mars has polar ice caps, water-carved valleys, chasms, and giant volcanoes. Its red colour is caused by iron oxide dust spread across its surface.

Silicate rock mantle

Rock crust with under ice permafrost

MARS DATA

- Distance from Sun: 227.9 million km (141.6 million miles)
- Time taken to orbit Sun: 687 Earth days
- Diameter at equator: 6,786 km (4,217 miles)

THE OUTER PLANETS

BEYOND THE ORBIT of Mars lie four giant
planets formed from liquefied
gas – Jupiter, Saturn, Uranus,
and Neptune. Farther out
still is Pluto, a small,
icy, rock planet.

*Liquid hydrogen and
helium outer mantle*

*Rock core about
twice the size
of Earth*

JUPITER DATA

• Distance from Sun:
778.3 million km
(484 million miles)

• Time taken to orbit
Sun: 12 Earth years

• Diameter at
equator: 142,984 km
(88, 849 miles)

16
MOONS

*Great
Red Spot*

JUPITER
The largest, fastest-
spinning planet, Jupiter
could contain 1,300 Earths. Composed mainly
of swirling gases, its most prominent feature is the
Great Red Spot, a rotating storm bigger than the Earth.

*Metallic
hydrogen
inner mantle*

*Metallic
hydrogen
inner mantle*

18
MOONS

*Liquid
hydrogen
outer mantle*

SATURN
The second largest planet
is Saturn, its famed ring
system made up of
tiny ice-coated rock
fragments and dust
particles. The
planet's mass is so
thinly spread that
on average it
is less dense
than
water.

*Rock
and ice
core*

SATURN DATA

• Distance from Sun:
1,427 million km
(887 million miles)

• Time taken to
orbit Sun:
29.5 Earth years

• Diameter at
equator:
20,536 km
(74,900 miles)

URANUS

The frozen methane atmosphere of Uranus gives it a blue-green appearance. The planet, and its rings and moons, are all tilted by more than 90°, travelling around the Sun on their side.

Rings of rock fragments about 1 m (39 in) across

15 MOONS

Mantle of water-ice, ammonia, and methane

Solid rock core

URANUS DATA

- Distance from Sun: 2,871 million km (1,784 million miles)
- Time taken to orbit Sun: 84 Earth years
- Diameter at equator: 51,118 km (31,764 miles)

NEPTUNE

The outermost gas giant, Neptune's atmosphere is very similar to Uranus, but thinner methane in its outer layer gives it a deeper blue colour. Huge, cyclonic storms form the planet's Great Dark Spot.

Silicate rock core

Methane, ammonia, and water-ice mantle

Great Dark Spot

8 MOONS

Dark, low clouds of hydrogen sulphide

NEPTUNE DATA

- Distance from Sun: 4,497 million km (2,794 million miles)
- Time taken to orbit Sun: 165 Earth years
- Diameter at equator: 49,528 km (30,776 miles)

PLUTO

The smallest and most distant of all the planets, Pluto is made of ice, rock, and frozen gases. Its orbit around the Sun is uniquely tilted at 17°, and for about ten per cent of its journey it is closer to the Sun than Neptune is.

Icy surface of water and methane

Thin atmosphere of methane and nitrogen

Ice mantle

1 MOON

Large rock core

PLUTO DATA

- Distance from Sun: 5,914 million km (3,675 million miles)
- Time taken to orbit Sun: 248 Earth years
- Diameter at equator: 2,284 km (1,419 miles)

EARTH'S MOON

THE MOON IS the Earth's only natural satellite,
a ball of rock held in place by our planet's gravity.
A quarter of the size of the Earth, the Moon is a dead,
waterless, and airless place. As the Earth orbits the
Sun, the Moon in turn rotates around the Earth.
Each rotation, or lunar cycle, takes
about a month.

Waning

*New
Moon*

*Full
Moon*

SUNLIGHT

Waxing

PHASES OF THE MOON
The Moon shines when
light from the Sun is reflected off the
lunar surface. As it travels around the Earth, the sunlit
area we can see changes, producing a monthly cycle of
lunar phases as it waxes (grows) from New Moon to
Full Moon and wanes (shrinks) back to New Moon.

*Asteroid
collides with
Earth*

LUNAR ORIGINS
Most astronomers
believe that a huge
asteroid collided with
Earth 4.6 billion years
ago. Vast amounts of
rock fragments thrown into
space by the impact came
together, forming the Moon.

MOON DATA

- Distance from
  Earth: 384,400 km
  (238,860 miles)

- Time to rotate on
  axis: 27.3 Earth days

- Diameter: 3,476 km
  (2,160 miles)

- Lunar temperature:
  −155°C to +105°C
  (−247°F to +221°F)

BATTERED SURFACE

Meteorite impacts scar the lunar surface with craters.

The lunar seas form from volcanic lava.

Rays of rock fan out from the rim of new craters.

3,800 million years ago
The Moon's surface receives a heavy meteorite bombardment.

2,800 million years ago
Volcanic eruptions fill the largest craters with dark lava.

Today
The surface has hardly changed apart from a few recent ray craters.

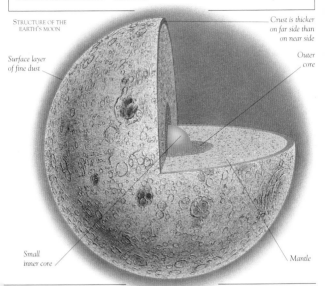

STRUCTURE OF THE EARTH'S MOON

Crust is thicker on far side than on near side

Surface layer of fine dust

Outer core

Small inner core

Mantle

ASTRONOMY

THE VISIBLE STARLIGHT magnified
by optical telescopes is only a
small part of the electromagnetic
spectrum, which includes all forms
of radiation. Astronomers learn
about the visible and invisible parts
of the universe by looking at other
types of radiation, such as radio
waves and X-rays. Space telescopes
provide the best view, collecting
information from wavelengths
usually absorbed by the atmosphere.

HIGH AND DRY
The domes of the Cerro
Tololo International
American Observatory are
sited in the Andes foothills
of Chile. A dry climate
with cloud-free nights and
a steady atmosphere makes
this an ideal location for
clear viewing through an
optical telescope.

DIFFERENT IMAGES OF THE CRAB NEBULA

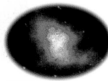

VISIBLE LIGHT
This visible light image
of the nebula has been
computer-enhanced to
show hydrogen (red)
and sulphur (blue) gas
filaments still streaming
out from the explosion.

UV LIGHT
The Crab Nebula is the
remnant of a supernova
explosion. Viewing the
ultraviolet light (UV)
produced by the explosion
reveals glowing, energetic
particles interacting with
the surrounding space.

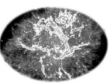

X-RAY
The X-rays emitted
by the Crab Nebula
explosion show a
bright object at the
centre of the nebula.
This pulsating star, or
pulsar, is the remains of
the pre-supernova star.

RADIO VISION

A radio telescope, like an ordinary radio set, can be tuned to pick up a particular wavelength. After measuring the intensity of the radio energy, computers are used to produce a "radio map" of the sky. Radio astronomy was responsible for the discovery of quasar galaxies and pulsar stars.

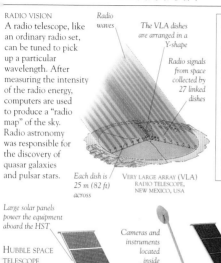

Radio waves

The VLA dishes are arranged in a Y-shape

Radio signals from space collected by 27 linked dishes

Each dish is 25 m (82 ft) across

VERY LARGE ARRAY (VLA) RADIO TELESCOPE, NEW MEXICO, USA

ASTRONOMY FACTS

• The world's largest radio telescope is at Arecibo, Puerto Rico, with a dish 305 m (1,000 ft) across.

• The largest optical telescope is the Keck Telescope, situated at Mauna Kea, Hawaii.

• The oldest existing observatory was built in South Korea in AD 72.

HUBBLE SPACE TELESCOPE

Operating outside the Earth's atmosphere, the orbiting Hubble Space Telescope (HST) can see much farther than Earth-based telescopes. Its large mirror detects very faint light, which is then directed by a secondary mirror into an onboard scientific instrument package or high-resolution camera.

Large solar panels power the equipment aboard the HST

Cameras and instruments located inside

Protective hinged cover

NASA

esa

Antenna transmits information to Earth via a communication satellite

ROCKETS AND SPACECRAFT

THE FIRST ARTIFICIAL satellite, Sputnik 1, was launched into space in 1957. Since then, hundreds of spacecraft have been launched, including manned missions of exploration, orbiting space laboratories, and probes to other planets. Powerful rocket engines enable spacecraft to escape the pull of Earth's gravity.

STAGE FLIGHT
Rockets are designed in separate stages, so that when all the fuel from a stage has been used up, that stage drops away and the next takes over. The giant three-stage Saturn V rocket carried astronauts to the Moon.

Solid fuel boosters jettisoned 2 mins 5 secs after lift-off, at an altitude of 45 km (28 miles). Shuttle now travelling at 4.5 times the speed of sound (Mach 4.5)

Shuttle reaches altitude of 130 km (81 miles) at Mach 15. External tank released, burning up in Earth's atmosphere

Shuttle engines put orbiter into circular orbit

THE SPACE SHUTTLE
The US space shuttle is the world's first reusable spacecraft. Typical shuttle missions include launching, retrieving, or repairing satellites, and performing scientific experiments. The shuttle is launched by reusable solid fuel rockets, and protected from the heat of re-entry by 32,000 carbon or silica insulating tiles.

Solid fuel burns for two minutes. Each solid fuel rocket produces the thrust of 11 Boeing 747 airliners at take-off

Main engines on orbiter take fuel from external tank. Two solid-fuel rocket boosters fire for lift-off

External tank

Orbiter

Solid-fuel boosters

SATURN V

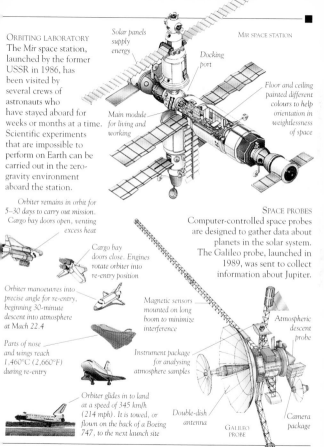

ORBITING LABORATORY

The *Mir* space station, launched by the former USSR in 1986, has been visited by several crews of astronauts who have stayed aboard for weeks or months at a time. Scientific experiments that are impossible to perform on Earth can be carried out in the zero-gravity environment aboard the station.

Solar panels supply energy

MIR SPACE STATION

Docking port

Floor and ceiling painted different colours to help orientation in weightlessness of space

Main module for living and working

Orbiter remains in orbit for 5–30 days to carry out mission. Cargo bay doors open, venting excess heat

Cargo bay doors close. Engines rotate orbiter into re-entry position

Orbiter manoeuvres into precise angle for re-entry, beginning 30-minute descent into atmosphere at Mach 22.4

Parts of nose and wings reach 1,460°C (2,660°F) during re-entry

Orbiter glides in to land at a speed of 345 km/h (214 mph). It is towed, or flown on the back of a Boeing 747, to the next launch site

SPACE PROBES

Computer-controlled space probes are designed to gather data about planets in the solar system. The Galileo probe, launched in 1989, was sent to collect information about Jupiter.

Magnetic sensors mounted on long boom to minimize interference

Atmospheric descent probe

Instrument package for analysing atmosphere samples

Double-dish antenna

Camera package

GALILEO PROBE

1926–1968

1926 US engineer Robert Goddard designs and launches first liquid fuel rocket.
1942 Wernher von Braun, later to play a major role in the post-war US space programme, develops Nazi Germany's rocket-powered *V2* flying bomb.
1957 Launch of USSR's *Sputnik 1*, the world's first artificial satellite.
1957 Russian dog Laika becomes first living creature in space aboard *Sputnik 2*.
1961 The first manned spacecraft, *Vostok 1*, carries Soviet cosmonaut Yuri Gagarin into Earth orbit.

Yuri Gagarin

1962 US probe *Mariner 2* flies past Venus, becoming first human-made object to "fly-by" another planet.
1963 First woman in space is USSR's Valentina Tereshkova, orbiting the Earth 48 times in two days in *Vostok 6*.
1965 Russian cosmonaut Alexei Leonov takes the first walk in space. US probe *Mariner 4* finds no sign of water or life on Mars.
1966 Unmanned Soviet probe *Lunar 9* lands on Moon.
1968 US astronauts enter lunar orbit in *Apollo 8*.

1969–1976

1969 US astronauts Neil Armstrong and Edwin M. Aldrin are the first humans to walk on the Moon.

Edwin M. Aldrin steps onto the lunar surface

1970 USSR's *Venera 7* lands on Venus. It is the first probe to touch down on another planet.
1970 Soviet robot *Lunokhods*, the first extra-terrestrial land vehicles, are driven across the Moon's surface.
1971 The first orbiting space station, the USSR's *Salyut 1*, is launched.
1972 *Apollo 17* is sixth and last US manned mission to the moon.
1973 Launch of *Skylab*, the first US space station. Close-up images of Jupiter taken by US *Pioneer 10*.
1974 US *Mariner 10* transmits first pictures of Mercury.
1975 First images of the surface of Venus sent by USSR's *Venera 9*.
1976 Surface tests carried out by US probe *Viking 1* confirm no life on planet Mars.

Martian surface

1977–1983

1977 US *Voyagers 1* and *2* launched on their long journey to the outer planets and beyond.
1979 US *Pioneer 11* reaches Saturn after a six-year voyage, finding a new ring and new moons.
Voyagers 1 and *2* pass Jupiter, observing active volcanoes on the moon, Io, and discovering three new moons.
1980 *Voyager 1* takes the first detailed close-up photographs of Saturn's ring systems and discovers an additional six moons.

Saturn, photographed by Voyager 1

1981 Launch of US space shuttle *Columbia*, the world's first reusable spacecraft. *Voyager 2* finds more moons around Saturn, bringing the total to 18.
1982 USSR's *Venera 13* probe approaches Venus, sending back colour photographs of the planet's surface. US astronauts Mark Lee and Judy Davis become the first married couple in space aboard the shuttle *Endeavor*.

1984–1996

1984 Manned Manoeuvring Unit (MMU) used by US astronaut Bruce McCandless to manoeuvre independently alongside space shuttle *Challenger*.

Bruce McCandless in MMU

1986 Shuttle programme halted after *Challenger* explosion kills the crew of seven. *Voyager 2* reaches Uranus and finds a ring system and 15 moons.
1988 Launch of *Columbia* resumes the US space shuttle programme.
1989 *Voyager 2* reaches Neptune and discovers six new moons.
1990 Hubble space telescope launched (with faulty mirror).
1992 US COBE (Cosmic Background Explorer) finds hotspots in "microwave background" radio energy, providing evidence for the Big Bang theory.

COBE image of microwave background

1994 Hubble telescope repaired.
1996 US scientists find fossil evidence in meteor fragments that microbes may once have existed on Mars.

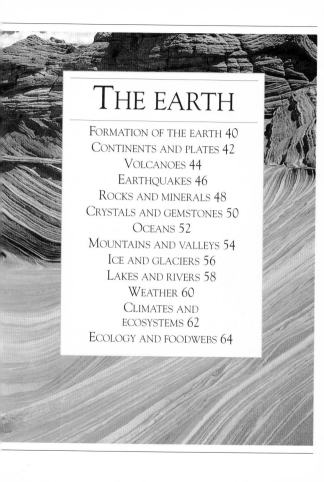

THE EARTH

FORMATION OF THE EARTH

ABOUT 4,600 MILLION years ago, the planets of the solar system were just a vast cloud of gas swirling around the newly formed Sun. The Earth and the other planets formed when parts of this cloud began to cluster together.

3 THE EARTH'S CRUST
About 4,000 million years ago, the Earth's crust began to form. Blocks of cooling, solid rock floated on a molten rock layer. The rock sometimes sank and remelted before rising again.

1 FORMING THE SUN
A spinning cloud of dust and gas contracted to form the Sun. Cooler matter from this dust cloud combined to shape the planets.

Dense cosmic gases surrounded the forming Earth

2 FORMING THE EARTH
Radioactivity in the Earth's rocks caused the planet's surface to melt. Lighter minerals floated to the surface, and heavier elements, such as iron and nickel, sank to form the Earth's core.

4 MAKING THE ATMOSPHERE
Over millions of years the Earth's crust thickened, while gases from erupting volcanoes began to form the atmosphere. Water vapour condensed to make oceans.

Sea 70.8%

Land 29.2%
PROPORTION OF LAND AND SEA

EARTH DATA

- Distance from Sun: 150 million km (93 million miles)

- Time to rotate on axis: 23 hours, 56 minutes

- Time to orbit Sun: 365 days, 6 hours

- Speed of Earth's orbits of Sun: 29.8 km/sec (18.5 miles/sec)

Crust composed of rocks similar to those on surface – 6–70 km (4–43 miles) deep

Atmosphere – about 640 km (400 miles) deep

Mantle of mostly solid rock – 2,900 km (1,800 miles) deep

COMPOSITION OF THE EARTH
Our planet is composed of several layers of rock around a core of iron and nickel. The deeper the layer, the higher the temperature.

Outer core of liquid iron, nickel, and oxygen – 2,000 km (1,240 miles) deep

Inner core of solid iron and nickel – 2,740 km (1,700 miles) deep

5 LAND FORMS
Large landmasses, or proto-continents, began to form on the planet's crust about 3,500 million years ago. Today's continents look very different.

6 THE EARTH TODAY
The planet is still changing – the huge tectonic plates (see pp. 42–43) that make up the Earth's crust are constantly moving, pulling some continents nearer and pushing others apart.

CONTINENTS AND PLATES

THE SEVEN HUGE landmasses that make up most of the Earth's surface are called continents. They are always slowly moving, shifted around by forces deep inside the Earth. This movement is known as continental drift.

The crack or boundary between two plates sliding past each other is called a transform fault

TECTONIC PLATES
The Earth's crust, or lithosphere, is made up of vast pieces of rock, called tectonic plates.

The Earth's tectonic plates fit together like pieces of a jigsaw

PLATE BOUNDARIES
Where they meet, tectonic plates may be sliding past each other, pulling apart, or colliding. These different types of motion cause earthquakes and volcanoes, create steep-sided valleys, form deep-sea trenches, and build mountains.

CONTINENTAL DRIFT

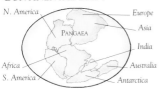

N. America — Europe
— Asia
PANGAEA
— India
Africa — — Australia
S. America — Antarctica

1 Some 220 million years ago (mya) the continents were joined together in the giant supercontinent of Pangaea (a Greek word meaning "all lands").

N. America — Asia
LAURASIA — Europe
Africa — India
GONDWANALAND — Australia
S. America — Antarctica

2 By 200 mya, Pangaea had split into two landmasses, Gondwanaland and Laurasia. Around 135 mya, these landmasses also began to divide.

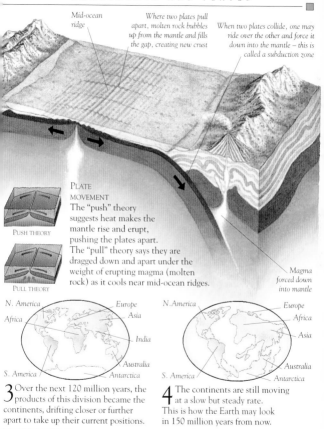

Mid-ocean ridge

Where two plates pull apart, molten rock bubbles up from the mantle and fills the gap, creating new crust

When two plates collide, one may ride over the other and force it down into the mantle – this is called a subduction zone

PLATE MOVEMENT
The "push" theory suggests heat makes the mantle rise and erupt, pushing the plates apart. The "pull" theory says they are dragged down and apart under the weight of erupting magma (molten rock) as it cools near mid-ocean ridges.

PUSH THEORY

PULL THEORY

Magma forced down into mantle

N. America   Europe
Africa   Asia
    India
    Australia
S. America   Antarctica

N. America   Europe
    Africa
    Asia
    Australia
S. America   Antarctica

3 Over the next 120 million years, the products of this division became the continents, drifting closer or further apart to take up their current positions.

4 The continents are still moving at a slow but steady rate. This is how the Earth may look in 150 million years from now.

VOLCANOES

A VOLCANIC ERUPTION takes place when hot, molten rock called magma rises up from deep inside the Earth and forces its way to the surface. The magma may erupt as a flow of red-hot lava, or explode into clouds of ash, rock, and dust.

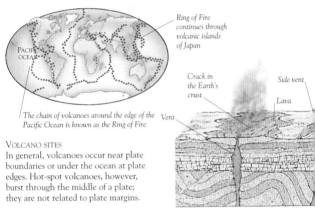

Ring of Fire continues through volcanic islands of Japan

PACIFIC OCEAN

The chain of volcanoes around the edge of the Pacific Ocean is known as the Ring of Fire

Crack in the Earth's crust

Side vent

Lava

Vent

VOLCANO SITES
In general, volcanoes occur near plate boundaries or under the ocean at plate edges. Hot-spot volcanoes, however, burst through the middle of a plate; they are not related to plate margins.

ERUPTION SIZES
The amount of ash thrown out during an eruption is a good indicator of the size of an eruption.

MT. ST. HELENS USA 1980   MT. VESUVIUS ITALY AD 79   MT. KATMAI ALASKA 1912   MT. KRAKATOA INDONESIA 1883   MT. TAMBORA INDONESIA 1815

FISSURE VOLCANO
This type of volcano is a long crack in the crust Runny lava seeps out along its length and forms a plateau.

VOLCANO FACTS
• The worst volcanic eruption was Mount Tambora, Indonesia, which killed 92,000 people in 1815.
• Kilauea, Hawaii, is the most frequently active volcano.

COMPOSITE VOLCANO

Cone-shaped volcanoes build up from hardening sticky lava. Inside are layers of thick lava and ash from previous eruptions. Gas builds up pressure inside the volcano until it erupts violently.

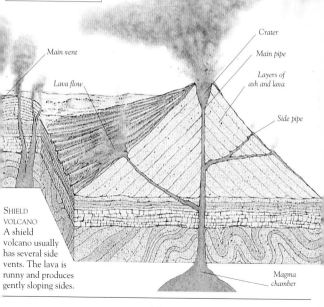

Clouds of ash, rock, and dust

Main vent

Lava flow

Crater

Main pipe

Layers of ash and lava

Side pipe

SHIELD VOLCANO

A shield volcano usually has several side vents. The lava is runny and produces gently sloping sides.

Magma chamber

EARTHQUAKES

A MAJOR EARTHQUAKE
occurs when the massive
tectonic plates that make
up the Earth's crust
suddenly move. A mild
earthquake can feel like
a truck passing; a severe
one can destroy roads and
buildings and cause the
sea to rise in huge waves.

*The focus is
usually deep
inside the
Earth*

*The earthquake is
strongest at the
epicentre*

*Shock
waves can
travel right through
the Earth to the
other side*

FOCUS
AND EPICENTRE
The point at which an
earthquake begins is the
focus. The point on the
Earth's surface directly above
the focus is the epicentre.

CLOSE-UP OF AN EARTHQUAKE
At transform faults, where two plates are
moving in opposite directions, the jagged
edges of two plates may lock
together. Stress builds up
within the plates, until
suddenly they slip,
making the ground
shake violently
as they jolt
into
a new
position.

BEFORE AN
EARTHQUAKE

AFTER AN
EARTHQUAKE

*The plates slip
and lurch past each
other, causing an
earthquake.*

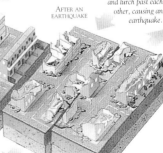

*This fault line marks
the boundary of two plates*

EARTHQUAKE FAULT ZONES

Most earthquakes occur on or near to the edges of the Earth's tectonic plates (see pp. 42–43) at cracks in the crust called faults. Deep earthquakes take place where one plate is sliding under another.

EARTHQUAKE-PROOF BUILDINGS

In earthquake-prone areas, specially designed buildings can lessen the effects of an earthquake.

Earthquake belts usually follow the edges of the Earth's tectonic plates

Many earthquakes occur on the northeast coast of Asia. This is at the boundary of two of the Earth's plates

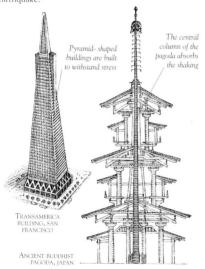

Pyramid-shaped buildings are built to withstand stress

The central column of the pagoda absorbs the shaking

TRANSAMERICA BUILDING, SAN FRANCISCO

ANCIENT BUDDHIST PAGODA, JAPAN

EARTHQUAKE FACTS

• The strongest known earthquake occurred in Colombia in 1906, with a magnitude of 8.9 on the Richter scale.

• The highest recorded number of deaths from an earthquake is 830,000, occurring in Shansi, China, in 1556.

• The worst earthquake damage on record took place in Kwanto, Japan, in 1923, destroying 375,000 homes and killing 144,000 people.

ROCKS AND MINERALS

THERE ARE MANY different types of
rock, all of which are composed of
one or more minerals. Rocks are
the building blocks from which
the Earth's crust is formed.

Earth's surface

Extrusive igneous rock   *Intrusive igneous rock*

TYPES OF ROCK

The study of rock is called
geology. All types of rock fall into
one of three categories: igneous,
sedimentary, or metamorphic.

EXTRUSIVE AND INTRUSIVE ROCKS
Igneous rock either settles within
Earth's crust (intrusive igneous rock)
or erupts from volcanoes onto the
surface (extrusive igneous rock).

METAMORPHIC ROCK
When igneous or
sedimentary rock is changed
by heat and/or pressure, it is
called metamorphic rock.

Gneiss is a metamorphic rock.

Basalt is an igneous rock.

IGNEOUS ROCK
When molten magma
rising from deep within
the Earth begins to cool
and solidify, it forms
igneous rock.

SEDIMENTARY ROCK
Wind and rainwater
deposit rock fragments as
sediments in lakes, rivers, sand
dunes, and on the sea floor. They
are compressed over millions of years
into layers of sedimentary rock.

Sandstone is a sedimentary rock.

MINERAL HARDNESS
The hardness of a mineral is
graded on a scale of 1 to 10,
devised by German mineralogist
Friedrich Mohs (1773–1839).

MOHS' SCALE

1: TALC   2: GYPSUM   3: CALCITE   4: FLUORITE

MINERALS

A mineral is a non-living substance occurring naturally in the Earth's crust. Most minerals are formed from silicates (compounds of oxygen and silicon).

Granite is composed of the minerals quartz, feldspar, and mica.

Chalcopyrite (copper ore); copper is a good conductor, widely used in the electricity industry.

ROCK-FORMING MINERALS

Different combinations of minerals form different types of rock.

ORE MINERALS

About 80 types of pure metal are extracted from ore minerals.

THE ROCK CYCLE

All rocks are constantly passing through a recycling process.

Igneous rocks are weathered away and washed into the ocean

Mineral particles sink to the sea floor where they are compacted into sedimentary rock

Rock may melt and rise to the surface where it cools to form igneous rock

Heat from molten rock changes surrounding sedimentary and igneous rock into metamorphic rock

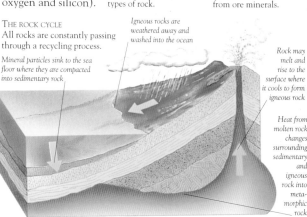

5: APATITE   6: ORTHOCLASE   7: QUARTZ   8: TOPAZ   9: CORUNDUM   10: DIAMOND

CRYSTALS AND GEMSTONES

A CRYSTAL IS a solid material in which the atoms are arranged in a regular pattern. Crystals form, or crystallize, from either molten minerals or minerals that are dissolved in liquids.

CRYSTAL HABIT

The characteristic general shape of a crystal is called its habit.

PRISMATIC;
UNIFORM
CROSS-SECTION
(BERYL)

DENDRITIC;
TREE-LIKE
SHAPE
(COPPER)

MASSIVE;
UNDEFINED
SHAPE
(LIMONITE)

ACICULAR;
NEEDLE-LIKE
(SCOLECITE)

RENIFORM;
SHAPED LIKE
KIDNEYS
(HEMATITE)

CRYSTAL SYSTEMS

The geometrical shape in which a mineral crystallizes is called its crystal system.

CUBIC SYSTEM
Every angle 90°. All three edges equal in length.

TETRAGONAL SYSTEM
Every angle 90°. Two edges equal in length.

ORTHORHOMBIC SYSTEM
Every angle 90°. No edges equal in length.

MONOCLINIC SYSTEM
Two edges meet at 90°. No edges equal in length.

HEXAGONAL SYSTEM
Edges form angles of 90° and 120°. Two equal-length edges.

TRIGONAL SYSTEM
No angles meet at 90°. All edges of equal length.

TRICLINIC SYSTEM
No edges meet at 90°. No edges equal in length.

GEMSTONES

Minerals valued for their beauty, rarity, and durability are called gemstones. There are about 100 types, the most valued including diamonds and rubies.

RUBY
HARDNESS: 9
SYSTEM: TRIGONAL/
HEXAGONAL

EMERALD
HARDNESS:
7–7.8
SYSTEM: TRIGONAL/
HEXAGONAL

DIAMOND
HARDNESS: 10
SYSTEM: CUBIC

LARGEST GEMS

• Cullinan diamond, found in South Africa, 1905. Gemstone weight: 3,106 carats (0.62 kg/1.37 lb)

• Pearl of Lao-tze, Philippines, 1934. Gemstone weight: 31,850 carats (6.37 kg /14 lb 1 oz)

ORGANIC GEMS

A gemstone that has a plant or animal origin is called an organic gem.

Spider trapped in amber, the fossilized resin of trees

AMBER

MOTHER OF PEARL

The best pearls come from oysters and mussels. Pinctada maxima is the largest pearl oyster

CARATS AND BEANS

A gemstone's weight is measured in carats: one carat = 0.2 g (0.007 oz). The term carat is the Greek word for carob seed. These were once used as weights.

CAROB SEED   1-CARAT RUBY

23.5 CARAT GOLD BAR

The purity of gold is also measured in carats

XXIII

OCEANS

MORE THAN TWO-THIRDS of the Earth's surface lies beneath the oceans. The water in these oceans is never still, and is constantly moved by currents, tides, and waves.

OCEAN CURRENTS

Major currents circulate the oceans in a clockwise direction in the northern hemisphere and anticlockwise in the southern hemisphere. Currents may be warm or cold, flowing across the surface of the ocean or deep beneath it.

Warm current (red arrow)   *Cold current (blue arrow)*

FORMATION OF THE OCEAN

1 Volcanic gases form Earth's early atmosphere.

2 Atmospheric water vapour falls as rain and collects in vast hollows.

3 Earth cools, eruptions reduce, sea level stabilizes.

FEATURES OF THE OCEAN FLOOR

Island arc

Deep-sea trenches are about 100 km (62 miles) wide and may be thousands of km long

Guyot (flat-topped seamount)

Escaping magma forms mid-ocean ridge

ISLAND ARC
Molten rock from a melting, subducted oceanic plate rises through the upper plate, forming volcanic islands.

TRENCH
Where the ocean floor sinks into the mantle, long, deep trenches occur.

WAVES

Wind blowing over the surface of the ocean causes waves. The height and power of waves depend on the strength of the wind.

Particles near the surface turn over and over

The top part of the wave, the crest, continues up the beach

The beach slows down the base of the wave

TIDES

High and low tides occur daily or twice daily. Twice each month tides are greater (spring tides) or smaller (neap tides). The tidal cycle is based on the relative positions of the Moon, Sun, and Earth.

The Earth's rotation balances the Moon's gravitational pull.

Earth spinning on its axis affects the tides.

The Moon's gravity pulls the oceans.

A seamount is an underwater volcano that rises over 1,000 m (3,280 ft)

A sediment-covered plain lying at a depth of 4,000 m (13,000 ft) is called an abyssal plain

Rivers flowing into the sea can erode submarine (underwater) canyons

Tectonic plates move apart

Magma rises to fill gap between plates

The steep incline descending from the continental shelf is called the continental slope

A continental shelf is a vast ledge of land under the sea. It can be up to 70 km (43 miles) wide

MOUNTAINS AND VALLEYS

WHEN THE EARTH'S rocky tectonic plates collide, the crust may buckle and fold, forcing up lofty mountain peaks. Volcanoes also erupt at plate boundaries and sometimes build into mountains. All are slowly weathered away, as erosion wears down peaks, carves out valleys, and opens up underground caves.

LIFE OF A MOUNTAIN

1 YOUNG
High-peaked mountains that formed in the last few million years.

2 MATURE
Eroded mountains created several hundred million years ago.

3 ANCIENT
Mountains so old and worn down that only a few hills remain.

TYPES OF MOUNTAIN

FOLD MOUNTAIN
Where two of Earth's plates collide, the rock layers buckle and bend, forcing the rocky crust up into a mountain range.

VOLCANO
Layers of volcanic lava, ash, and rock ejected from the Earth's interior build up into a mountain.

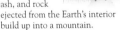

FAULT-BLOCK MOUNTAIN
When Earth's plates push together, faults or cracks appear in the crust, forcing up huge blocks of rock.

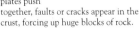

DOME MOUNTAIN
Rising magma makes the rock above bulge upwards, creating a dome-shaped mountain.

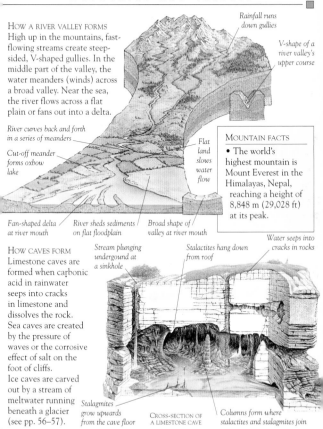

HOW A RIVER VALLEY FORMS
High up in the mountains, fast-flowing streams create steep-sided, V-shaped gullies. In the middle part of the valley, the water meanders (winds) across a broad valley. Near the sea, the river flows across a flat plain or fans out into a delta.

Rainfall runs down gullies

V-shape of a river valley's upper course

River curves back and forth in a series of meanders

Cut-off meander forms oxbow lake

Flat land slows water flow

Fan-shaped delta at river mouth

River sheds sediments on flat floodplain

Broad shape of valley at river mouth

MOUNTAIN FACTS
• The world's highest mountain is Mount Everest in the Himalayas, Nepal, reaching a height of 8,848 m (29,028 ft) at its peak.

HOW CAVES FORM
Limestone caves are formed when carbonic acid in rainwater seeps into cracks in limestone and dissolves the rock. Sea caves are created by the pressure of waves or the corrosive effect of salt on the foot of cliffs.
Ice caves are carved out by a stream of meltwater running beneath a glacier (see pp. 56–57).

Stream plunging undergound at a sinkhole

Stalactites hang down from roof

Water seeps into cracks in rocks

Stalagmites grow upwards from the cave floor

CROSS-SECTION OF A LIMESTONE CAVE

Columns form where stalactites and stalagmites join

ICE AND GLACIERS

MORE THAN ONE-TENTH of the
Earth's surface is permanently
covered with ice. At the Poles
and in high mountain
regions, vast areas are
covered by ice sheets
and rivers of ice
called glaciers.

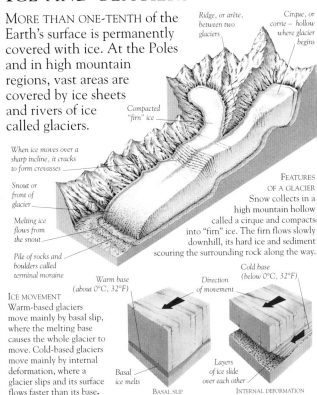

*Ridge, or arête,
between two
glaciers*

*Cirque, or
corrie – hollow
where glacier
begins*

*Compacted
"firn" ice*

*When ice moves over a
sharp incline, it cracks
to form crevasses*

*Snout or
front of
glacier*

*Melting ice
flows from
the snout*

*Pile of rocks and
boulders called
terminal moraine*

FEATURES
OF A GLACIER
Snow collects in a
high mountain hollow
called a cirque and compacts
into "firn" ice. The firn flows slowly
downhill, its hard ice and sediment
scouring the surrounding rock along the way.

*Warm base
(about 0°C, 32°F)*

*Direction
of movement*

*Cold base
(below 0°C, 32°F)*

ICE MOVEMENT
Warm-based glaciers
move mainly by basal slip,
where the melting base
causes the whole glacier to
move. Cold-based glaciers
move mainly by internal
deformation, where a
glacier slips and its surface
flows faster than its base.

*Basal
ice melts*

*Layers
of ice slide
over each other*

BASAL SLIP

INTERNAL DEFORMATION

ICEBERGS

Fragments of ice that float out to sea after breaking off ice sheets, ice caps, and glaciers are called icebergs. This process is called calving. Only 12 per cent of an iceberg is visible above the sea's surface.

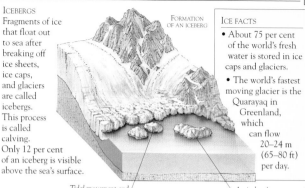

FORMATION OF AN ICEBERG

Tidal movement and buffeting by waves breaks off iceberg

An iceberg's movement is controlled by ocean currents and the wind

ICE FACTS

- About 75 per cent of the world's fresh water is stored in ice caps and glaciers.

- The world's fastest moving glacier is the Quarayaq in Greenland, which can flow 20–24 m (65–80 ft) per day.

PLEISTOCENE EPOCH – THE LAST ICE AGE

EXTENT OF ICE IN THE WORLD TODAY

ICE AGES

There have been many ice ages in Earth's history, interspersed with warmer periods called interglacials. During the most recent ice age about 30,000 years ago, ice covered much of North America and Europe.

GLACIAL DEPOSITION

The ice in a glacier is choked with rocky debris. When the ice melts, it leaves behind piles of debris (moraine), which form small mounds or hummocks.

Horn peak

Cirque with tarn

Arête

Hanging valley

Striations

U-shaped valley

Lake chains jammed with moraine

LAKES AND RIVERS

WHEN RAINWATER falls on the land, it may seep into the ground, collect in lakes, or form rivers running down to the sea. Rivers gradually mould the land, wearing down material in some places and depositing it in others.

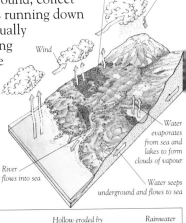

Water vapour from plants released into atmosphere

Rain and snow fall on high ground

Wind

Water evaporates from sea and lakes to form clouds of vapour

River flows into sea

Water seeps underground and flows to sea

THE WATER CYCLE
The Sun's heat causes water to evaporate from seas, lakes, and rivers. As it rises into the atmosphere, the water vapour cools and condenses into clouds. Eventually the droplets fall back to Earth as rain.

TYPES OF LAKE

Water fills depressions or hollows

Hollow eroded by glacier forms lake

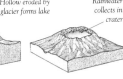

Rainwater collects in crater

KETTLE LAKE
Melting ice blocks from glaciers fill depressions in rocky glacial debris to form kettle lakes.

TARN
Circular mountain lake that forms in hollows worn by glacial erosion or blocked by ice debris.

VOLCANIC LAKE
Ancient volcanic craters fill with water, producing lakes such as Crater Lake, Oregon, USA.

SOURCES OF RIVER WATER

All rivers receive their water, either directly or indirectly, from precipitation (rainfall).

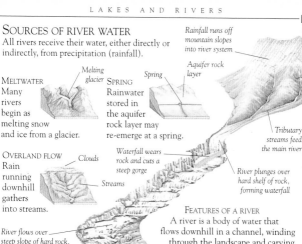

Rainfall runs off mountain slopes into river system

Aquifer rock layer

METLWATER Many rivers begin as melting snow and ice from a glacier.

Melting glacier

SPRING Rainwater stored in the aquifer rock layer may re-emerge at a spring.

Spring

Tributary streams feed the main river

OVERLAND FLOW Rain running downhill gathers into streams.

Clouds

Streams

Waterfall wears rock and cuts a steep gorge

River plunges over hard shelf of rock, forming waterfall

River flows over steep slope of hard rock, forming swirling rapids

FEATURES OF A RIVER

A river is a body of water that flows downhill in a channel, winding through the landscape and carving out deep valleys in solid rock. Rivers carry huge amounts of silt that are eventually laid down to form broad floodplains.

Meander cut off after flooding forms an oxbow lake

River cuts into bank, widening meander (loop)

Wide, flat floodplain is submerged when the river floods

Sediment deposits cause river to split into separate streams, which fan out to form a delta

Fresh riverwater meets salty seawater at estuary

RIVER FACTS

• The world's longest river is the Nile, Africa, at 6,695 km (4,160 miles) long.

• The world's highest waterfall is Angel Falls, Venezuela, at a height of 979 m (3,212 ft).

WEATHER

THE CONSTANT motion of the lower layers of the atmosphere means that air conditions are always changing, creating weather variations such as wind and rain, snow, frost, fog, and sunshine.

Trade winds

Polar easterly

Westerlies

Cold polar air

Cells of air circulate above the planet

Warm air rises, spreading over cold air

FORMATION OF CLOUDS
Clouds form when water vapour in warm air rises, cools, and condenses.

THE WORLD'S WINDS
Wind is simply air moving from areas of high pressure to areas of low pressure.

Three bands of prevailing (persistent) winds are found around the world – dry trade winds, warm westerlies, and cold polar easterlies.

Warm air containing water vapour rises.

Water vapour cools and condenses, forming clouds.

Cloud continues to form as long as warm, moist air rises.

AIR MASSES AND FRONTS
Huge bodies of air that form over continents and oceans are called air masses. They can be warm, cold, moist, or dry depending on where they form. A front is the boundary between two air masses.

Warm, moist air mass rises above cold air mass

Thin cloud

Dense, high clouds

Cold air moves over warmer air along Earth's surface

Thick rain clouds

Rain at base of front

Shallow gradient

WARM FRONT

Steep gradient

Heavy rain

COLD FRONT

TYPES OF CLOUD
Clouds are classified according to their shape and their height above the ground.

Freezing level

Cumulonimbus – giant, dark, anvil-headed thundercloud – forms at 15,000 m (49,000 ft)

Stratocumulus – white or grey lumpy cloud at top of cumulus – forms at 0–2,000 m (0–6,500 ft)

Nimbostratus – thick, grey rain cloud – forms at 0–2,000 m (0–6,500 ft)

Stratus – low-level, flat, grey sheet of misty cloud – forms at 0–2,000 m (0–6,500 ft)

Cirrus – wisps of cloud made of ice crystals – forms at 5,000–13,000 m (16,000–42,000 ft)

Cirrocumulus – rippled ice crystal cloud like fish scales – forms at 5,000–13,000 m (16,000–42,000 ft)

Altocumulus – fluffy cloud – forms at 2,000–7,000 m (6,500–23,000 ft)

Altostratus – grey or white sheet of cloud. forms at 2,000–7,000 m (6,500–23,000 ft)

Cumulus – large, white, fluffy cloud, forms at 0–2,000 m (0–6,500 ft)

TYPES OF RAIN
Most of the world's rain comes from water droplets freezing into icy particles high in a cloud. The particles grow into snowflakes, turning to raindrops as they fall. In the tropics, small raindrops join up to make bigger drops heavy enough to fall as rain.

Drops smaller than 5 mm (0.2 in) fall as drizzle

Larger raindrops

Water droplets freeze into ice crystals

Snowflakes melt inside cloud or on their way to ground

Rising air

Some rain falls without freezing

Sleet

TROPICAL RAIN

MELTED SNOW

CLIMATES AND ECOSYSTEMS

THE TYPICAL LONG-TERM weather conditions of an area are referred to as its climate. A region's climate varies according to its distance from the Equator and the sea, and its height above sea level. The interacting range of plants and animals within a climate is called an ecosystem.

MAP OF WORLD CLIMATE ZONES

TYPES OF CLIMATE
The world's climates are split into three broad zones: tropical, temperate, and polar. The farther from the Equator and above sea level a zone lies, the colder the climate. The farther from the sea it is, the more extreme its winters and summers.

KEY TO CLIMATE ZONES
- Polar
- Taiga
- Mountain
- Temperate
- Tropical rainforest
- Hot desert

HOT DESERT
Few species can survive in desert climates. Temperatures can exceed 38°C (100°F) and it may not rain for several years.

TROPICAL RAINFOREST
Heavy rain and high temperatures all year round make rainforests the world's richest plant and animal habitats.

POLAR AND TUNDRA

In the polar regions, temperatures rarely rise above freezing for more than a few months of the year. Fresh water is permanently frozen, and so plants cannot grow. The cold, dry land bordering the ice caps is known as the tundra.

CLIMATES AND ECOSYSTEMS FACTS

• The highest recorded temperature, taken at al'Aziziyah, Libya, measured 58°C (136°F).

• The coldest inhabited place is Oymyakon, Siberia, with a temperature of –68°C (–90°F).

TAIGA (COLD TEMPERATE)

The vast coniferous forest called the Taiga stretches across Canada, Scandinavia, and the Russian Federation. Six months of the year are dark, with temperatures below 0°C (32°F).

TEMPERATE

Winters are cool and summers warm in temperate climates, with many plants and trees becoming dormant in winter.

MOUNTAIN REGIONS

Low temperatures stop most vegetation growing on mountain peaks, but trees and plants thrive on the lower slopes.

ECOLOGY AND FOOD WEBS

THE LIVING WORLD is built on complex relationships
between plants, animals, and the places they inhabit.
Ecology is the study of these relationships and
how communities of living things interact
with their habitats.

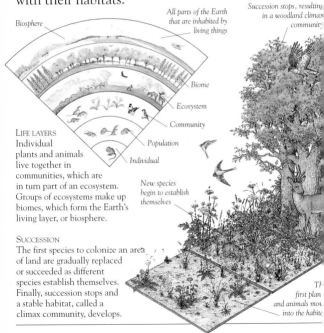

Biosphere

*All parts of the Earth
that are inhabited by
living things*

*Succession stops, resulting
in a woodland clima*
communit

Biome

Ecosystem

Community

Population

Individual

LIFE LAYERS
Individual
plants and animals
live together in
communities, which are
in turn part of an ecosystem.
Groups of ecosystems make up
biomes, which form the Earth's
living layer, or biosphere.

*New species
begin to establish
themselves*

SUCCESSION
The first species to colonize an area
of land are gradually replaced
or succeeded as different
species establish themselves.
Finally, succession stops and
a stable habitat, called a
climax community, develops.

*Th
first plan
and animals mo
into the habit*

FOOD WEBS

Some organisms within an ecosystem may feed off each other. In a salt marsh, for example, shrews feed on snails, and marsh hawks feed on shrews. This series of feeding links is called a food chain. Each species is involved in a number of chains, and these chains link up to form interconnecting food webs.

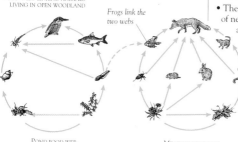

FOOD WEBS LINKING ANIMALS LIVING IN OPEN WOODLAND

Frogs link the two webs

Arrows link food source to consumer

POND FOOD WEB   MEADOW FOOD WEB

ECOLOGY FACTS

• The Earth's biosphere stretches from the ocean depths to about 15 km (9 miles) up into the atmosphere.

• The composition of nearly all plants and animals, including humans, is 75% water.

FEEDING LEVELS

In most food chains there are various stages or trophic levels.

SUN   CABBAGE   CATERPILLAR   THRUSH   FUNGI

Producers
Green plants use sunlight to make their own food.

Primary consumer
Herbivores such as caterpillars eat producers.

Secondary consumer
Carnivores eat herbivores and other carnivores.

Decomposer
Fungi and bacteria decompose dead organisms.

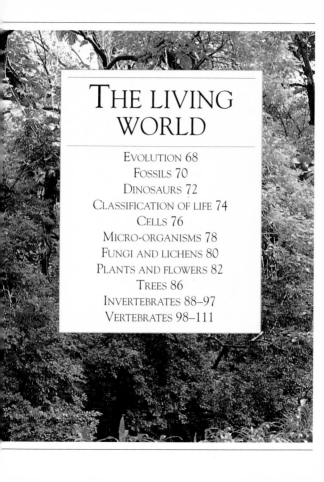

THE LIVING WORLD

EVOLUTION

SINCE LIFE appeared 3.8 billion years ago, millions of different creatures have come and gone. As habitats changed, some species survived by adapting, while others died out quickly. This gradual turnover of species is called evolution.

PORPOISE'S
FRONT
FLIPPER

"Finger"
bones form a
powerful flipper
for swimming

Two sets of short
"arm" bones

Two sets of long
bones make up
the arm

Five sets of finger
bones make up
hand

HUMAN
ARM

ADAPTATION
Evolution works by slowly adapting existing features to suit different purposes. Although they look very different, humans and porpoises both have two "arm" bones and five "finger" bones.

LIFE FORMS
THROUGH THE AGES
By working out when certain rocks formed, and then studying the fossils found in them, paleontologists – who study the life forms of the past – have built up a remarkable picture of the way species have changed since the dawn of the Cambrian period 590 million years ago. Little is known of Precambrian life forms because very few fossils remain.

PRECAMBRIAN	PALEOZOIC	
	Cambrian	Ordovician
4600–590 mya Single-celled life forms, such as bacteria and algae, appear, then soft multi-celled life forms, such as worms and jellyfish.	590–505 mya No life on land. Invertebrates flourish in the seas. First molluscs and trilobites.	505–438 mya First crustaceans and early jawless fish appear. Coral reefs form. Sahara glaciated.

HOW EVOLUTION WORKS

According to Darwin's theory of evolution, animals and plants developed over millions of years, surviving according to their ability to adapt to a changing environment. Darwin's theory challenged the accepted 19th-century view that life forms did not change after being created by a deity (god).

CHARLES DARWIN (1809–1882)

The theory of evolution was developed by English naturalist Charles Darwin after studying the animals of the Galápagos Islands. He published his findings in 1859 in his book *On the Origin of Species*.

EVOLUTION OF THE HORSE

Eohippus
This hare-sized creature browsed in woodland.

Mesohippus
Over millions of years, Eohippus evolved into a larger grazing animal.

Merychippus
As early horses adapted to the grasslands, they developed longer limbs to escape from predators.

Modern horse
The horses of today are highly developed grazers, with long legs for running and keen senses.

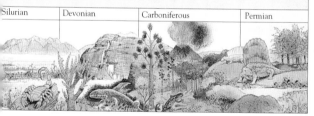

Silurian	Devonian	Carboniferous	Permian
438–408 mya First jawed fish. Huge sea scorpions hunt in the sea. Small land plants colonize the shore.	408–355 mya Age of sharks and fish. Insects and amphibians appear on land. Giant ferns form forests.	355–290 mya Warm swampy forests leave remains that will turn to coal. First reptiles.	290–250 mya Reptiles diversify, conifers replace tree ferns. Mass extinction as Earth turns cold.

FOSSILS

THE REMAINS of living things
preserved naturally, often for many
millions of years, are called fossils.
Most fossils are formed in rocks;
however, remains can also be
preserved in ice, tar, peat, and
amber. Fossils tell us nearly all
we know about the history
of life on Earth.

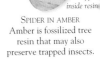

Spider
trapped
inside resin

SPIDER IN AMBER
Amber is fossilized tree
resin that may also
preserve trapped insects.

AMMONITES
BECAME
EXTINCT 65 MYA

KINDS OF FOSSIL
Most fossils form on the sea bed, so shells and sea
creatures are the most common. Fossils of land
animals and plants are more rare. Footprints,
burrows, or droppings may also be preserved.

Fossilized
shell

MESOZOIC			CENOZOIC	
Triassic	Jurassic	Cretaceous	Tertiary	
			Palaeocene	Eocene

250–205 mya *Mammals and* *dinosaurs appear.* *The climate warms* *and seed-bearing* *plants dominate.*	*205–135 mya* *The age of the* *dinosaurs. The* *first known bird,* *Archaeopteryx,* *appears.*	*135–66 mya* *First flowering* *plants. Period* *ends with a mass* *extinction that* *wipes out dinosaurs.*	*66–53 mya* *Warm, humid* *climate. Mammals,* *insects, and* *flowering plants* *flourish.*	*53–36 mya* *Mammals* *grow larger* *and diversify.* *Primates* *evolve.*

1 ANIMAL DIES
The body of a dead animal lies decaying on the surface of the land.

2 REMAINS SINK
Gradually, the body becomes covered with sand or mud.

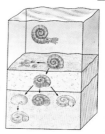

FOSSILIZATION AT SEA
Dead organisms sink to the sea bed and are buried. As the sediment turns to rock, their remains are either chemically altered or dissolve to leave a cavity, which may fill with minerals to form a cast.

3 BONES ALTER
Over time, the bones are altered, and the sand and mud turn to rock.

4 FOSSIL IS EXPOSED
Eventually, weather and erosion expose the fossil at the surface.

Oligocene	Miocene	Pliocene	Quaternary	
			Pleistocene	Holocene

36–23 mya
First human-like creatures appear. Hunting birds thrive. Some mammals die out.

23–6.3 mya
Climate cools, and forests shrink. Deer-like hoofed mammals flourish. First hominids.

6.3–1.6 mya
Cold and dry. Mammals reach maximum diversity. Many modern mammals appear.

1.6m–10,000 ya
Ice Ages. Homo sapiens evolves. Mammoths and sabre-toothed tigers die out.

10,000 ya to present
Humans develop agriculture and technology. Human activity threatens many species.

DINOSAURS

FOR 150 MILLION YEARS the Earth was dominated by giant reptiles called dinosaurs, including *Seismosaurus*, the largest creature ever to walk on land. Then, 65 million years ago, all the dinosaurs mysteriously died out.

Light bones for flying

Wings of skin

Furry body

PTEROSAUR
While dinosaurs ruled the land, giant reptiles, like Pterosaur, flew in the air.

DINOSAUR GROUPS
Scientists divide dinosaurs into two orders according to the arrangement of their hip bones. Saurischians have lizard-like hips and include both plant and meat-eaters. Ornithischians have bird-like hips and are all plant eaters. The two orders are divided into five subgroups.

Muscular tail balanced the front of the body

Long neck for browsing in treetops

Ruff

Horn

SALTASAURUS

STYRACOSAURUS

Sauropods (Saurischians) were huge, long-necked four-legged plant eaters.

Marginocephalians (Saurischians) had a bony ruff and horns for self-defence.

TYRANNOSAURUS

STEGOSAURUS

CORYTHOSAURUS

Thyreophorans (Ornithischians) were spiny-backed plant eaters.

Theropods (Saurischians) were two-legged meat-eaters.

Ornithopods (Ornithischians) had a horny beak and bird-like feet

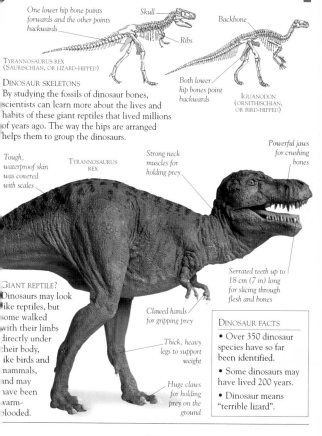

One lower hip bone points
forwards and the other points
backwards

Skull

Backbone

TYRANNOSAURUS REX
(SAURISCHIAN, OR LIZARD-HIPPED)

Ribs

Both lower
hip bones point
backwards

IGUANODON
(ORNITHISCHIAN,
OR BIRD-HIPPED)

DINOSAUR SKELETONS

By studying the fossils of dinosaur bones,
scientists can learn more about the lives and
habits of these giant reptiles that lived millions
of years ago. The way the hips are arranged
helps them to group the dinosaurs.

Tough,
waterproof skin
was covered
with scales

TYRANNOSAURUS
REX

Strong neck
muscles for
holding prey

Powerful jaws
for crushing
bones

Serrated teeth up to
18 cm (7 in) long
for slicing through
flesh and bones

Clawed hands
for gripping prey

GIANT REPTILE?

Dinosaurs may look
like reptiles, but
some walked
with their limbs
directly under
their body,
like birds and
mammals,
and may
have been
warm-
blooded.

Thick, heavy
legs to support
weight

Huge claws
for holding
prey on the
ground

DINOSAUR FACTS

• Over 350 dinosaur
species have so far
been identified.

• Some dinosaurs may
have lived 200 years.

• Dinosaur means
"terrible lizard".

CLASSIFICATION OF LIFE

THE NATURAL WORLD contains
millions of living things, which
can be classified according to the
features they have in common.
The largest groups are the five
kingdoms: animals, plants, fungi,
protists, and monerans.

ALGAE

PROTOZOA

MONERANS
These simple
single-celled organisms,
such as bacteria, are
visible only under a
microscope. They were
the first life forms and
there are now around
4,000 species.

BACTERIA

PROTISTS
Complex single-celled
organisms, such as protozoa
and amoebas, are called
protists. Protozoa are like
animals. Algae are like
plants. There are over
50,000 protist species.

THE PANTHER

COMMON OYSTER MUSHROOM

MEADOW
CORAL
FUNGUS

CURLY-HAIRED ELF CUP

FUNGI
Fungi often look like plants
but have no leaves and
absorb food from other living
or dead matter. There are
about 100,000 species.

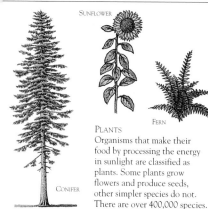

SUNFLOWER

FERN

CONIFER

PLANTS

Organisms that make their food by processing the energy in sunlight are classified as plants. Some plants grow flowers and produce seeds, other simpler species do not. There are over 400,000 species.

CLASSIFICATION

Each kingdom is divided into smaller and smaller groups according to its characteristics. This is how a serval (*Felis serval*) would be classified.

Kingdom
Animal (Animalia)
Many-celled, must find food

Phylum
Chordate (Chordata)
Single nerve cord during life

Class
Mammal (Mammalia)
Suckles young

Order
Carnivores (Carnivora)
Adapted to hunting

Family
Cats (Felidae)
Sharp, retractable claws

Genus
(*Felis*)
Short tail, tufted ears

Species
serval
(*Felis serval*)

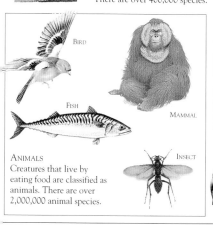

BIRD

MAMMAL

FISH

INSECT

ANIMALS

Creatures that live by eating food are classified as animals. There are over 2,000,000 animal species.

FELIS SERVAL

CELLS

ALL LIVING THINGS are made up
of tiny, self-contained units called
cells, usually so small that they are
visible only under a microscope.
A cell takes in energy and uses
it to grow and reproduce. Some
organisms consist of just a single
cell, others have billions.

EGG CELL
Cells vary in size from
minute fractions of a
millimetre to eggs, which
are the largest cells of all.

ANIMAL CELL
An animal cell is a tiny jelly-filled
sac with a soft and flexible
skin or membrane.
Different kinds
of cell, such as
blood cells and
skin cells, perform
different tasks in
the body. Inside
each cell are
organelles that
control and
run the cell.

*Vacuoles are used
to store fats*

*The nucleus is the control
centre of the cell, and
contains the cell's
instructions in the
form of DNA*

*Endoplasmic
reticulum is
the cell's
warehouse
and factory,
making and
storing vital
substances*

*Ribosomes are
tiny granules
scattered through
the cell that
make proteins*

*Mitochondria are
organelles that act like
the cell's power stations,
breaking down food
to release energy*

*The cytoplasm is
the jelly-like fluid
that fills the cell*

*The Golgi body is the
cell's distribution centre,
packaging and transporting
chemicals made in the cell*

*Plasma membrane
holds cell together and
filters materials
passing in and out*

PLANT CELL

The features of a plant cell are very similar to those of an animal cell, but plant cells are enclosed in a rigid shell of cellulose. They also have organelles called chloroplasts, made bright green by a pigment called chlorophyll. Chloroplasts are like solar batteries, enabling plants to trap energy from the sun in a process called photosynthesis.

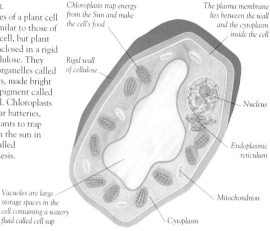

Chloroplasts trap energy from the Sun and make the cell's food

The plasma membrane lies between the wall and the cytoplasm inside the cell

Rigid wall of cellulose

Nucleus

Endoplasmic reticulum

Mitochondrion

Vacuoles are large storage spaces in the cell containing a watery fluid called cell sap

Cytoplasm

CELL DIVISION

Living cells multiply by splitting in two again and again. This is how worn-out cells are replaced and plants and animals grow. To ensure that the chromosomes (the cell's life plan) are passed on to each new cell equally, most cells divide by a complex process called mitosis.

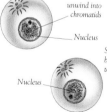

Chromosomes unwind into chromatids

Nucleus

Chromatids prepare to split

Spindle begins to form

Nucleus

Two genetically identical cells prepare to divide.

The old nucleus disintegrates and the spindle pulls equal numbers of chromatids to opposite ends of the cell to form two new nuclei. The cytoplasm then divides to form two new, identical cells.

MICRO-ORGANISMS

THE MOST NUMEROUS living things in the world are usually too small to see except under a microscope. These micro-organisms, including bacteria and protozoa, are everywhere – there are 100,000 billion in your body alone. All are made of just a single cell.

A tough, slimy capsule protects the cell wall

Long, hair-lik[e] flagella on som[e] bacteria whi[p] from side t[o] side to mov[e] the cell alon[g]

Cell wall

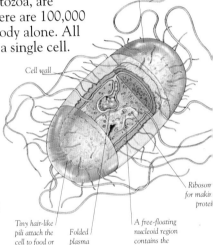

BACTERIA
The most abundant living things on Earth, and among the most ancient, bacteria live everywhere from the upper atmosphere to the ocean depths. Many feed on dead matter and help to recycle nutrients. Others, called germs, feed on living things and cause disease. Bacteria cells are prokaryotic, which means they have no nucleus.

Ribosom[es] for makin[g] protein[s]

Tiny hair-like pili attach the cell to food or other cells

Folded plasma membrane

A free-floating nucleoid region contains the bacteria's instructions

COCCUS

BACILLUS

SPIRILLUM

BACTERIA SHAPES
Bacteria may be classified by shape – coccus (round), bacillus (rod-shaped), or spirillum (coiled).

PROTOZOA

Like bacteria, protozoa are single-celled organisms, but they have a nucleus and grow much bigger. They live in damp habitats, like soil, ponds, and oceans. Amoebae are protozoans with no fixed shape. They move by changing shape, and feed by engulfing food. Some live in water and soil. Others are parasites living inside plants and animals.

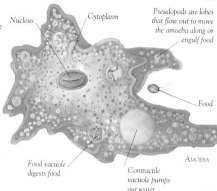

Nucleus

Cytoplasm

Pseudopods are lobes that flow out to move the amoeba along or engulf food

Food

Food vacuole digests food

Contractile vacuole pumps out water

AMOEBA

INFLUENZA VIRUSES SEEN THROUGH AN ELECTRON MICROSCOPE

VIRUSES

A virus is a tiny package of chemicals coated with protein. It is not a living organism – it must invade a living host to reproduce itself.

USEFUL BACTERIA

Bacteria play a vital role in breaking down dead matter and recycling nutrients, helping us digest food. Bacteria are important in the production of many foods such as cheese, yoghurt, vinegar, and beer.

YOGHURT

CHEESE

VINEGAR

MICRO-ORGANISM FACTS

• One gram of soil may contain 150,000 protozoa.

• There may be 800 bacteria per square millimetre of human armpit.

• The largest protozoa (now extinct) grew to 20 cm (7.9 in) across.

• Viruses can be seen only under an electron microscope.

FUNGI AND LICHENS

MUSHROOMS, toadstools, mildew, and mould are all kinds of fungi. Like plants, fungi often grow in soil, but they cannot make food from sunlight. Instead they absorb chemicals from living and dead plants and animals, dung, and other organic material.

FUNGUS VARIETY
There are fungi of all shapes and sizes. Some are good to eat, but many are so poisonous they can kill.

FUNGUS STRUCTURE
The stalk and head of the toadstool are the fungi's "fruiting body", which releases tiny, seed-like spores. Wherever these spores land, they send out new hyphae (threads).

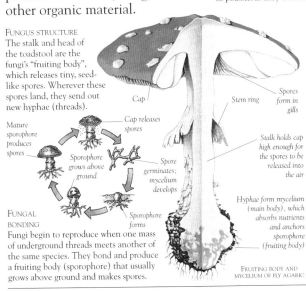

Cap

Mature sporophore produces spores

Cap releases spores

Sporophore grows above ground

Spore germinates; mycelium develops

Sporophore forms

FUNGAL BONDING
Fungi begin to reproduce when one mass of underground threads meets another of the same species. They bond and produce a fruiting body (sporophore) that usually grows above ground and makes spores.

Spores form in gills

Stem ring

Stalk holds cap high enough for the spores to be released into the air

Hyphae form mycelium (main body), which absorbs nutrients and anchors sporophore (fruiting body)

FRUITING BODY AND MYCELIUM OF FLY AGARIC

BRACKET FUNGI
Instead of growing in soil, some fungi grow in tiers on dead or dying trees and logs. Knowing which types of wood attract which types of fungus makes it easier to identify different fungus species.

Fruiting bodies grow in tiers on dead wood

LICHENS

STRUCTURE
Lichens are a partnership between fungi and algae, a bit like a sandwich, with fungal "bread" and algal "filling". The green algae trap sunlight to make food to feed the fungi, which in turn protect the algae and retain water.

Lichens attach themselves to stones or wood. They eventually break down rocks and help to form soil.

FOLIOSE
(*Hypogymnia physodes*)

The many species of lichen grow in five distinct ways. Three are shown here.

FRUTICOSE (*Cladonia portentosa*)

SQUAMULOSE
(*Cladonia floerkeana*)

PLANTS

PLANTS make their own food
out of water, air, and sunlight.
This makes them the starting
point of most food chains, and
most other living organisms
depend on them for food.
Plants have adapted to the
most extreme habitats, from hot
desert to icy tundra.

Seeds
ripen

Seeds germinates
leaves and
roots
grow

Seed

Ova is
pollinated

Plant
grows

SEXUAL REPRODUCTION
Many plants reproduce by
ova being fertilized by pollen,
whether from the same flower
or plant or a different one.
This is sexual reproduction.

ASEXUAL REPRODUCTION
Many plants can
reproduce without
pollination or
fertilization taking
place. This is called
asexual reproduction.

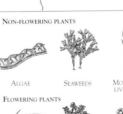

Parent
plant

Runner

New plant
develop from tip of
underground
runner

STRAWBERRY PLANT

TYPES OF PLANT
The earliest plants
on Earth did not have
flowers or produce seeds.
Simple plants like this
still exist, but now they
share the Earth with
their flowering relatives.
Plants come in all
shapes and sizes, from
tiny algae to grasses
and giant trees.

NON-FLOWERING PLANTS

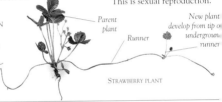

ALGAE

SEAWEEDS

MOSSES AND
LIVERWORTS

FERNS

FLOWERING PLANTS

GRASSES

SHRUBS

HERBS

TREES

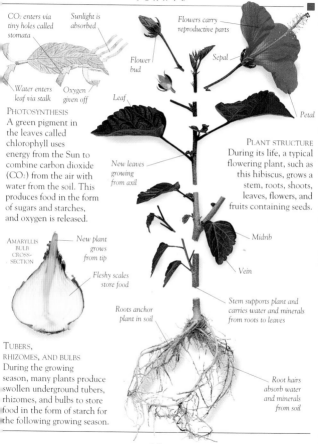

CO₂ enters via tiny holes called stomata

Sunlight is absorbed

Flowers carry reproductive parts

Flower bud

Sepal

Water enters leaf via stalk

Oxygen given off

Leaf

Petal

PHOTOSYNTHESIS
A green pigment in the leaves called chlorophyll uses energy from the Sun to combine carbon dioxide (CO_2) from the air with water from the soil. This produces food in the form of sugars and starches, and oxygen is released.

New leaves growing from axil

PLANT STRUCTURE
During its life, a typical flowering plant, such as this hibiscus, grows a stem, roots, shoots, leaves, flowers, and fruits containing seeds.

AMARYLLIS BULB CROSS-SECTION

New plant grows from tip

Fleshy scales store food

Midrib

Vein

TUBERS, RHIZOMES, AND BULBS
During the growing season, many plants produce swollen underground tubers, rhizomes, and bulbs to store food in the form of starch for the following growing season.

Roots anchor plant in soil

Stem supports plant and carries water and minerals from roots to leaves

Root hairs absorb water and minerals from soil

8 3

FLOWERS AND FRUITS

FLOWERS help ensure that a
plant is pollinated so that it can
produce seeds and fruit. A fruit is
anything that contains a seed or
seeds, from a coconut to a tomato.

Tough,
bumpy
surface

POLLEN GRAIN
Microscopic pollen grains,
which look like orange
dust, are produced by a
flower's anthers. A plant
is fertilized when a single
grain lands on the stigma
of the same type of flower.

FLOWER PARTS
The reproductive organs of a flowering
plant are found within the flower.
The flowerheads of some plants
have a stamen (male parts) and a pistil
(female), while in others they are
separate.

Filament

Anther – pollen is made in
pollen sacs inside anther, which
split open when ripe to release
the pollen

Stigma – sticky
head for trapping
pollen

Stamens – the
male parts of the
flower that consist
of an anther and
a filament

Style carries
pollen from the
stigma to the
ovary

Pistil – female
parts of the flower
consisting of an
ovary, stigma,
and style

Ovary – where
the ova (eggs)
are made.
Once the
ova are
fertilized,
the ovary
swells to
become
a fruit

Sepal – protects
flower when it
is in bud

Petal –
guides insects
to anthers
and stigma

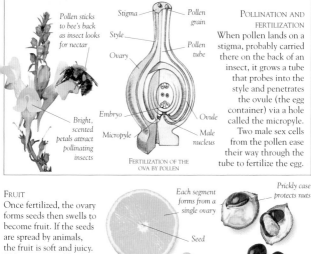

Pollen sticks to bee's back as insect looks for nectar

Bright, scented petals attract pollinating insects

Stigma
Pollen grain
Style
Pollen tube
Ovary
Embryo
Ovule
Micropyle
Male nucleus

FERTILIZATION OF THE OVA BY POLLEN

POLLINATION AND FERTILIZATION

When pollen lands on a stigma, probably carried there on the back of an insect, it grows a tube that probes into the style and penetrates the ovule (the egg container) via a hole called the micropyle. Two male sex cells from the pollen ease their way through the tube to fertilize the egg.

FRUIT

Once fertilized, the ovary forms seeds then swells to become fruit. If the seeds are spread by animals, the fruit is soft and juicy. If they are spread by the wind, they are hard and dry.

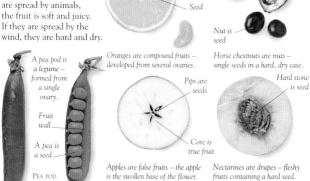

Each segment forms from a single ovary

Seed

Oranges are compound fruits – developed from several ovaries.

Prickly case protects nuts

Nut is seed

Horse chestnuts are nuts – single seeds in a hard, dry case.

A pea pod is a legume – formed from a single ovary.

Fruit wall

A pea is a seed

PEA POD

Pips are seeds

Core is true fruit

Apples are false fruits – the apple is the swollen base of the flower.

Hard stone is seed

Nectarines are drupes – fleshy fruits containing a hard seed.

TREES

TREES ARE WOODY PLANTS, which
means they have hard stems and
grow for years – often to immense
sizes. Leaves growing on trees can
be broad, like oak and beech
leaves, or narrow, such as pine
needles and palm fronds.

TALLEST TREE
The tallest
living tree is a
coast redwood
in Redwood
National Park,
USA. It soars
111.25 m
(365 ft) into
the air, as tall
as an Apollo
space rocket.

*Leaves
range from long
"needles" like these to
short, flat scales.*

CONIFERS
Most conifers are
evergreen with leaves
that last three to four
years and often have a
dark, waxy skin to help
save water.

*Most conifers
bear their seeds
under the scales
of hard cones.*

PALM TREES
Palm trees grow
mainly in the
tropics. They
have no branches
but giant multiple
leaves that grow
from a single
point, called the
apical bud.

*Palm trees
get their name
because leaves are
sometimes shaped
like a hand*

*Palm trees
are flowering
plants*

BROAD-LEAVED TREES

Most broad-leaved trees are deciduous, which means they shed their leaves seasonally to save water.

Many broad-leaved trees can be identified by the shape of their leaves.

Crown

Leaves absorb sunlight and convert it to food

Heartwood

Sapwood

One year's growth

Cambium

Waterproof bark

THE TRUNK

The series of rings, called growth rings, on a sawn log mark each year's growth. The dark centre of the tree is dead "heartwood". Around this is paler, living, sapwood with a thin rim, or "cambium", where it grows. Protecting the sapwood is a layer of bark.

COMMON OAK

Oak trees produce nuts called "acorns" in autumn

Single trunk carries nutrients from roots to leaves

All broad-leaved trees are flowering plants and bear flowers and fruits.

TREE FACTS

• Mangroves are the only trees that can grow in salty water.

• The oldest living trees on Earth are 5,000-year-old bristlecone pines from Arizona, USA.

INVERTEBRATES

NINE-TENTHS of all animals are invertebrates, which means they have no backbone. They include jellyfish, sponges, starfish, coral, worms, crabs, spiders, and insects.

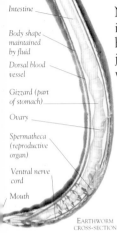

Intestine

Body shape maintained by fluid

Dorsal blood vessel

Gizzard (part of stomach)

Ovary

Spermatheca (reproductive organ)

Ventral nerve cord

Mouth

EARTHWORM CROSS-SECTION

Hard shell to protect soft body

Soft body

Eyes on stalks

MOLLUSCS
These soft-bodied invertebrates are often protected by a hard shell. Most molluscs, such as squid and octopuses, clams, mussels, and scallops, live in water, but some, like snails and slugs, live on land.

WORMS
A worm is an animal with a long soft body and no legs. There are many different kinds, including flatworms, tapeworms, earthworms, roundworms, and leeches.

STARFISH AND URCHINS
Starfish, sea urchins, and sea cucumbers are all echinoderms. All are predators, and most have sucker-tipped "tube feet" through which they pump water to move along and feed. The five broad arms of a starfish can wrench open a shellfish to suck out the contents.

Echinoderms have a five-part body plan.

Arm

Ossicles are hard plates just under the skin that keep the body rigid.

Underside of arm is covered with fluid-filled tube feet for moving and feeding

Arm

LIFE CYCLE
Each invertebrate has its own life cycle, but most species lay eggs. Some go through several larval stages, while others hatch as miniature adults.

Jellyfish

Buds break away as free-swimming adults

Fertilized larva

Polyp divides into eight-part buds

Larva grows into a polyp

SPIDER

ARTHROPODS
Insects, spiders, and lobsters are all arthropods. They have jointed limbs and a tough external skeleton.

CROSS-SECTION OF A JELLYFISH

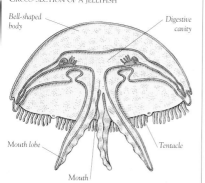

Bell-shaped body

Digestive cavity

Mouth lobe

Tentacle

Mouth

Jellyfish, anemones, and coral are all kinds of coelenterate – sea creatures with a mouth surrounded by tentacles. These tentacles usually carry a sting to stun or kill prey. Some coelenterates, called polyps, always attach to solid objects, such as a rock; others, called medusas, move by contracting their bell-shaped bodies.

SPONGES
These primitive sea creatures feed by drawing water into the holes in their soft bodies and filtering out any food.

INVERTEBRATE FACTS

• Up to 500 million hookworms may be found in a single human.

• Roundworms are probably the most numerous animals on Earth.

Molluscs

AFTER ARTHROPODS, molluscs are the largest group of animals on Earth. There are over 50,000 species, ranging from tiny snails to giant squid as big as sperm whales. Most molluscs, except slugs, squid, cuttlefish, and octopuses, have soft, moist bodies protected by hard shells.

WHELK

MOLLUSC SHELLS
The shells produced by molluscs are made of layers of calcium carbonate. They form in many shapes, sizes, patterns, and colours.

COCKLE SHELLS

ROYAL CLOAK SCALLOP

PACIFIC THORNY OYSTER

TYPES OF MOLLUSC

GASTROPODS
There are 35,000 species of gastropod, including snails, slugs, and whelks.

CEPHALOPODS
There are 600 species of these complex molluscs including octopus, squid, and cuttlefish.

BIVALVES
There are 8,000 species of these double-shelled molluscs, such as oysters, clams, and cockles.

SNAILS AND SLUGS

Slugs and snails are gastropods. They move by a wave of contractions that runs from the rear of the foot to the front, sliding along on a trail of slime. They have soft bodies, but snails are protected by a hard, coiled shell.

Lung — Heart — Kidney

Mucus gland — Mantle

Shell

Eye

Tentacle

Mouth — Foot — Reproductive organs

GIANT AFRICAN
LAND SNAIL

LIFE CYCLE

Molluscs start life as eggs. Many marine molluscs, like this oyster, hatch first as larvae and then develop into adults. Land snails, however, hatch as miniature adults.

Oyster egg

Young adult sinks to sea bed and settles in a suitable place

Larva grows larger; shell develops

Free-swimming larva

MOLLUSC FACTS

- Great grey slugs mate for 7–24 hours, hanging from a trail of mucus.
- Giant clams can live for over 200 years.
- Limpets' teeth are so strong that they leave scratch marks on rocks.

TUSK SHELLS
There are 350 species of these rare sea creatures with tusk-shaped shells.

SOLENOGASTERS
There are 5,540 species of these worm-like marine molluscs.

MONOPLACOPHORANS
There are only ten species of these limpets. They live in the depths of the ocean.

CHITONS
There are 500 species of these coat-of-mail shelled creatures.

INSECTS

INSECTS MAY BE TINY, but there are more of them than all other animals put together. Over five million species, from tiny flies to giant beetles, are known, and there may be over 200 million insects for every human. They have existed for over 400 million years and are found everywhere from the Arctic to the Sahara.

WASP'S HEAD

Antenna

Compound eye

COMPOUND EYES
The compound eyes of most insects have six or more facets. Dragonfly eyes have 30,000 facets in each eye, which help to spot movement.

DRAGONFLY

Compound eye

Head

Veins in wing keep it rigid

Wing

Thorax (middle section of the body) which bears the legs

Abdomen (rear part of the body)

FEELERS AND HAIRS
Insects use antennae to sense the world in different ways. Most work by smell or touch. Ants, bees, and wasps use their antennae for tasting.

BEETLE ANTENNAE

Branched antennae are super-sensitive

INSECT BODY
An insect's body is divided into three parts – head, thorax, and abdomen – and has six legs. The body is encased in a tough shell, or exoskeleton, made of a substance called chitin. Some insects have two or four wings.

Egg · Caterpillar

Adult butterfly · Chrysalis

COMPLETE METAMORPHOSIS

Insects such as butterflies, beetles, and flies start life as larvae, which hatch from eggs. The larvae then turn into pupae, from which an adult emerges. This process is known as complete metamorphosis. The larva bears no resemblance to the adult it becomes.

WASPS' NEST · Nest of chewed wood

INSECT NESTS

Some insects, such as bees, wasps, termites, and ants, live in ordered societies and build elaborate homes.

INCOMPLETE METAMORPHOSIS

Insects such as grasshoppers or damselflies hatch into wingless "nymphs" before moulting and growing into adults. This is known as incomplete metamorphosis.

Winged adult emerges from final moult

Egg

Winged nymph

Nymph grows and moults

Final nymph resembles adult

INSECT FACTS

• A queen termite lays 440 million eggs – one per second for 14 years.

• A bee must visit more than 4,000 flowers to make one tablespoon of honey.

MOULTING

A young insect's tough exoskeleton cannot stretch. Instead it is discarded and replaced with a new one several times. This sequence shows the final moult of a damselfly as it changes from nymph to adult.

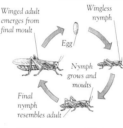

Legs grip stem

Old skin

Crinkled wings

Blood pumps into wings

Wing buds

Nymph crawls out of water up a stem

Soft-bodied adult emerges

Adult rests before flying off

Abdomen turns blue

Types of insect

Insects range from fairyfly wasps only 0.2 mm long, to giant stick insects, up to 45 cm (17.7 in) long. They are divided into 32 orders, six of which are shown here. Other insects include flies, grasshoppers, earwigs, and fleas.

TERMITES
(ISOPTERA)
2,300 SPECIES

PRAYING MANTIDS
(MANTODEA)
1,800 SPECIES

COCKROACHES
(BLATTODEA)
3,700 SPECIES

ANTS, BEES, WASPS
(HYMENOPTERA)
110,000 SPECIES

BEETLES
(COLEOPTERA)
300,000 SPECIES

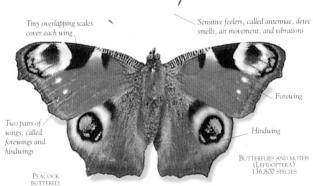

Tiny overlapping scales cover each wing

Sensitive feelers, called antennae, detect smells, air movement, and vibrations

Forewing

Hindwing

Two pairs of wings, called forewings and hindwings

PEACOCK BUTTERFLY

BUTTERFLIES AND MOTHS
(LEPIDOPTERA)
136,800 SPECIES

ARACHNIDS

SPIDERS, SCORPIONS, ticks, and mites belong to a group of arthropods called arachnids. There are more than 73,000 species, living in almost every habitat.

Eight jointed legs

CHILEAN RED-LEG SPIDER

Powerful jaws

SPIDERS
All spiders are meat-eaters. Some jump on prey; others trap prey in a web, paralyze it with venom, then eat it.

MITES AND TICKS (ACARI) 30,000 SPECIES

SPIDERS (ARANEAE) 40,000 SPECIES

ARACHNID ANATOMY

Arachnids usually have eight legs and their body is divided into the cephalothorax (front and middle) and the abdomen (rear). Scorpions have six legs and two pincer-like pedipalps for gripping prey.

Poisonous sting in the tail for paralyzing prey

Waterproof, flexible outer covering, or exoskeleton

Legs are jointed in several places for flexibility

SCORPION

Powerful claws, called pedipalps, hold on to prey

ARACHNID FACTS

• The biggest arachnid is a bird-eating spider (*Theraphosa leblondi*), with a leg span of 28 cm (11 in).

• The largest web is spun by the tropical orb spider (*Nephila*) and measures up to 3 m (10 ft) across.

CRUSTACEANS

THESE ARTHROPODS get their name from their crusty skin. They include lobsters, crabs, and shrimps, which live in the sea. Only a few, such as woodlice, live on land. There are more than 55,000 species of crustacean.

Long antenna, or feeler

Saw-like pincer for cutting up prey

Compound eyes on stalks for spotting prey

Blunt pincer for gripping and crushing prey

Hard body case, or carapace, protects internal organs

Tail allows lobster to swim backwards to escape danger

Lobsters and crabs have ten legs and are called decapods

EUROPEAN LOBSTER

ANATOMY OF A LOBSTER
Lobsters have a tough body case, or carapace, two long antennae, and a pair of compound eyes on stalks for spotting prey. Lobsters also have large, strong pincers for gripping victims and pulling them apart.

DECORATOR CRAB

CRAB CAMOUFLAGE
Most crabs are sand-coloured to make them less visible on the sea-bed. This decorator crab covers its whole body with plants and sea creatures to disguise itself completely.

CRABS

Most crabs have a hard, shield-like shell called
a carapace for defence. The flexible
abdomen is usually tucked underneath
for protection. Crabs move by
scuttling sideways.

Huge pincers
for gripping and
tearing food

Hard outer
shell, called
the carapace

FURROWED
CRAB

Jointed legs
with clawed toes

LIFE CYCLE

Crustaceans begin
life as eggs, which are
usually laid in water.
After the eggs hatch,
they pass through
several larval stages
before taking on
their adult form. As
adults, they grow
bigger by moulting,
or shedding their
outer layer.

Adult
shrimp

Egg

Egg hatches
into first
larval
stage

LIFE CYCLE OF
A SHRIMP

Final
post-larval stage

Second
larval stage

CRUSTACEAN FACTS

• The largest
crustacean is the
Japanese spider crab
(*Macrocheira
kaempferi*), with a leg
span of almost 4 m
(13 ft).

• The smallest
crustaceans are tiny
water-fleas (*Alonella*),
which measure less
than 0.25 mm long.

VERTEBRATES

ONLY ABOUT three per cent of all
animals have backbones, and these
are called vertebrates. There are
more than 40,000 different species
of vertebrate, divided into
classes of mammals, birds, fish,
reptiles, and amphibians. Their
sense organs and nervous systems
are well developed, and they have
adapted to almost every habitat.

GORILLA
SKELETON

BACKBONE
Vertebrates have a skeleton
of bone, with a backbone,
two pairs of limbs, and a
skull that protects the
brain. Inside are the heart,
lungs, and other organs.

REPTILES
Lizards, snakes, crocodiles, and geckos
are reptiles. They all have a tough,
scaly skin. Young reptiles hatch
from eggs, and look like
tiny versions of their
parents. This chameleon
is a type of lizard.

*Spines along
backbone give
protection
from attack*

*Scaly
skin*

*Female frog lays eggs,
called frogspawn*

MADAGASCAN
CHAMELEON

*Male
fertilizes
spawn*

ANIMAL REPRODUCTION
In vertebrates, offspring are created when
males and females come together and the
male's sperm join the female's eggs.
This is called sexual reproduction,
and usually involves
mating. A few animals are
neither male nor female,
and they reproduce asexually.

*Prehensile
tail for
holding on to
branches*

SENSES

Mammals and other vertebrate animals have senses to help them find their way, locate food, and avoid enemies. For land animals, such as this caracal, sight, hearing, and smell are the most important senses. Sea creatures rely more on smell and taste to escape danger and find food.

Sharp eyesight for hunting, even at night

Long, sensitive ears pick up even the faintest sounds

Strong sense of smell

Sharp teeth

CARACAL

FISH

With streamlined bodies covered in slippery scales, these vertebrates are perfectly suited to life in the water.

TWINSPOT WRASSE

Scales covered in slimy mucus

BIRDS

The only animals that have feathers are birds, and most of them are powerful fliers. Birds have a beak, or bill, instead of teeth, and all reproduce by laying eggs.

RED-EYED TREE FROG

Large eyes spot prey

AMPHIBIANS

Frogs, toads, newts, and salamanders are amphibians. These vertebrates spend part of their lives in water and part on land. They all reproduce by laying eggs.

COUNT RAGGI'S BIRD OF PARADISE

Long legs for jumping

PORCUPINE

Spiny quills protect body

Fur helps keep body warm

MAMMAL

A mammal is usually covered in fur or hair. It gives birth to live young, which it feeds with milk.

AMPHIBIANS

THERE ARE more than 4,200 species of amphibian. They begin life in water as fish-like tadpoles, after hatching from clusters of eggs called spawn. The tadpoles soon grow legs and lungs for life on land. Young amphibians breathe using gills, while adults take in oxygen through their skin.

TIGER SALAMANDER

Damp skin absorbs oxygen

Bright warning spots

NEWTS AND SALAMANDERS

Salamanders have long bodies, short, thin legs, and cylindrical tails. They usually spend their adult life on land and breathe by absorbing oxygen through their damp skin. Their skin's bright colour warns predators that they are poisonous.

Large, bulging eyes for spotting prey

Round external eardrum called a "tympanum"

Thick, knobbly skin covered with bumps, or warts

FROGS AND TOADS

Both frogs and toads have short, compact bodies, and strong back legs for jumping long distances. As they grow up from tadpole to adult, they lose their tails. There is no clear distinction between frogs and toads, but frogs tend to spend more of their life in or near water, while toads can survive in damp spots on land, returning to water to breed.

Squat body

Feet are webbed for swimming

EUROPEAN COMMON TOAD

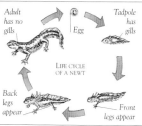

Adult
has no
gills

Egg

Tadpole
has gills

LIFE CYCLE
OF A NEWT

Back
legs
appear

Front
legs appear

LIFE CYCLE OF AN AMPHIBIAN
Amphibians lay their eggs in water; the
eggs are not waterproof and would dry out
on land. After a week or so, the eggs hatch
into tadpoles, and these become strong
swimmers. In newts, the front legs appear
about three weeks after hatching. The
back legs appear at seven to eight weeks.
Finally, the gills disappear and the newt
metamorphoses (changes) into an adult.

MIDWIFE TOAD
The female midwife toad lays about
50 eggs. After the male has fertilized
the eggs, he carries them on his back
for up to one-and-a-half months until
they are ready to hatch.

Male wraps
eggs around
back legs

MIDWIFE
TOAD (MALE)

Vivid colours act as
warning signal to
predators

DEADLY POISONS
Some amphibians produce powerful
poisons from glands in their skin. These
creatures are often brightly coloured to
warn predators of the danger. Poison-dart
frogs are the most poisonous amphibians.

POISON-DART FROG

AMPHIBIAN CAMOUFLAGE
Some amphibians manage to
avoid predators by the unusual
colours and patterns on their bodies.
This European yellow-bellied toad
hardly shows up against the tree bark.

Patches of green
complete the
toad's disguise

EUROPEAN
YELLOW-
BELLIED
TOAD

REPTILES

SCALY-SKINNED crocodiles, lizards, and snakes are all reptiles. There are almost 6,000 species. Reptiles are found on land and in water, but they cannot live in cold places as they need the sun's warmth to give them energy.

EGGS
Most reptiles hatch from eggs with thick, leathery shells that stop them from drying out. Some reptiles are "viviparous", giving birth to live young.

IGUANA
These large American lizards often have a crest on their backs

Thick, scaly skin acts as a suit of armour

Crest

COMMON
IGUANA

Long tail helps with balance

Sharp claws on each toe

LIZARDS
Iguanas, geckos, skinks, and chameleons are all lizards. Most lizards are swift-moving hunters, with sharp claws for catching prey and long tails to help with balance.

After eight months, the whole tail has grown back

Lizard has lost part of its tail

GROWING A TAIL
If a predator catches a lizard by its tail, the tail may break off, which confuses the attacker. The lizard grows a new tail within about eight months

Tail begins to grow back after two months

TURTLES AND TORTOISES

Tortoises, turtles, and terrapins are called chelonians. They have a hard shell made of bony plates. By hiding inside the shell they can escape most predators, so they do not need to move quickly. Tortoises live on land and terrapins and turtles live in water.

Shell made of horn

STARRED
TORTOISE
SHELL

RED-EARED
TERRAPIN

Cobra inflates hood to make itself appear bigger

MONOCLED
COBRA

SNAKES

Snakes are long, legless reptiles. They hunt prey by smelling the air with their forked tongue. Constrictors such as pythons coil around prey and suffocate them. Venomous snakes such as this cobra stun or kill their prey with poison from hollow teeth called fangs.

Long, thin body

REPTILE FACTS

• A giant turtle found in Mauritius in 1766 survived for another 152 years.

• The venom glands of the Australian taipan snake hold enough poison to kill 200 people.

CROCODILES AND ALLIGATORS

Alligators, crocodiles, caimans, and gavials are called crocodilians. These hunters with huge jaws and sharp teeth live in tropical swamps and rivers.

Crocodile swims by waving its flattened tail

Peg-like teeth for tearing flesh apart

Female carries young in her mouth and guards them until they can fend for themselves

Short, strong legs

ESTUARINE
CROCODILE

FISH

THERE ARE more than 20,000 species of fish, all of which live in water from deep oceans to ponds, rivers, and lakes. Most fish have streamlined, scaly bodies, fins for swimming, and gills for breathing. They reproduce by laying eggs.

Water flows into mouth

Gill rakers sieve water

Water flows over gills

HOW FISH BREATHE
Fish are able to breathe underwater using their gills. As water flows over the gills, oxygen passes into the bloodstream through special, thin skins called membranes.

BONY FISH
The largest group of fish includes carp and other bony fish. These fish have bony skeletons and an internal air bag called the swim bladder that keeps them afloat in the water.

Dorsal fin

Scales

Eye

Mouth

Caudal fin

Gill cover

CARP

Anal fin

Pelvic fin

Pectoral fin

HOW CARTILAGINOUS FISH SWIM
A cartilaginous fish, such as a dogfish, swims by swinging its tail in an "S" shape; it steers by waving its pectoral and pelvic fins. The dorsal fin helps keep the fish upright as it swims. Bony fish swim by moving their fins only.

Tail

Head

First dorsal fin

Pelvic fin

The fish swings its head to the right, and an S-shaped wave begins to travel along the body.

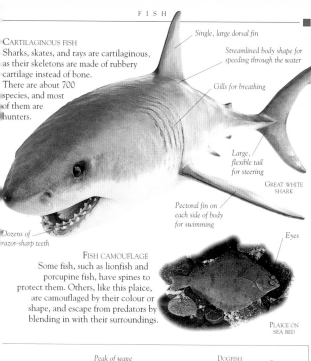

CARTILAGINOUS FISH

Sharks, skates, and rays are cartilaginous, as their skeletons are made of rubbery cartilage instead of bone. There are about 700 species, and most of them are hunters.

Single, large dorsal fin

Streamlined body shape for speeding through the water

Gills for breathing

Large, flexible tail for steering

GREAT WHITE SHARK

Pectoral fin on each side of body for swimming

Dozens of razor-sharp teeth

FISH CAMOUFLAGE

Some fish, such as lionfish and porcupine fish, have spines to protect them. Others, like this plaice, are camouflaged by their colour or shape, and escape from predators by blending in with their surroundings.

Eyes

PLAICE ON SEA BED

Peak of wave

DOGFISH

Peak of wave

Peak of wave

The peak of the wave reaches the area of pelvic and first dorsal fins.

The peak of the wave is now between the two dorsal fins, and the tail thrusts to the right.

The peak of the wave reaches the tail, and the fish's head swings for the next wave.

BIRDS

RED-TAILED MINLA

FROM THE TINY BEE hummingbird, which weighs only 1.6 g (0.056 oz), to the ostrich, which weighs up to 156 kg (344 lb) and grows up to 2.7 m (8.9 ft) tall, birds are the only animals with feathers. They also have wings and beaks, and most are expert fliers. Birds reproduce by laying eggs.

Wing size and shape depends on a bird's lifestyle

Wing feathers spread in flight to give lift

Beak made of bone covered by layer of horn

Tail helps bird to balance and change direction

Scaly, clawed feet for gripping branches

BIRDS IN FLIGHT
Birds fly by flapping their wings, or by gliding. Each bird has its own flight pattern. Small birds have a bouncing flight, and glide between flaps to save energy. Larger birds fly level and flap their wings all the time. Some birds take to the air for a few minutes at a time; others stay airborne for weeks or even months.

FROM EGG TO CHICK
As a chick develops inside an egg, the parent birds sit on the egg to keep it warm. This is called incubation. Small birds incubate their eggs for two weeks, eagles for seven weeks, and albatrosses for eleven weeks.

The chick hatches by pecking the shell with the "egg tooth" on its bill.

The chick pecks a circle around the top of the egg and pushes.

*Flight feathers
in wings and tail
enable bird to fly*

*Body feathers
overlap and keep
bird waterproof*

*Down feathers
trap warm air
next to the skin*

FEATHERS

A bird's feathers keep it warm and enable it to fly. Feathers are light yet strong because each strand is linked together with hooks called barbs and barbules.

NESTS AND YOUNG

Most birds build nests. A nest keeps the eggs warm and safe until they are ready to hatch, and provides a home for the newly hatched young. Each bird species has its own way of building a nest. Magpies build nests of twigs in trees; weaver birds weave elaborate nests from grass.

Tail feathers are extra long for steering, balancing, and braking

NESTLINGS

CHICK EMERGING FROM EGG

The top of the shell breaks off and the chick struggles free. Its feathers are still wet.

The fluffy down soon dries out and will be replaced by feathers as the chick grows.

Types of bird

Birds have adapted to life in almost all parts of the world. Some, like birds of prey, are meat eaters, while others eat only seeds and fruits. There are at least 9,000 species divided into 28 orders.

OSTRICH
(STRUTHIONIFORMES)
1 SPECIES

CRANES, RAILS, AND BUSTARDS
(GRUIFORMES)
190 SPECIES

KIWIS
(APTERYGIFORMES)
3 SPECIES

TINAMOUS
(TINAMIFORMES)
46 SPECIES

ALBATROSSES, PETRELS
(PROCELLARIIFORMES)
110 SPECIES

EMUS, CASSOWARIES
(CASUARIIFORMES)
4 SPECIES

LOONS OR DIVERS
(GAVIIFORMES)
5 SPECIES

BIRDS OF PREY
(FALCONIFORMES)
290 SPECIES

RHEAS
(RHEIFORMES)
2 SPECIES

OWLS
(STRIGIFORMES)
174 SPECIES

WATERFOWL
(ANSERIFORMES)
150 SPECIES

GAME BIRDS
(GALLIFORMES)
274 SPECIES

SHOREBIRDS,
GULLS,
TERNS, AUKS
(CHARADRIIFORMES)
337 SPECIES

PELICANS, GANNETS,
CORMORANTS
(PELECANIFORMES)
55 SPECIES

PARROTS, LORIES, COCKATOOS
(PSITTACIFORMES)
342 SPECIES

MOUSEBIRDS
(COLIIFORMES)
6 SPECIES

HERONS,
STORKS, IBISES
(CICONIIFORMES)
117 SPECIES

NIGHTJARS, FROGMOUTHS
(CAPRIMULGIFORMES)
109 SPECIES

KINGFISHERS,
BEE-EATERS, HOOPOES
(CORACIIFORMES)
204 SPECIES

SANDGROUSE
(PTEROCLIDIFORMES)
16 SPECIES

PASSERINES
(PASSERIFORMES)
5,414 SPECIES

CUCKOOS,
TURACOS
(CUCULIFORMES)
159 SPECIES

PIGEONS
(COLUMBIFORMES)
300 SPECIES

SWIFTS,
HUMMINGBIRDS
(APODIFORMES)
429 SPECIES

GREBES
(PODICIPEDIFORMES)
21 SPECIES

WOODPECKERS,
TOUCANS, BARBETS
(PICIFORMES)
381 SPECIES

TROGONS
(TROGONIFORMES)
39 SPECIES

PENGUINS
(SPHENISCIFORMES)
18 SPECIES

MAMMALS

DOLPHIN

ALL MAMMALS are warm-blooded animals, so their blood is always at the correct temperature for their body processes to work well. To keep warm, mammals usually have thick fur or a layer of fat or blubber. Mammals are found all over the world, on land, in water, and even in the air.

CARNIVORES

Some mammals are carnivores (meat-eaters), and most carnivores are hunters. The deadliest hunters of the mammal world are the big cats, such as lions, tigers, cheetahs, and leopards. They have strong, agile bodies for chasing prey, and sharp claws and teeth for killing it.

SEA MAMMALS

Whales and dolphins spend their live in the sea and come to the surface to breathe. They are called cetaceans

Excellen
hearin

Keen senses o
sight and sme

Striped pattern
camouflages
tiger in long
grass

Body covered in
fur for warmth

INDIAN TIGER

Powerful,
low-slung
body

Massive pau
and sharp clau
can strike
fatal blo

HERBIVORES

Mammals that eat only plants are called herbivores. Some herbivores, such as giraffes, browse on the buds of bushes and trees. Others, including zebras and cattle, graze on grass. Herbivores often have special teeth for grinding plant matter.

GUERNSEY COW

Tiny new-born kangaroo crawls into pouch

MARSUPIALS

Kangaroos, koalas, and other marsupial mammals have a pouch into which their new-born baby crawls. The young animal lives in its mother's pouch until it is fully developed and able to fend for itself.

GREY KANGAROO

Young kangaroos are called joeys

MONOTREMES

Platypuses such as this Australian duck-billed platypus are the only mammals that lay eggs.

MOTHER'S MILK

Mammals are the only animals to feed their young on milk, produced in the mother's teats. Milk is nourishing, and it contains substances that protect the young from disease.

Kittens feed on their mother's milk

MAMMAL FACTS

• Pygmy shrews lose body heat quickly because of their small size, so they must eat three times their body weight of food every day to survive.

• Elephants eat about 228 kg (500 lb) of vegetation every day.

Types of mammal

Mammals range from Kitti's
long-nosed bat, which is
the size of a bee, to the
massive blue whale, which is
the size of a jumbo jet. There
are more than 4,600 species of
mammal, found all over the
world. Mammals are
divided into 21
orders, shown here.

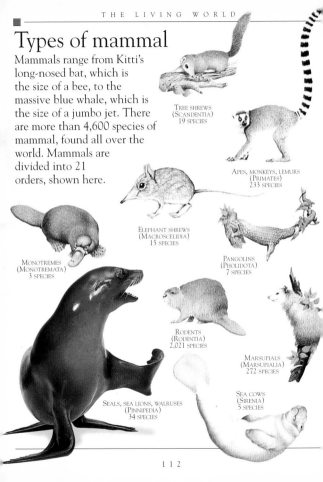

TREE SHREWS
(SCANDENTIA)
19 SPECIES

APES, MONKEYS, LEMURS
(PRIMATES)
233 SPECIES

ELEPHANT SHREWS
(MACROSCELIDIA)
15 SPECIES

PANGOLINS
(PHOLIDOTA)
7 SPECIES

MONOTREMES
(MONOTREMATA)
3 SPECIES

RODENTS
(RODENTIA)
2,021 SPECIES

MARSUPIALS
(MARSUPIALIA)
272 SPECIES

SEA COWS
(SIRENIA)
5 SPECIES

SEALS, SEA LIONS, WALRUSES
(PINNIPEDIA)
34 SPECIES

ELEPHANTS
(PROBOSCIDEA)
2 SPECIES

FLYING LEMURS
(DERMOPTERA)
2 SPECIES

EDENTATES
(EDENTATA)
29 SPECIES

EVEN-TOED HOOFED MAMMALS
(ARTIODACTYLA)
220 SPECIES

AARDVARK
(TUBULIDENTATA)
1 SPECIES

WHALES, DOLPHINS
(CETACEA)
78 SPECIES

BATS
(CHIROPTERA)
925 SPECIES

HYRAXES
(HYRACOIDEA)
6 SPECIES

HARES, RABBITS, PIKAS
(LAGOMORPHA)
80 SPECIES

INSECTIVORES
(INSECTIVORA)
428 SPECIES

ODD-TOED HOOFED MAMMALS
(PERISSODACTYLA)
18 SPECIES

CARNIVORES
(CARNIVORA)
237 SPECIES

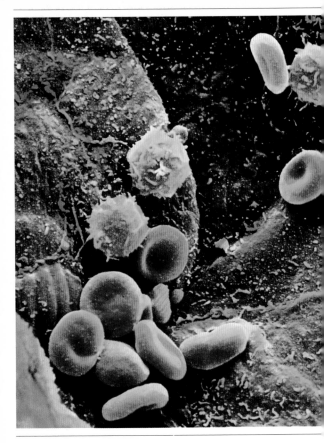

THE HUMAN BODY

BODY SYSTEMS

THE HUMAN BODY is an amazingly complex organism made up of 50 trillion microscopic cells. There are more than 200 kinds of cell, all organized into a dozen or so body systems, each with its own function. Here are the major systems that are common to both sexes.

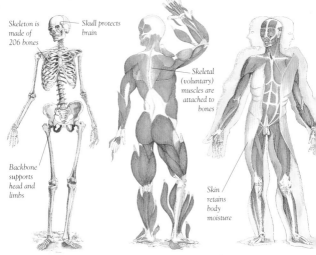

Skeleton is made of 206 bones

Skull protects brain

Skeletal (voluntary) muscles are attached to bones

Backbone supports head and limbs

Skin retains body moisture

SKELETAL SYSTEM
The skeleton is the rigid framework of bone that supports the body and protects its internal organs.

MUSCULAR SYSTEM
Every movement of the body (both involuntary and voluntary) is caused by muscles contracting.

INTEGUMENTARY SYSTEM
This system consists of the skin, hair, and nails. Skin and hair cover the body, and help to protect it.

RESPIRATORY SYSTEM
This takes oxygenated air into the lungs and pushes out waste gases.

DIGESTIVE SYSTEM
The digestive tract breaks down and absorbs food, and gets rid of solid waste.

URINARY SYSTEM
This filters soluble wastes from the blood for disposal as urine.

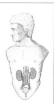

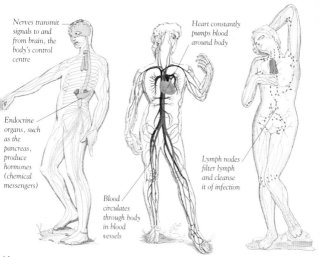

Nerves transmit signals to and from brain, the body's control centre

Heart constantly pumps blood around body

Endocrine organs, such as the pancreas, produce hormones (chemical messengers)

Lymph nodes filter lymph and cleanse it of infection

Blood circulates through body in blood vessels

NERVES AND HORMONES
The nervous system and hormones co-ordinate all the body systems and direct our actions.

CARDIOVASCULAR SYSTEM
Blood pumped around the body by the heart supplies tissues with oxygen and removes waste products.

LYMPHATIC SYSTEM
Lymph, containing immune cells, is collected by a network of lymph vessels.

BONES AND TEETH

THE INNER FRAMEWORK of the human body consists of interconnecting bones that form the skeleton. Without a skeleton we could not stand or move.

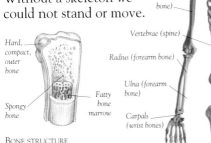

Hard, compact, outer bone

Spongy bone

Fatty bone marrow

BONE STRUCTURE
The hardest part of a bone is the outer layer, containing calcium and phosphorus. Inside long bones there is a soft, living tissue called marrow. Yellow marrow stores fat, and red marrow forms blood cells.

SKELETON FACTS
• The femur is the longest, strongest bone.

• A woman's pelvic bones are shallower and wider than a man's to allow childbirth.

SKELETON
The skeleton supports and protects delicate internal organs such as the brain, lungs, and heart. It also provides strong, fixed points of attachment for the muscles.

Cranium (skull)

Clavicle (collarbone)

Scapula (shoulder blade)

Humerus (upper arm bone)

Rib

Vertebrae (spine)

Radius (forearm bone)

Ulna (forearm bone)

Carpals (wrist bones)

Coccyx (tail bone)

Phalanges (finger bones)

Femur (thigh bone)

Tibia (shinbone)

Patella (kneecap)

Tarsals (ankle bones)

Fibula (calf bone)

Metatarsals (foot bones)

JOINTS

Where bones meet, a joint forms. In a mobile joint, the bone surface is coated with slippery cartilage and is lubricated with synovial fluid. Most joints are held together by cords called ligaments.

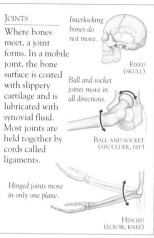

Interlocking bones do not move.

FIXED
(SKULL)

Ball and socket joints move in all directions.

BALL AND SOCKET
(SHOULDER, HIP)

Hinged joints move in only one plane.

HINGED
(ELBOW, KNEE)

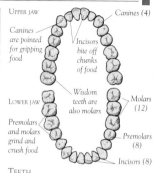

UPPER JAW

Canines are pointed for gripping food

Canines (4)

Incisors bite off chunks of food

Wisdom teeth are also molars

Molars (12)

LOWER JAW

Premolars and molars grind and crush food

Premolars (8)

Incisors (8)

TEETH

Humans have two sets of teeth. Children lose their first "milk" teeth when they are about six years old. These are gradually replaced by a second, permanent set of 32 teeth, each with a different job to do.

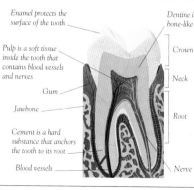

Enamel protects the surface of the tooth

Pulp is a soft tissue inside the tooth that contains blood vessels and nerves

Gum

Jawbone

Cement is a hard substance that anchors the tooth to its root

Blood vessels

Dentine is a bone-like layer

Crown

Neck

Root

Nerve

TOOTH STRUCTURE

Teeth are harder than bone, and consist of several layers. The enamel is the hardest substance in the body, and forms the tough, non-living exterior surface of the tooth. The dentine is the living tissue that gives the tooth its shape. The pulp contains vessels that bring blood to the tooth, enabling it to live and grow.

MUSCLES

ALL THE body's functions are controlled by muscles, which convert chemical energy into movement. We consciously control voluntary muscles, but involuntary muscles work automatically.

MUSCLE USE

When muscles are used, they warm up, providing the body with about one-fifth of its heat. Regular exercise increases the flow of blood to the muscles. This keeps them toned and makes them grow in size.

TENDONS
Skeletal muscles are attached to bones at either end by tough cords called tendons.

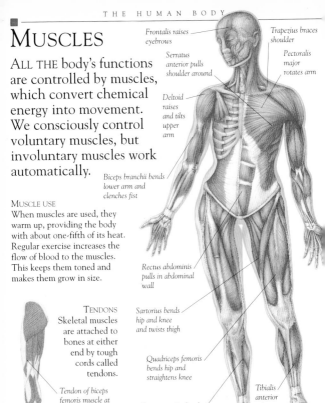

Frontalis raises eyebrows

Trapezius braces shoulder

Serratus anterior pulls shoulder around

Pectoralis major rotates arm

Deltoid raises and tilts upper arm

Biceps branchii bends lower arm and clenches fist

Rectus abdominis pulls in abdominal wall

Sartorius bends hip and knee and twists thigh

Quadriceps femoris bends hip and straightens knee

Tibialis anterior raises foot

Gastrocnemius bends knee and lifts heel

Tendon of biceps femoris muscle at back of knee

Achilles tendon

MUSCLE ACTION

A muscle can pull, but it cannot push, as it works by contracting. Muscles often work in pairs. A "flexor" muscle flexes, or bends a joint, and an "extensor" muscle straightens it again.

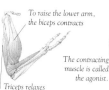

To raise the lower arm, the biceps contracts

To lower the arm, the triceps contracts, and the biceps relaxes

The contracting muscle is called the agonist.

The relaxing muscle is called the antagonist.

Triceps relaxes

MUSCLE STRUCTURE

Voluntary muscles consist of bundles of cells called myofibres. Inside are strands of myofibrils containing the proteins actin and myosin. When a muscle contracts, the myosin tightens on the actin, making the muscle shorter.

Contracted myofibril *Relaxed myofibril*

Myofibril

Myofibre

Bundle of myofibres

MUSCLE FACTS

- There are more than 600 different voluntary muscles in the body.

- Muscles make up 40 per cent of a person's total weight.

- The largest muscle is the gluteus maximus, in the buttock.

TYPES OF MUSCLE

The three types of muscle are skeletal, cardiac, and smooth.

Skeletal muscles enable the body to move.

Cardiac muscles are found only in the heart and cause it to contract rhythmically.

Smooth muscles perform automatic tasks such as propelling food through the stomach and gut.

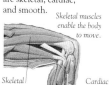

Skeletal muscle attached to bone

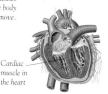

Cardiac muscle in the heart

Smooth muscle in the stomach

SKELETAL MUSCLES   CARDIAC MUSCLES   SMOOTH MUSCLES

SKIN, NAILS, AND HAIR

THE SKIN is the body's waterproof coat, protecting it from the outside world and preventing it from drying out. It is also a sense organ, sensitive to touch, pressure, warmth, and pain. The skin produces nails, which shield the tips of fingers and toes, and hair to provide extra warmth and protection.

SKIN STRUCTURE

The skin has two main layers. The thin, tough, outer epidermis consists mostly of dead cells that are constantly shed and replaced by new skin cells. The thick, living inner dermis layer contains nerves, blood vessels, sense receptors, glands, and hair follicles.

Each hair is coated in dead cells

Outer layers of epidermis consist of dead cells made of a hard protein called keratin

Movement of hair gives sensation of touch

Hair erector muscle makes hair stand on end in the cold to help trap warmth

Sebaceous glands make sebum (oil) to keep hair and skin supple

Hair follicle

Sweat glands produce sweat to help keep the skin cool

BLOOD CLOTTING

When skin is cut, the damaged blood vessels bleed. White blood cells fight infection. Fibrin threads bind small, sticky blood cells (platelets) together to form a clot. This clot dries as a scab.

Damaged blood vessel

White blood cells attack germs

Scab forms a protective layer over wound

Fibrin threads bind platelets together to stop blood flow

NAIL STRUCTURE

The dead tissue made from a tough protein called keratin forms our nails. Keratin is made by living cells at the base and side of each nail, which are protected by folds of skin called cuticles.

Finger bone

Cuticle

Nail

Nail root

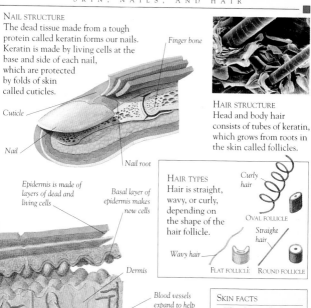

HAIR STRUCTURE

Head and body hair consists of tubes of keratin, which grows from roots in the skin called follicles.

Epidermis is made of layers of dead and living cells

Basal layer of epidermis makes new cells

HAIR TYPES

Hair is straight, wavy, or curly, depending on the shape of the hair follicle.

Curly hair

OVAL FOLLICLE

Straight hair

Wavy hair

FLAT FOLLICLE   ROUND FOLLICLE

Dermis

Blood vessels expand to help heat loss when body is hot

Layer of subcutaneous fat to insulate body from cold

Pain, pressure, warmth, and touch receptors

SKIN FACTS

• The skin is the body's largest organ.

• In a normal lifespan, the body sheds 18 kg (40 lb) of skin.

• Household dust is mainly dead skin.

• About 80 scalp hairs fall out every day.

BRAIN AND NERVES

THE NERVOUS SYSTEM is a dense, branching network of nerve fibres. It co-ordinates the body's actions and sends a never-ending stream of sense data to the brain.

Touch   Vision

Skilled movement

Behaviour and emotion

Speech

Hearing

Taste

SENSORY AREAS
Certain parts of the brain have particular functions. "Sensory" areas receive and interpret data from sense organs; "motor" areas control voluntary muscles.

BRAIN STRUCTURE
The human brain is a complex network of nerve cells linked to the rest of the body via the cranial nerves and spinal cord. The brain has two halves, or hemispheres. Each controls the *opposite* side of the body.

Cerebrum is a folded mass of nerves where conscious activity takes place

Thalamus transmits nerve signals between brain and spinal cord

Hypothalamus controls hunger, thirst, body temperature, sleeping, and waking

Pituitary gland sends out hormones (chemical messengers) that stimulate other glands to release hormones

Brain stem, or medulla, controls basic bodily functions such as breathing and heart rate

Cerebellum works subconsciously to co-ordinate all our body movements

Spinal cord

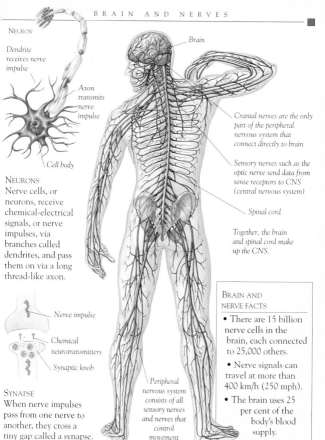

NEURON

Dendrite receives nerve impulse

Axon transmits nerve impulse

Cell body

NEURONS
Nerve cells, or neurons, receive chemical-electrical signals, or nerve impulses, via branches called dendrites, and pass them on via a long thread-like axon.

Nerve impulse

Chemical neurotransmitters

Synaptic knob

SYNAPSE
When nerve impulses pass from one nerve to another, they cross a tiny gap called a synapse.

Brain

Cranial nerves are the only part of the peripheral nervous system that connect directly to brain

Sensory nerves such as the optic nerve send data from sense receptors to CNS (central nervous system)

Spinal cord

Together, the brain and spinal cord make up the CNS.

Peripheral nervous system consists of all sensory nerves and nerves that control movement

BRAIN AND NERVE FACTS

• There are 15 billion nerve cells in the brain, each connected to 25,000 others.

• Nerve signals can travel at more than 400 km/h (250 mph).

• The brain uses 25 per cent of the body's blood supply.

SIGHT

AT THE FRONT of each eye is a lens system that projects an image on to the lining of the eye, called the retina. Millions of light-sensitive cells in the retina, called rods and cones, respond to the image and send signals to the brain.

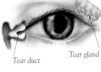

Tear duct

Tear gland

TEARS

The tear glands above each eye continually produce tears. Tears keep the eyes moist and clean. Excess tears are drained down into the nose via the tear ducts.

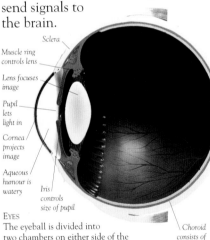

Sclera

Muscle ring controls lens

Lens focuses image

Pupil lets light in

Cornea projects image

Aqueous humour is watery

Iris controls size of pupil

Retina contains light-sensitive rods and cones

Vitreous humour is jelly-like

Optic nerve leads to brain

Choroid consists of blood vessels

EYES

The eyeball is divided into two chambers on either side of the lens. One chamber is filled with aqueous humour, the other with vitreous humour. The casing consists of three layers: the sclera (the white of the eye), the choroid, and the retina.

EYE FACTS

• Rods respond to light but cannot see colour.

• Cones can see colour but cannot see well in the dark.

• Most people blink about 15 times a minute.

HEARING

SOUND CONSISTS of tiny vibrations in the air. We hear sound because the ear amplifies the vibrations, channelling them towards sensitive hairs in the inner ear. These hairs are stimulated by the vibrations and send signals to the brain.

EAR FACTS

• The ear canal is about 2.5 cm (1in) in length.

• Humans can detect 1,500 different tones.

• The sensation of ears "popping" is caused by air pressure equalizing in the middle ear.

EARS

The ear consists of three parts – the outer ear (including the pinna and the ear canal), the middle ear (including the eardrum and ossicles), and the inner ear (including the cochlea).

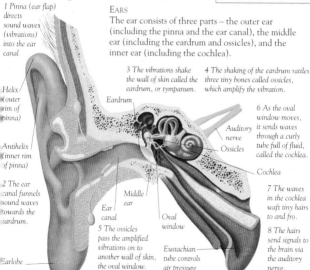

1 Pinna (ear flap) directs sound waves (vibrations) into the ear canal

Helix (outer rim of pinna)

Antihelix (inner rim of pinna)

2 The ear canal funnels sound waves towards the eardrum.

Earlobe

3 The vibrations shake the wall of skin called the eardrum, or tympanum.

Eardrum

Middle ear

Ear canal

5 The ossicles pass the amplified vibrations on to another wall of skin, the oval window.

Oval window

Eustachian tube controls air pressure

4 The shaking of the eardrum rattles three tiny bones called ossicles, which amplify the vibration.

Auditory nerve

Ossicles

6 As the oval window moves, it sends waves through a curly tube full of fluid, called the cochlea.

Cochlea

7 The waves in the cochlea waft tiny hairs to and fro.

8 The hairs send signals to the brain via the auditory nerve.

127

TASTE

THE SENSES OF taste and smell are closely related, and work together to help us identify flavours. The microscopic chemical receptor cells on the tongue called taste buds are the main organs of taste.

TONGUE SURFACE MAGNIFIED

TONGUE

This muscular structure is used in talking, eating, and tasting. It is covered with taste buds which can detect sweet, sour, bitter, and salty flavours.

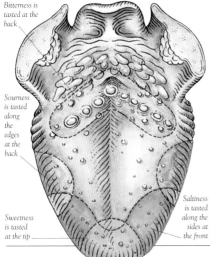

Bitterness is tasted at the back

Sourness is tasted along the edges at the back

Sweetness is tasted at the tip

Saltiness is tasted along the sides at the front

Pore — Tongue tissue

Nerve fibres — Taste bud receptors

TASTE BUDS

There are about 10,000 taste buds on the tongue's surface. Each taste bud contains 10–20 receptors. Chemicals dissolved in saliva reach these taste receptors through pores.

TASTE FACTS

• Babies have taste buds all over the inside of their mouths.

• Taste bud cells last only a week before they are renewed.

SMELL

THE SENSE of smell detects chemicals in the air. These chemicals dissolve in the nasal mucus inside the nose and stimulate hair-like endings on the olfactory bulb. The fine hairs are so sensitive that they can detect even faint traces of chemicals.

There are five million receptors in the olfactory area

Fine hairs, or cilia, on the olfactory bulb are sensitive to the chemicals in mucus

15,000 fibres in the olfactory nerve send messages to the brain

NOSE

The septum divides the nose into two nostrils, each lined with hairs and membranes that secrete sticky mucus. Smell relies on the olfactory area at the top of the nose.

Nose warms and moistens air before it reaches the lungs

Nasal hairs filter out large particles as they are breathed in

Chemicals from the air dissolve in mucus before they reach smell receptors

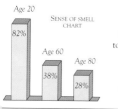

Age 20

SENSE OF SMELL CHART

82%

Age 60

38%

Age 80

28%

LOSS OF SENSITIVITY
Babies are very sensitive to smells, which may help them to identify their mother. But as we grow older, our sensitivity to smell diminishes, as this chart shows.

SMELL FACTS

• Humans can identify about 3,000 different smells.

• Smell is processed by the part of the brain that also deals with memory and emotions.

LUNGS AND BREATHING

LUNGS

OXYGEN IS VITAL to every cell in the body. Without it, brain cells die in minutes. To keep up the supply of oxygen, we breathe air continuously into the lungs. From there the oxygen enters the bloodstream.

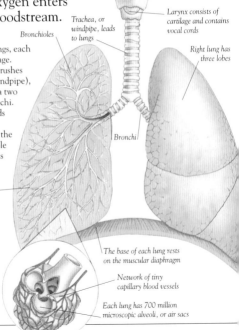

LUNG STRUCTURE
Humans have two lungs, each protected by the ribcage. As we breathe in, air rushes down the trachea (windpipe), and into the lungs via two branches, called bronchi. From there, air spreads through the smaller bronchioles. Around the end of each bronchiole are bunches of air sacs called alveoli.

Trachea, or windpipe, leads to lungs

Larynx consists of cartilage and contains vocal cords

Bronchioles

Right lung has three lobes

Bronchi

Left lung has two lobes

OXYGEN EXCHANGE
As the air enters the alveoli, it seeps through the thin walls into the bloodstream. At the same time, carbon dioxide seeps from the blood back into the lungs, to be breathed out.

The base of each lung rests on the muscular diaphragm

Network of tiny capillary blood vessels

Each lung has 700 million microscopic alveoli, or air sacs

BREATHING

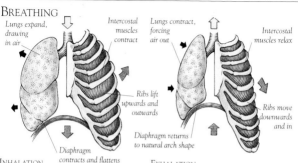

Lungs expand, drawing in air

Intercostal muscles contract

Lungs contract, forcing air out

Intercostal muscles relax

Ribs lift upwards and outwards

Ribs move downwards and in

Diaphragm contracts and flattens

Diaphragm returns to natural arch shape

INHALATION
When we breathe in, the diaphragm contracts and the ribcage expands. Pressure in the chest cavity drops and draws air into the lungs.

EXHALATION
When we breathe out, the diaphragm and the ribcage relax. Pressure in the chest cavity rises and pushes air out of the lungs.

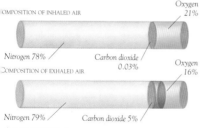

COMPOSITION OF INHALED AIR

Oxygen 21%

Nitrogen 78%

Carbon dioxide 0.03%

COMPOSITION OF EXHALED AIR

Oxygen 16%

Nitrogen 79%

Carbon dioxide 5%

AIR COMPOSITION
Every minute, we breathe in and out about 6 litres (10.14 pints) of air containing oxygen, nitrogen, and carbon dioxide. The air that we exhale contains about 100 times more carbon dioxide than the air we inhale.

BREATHING FACTS

• The average human takes 600 million breaths in a 70-year lifetime.

• If the lungs were opened out and laid flat, they would cover a tennis court.

• The lungs contain 2,400 km (1,490 miles) of airways.

• Humans can survive with only one fully working lung.

HEART AND BLOOD

THE BODY'S transport network, consisting of the heart, blood, and blood vessels, is called the cardiovascular system. Blood carries oxygen to cells and also transports food, hormones, waste, and warmth.

1 During "diastole" (resting), both atria fill with blood and some flows into the ventricles below.

2 During atrial "systole" (pumping), the atria contract, forcing blood into the ventricles.

3 During ventricular systole, the ventricles contract, forcing blood out into the arteries.

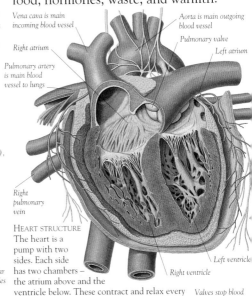

Vena cava is main incoming blood vessel

Aorta is main outgoing blood vessel

Pulmonary valve

Right atrium

Left atrium

Pulmonary artery is main blood vessel to lungs

Right pulmonary vein

Left ventricle

Right ventricle

Valves stop blood flowing backwards.

HEART STRUCTURE

The heart is a pump with two sides. Each side has two chambers – the atrium above and the ventricle below. These contract and relax every 0.8 seconds to pump blood around the body.

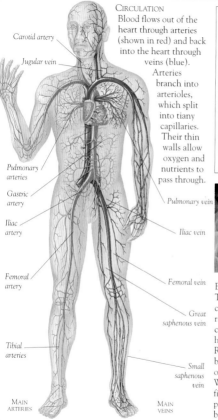

CIRCULATION

Blood flows out of the heart through arteries (shown in red) and back into the heart through veins (blue). Arteries branch into arterioles, which split into tiany capillaries. Their thin walls allow oxygen and nutrients to pass through.

Carotid artery

Jugular vein

Pulmonary arteries

Gastric artery

Iliac artery

Femoral artery

Tibial arteries

MAIN ARTERIES

Pulmonary vein

Iliac vein

Femoral vein

Great saphenous vein

Small saphenous vein

MAIN VEINS

HEART FACTS

- The circulatory system contains around 150,000 km (93,000 miles) of blood vessels.

- The heart rate increases with exercise to provide muscles with extra oxygen.

- With every heart beat, the heart pumps out about 80 ml (2.8 fl oz) of blood.

BLOOD

The liquid part of blood, called plasma, contains a rich mixture of blood cells, proteins, antibodies, hormones, and minerals. Red blood cells are button-shaped, and carry oxygen around the body. White cells, or leucocytes, fight infection. The tiny platelets help to plug leaks by forming blood clots.

DIGESTION

FOOD IS BROKEN down by a process called digestion. Once food has been swallowed, it slips into the alimentary canal, or gut, which runs from mouth to anus. As food passes through the gut, it is gradually digested and absorbed until all that emerges at the far end is waste.

ALIMENTARY CANAL
The digestive tract runs from the mouth to the anus and is about 9 m (30 ft) long. Food passes from the mouth, down the oesophagus into the stomach. From here, it passes into the small intestine, made up of the duodenum, jejunum, and ileum, and into the large intestine, made up of the colon and rectum. Several organs and glands are connected to the tract to help digestion.

Teeth soften food by chewing it

Saliva helps to dissolve starch

Food is swallowed as a bolus

Waves of muscular action push food down oesophagus into stomach

Liver

Stomach

Digestive enzymes in duodenum break down food into semi-fluid called chyme

Ileum absorbs digested minerals and nutrients into bloodstream

Indigestible food passes on into colon where water is absorbed

Muscular rectum expels waste through anus

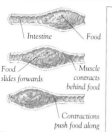

Intestine — *Food*

Food slides forwards — *Muscle contracts behind food*

Contractions push food along

PERISTALSIS
The walls of the digestive tract contain strong muscle fibres that produce wave-like contractions to propel food along. This process is called peristalsis.

STOMACH ACTION
The stomach is a bag-like chamber that stores food. As the stomach fills with food, its walls stretch. Powerful muscles churn up the food, and gastric juices break it down so it can be digested. The food passes from the stomach into the intestines.

Undigested food enters the stomach

Gastric juices digest the food

Broken-down food is pushed into the duodenum

VILLI
The lining of the small intestine has millions of microscopic finger-like villi that absorb nutrients.

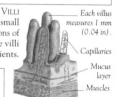

Each villus measures 1 mm (0.04 in).

Capillaries

Mucus layer

Muscles

LIVER
The liver has many functions. It stores vitamins, turns digested food into blood proteins, and makes bile, which helps break fat into tiny globules.

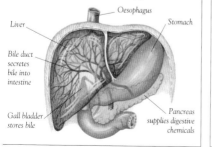

Oesophagus

Liver

Stomach

Bile duct secretes bile into intestine

Gall bladder stores bile

Pancreas supplies digestive chemicals

DIGESTION FACTS

• Food stays in the stomach for up to five hours, and spends up to 20 hours in the colon.

• The wall of the stomach is protected by a lining of mucus so it cannot digest itself.

• The digestive process begins as soon as you take a bite of food.

URINARY SYSTEM

AS BLOOD FLOWS through the kidneys, they filter out waste and drain off excess water. This is expelled from the body as urine, via the ureter, bladder, and urethra. In this way the urinary system clears the blood of toxins and regulates its water content.

THE URINARY SYSTEM

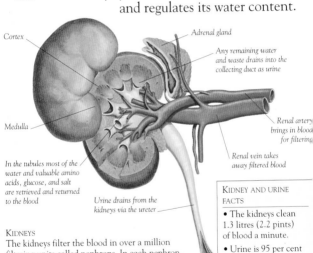

Cortex

Adrenal gland

Any remaining water and waste drains into the collecting duct as urine

Medulla

Renal artery brings in blood for filtering

Renal vein takes away filtered blood

In the tubules most of the water and valuable amino acids, glucose, and salt are retrieved and returned to the blood

Urine drains from the kidneys via the ureter

KIDNEYS

The kidneys filter the blood in over a million filtering units called nephrons. In each nephron, water and tiny molecules are drawn off and channelled through little tubes called tubules. Inside these, valuable molecules and most of the water are retrieved and returned to the blood, leaving only a little water and waste to drain off as urine.

KIDNEY AND URINE FACTS

• The kidneys clean 1.3 litres (2.2 pints) of blood a minute.

• Urine is 95 per cent water. The rest is toxic waste such as urea, which is produced in the liver.

HORMONES

ENDOCRINE glands secrete chemical messengers called hormones into the blood. These stimulate, regulate, and co-ordinate a whole range of body processes.

TESTOSTERONE
In men, the testes produce the hormone testosterone to control the development of sexual characteristics.

Testis

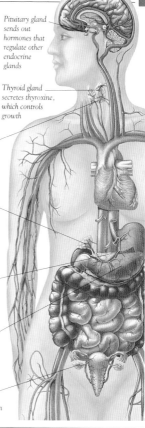

Pituitary gland sends out hormones that regulate other endocrine glands

Thyroid gland secretes thyroxine, which controls growth

Parathyroid glands secrete hormone that raises blood calcium levels

Adrenal glands secrete cortisone, which boosts metabolism, and adrenalin, which primes body for action

Pancreas secretes glucagon and insulin, which regulate blood sugar levels

Stomach and intestines secrete hormones that aid digestion

Ovaries in women make female sex hormones, oestrogen and progesterone

HORMONE FACTS

• Too much growth hormone can cause gigantism (excess growth); too little can cause slow growth.

• The hormone adrenalin can give short bursts of superhuman strength.

REPRODUCTION

FROM PUBERTY ONWARDS, the reproductive system in males and females is sufficiently developed for them to have sexual intercourse and create new human beings. A new life begins when a man's sperm cell fertilizes, or joins with, a woman's egg cell.

THE MALE REPRODUCTIVE SYSTEM

MALE REPRODUCTIVE SYSTEM
Male sex cells, or sperm, are made inside the testicles in tubes called seminiferous tubules. These mature in tubes called the epididymides. When the penis is stimulated, muscles pump sperm from the epididymis along the vas deferens, where they mix with seminal fluid to make semen.

SINGLE SPERM

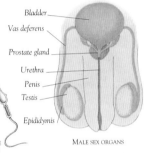

Bladder
Vas deferens
Prostate gland
Urethra
Penis
Testis
Epididymis

MALE SEX ORGANS

THE FEMALE REPRODUCTIVE SYSTEM

FEMALE REPRODUCTIVE SYSTEM
Female sex cells, or ova, are stored in the ovaries. Every 28 days or so, one ovum, or egg, is released during ovulation. The egg passes down one of two fallopian tubes to the uterus, or womb. If the ovum is fertilized, it is embedded in the womb lining. If not, both the ovum and lining are shed during menstruation.

Fallopian tube

SINGLE OVUM

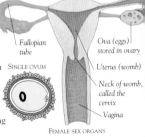

Ova (eggs) stored in ovary
Uterus (womb)
Neck of womb, called the cervix
Vagina

FEMALE SEX ORGANS

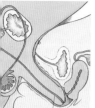

SEXUAL INTERCOURSE
During sexual intercourse,
the man's penis fills with
blood, becomes hard and
erect, and is slid into the
woman's vagina. Semen is
released (ejaculated) into
the vagina. If one of the
300 million sperm reaches
the egg, it may fertilize it.

*Oral
contraceptive pills*

The cap

Condom

CONTRACEPTIVES
Condoms and other
contraceptives are used
to stop conception during
intercourse. They prevent
sperm fertilizing the egg.

nis inside vagina

*Umbilical cord consists
of three intertwined
blood vessels*

*Amnion membrane
containing amniotic
fluid*

*The placenta is a
spongy organ on
the womb lining*

*by turns upside
wn during last
w weeks of
egnancy*

Pregnancy

The fertilized
egg becomes an
embryo, which
grows rapidly in
the uterus. After
eight weeks, it is
a foetus, with
recognizable features
and all its internal
organs. Fed via the
umbilical cord
with food and
oxygen from the
placenta, the foetus
is ready to be born
after 40 weeks.

GENES AND HEREDITY

STORED IN a cell's nucleus are packages called chromosomes, made up of long spirals of the molecule DNA. Each DNA molecule consists of genes, which are responsible for characteristics such as eye colour.

A chromosome has two ident[...] arms called chrom[...]

GENES

Each DNA molecule consists of millions of genes. Each gene provides instructions to make a single protein, used to build a new cell or to control a cell's activities. Genes are passed on to the next generation during sexual reproduction.

Cell

Nucleus

Each cell has 46 chromosomes, except for sex cells, which have 23

Chromosome unwinds

MITOSIS

As the body grows, or when worn-out cells need replacing, the cells divide into two by a process called mitosis. The normal number of chromosomes in each cell is 46. When the cells divide, each new cell has the same number of chromosomes – 46.

Cell copies chromosomes before it divides

Each new cell has 46 chromosomes

MITOSIS

MEIOSIS

Genes are reshuffled in original cell

MEIOSIS

Sex cells are produced during the cell division called meiosis. The original cell's genes are mixed and recombined so that the new cells produced are genetically unique.

Each pair of chromosomes splits in half and the two new cells receive half each

Chromatid

140

Each DNA strand is made up of sections called genes

Genes consist of linked pairs of four different chemicals called bases

Copies of the gene are made and tell the cell to make a particular protein

As the DNA unwinds, the genes are exposed

Each DNA molecule is made up of two spiral strands

GIRL OR BOY
A child's sex depends on the sperm that reaches the mother's X egg; another X chromosome means a girl; a Y means a boy.

GENETIC FACTS
• DNA stands for deoxyribonucleic acid.

• Red blood cells have no nucleus and do not contain genes.

• Women have two X chromosomes. Men have one X chromosome paired with a Y chromosome.

HEREDITY
The passing on of characteristics via the genes is called heredity. A baby inherits half its genes from its mother and half from its father. The reshuffling of genes means that brothers and sisters inherit different genes, but there may be a resemblance.

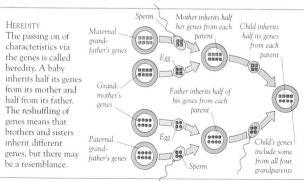

Sperm

Maternal grandfather's genes

Mother inherits half her genes from each parent

Egg

Grandmother's genes

Father inherits half of his genes from each parent

Paternal grandfather's genes

Egg

Sperm

Child inherits half its genes from each parent

Child's genes include some from all four grandparents

FIGHTING INFECTION

IF BACTERIA or viruses enter the body and multiply, you can become ill. To fight infection, the body has a defence mechanism called the immune system.

Adenoid glands

Tonsils

Tonsils and adenoids produce antibodies to fight infection.

Spleen stores special white blood cells called lymphocytes

Small intestine contains lymph tissues that help fight infection

Bone marrow produces lymphocytes

Lymph capillaries drain tissue fluids into lymphatic system

A single macrophage can inject 100 bacteria

MACROPHAGE (BLUE) ENGULFING A YEAST CELL (YELLOW)

SCAVENGER CELLS
Lymphocytes called phagocytes, and larger ones called macrocytes, roam through the blood, engulfing unwanted matter, such as the dirt in a cut.

IMMUNE FACTS
• A fever is caused when white blood cells release proteins called pyrogens, raising the body's temperature.
• Swollen glands are a sign of infection.

LYMPHATIC SYSTEM
Lymph fluid drains waste from the body's tissues into the ducts of the lymphatic system. Germs that enter the lymphatic system are swept towards lymph nodes, where there is a cluster of lymphocytes waiting to fight them.

THE LYMPHATIC SYSTEM

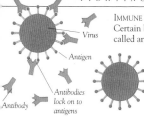

IMMUNE RESPONSE
Certain bacteria and viruses possess substances called antigens, which trigger the immune system into action. When the immune system first meets an antigen, it produces antibodies to fight it. Lymphocytes called B-cells make these antibodies, and each one targets a specific antigen.

Virus

Antigen

Antibodies lock on to antigens

Antibody

Medicine

The body's immune system is remarkably effective at dealing with infection, but sometimes it breaks down or takes a long time to work. Modern drugs and traditional forms of medicine such as herbalism can help the body to combat illness.

DRUGS
The drugs we use to treat illness and disease are made from plant extracts or from chemicals produced in a laboratory. They are commonly taken in the form of tablets, capsules, or liquid.

IMMUNIZATION
Active or passive immunization by injection provides the body with protection from certain diseases.

ACTIVE IMMUNIZATION

PASSIVE IMMUNIZATION

Harmless extracts that cannot cause disease are injected into the body.

People donate blood that contains antibodies.

Vaccine causes B-cells to produce antibodies.

Antibodies to a disease are injected into patient.

Immune system will respond more quickly.

If disease attacks, the antibodies will fight it.

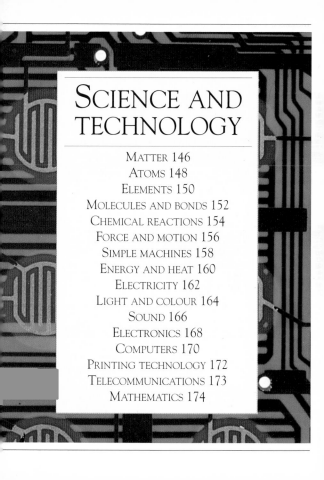

SCIENCE AND TECHNOLOGY

MATTER

FROM THE TINIEST speck of dust to giant stars, everything that exists in the universe is made up of matter. Most matter consists of minute particles called atoms. On Earth, matter usually occurs in one of three forms, or "states", called solid, liquid, or gas.

Electrode

Plasma streaks

PLASMA
A rare fourth state of matter called plasma forms when a gas becomes so hot, electrons (see p.148) break away from its atoms.

GAS
A gas has no fixed volume or shape. Gas particles are widely spaced and loosely bound, with the ability to move freely in all directions. A gas will expand to fill any container it is put in.

Gas dispersing from a chemical reaction

LIQUID
A liquid has a definite volume but no fixed shape. Liquid particles are more loosely bound than solid particles and can move over small distances. A liquid will flow and take the shape of its container.

Every liquid takes the shape of its container

Coins have a rigid shape

SOLID
A solid has a fixed shape and volume. Solid particles are tightly packed in regular patterns. Strong bonds allow the particles to vibrate, but prevent them moving far.

CHANGING STATE

The particles of a substance are held together by bonds that weaken when heated and strengthen when cooled. Heat changes solids to liquids, and liquids to gases. When cooled sufficiently, gases condense to liquids, and liquids freeze to solids.

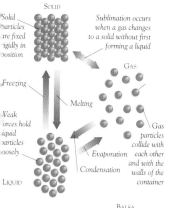

SOLID

Solid particles are fixed rigidly in position

Sublimation occurs when a gas changes to a solid without first forming a liquid

Freezing

Melting

GAS

Weak forces hold liquid particles loosely

Evaporation

Condensation

Gas particles collide with each other and with the walls of the container

LIQUID

Blocks of equal mass but unequal density

LEAD

WAX

BALSA

HIGH DENSITY   MEDIUM DENSITY   LOW DENSITY

MASS, VOLUME, AND DENSITY

The amount of matter in an object is its mass. Volume is the space it occupies. The object's density is its mass divided by its volume.

GAS LAWS

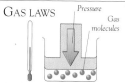

Pressure

Gas molecules

BOYLE'S LAW

At constant temperature (T), the volume of a gas (V) is inversely proportional to the pressure (P) (the gas contracts as the pressure rises): PV=constant.

PRESSURE LAW

At constant volume, the pressure of a gas is proportional to the temperature (increasing the temperature raises the gas's pressure): P/T=constant.

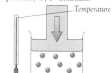

Temperature

CHARLES' LAW

At constant pressure, the gas's volume is proportional to the temperature (the gas expands if temperature rises): V/T=constant.

ATOMS

MATTER IS MADE UP of tiny particles called atoms.
Atoms form the building blocks for everything in
the universe. There are just over a hundred types of
atom, which are themselves made up of even smaller
"subatomic" particles. Atoms and subatomic particles
are not solid – they are clouds of energy.

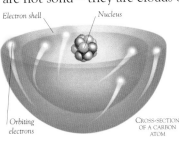

Electron shell

Nucleus

Orbiting electrons

CROSS-SECTION
OF A CARBON
ATOM

INSIDE THE ATOM
The centre, or nucleus, of all
but the hydrogen atom contains
protons (with a positive electrical
charge) and neutrons (with no
charge). Negatively charged
particles called electrons orbit
the nucleus at very high speeds,
forming layers or "shells".

NUCLEON NUMBER
The total number of protons and neutrons contained
in the nucleus of an atom is called
the nucleon number. The most common
form of carbon is referred to as carbon–12,
as it contains 6 protons and 6 neutrons.

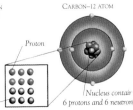

CARBON–12 ATOM

Proton

Neutron

*Nucleus contain
6 protons and 6 neutron*

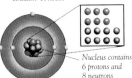

CARBON–14 ATOM

*Nucleus contains
6 protons and
8 neutrons*

ISOTOPES
All atoms of a particular element have the
same number of protons, but some forms of
the element may have different numbers of
neutrons. These variations are called isotope
The isotope carbon–14, for example, has two
more neutrons than the isotope carbon–12.

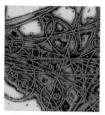

PARTICLE COLLISIONS

Scientists have discovered many new particles by smashing together subatomic particles at high speed. Most new particles exist for only a fraction of a second after the collision, but their movements can be recorded by computers.

PATHS OF PARTICLES CREATED AFTER SUBATOMIC COLLISION

QUARKS

Particles such as neutrons and protons are called hadrons. A hadron is made up of three smaller particles called quarks, which are stuck together by tiny particles called gluons. Quarks occur in two types: "down" quarks have one-third of a unit of negative electric charge, while "up" quarks have two-thirds of a unit of positive charge.

$-\frac{1}{3}$ $+\frac{2}{3}$ $-\frac{1}{3}$ $+\frac{2}{3}$

$-\frac{1}{3}$ $+\frac{2}{3}$

QUARKS IN A NEUTRON

A neutron has one up quark and two down quarks, giving an overall neutral charge.

QUARKS IN A PROTON

A proton has two up quarks and one down quark, giving an overall positive charge.

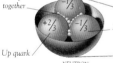

Gluon particles hold quarks together

$+\frac{2}{3}$ $-\frac{1}{3}$ $-\frac{1}{3}$

Down quark

Up quark

NEUTRON

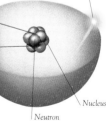

Electron

Nucleus

Neutron

BINDING FORCES

Atoms are held together by four fundamental forces, or interactions. Electrons are attracted to protons by electromagnetic force, while "strong" and "weak" nuclear forces bind together particles inside the nucleus. These basic forces, plus the pull of gravity, hold the entire universe together.

ELEMENTS

AN ELEMENT is a substance
made from only one type of atom.
The known elements are set out in a
chart called the periodic table. This chart
arranges elements into "groups"
(columns) and "periods" (rows).

Veins of pure gold

QUARTZ

Atomic number

Chemical symbol

Name of element

NAME, NUMBER, AND SYMBOL
Each box carries basic details about
an element. The atomic number is
the number of protons in the nucleus
of one of the element's atoms.

GROUP I   GROUP II

*The number of electron
shells circling the nuclei of
an element's atoms increases
down each group. Elements
in the same group have
similar chemical properties.*

Group I	Group II	3	4	5	6	7	8	9
1 H Hydrogen								
3 Li Lithium	4 Be Beryllium					15 P Phosphorus		
11 Na Sodium	12 Mg Magnesium							
19 K Potassium	20 Ca Calcium	21 Sc Scandium	22 Ti Titanium	23 V Vanadium	24 Cr Chromium	25 Mn Manganese	26 Fe Iron	27 Co Cobalt
37 Rb Rubidium	38 Sr Strontium	39 Y Yttrium	40 Zr Zirconium	41 Nb Niobium	42 Mo Molybdenum	43 Tc Technetium	44 Ru Ruthenium	45 Rh Rhodium
55 Cs Caesium	56 Ba Barium	57-71 Lanthanides	72 Hf Hafnium	73 Ta Tantalum	74 W Tungsten	75 Re Rhenium	76 Os Osmium	77 Ir Iridium
87 Fr Francium	88 Ra Radium	89-103 Actinides	104 Unq Unnilquadium	105 Unp Unnilpentium	106 Unh Unnilhexium	107 Uns Unnilseptium	108 Uno Unniloctium	109 Une Unnilennium

57 La Lanthanum	58 Ce Cerium	59 Pr Praseodymium	60 Nd Neodymium	61 Pm Promethium	62 Sm Samarium
89 Ac Actinium	90 Th Thorium	91 Pa Protactinium	92 U Uranium	93 Np Neptunium	94 Pu Plutonium

150

TYPES OF ELEMENT KEY

- ALKALI METALS
- ALKALINE-EARTH METALS
- TRANSITION METALS
- LANTHANIDES
- ACTINIDES
- POOR METALS
- SEMI-METALS
- NON-METALS
- NOBLE GASES

GROUPS AND PERIODS

Each period starts on the left with a highly reactive alkali metal that has one electron in its outer shell. It ends on the right with a stable noble gas in group 18 (0) with eight electrons in its outer shell. Elements in the same group have the same number of electrons in their outer shells.

18
2 **He** Helium

As the atomic number increases by one along each period, the chemical properties of the element gradually change

13	14	15	16	17
5 **B** Boron	6 **C** Carbon	7 **N** Nitrogen	8 **O** Oxygen	9 **F** Fluorine	10 **Ne** Neon
13 **Al** Aluminium	14 **Si** Silicon	15 **P** Phosphorus	16 **S** Sulphur	17 **Cl** Chlorine	18 **Ar** Argon

10	11	12					
28 **Ni** Nickel	29 **Cu** Copper	30 **Zn** Zinc	31 **Ga** Gallium	32 **Ge** Germanium	33 **As** Arsenic	34 **Se** Selenium	35 **Br** Bromine	36 **Kr** Krypton
46 **Pd** Palladium	47 **Ag** Silver	48 **Cd** Cadmium	49 **In** Indium	50 **Sn** Tin	51 **Sb** Antimony	52 **Te** Tellurium	53 **I** Iodine	54 **Xe** Xenon
78 **Pt** Platinum	79 **Au** Gold	80 **Hg** Mercury	81 **Tl** Thallium	82 **Pb** Lead	83 **Bi** Bismuth	84 **Po** Polonium	85 **At** Astatine	86 **Rn** Radon

GROUP III GROUP IV GROUP V GROUP VI GROUP VII GROUP 0

An element's atomic number also corresponds to the total number of electrons orbiting the nucleus of one of its atoms.

Two alternative number systems are used to group the elements

Lanthanides and actinides are set apart from the main table to make it easier to understand

63 **Eu** Europium	64 **Gd** Gadolinium	65 **Tb** Terbium	66 **Dy** Dysprosium	67 **Ho** Holmium	68 **Er** Erbium	69 **Tm** Thulium	70 **Yb** Ytterbium	71 **Lu** Luterium
95 **Am** Americium	96 **Cm** Curium	97 **Bk** Berkelium	98 **Cf** Californium	99 **Es** Einsteinium	100 **Fm** Fermium	101 **Md** Mendelevium	102 **No** Nobelium	103 **Lr** Lawrencium

MOLECULES AND BONDS

A GROUP OF ATOMS that are linked together is called a molecule. A molecule may be made up of a few or very many atoms. Molecules are formed when the electrical forces created by electron movement "bond" atoms together. Electron transfer between atoms occurs because some atoms require extra electrons to fill their outer shell.

WATER MOLECULE

CHEMICAL FORMULAE
A chemical formula uses letters and numbers to show how elements combine in a compound. The formula for a water molecule is H_2O, as it is made up of two atoms of hydrogen linked to a single atom of oxygen.

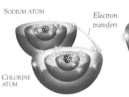

SODIUM ATOM

Electron transfers

CHLORINE ATOM

POSITIVELY CHARGED SODIUM ION

Both ions now have eight electrons in their outer shells

Ionic bond

NEGATIVELY CHARGED CHLORIDE ION

IONIC BONDS
In ionic bonding, excess electrons transfer from the full outer shell of one atom to the outer shell of another that requires extra electrons to fill it. The transfer leaves both atoms as charged particles called ions. The atom losing the electron becomes a positively charged ion, or cation, and the atom gaining the electron becomes a negative ion, or anion. The force of attraction between the opposite charges binds the ions together.

GIANT IONIC STRUCTURE

A crystal of salt (sodium chloride) contains
sodium and chloride ions arranged in a regular,
connected network that extends throughout
the crystal. This network is called a
giant ionic lattice.

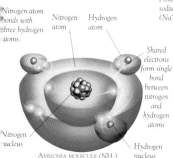

Nitrogen atom
bonds with
three hydrogen
atoms.

Nitrogen
atom

Hydrogen
atom

Shared
electrons
form single
bond
between
nitrogen
and
hydrogen
atoms

Nitrogen
nucleus

Hydrogen
nucleus

AMMONIA MOLECULE (NH_3)

Positive
sodium ion
(Na^+)

Negative
chloride
ion (Cl^-)

SODIUM CHLORIDE

COVALENT BONDS

Ionic bonds are formed between
metals and non-metals. In covalent
bonds, non-metals bind together
by sharing electrons. Two atoms
each "donate" an electron, and
the electrons form a pair that
orbits both nuclei, holding the
atoms together as a molecule.
In a double bond, each atom
donates two electrons.

ORGANIC CHEMISTRY

Carbon compounds are extremely common
because carbon atoms link up easily with
atoms of most other elements, and have the
ability to form very stable bonds with other
carbon atoms. All living things contain some
compounds of carbon. The study of substances
containing carbon is known as
organic chemistry.

MATERIALS CONTAINING
CARBON COMPOUNDS

Plants

Fuels
(butane,
petrol)

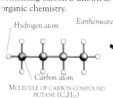

Hydrogen atom

Earthenware

Foods

Carbon atom

MOLECULE OF CARBON COMPOUND
BUTANE (C_4H_{10})

Textiles

Natural
sponge

Plastics

Soaps

CHEMICAL REACTIONS

WHEN A CHEMICAL reaction occurs, new substances (called products) form from the original chemicals taking place in the reaction (called reactants). The atoms of the reactants rearrange themselves to form products.

Electron

ELECTRON TRANSFER
During the oxidation process atoms lose electrons and are "oxidized". During reduction atoms gain electrons and are "reduced".

EXOTHERMIC REACTIONS
A reaction that gives out more heat than it takes in, such as burning, is called an exothermic reaction. Oxidation and reduction are both types of exothermic reaction. Oxidation occurs when a substance combines with oxygen. Reduction takes place when a substance loses oxygen.

Heat is produced, warming surrounding air

Log burns, combining with oxygen in an oxidation reaction

Heat is absorbed during cooking

ACIDS
An acid is a compound that forms hydrogen ions when it dissolves in water. The greater the concentration of ions, the stronger the acid. Strong acids are corrosive and can burn skin and dissolve metals. The pH scale measures acidity; pH 1 is the strongest acid, pH 7 is neutral.

ENDOTHERMIC REACTIONS
Reactions that take in more heat than they give out, such as those during cooking, are endothermic

UNIVERSAL INDICATOR COLOUR/PH CHART OF ACIDS						
DIGESTIVE JUICES	CAR BATTERY	LEMON JUICE	VINEGAR	ACID RAIN	TAP WATER	PURE WATER

Mixtures and compounds

Most substances are
made of two or more
elements, either
mingled loosely as
mixtures or, after
chemical reactions,
combined strongly
as compounds.

CHLORINE
(GAS)

+

SODIUM
(METAL)

=

SODIUM CHLORIDE
OR COMMON SALT

COMPOUNDS

A compound is a substance in which the atoms
of two or more elements are combined together.
Common salt (sodium chloride), for example, is
a compound of sodium and chlorine atoms.

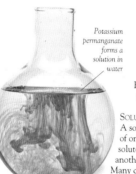

*Potassium
permanganate
forms a
solution in
water*

COLLOIDS

In a colloid, tiny
particles of one
substance are
dispersed evenly
throughout another.
Hair gel is a colloid of solid
fat particles suspended in water.

HAIR GEL

SOLUTIONS

A solution is a mixture
of one substance (the
solute) dissolved in
another (the solvent).
Many compounds
dissolve in water, forming
weak bonds with water molecules.

BASES AND ALKALIS

A base is a compound that
neutralizes acidity. Alkalis
are bases that dissolve in
water. The pH scale for
bases ranges from neutral
pure water (pH 7) to the
strongest alkali (pH 14).

UNIVERSAL INDICATOR COLOUR/PH CHART OF BASES

PURE WATER	SOAP	BICARBONATE OF SODA	DISINFECTANT	HOUSEHOLD CLEANER	CALCIUM HYDROXIDE	OVEN CLEANER	SODIUM HYDROXIDE

FORCE AND MOTION

ALL MOVEMENT, or motion, is caused
by forces. A force is invisible, but its
effects are observable. Forces push or
pull, causing objects to start or stop
moving, change speed or direction,
bend, twist, or change shape.

ATHLETES ACCELERATING UNDER
FORCE FROM MUSCLES

*Cue strikes white ball,
transmitting momentum
that overcomes ball's inertia*

Ball accelerates away

*White ball strikes red
ball, transferring
some of its
momentum*

INERTIA AND MOMENTUM

The tendency of all objects to resist efforts to
change their state or motion, whether they
are actually moving or at rest, is called inertia.
Momentum is the transferable force possessed
by an object moving in a straight line, a
circle, or back and forth. It is calculated by
multiplying the object's mass by its velocity.

VELOCITY AND
ACCELERATION

The speed of an object
in a particular direction
is called its velocity.
A cornering motorcycle,
for example, keeps a
constant speed but
changes velocity as the
direction of motion shifts.
An increase in
the velocity of an object
is called acceleration.
As its velocity decreases,
the object undergoes
deceleration.

*Transferred momentum
accelerates red ball away*

NEWTON'S LAWS OF MOTION

• **First Law**: An object will
remain at rest or continue
travelling at a uniform
velocity unless a force
acts on it.

• **Second Law**: An object's
acceleration is equal to the
force acting on it, divided
by the object's mass.

• **Third Law**: When two
objects act on each other,
they experience equal
forces in opposite directions.

Athlete pulls on hammer, producing centipetal force

Centripetal force pulls hammer inwards

Hammer's direction changes constantly

Hammer's inertia pulls it outwards

Hammer flies off when released

CIRCULAR MOTION
A whirling object, such as an athlete's hammer, tries to fly off in a straight line, but circular motion, or centripetal force, pulls it towards the centre of the circle. This force constantly changes the object's direction, keeping it moving in a circle.

Gravity

A force of attraction between all objects is called gravity. The greater the object's mass, the stronger the pull. The large mass of the Earth generates a strong gravitational pull, keeping us on the ground.

Equal mass but different weight

ON THE MOON   ON EARTH

WEIGHT AND MASS
The force exerted on an object by gravity is called weight. Mass is the amount of matter an object contains.

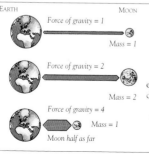

EARTH   MOON

Force of gravity = 1

Mass = 1

Force of gravity = 2

Mass = 2

Force of gravity = 4

Mass = 1

Moon half as far

NEWTON'S LAW OF GRAVITATION
According to Newton's law, the force of gravity between two objects is calculated by multiplying their masses and dividing the result by the square of the distance between them. For example, if the Moon was half its actual distance from Earth, the force of gravity between them would be four times as strong. If the Moon had twice as much mass, the gravity between the Earth and Moon would be twice as great.

SIMPLE MACHINES

MACHINES can make tasks easier by changing the size or direction of a force. Many machines magnify effort, which is the level of force needed to overcome a resisting force, or load.

Axle turns with greater force

Effort applied to wheel rim magnified by axle

WHEEL AND AXLE
Effort applied to the wheel rim is magnified by the axle, which turns with greater force over a shorter distance. Applying effort to an axle turns the wheel rim with less force over a greater distance.

INCLINED PLANE
An inclined plane is an angled surface, or slope, that reduces the effort required to move an object. Moving a car by pulling it up a ramp, for example, is easier than lifting it vertically. The car must travel further, but less effort is needed to move it.

Force of tension in rope pulls car up slope

Car has to travel further than if lifted vertically

Weight of car pulls it downwards

Winch magnifies force applied to a handle

Ramp (inclined plane)

A winch is a form of wheel and axle

Force used to wield axe magnified and transferred into log, pushing it apart

WEDGE
A wedge is a moving inclined plane that pushes an object with more force than the effort needed to move the wedge. Cutting blades, such as axes, make use of the wedge.

Screw head

Screw thread

SCREW
A screw's spiral groove, or thread, is a type of inclined plane wrapped around a shaft. When the screw head is turned, the thread moves the whole screw forward with more force than the turning effort.

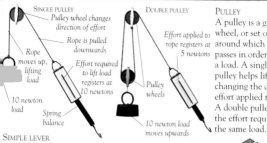

SINGLE PULLEY
Pulley wheel changes direction of effort
Rope is pulled downwards
Rope moves up, lifting load
Effort required to lift load registers at 10 newtons
10 newton load
Spring balance

DOUBLE PULLEY
Effort applied to rope registers at 5 newtons
Pulley wheels
10 newton load moves upwards

PULLEY
A pulley is a grooved wheel, or set of wheels, around which a rope passes in order to move a load. A single-wheeled pulley helps lift a load by changing the direction of effort applied to the rope. A double pulley halves the effort required to lift the same load.

SIMPLE LEVER
A lever is a bar that exerts a force by turning on a pivot, or "fulcrum". A small effort moved through a great distance at one end moves a larger load through a shorter distance at the other end.

Small force is applied
Lever magnifies force
Fulcrum
Direction of movement
Rotary (circular) motion
Linear (straight) motion
Rack
Pinion
Large load to be moved
Worm gear (cog meshes with screw-threaded shaft)
Direction of motion
Spur gear

MACHINE FACTS
• A machine's force ratio (FR) shows how effective it is as a force magnifier. Force ratio is the force of the load divided by the effort needed to move it.

• A machine's velocity ratio (VR) shows how effective it is as a distance magnifier. Velocity ratio is the distance moved by the effort divided by the distance moved by the load.

• Units of force are called newtons (N).

GEARS
Intermeshing toothed wheels, or cogs, that transmit and direct force and motion are called gears. A gear system uses large cogs to turn small cogs with less force but greater speed, and small cogs to turn large cogs with more force but less speed.

ENERGY AND HEAT

THE ABILITY to cause an action is
called energy. Light, sound, heat,
and electricity are forms of energy.
Human energy comes from the
chemical energy in food. Movement
energy is also called kinetic energy.

*Jack has
kinetic energy*

*Spring in
box has
potential
energy.*

POTENTIAL ENERGY
Stored energy is
called potential energy.
Squeezing or stretching
an object makes it gain
potential energy, which
is stored until the object
is released. Dropping a
raised object converts its
potential to fall to Earth
into kinetic energy.

200 N

200 N

*Total
weight is
400 N*

*Raised
weights have
gravitational
potential energy*

*Bar carries
two sets of
200 N
weights*

*Weights are
raised about
1.5 m (4.9 ft)*

WORK AND POWER
Work is done
when a force
moves something.
Energy provides
the ability to do
work. When work
is done, energy
converts from one
form to another.
The rate at which
work is done, or
energy changed
from one form to
another, is
called power.

*Weightlifter
raises weights
in two seconds*

WEIGHTLIFTER
RAISING
WEIGHTS

WORK FACTS

• The **joule** (J) is the
SI unit of energy and
work: 1 J of energy is
used when a force
of 1 newton moves
through a distance of
1 metre. A kilojoule
(kJ) is 1,000 joules.

• The **watt** (W) is the
SI unit of power: 1 W
is the conversion of
1 joule of energy from
one form to another in
1 second. A kilowatt
(kW) is 1,000 watts.

Heat and temperature

The more energy an object's particles have, the hotter the object is. Heat is the total kinetic energy of an object's moving particles.

MEASURING TEMPERATURE

Temperature is a measure of the average kinetic energy of an object's moving particles. Most liquid and electronic thermometers measure temperature on the Celsius and Fahrenheit scales.

LIQUID THERMOMETER

Temperature

Column of mercury or alcohol expands as temperature rises

Heat-sensitive tip

Liquid-crystal display

ELECTRONIC THERMOMETER

Heat
from feet conducts into stone, leaving feet feeling cold

CONDUCTION

Heat energy always passes from hot objects to cooler ones. Heat travels through solids by conduction. Particles in the heated part of the solid vibrate and excite neighbouring particles.

CONVECTION AND RADIATION

Heat travels through liquids and gases by convection. Hot fluids are less dense than cold ones and float upwards, sinking again as they cool. Matter can also lose or gain heat energy by radiation.

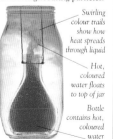

Swirling colour trails show how heat spreads through liquid

Hot, coloured water floats to top of jar

Bottle contains hot, coloured water

SCALE OF TEMPERATURE
Temperatures are measured in degrees on the Celsius (C) and Fahrenheit (F) scales, and in Kelvins (K).

250°C, 482°F, 523K
Burning point of wood

218°C, 424°F, 491K
Explosion point of nitro-glycerine

140°C, 284°F, 413K
Sauna bath

100°C, 212°F, 373K
Boiling point of water

56.7°C, 134°F, 329.7K
Midday heat in Death Valley, California

37°C, 98.6°F, 310K
Human body temperature

22°C, 71.6°F, 295K
Body temperature of spiny anteater

0°C, 32°F, 273K
Freezing point of pure water

–39°C, –32°F, 234K
Freezing point of mercury

–273°C, –459°F, 0K
Absolute zero

ELECTRICITY

THE MOVEMENT OF electrons between atoms creates a form of energy called electricity. A flow of electrons is called a current. Electric currents and certain materials generate a force called magnetism.

BALLOON CHARGED BY RUBBING (FRICTION)

ELECTROSTATIC INDUCTION
Electricity that does not flow in a current is called static electricity. A static charge can be produced by rubbing a balloon against an object such as a sweater. Friction causes electrons to transfer from the sweater's atoms to the balloon's atoms; the balloon gains a negative electric charge and the sweater a positive one. The charged balloon can also induce a static charge in other objects.

Negatively charged balloon repels electrons in pieces of paper, giving paper a positive static charge

Positively charged paper attracted to negatively charged balloon

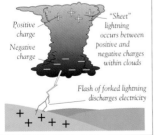

Positive charge

Negative charge

"Sheet" lightning occurs between positive and negative charges within clouds

Flash of forked lightning discharges electricity

LIGHTNING
Inside a thundercloud, positive and negative charges separate between the top and bottom of the cloud. The negative charge at the bottom of the cloud induces a positive charge to build up in the ground below. "Forked" lightning occurs when a strong pulse of electric current suddenly flows between the two opposite charges, discharging from the cloud's base to the ground and back again.

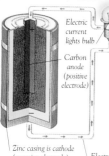

Electric current lights bulb

Carbon anode (positive electrode)

Zinc casing is cathode (negative electrode)

Electron flow

BATTERY

A battery is a device that produces and stores electric current. Many batteries produce current by using carbon and zinc conductors called electrodes and a chemical paste called an electrolyte. In a circuit, the current flows from the negative electrode (cathode) to the positive (anode). An electric current can be used to power anything from a light bulb to a computer.

Battery

Current flows through wires

Electrical contacts

Opposing magnetic fields cause coil to rotate

Rotating coil can be attached to a drive shaft or flywheel

ELECTRIC MOTOR

A current flows through a wire coil between the poles of a magnet. The current creates a magnetic field around the coil that interacts with the field produced by the magnet, forcing the coil to turn.

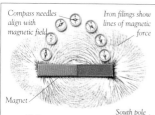

Compass needles align with magnetic field

Iron filings show lines of magnetic force

Magnet

MAGNETISM

A magnet exerts an invisible field of magnetic force that attracts objects made of iron, and a few other metals. Every magnet has two ends, called its north and south poles, where the forces it exerts are strongest. An electromagnet is a piece of iron that exerts magnetic force when a current is passed through it.

Unlike, or opposite, magnetic poles (a north pole and a south pole) attract each other. Like poles (two north or two south poles) repel each other. Iron filings scattered near the magnets show the lines of attraction and repulsion.

South pole

ATTRACTION   North pole

Two south poles   REPULSION

LIGHT AND COLOUR

THE FASTEST-MOVING form of energy is light. It travels in waves that are part of a range of radiation called the electromagnetic spectrum. Visible "white light" is a mixture of many different colours of light, each with its own frequency and wavelength.

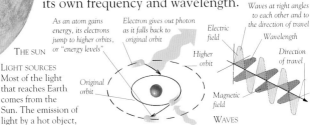

As an atom gains energy, its electrons jump to higher orbits, or "energy levels"

Electron gives out photon as it falls back to original orbit

THE SUN

Higher orbit

Original orbit

Waves at right angles to each other and to the direction of travel

Electric field

Wavelength

Direction of travel

Magnetic field

LIGHT SOURCES
Most of the light that reaches Earth comes from the Sun. The emission of light by a hot object, such as the Sun, is called incandescence. Luminescence is the emission of light without using heat.

PHOTONS
A photon is a particle of electromagnetic radiation that makes up light rays, X-rays, and radio waves.

WAVES
Electromagnetic radiation travels as waves of oscillating (fluctuating) electric and magnetic fields.

RADIO

TELEVISION

MICROWAVE OVEN

INFRARED HOB

Infrared (IR) rays

ELECTROMAGNETIC SPECTRUM

Radio waves

Microwaves

| 10^5 | 10^4 | 10^3 | 10^2 | 10 | 1 | 10^{-1} | 10^{-2} | 10^{-3} | 10^{-4} | 10^{-5} | 10^{-6} |

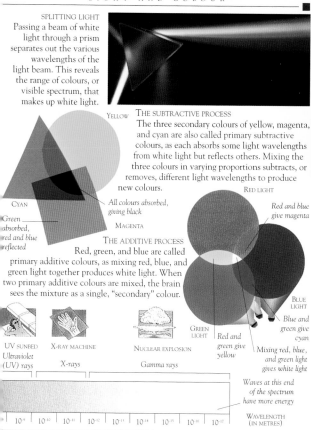

SPLITTING LIGHT

Passing a beam of white light through a prism separates out the various wavelengths of the light beam. This reveals the range of colours, or visible spectrum, that makes up white light.

YELLOW

THE SUBTRACTIVE PROCESS

The three secondary colours of yellow, magenta, and cyan are also called primary subtractive colours, as each absorbs some light wavelengths from white light but reflects others. Mixing the three colours in varying proportions subtracts, or removes, different light wavelengths to produce new colours.

CYAN

All colours absorbed, giving black

Green absorbed, red and blue reflected

MAGENTA

RED LIGHT

Red and blue give magenta

THE ADDITIVE PROCESS

Red, green, and blue are called primary additive colours, as mixing red, blue, and green light together produces white light. When two primary additive colours are mixed, the brain sees the mixture as a single, "secondary" colour.

BLUE LIGHT

Blue and green give cyan

GREEN LIGHT

Red and green give yellow

Mixing red, blue, and green light gives white light

UV SUNBED

Ultraviolet (UV) rays

X-RAY MACHINE

X-rays

NUCLEAR EXPLOSION

Gamma rays

Waves at this end of the spectrum have more energy

10^{-9}	10^{-12}	10^{-11}	10^{-12}	10^{-11}	10^{-14}	10^{-15}	10^{-16}	10^{-17}

WAVELENGTH (IN METRES)

SOUND

A SOUND source generates vibrations that pass though a material in waves. Our ears pick up sound waves travelling in the air around us. Sound waves can travel through solids, liquids, and gases, but not through a vacuum as there are no particles of matter to carry vibrations.

DECIBELS	
140	EAR DAMAGE (ROCKET LIFTING OFF)
120	PAIN THRESHOLD (JET PLANE TAKING OFF)
100	ROCK CONCERT
80	PNEUMATIC DRILL
60	NORMAL CONVERSATION
30	PEOPLE WHISPERING 5 M (18 FT) AWAY
10	LEAVES FALLING 1 M (3.3 FT) AWAY
0	THRESHOLD OF HUMAN HEARING – SOUND JUST AUDIBLE

Tuning fork vibrates, causing pressure variations in surrounding air

High pressure (compression)

Low pressure (rarefaction)

Sound wave

SOUND WAVES

A sound source produces vibrations that squeeze and stretch surrounding air. Squeezing air molecules together creates high pressure, or "compression". Stretching air creates an area of low pressure, or "rarefaction". Alternating compressions and rarefactions travel through air as sound waves.

LOUDNESS

The greater the pressure changes between a sound wave's highest and lowest points (amplitude), the louder the sound. Loudness is measured in decibels (dB). A 10 dB increase means the sound is ten times as loud.

HUMAN
HEARS: 20–20,000 Hz
MAKES: 85–1,100 Hz

PITCH

A sound's pitch is how high or low its soundwave is. Pitch depends on frequency vibrations a second, measured in hertz (Hz).

NUCLEAR EXPLOSION
MAKES: 0.01 Hz

ELEPHANT
HEARS: 1–20,000
MAKES: 12 Hz

RECORDING SOUND

COMPACT
DISC

SOUND SYSTEMS

All sound recording systems store sound by making copies of sound waves, either as spiral grooves on a vinyl record, magnetic patterns on tape, or tiny, laser-scanned pits on a compact disc.

Record
groove

Stylus picks
up sound
stored as
electrical
signals in
groove

VINYL RECORD

Magnetic field
aligns particles
on tape to
reproduce
sound

Pits pressed into
CD surface store
sound as a sequence
of binary numbers

CASSETTE TAPE

MICROPHONE

In a moving-coil microphone, sound waves cause a wire coil to vibrate, or move, within a magnetic field. This makes an electric current flow through the coil. The current fluctuates in strength as the sound waves change, producing electrical signals that mirror the sound waves.

Permanent
magnet

Diaphragm
of thin
plastic or
metal foil

Permanent
magnet

Wire coil
forms an
electromagnet

Electromagnet

Diaphragm

LOUDSPEAKER

Feeding electric signals to a loudspeaker generates a varying magnetic field around an electromagnet. The varying field causes a diaphragm to vibrate, producing sound waves.

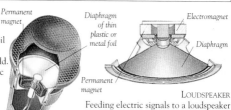

DOG
HEARS: 15–50,000 Hz
MAKES: 450–1,080 Hz

BAT
HEARS: 1,000–120,000 Hz
MAKES: 10,000–120,000 Hz

ULTRASOUND SCANNER
MAKES AND RECEIVES:
3,500,000–7,500,000
Hz

PORPOISE
HEARS: 150–150,000 Hz
MAKES: 7,000–120,000 Hz

ELECTRONICS

THE SCIENCE OF electronics is concerned with controlling and directing the movement of electrons. The complex operation of machines such as computers and jet aircraft is dependent on electronic technology.

Three layer "sandwich" of n- and p-type silicon

SEMICONDUCTORS

A semiconductor is a material used in most electronic components, which can vary its ability to conduct electricity. Adding impurities alters its electrical properties. Boron atoms in p-type silicon take up electrons from the outer shells of silicon atoms, leaving moving "holes" that carry current. In n-type silicon, extra electrons donated by added arsenic atoms carry current.

TRANSISTOR

A transistor is a semiconducting component that boosts or switches current. In computers, transistors switch on and off many times each second, enabling rapid information processing.

Hole in outer shell of silicon atom moves, carrying current

Extra electron moves, carrying current

P-TYPE SILICON (SEMICONDUCTOR)   *Boron atom*

N-TYPE SILICON (SEMICONDUCTOR)   *Arsenic atom*

INTERNATIONAL ELECTRICAL COMPONENT SYMBOLS

CAPACITOR
Stores charge

DIODE
Permits current to flow in one direction only; can also be used to convert a.c. signals to d.c. signals (a rectifier)

LIGHT-EMITTING DIODE
Emits light when current flows through it

MICROPHONE
Converts sound waves into a.c. signals (and vice versa)

LOUDSPEAKER
Converts a.c. signals into sound waves

n-p-n TRANSISTOR
Amplifies electric current, and turns it on and off

p-n-p TRANSISTOR
Amplifies electric current, and turns it on and off

INTEGRATED CIRCUITS

An integrated circuit, or "microchip" is a tiny piece, or "wafer", of silicon that contains a complete circuit of thousands of electronic components. Layers of n- and p-type semi-conductors and other materials are built up on the silicon wafer and linked by fine conducting wires.

MAGNIFIED OVERLAY OF AN INTEGRATED CIRCUIT

Circuits are "printed" onto wafer photographically through transparent overlay

Detailed overlay plans are made for each layer of the chip

Each plan is a different colour

BINARY CODE

Microchips store data as on/off electrical pulses called binary code. All information is broken down into sequences of ones (on) and zeros (off). The decimal number 13, for example, is 1101 in binary form.

ON — ON — OFF — ON

2^3 — 2^2 — 2 — 1

$(1 \times 8) + (1 \times 4) + (0 \times 2) + (1 \times 1) = 13$

Microchips, or "chips", are encased in a tough plastic or ceramic capsule

ENCASED INTEGRATED CIRCUIT

Conducting pins can be soldered or plugged into a circuit board

ENCASED CHIP

A microchip is housed in a protective casing that dwarfs the tiny chip itself. An encased chip stores data as electrical signals in binary code, and uses logic gates (see right) to process that data. A microprocessor is a chip that can store instructions in an electronic memory.

LOGIC GATES

Microchips use patterns of transistors called logic gates to process binary code. Different types of gate switch on (open) or off (close) depending on the type of input received.

OUTPUT

AND GATE
Gives an output signal when a signal is applied to one input AND to the other input.

A B

OUTPUT

OR GATE
Gives an output signal when a signal is applied to one input OR to the other input, OR to both.

A B

OUTPUT

NOT GATE
Gives an output signal when a signal does NOT arrive at its input.

INPUT

COMPUTERS

A COMPUTER IS an electronic machine that can perform a wide variety of complex tasks very quickly. Each task is reduced to a series of simple calculations, which enables rapid processing of data.

PERSONAL COMPUTER
The most familiar type of computer is the personal computer (PC), which can only be used by one person at a time. The machinery that makes up a PC, such as the keyboard and mouse, disk drive, and monitor screen, is called "hardware".

Monitor screen displays data

Disk drive uses magnetic "floppy" disks to store and run software

Keyboard and mouse for inputting data

COMPUTER PROGRAMS
A program is a set of instructions that tells a computer to carry out a specific task. This set of instructions may be written as long sets of numbers called "machine code", or in a computer language such as BASIC or FORTRAN. Computer programs are also called "software".

CENTRAL PROCESSING UNIT
A computer is controlled by a central processing unit (CPU), a single microchip containing a large number of circuits. The CPU processes data from the keyboard, ROM, and RAM. It also sends information to the RAM, outputs data to the printer, and displays software on the monitor.

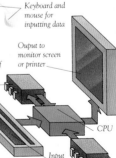

ROM (read-only memory) is permanent and contains the operating system, a set of instructions that tells the computer how to work

Keyboard

RAM (random-access memory) temporarily stores programs that are currently being run

Ouput to monitor screen or printer

CPU

Input

SUPERCOMPUTER

Computers designed to perform complex tasks at the highest possible speeds are called supercomputers. The world's fastest computers use parallel processing. While conventional computers handle tasks one after another (in series), parallel computers perform groups of operations at the same time. Their processing speed is also increased by cooling their components, which aids conductivity.

COMPUTER-AIDED DESIGN

Designers and architects test new ideas by using computer-aided design (CAD) to create 3D graphic models on screen.

This computer is used in the study of particle physics

CRAY X-MP/48
SUPERCOMPUTER

COMPUTER FACTS

• Neural networks are computers designed to imitate the workings of the human brain.

• The world's largest computer manufacturer is US company IBM, which employs about 220,000 people.

CD-ROM

A form of compact disc adapted for use in computers, a CD for CD-ROM can store 450 times more information than a standard floppy disk, including pictures, text, sound, and video.

CD-ROM
software page

VIRTUAL REALITY

A virtual-reality (VR) system enables the user to interact with a computer-generated "virtual" world. A headset supplies the user with 3-D images, while a "data glove" lets you "touch" what you see.

171

PRINTING TECHNOLOGY

THE PROCESS of reproducing words (text) and pictures (images) using ink is called printing. Printing presses enable numerous copies of text and images to be made very quickly. Modern print production uses computers at many stages in the printing process.

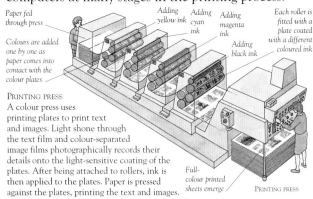

Paper fed through press

Colours are added one by one as paper comes into contact with the colour plates

Adding yellow ink

Adding cyan ink

Adding magenta ink

Adding black ink

Each roller is fitted with a plate coated with a different coloured ink

Full-colour printed sheets emerge

PRINTING PRESS

PRINTING PRESS
A colour press uses printing plates to print text and images. Light shone through the text film and colour-separated image films photographically records their details onto the light-sensitive coating of the plates. After being attached to rollers, ink is then applied to the plates. Paper is pressed against the plates, printing the text and images.

PRINTED FULL-COLOUR IMAGE

YELLOW

MAGENTA

CYAN

BLACK

COLOUR PRINTING
Only four colours are used in colour printing – yellow, magenta, cyan, and black. The image to be printed is scanned electronically, producing a separate piece of film for each colour. The details of these "separations" are transferred onto colour plates in the printing press. The separations are then printed on top of each other, reproducing the full-colour image.

TELECOMMUNICATIONS

THE SCIENCE OF broadcasting sound and pictures over long distances is called telecommunications.

WAVE MODULATION

Radio and television programmes are broadcast by radio waves, which must first be modulated (coded) so that they can carry sound and picture signals. A steady radio wave is modulated by a sound signal in one of two ways. Its amplitude (strength) may be modulated (AM) or its frequency may change (FM).

Wave strength modulated

AM RADIO WAVE

FM RADIO WAVE

Wave frequency modulated

HOW A TELEVISION WORKS

The aerial of a TV receives a modulated carrier wave (carrying sound and picture signals), which is then "demodulated" into electrical signals and sent to a cathode-ray tube. The tube contains three "electron guns" that fire beams of electrons at the phosphor-coated TV screen. Magnetic fields cause the beams to scan the screen. The picture builds as the electrons make the phosphors glow.

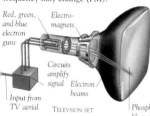

Red, green, and blue electron guns

Electromagnets

Circuits amplify signal

Electron beams

Input from TV aerial

TELEVISION SET

LONG-RANGE COMMUNICATIONS

Low-frequency radio waves can be sent long distances by bouncing them between the ionosphere (an ion-rich region of the atmosphere) and the ground. High-frequency waves are transmitted through the ionosphere to orbiting communication satellites, which relay the radio waves to receiving stations on Earth.

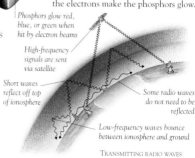

Phosphors glow red, blue, or green when hit by electron beams

High-frequency signals are sent via satellite

Short waves reflect off top of ionosphere

Some radio waves do not need to be reflected

Low-frequency waves bounce between ionosphere and ground

TRANSMITTING RADIO WAVES

MATHEMATICS

THE STUDY OF numbers and shapes is called
mathematics. The different branches of mathematics
enable us to create sophisticated machines, build
structures, and run businesses. Algebra, for example,
uses abstract symbols in place of numbers, while
geometry deals with shapes and lines.

MATHEMATICAL SYMBOLS

$=$
EQUAL TO

$-$
SUBTRACTION

$+$
ADDITION

$\div$
DIVISION

$\times$
MULTIPLICATION

TYPES OF NUMBERS
A written number consists
of digits, or numerals; the
number 313, for example,
has 3 digits. A positive
number is any number
greater than zero, such as
6. A negative number is
less than zero, such as –6.
A prime number can only
be divided by itself and 1.

ROTATION AND ANGLES

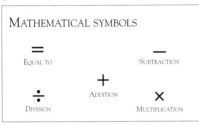

Obtuse angle
90°
130°
Reflex angle
45°
Acute angle
360°
0°
Right angle
Round angle
240°

CIRCLES AND CURVES

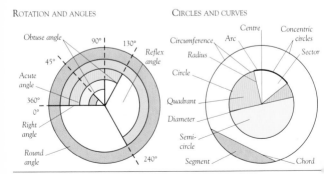

Centre
Concentric circles
Circumference
Arc
Radius
Sector
Circle
Quadrant
Diameter
Semi-circle
Segment
Chord

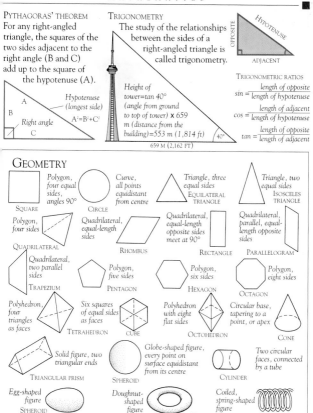

PYTHAGORAS' THEOREM

For any right-angled triangle, the squares of the two sides adjacent to the right angle (B and C) add up to the square of the hypotenuse (A).

A
B
Right angle
C
Hypotenuse (longest side)
$A^2 = B^2 + C^2$

TRIGONOMETRY

The study of the relationships between the sides of a right-angled triangle is called trigonometry.

HYPOTENUSE
OPPOSITE
ADJACENT

Height of tower=tan 40° (angle from ground to top of tower) x 659 m (distance from the building)=553 m (1,814 ft)

659 M (2,162 FT)

TRIGONOMETRIC RATIOS

$$sin = \frac{length\ of\ opposite}{length\ of\ hypotenuse}$$

$$cos = \frac{length\ of\ adjacent}{length\ of\ hypotenuse}$$

$$tan = \frac{length\ of\ opposite}{length\ of\ adjacent}$$

GEOMETRY

Polygon, four equal sides, angles 90°
SQUARE

Curve, all points equidistant from centre
CIRCLE

Triangle, three equal sides
EQUILATERAL TRIANGLE

Triangle, two equal sides
ISOSCELES TRIANGLE

Polygon, four sides
QUADRILATERAL

Quadrilateral, equal-length sides
RHOMBUS

Quadrilateral, equal-length opposite sides meet at 90°
RECTANGLE

Quadrilateral, parallel, equal-length opposite sides
PARALLELOGRAM

Quadrilateral, two parallel sides
TRAPEZIUM

Polygon, five sides
PENTAGON

Polygon, six sides
HEXAGON

Polygon, eight sides
OCTAGON

Polyhedron, four triangles as faces
TETRAHEDRON

Six squares of equal sides as faces
CUBE

Polyhedron with eight flat sides
OCTOHEDRON

Circular base, tapering to a point, or apex
CONE

Solid figure, two triangular ends
TRIANGULAR PRISM

Globe-shaped figure, every point on surface equidistant from its centre
SPHEROID

Two circular faces, connected by a tube
CYLINDER

Egg-shaped figure
SPHEROID

Doughnut-shaped figure
TORUS

Coiled, spring-shaped figure
HELIX

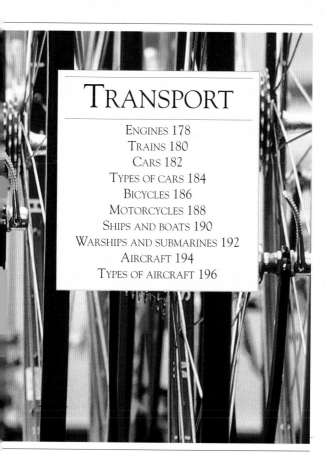

TRANSPORT

ENGINES

AN ENGINE harnesses one form of energy and converts it into motive force, or kinetic energy. Engines range in complexity from simple windmills to sophisticated turbofans.

WINDMILL
The sails of a windmill convert wind force into rotary motion, driving a central shaft that powers the milling machinery.

INTERNAL COMBUSTION
An internal combustion engine provides motive force by harnessing the energy released when a mix of fuel and air is burned (combusted) inside its cylinders. The stages of the combustion cycle are called strokes.

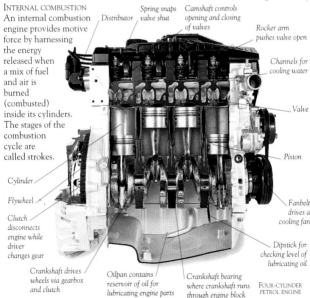

Distributor

Spring snaps valve shut

Camshaft controls opening and closing of valves

Rocker arm pushes valve open

Channels for cooling water

Valve

Piston

Fanbelt drives a cooling fan

Dipstick for checking level of lubricating oil

FOUR-CYLINDER PETROL ENGINE

Cylinder

Flywheel

Clutch disconnects engine while driver changes gear

Crankshaft drives wheels via gearbox and clutch

Oilpan contains reservoir of oil for lubricating engine parts

Crankshaft bearing where crankshaft runs through engine block

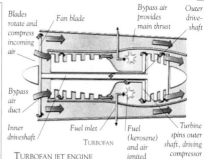

FOUR-STROKE ENGINE CYCLE

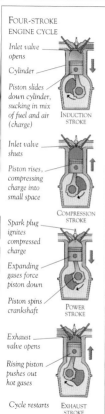

Inlet valve opens

Cylinder

Piston slides down cylinder, sucking in mix of fuel and air (charge)

INDUCTION STROKE

Inlet valve shuts

Piston rises, compressing charge into small space

COMPRESSION STROKE

Spark plug ignites compressed charge

Expanding gases force piston down

Piston spins crankshaft

POWER STROKE

Exhaust valve opens

Rising piston pushes out hot gases

Cycle restarts

EXHAUST STROKE

Blades rotate and compress incoming air

Fan blade

Bypass air provides main thrust

Outer drive-shaft

Bypass air duct

Inner driveshaft

Fuel inlet

TURBOFAN

Fuel (kerosene) and air ignited

Turbine spins outer shaft, driving compressor

TURBOFAN JET ENGINE

A turbofan jet engine sucks in and compresses air, which is then mixed with fuel and ignited. The hot gases produced create forward thrust and drive air-circulating turbines that cool the engine.

Casing of rocket

Most liquid-fuel rockets use liquid hydrogen and liquid oxygen

Liquid hydrogen and liquid oxygen mixture ignited in combustion chamber

Escaping gases provide thrust for rocket

ROCKET ENGINE

A rocket engine burns solid or liquid fuel in an open-ended combustion chamber. The escaping hot gases thrust the rocket upwards.

ENGINE FACTS

• The smallest internal combustion engine is the 0.1 cc model aircraft.

• Temperatures inside an internal combustion engine can reach 1,700°C (3,100°F).

TRAINS

PEOPLE AND GOODS are
transported along railways
in long trains of trucks and
carriages. These trains are
pulled by powerful engine
units called locomotives.

*The tracks rests on
concrete or wooden
beams known as
ties or sleepers*

Rail

*When a switch
takes place, short
sections of rail
swing across
to guide the
train
on to the new
track*

*Switch
(point)*

STEAM TRAVEL

Water in a steam locomotive's boiler is heated
by a coal fire in the firebox, making steam.
Pressure from the steam moves a piston back
and forth, which turns the wheels via a
connecting rod and crank. Steam locomotives
were used to pull the earliest trains, eventually
being replaced by electric and diesel
locomotives in the 1960s.

TRACKS AND SWITCHES

Rails are often welded into one
continuous track as they are laid,
allowing trains to run smoothly.
Trains change tracks at pivoting
sections called switches, or points.

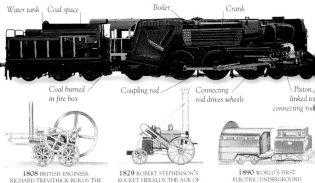

Water tank *Coal space* *Boiler* *Crank*

*Coal burned
in fire box* *Coupling rod* *Connecting
rod drives wheels* *Piston
linked to
connecting rod*

1808 BRITISH ENGINEER
RICHARD TREVITHICK BUILDS THE
FIRST STEAM LOCOMOTIVE

1829 ROBERT STEPHENSON'S
ROCKET HERALDS THE AGE OF
THE PASSENGER TRAIN

1890 WORLD'S FIRST
ELECTRIC UNDERGROUND
RAILWAY OPENS IN UK

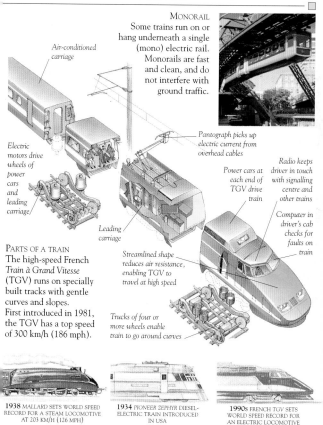

MONORAIL
Some trains run on or hang underneath a single (mono) electric rail. Monorails are fast and clean, and do not interfere with ground traffic.

Air-conditioned carriage

Electric motors drive wheels of power cars and leading carriage

Pantograph picks up electric current from overhead cables

Leading carriage

Radio keeps driver in touch with signalling centre and other trains

Power cars at each end of TGV drive train

Computer in driver's cab checks for faults on train

PARTS OF A TRAIN
The high-speed French *Train à Grand Vitesse* (TGV) runs on specially built tracks with gentle curves and slopes. First introduced in 1981, the TGV has a top speed of 300 km/h (186 mph).

Streamlined shape reduces air resistance, enabling TGV to travel at high speed

Trucks of four or more wheels enable train to go around curves

1938 MALLARD SETS WORLD SPEED RECORD FOR A STEAM LOCOMOTIVE AT 203 KM/H (126 MPH)

1934 PIONEER ZEPHYR DIESEL-ELECTRIC TRAIN INTRODUCED IN USA

1990S FRENCH TGV SETS WORLD SPEED RECORD FOR AN ELECTRIC LOCOMOTIVE

CARS

MODERN CARS use a variety of mechanical and electrical systems to provide the everyday transport we take for granted. Car manufacturers are always looking into new ways of making cars safer and more efficient.

Gear lever changes gears, which enable the engine to run at efficient speeds while the car slows down or speeds up

ENGINE LAYOUTS

FRONT ENGINE,
REAR-WHEEL DRIVE

REAR ENGINE,
REAR-WHEEL DRIVE

FRONT ENGINE,
FRONT-WHEEL DRIVE

MID ENGINE,
REAR-WHEEL DRIVE

Design features
Compromise between traction (road grip), handling, and internal space requirements.

Provides maximum traction, but reduces amount of internal space.

Maximizes internal space, and provides good traction. Used by most family cars.

Good handling and traction, but little internal space. Fast sports cars use this engine layout.

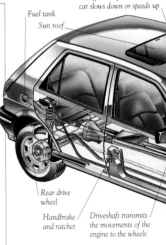

Fuel tank
Sun roof

Rear drive wheel

Handbrake and ratchet

Driveshaft transmits the movements of the engine to the wheels

THE ANATOMY OF A CAR
Most cars have four wheels, an engine at the front, and room for at least two passengers. This illustration shows the main features of a rear-wheel drive hatchback.

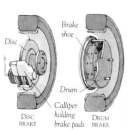

DISC BRAKE

Disc

Brake shoe

Drum

Calliper holding brake pads

DRUM BRAKE

TYPES OF BRAKES

Modern disc brakes use hydraulic pressure to squeeze a steel disc fixed to the wheel between two brake pads, slowing the car. In older drum brakes, curved brake "shoes" push against the inside of a metal drum attached to the wheel.

SUSPENSION SYSTEMS

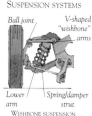

Ball joint

V-shaped "wishbone" arms

Lower arm

Spring/damper strut

WISHBONE SUSPENSION

Spring

Damper unit

Lower arm

Ball joint

MACPHERSON STRUT

Suspension isolates the wheels from the rest of the car, providing a smoother ride. Wishbone suspension uses hinged, swivelling V-shaped arms that enable the steered wheels to go up and down as well as swivel. A MacPherson Strut is a swivelling coil and damper unit that gives lighter suspension for front or rear wheels.

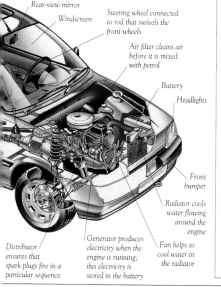

Rear-view mirror

Windscreen

Steering wheel connected to rod that swivels the front wheels

Air filter cleans air before it is mixed with petrol

Battery

Headlights

Front bumper

Radiator cools water flowing around the engine

Distributor ensures that spark plugs fire in a particular sequence

Generator produces electricity when the engine is running; this electricity is stored in the battery

Fan helps to cool water in the radiator

Types of car

Since 1901, when the Oldsmobile became the first mass-produced motor vehicle, car design has changed drastically. Today, there are many different designs to suit a wide variety of purposes, from driving to work to motor racing.

1898 BENZ VELO

1898 BENZ VELO
German engineer Karl Benz produced the first car to be sold to the public in 1885. The Benz Velo, introduced in 1894, was the first car to sell in significant numbers.

1903 DE DION BOUTON MODEL Q
Produced by the French De Dion Bouton company, the 698 cc Model Q is typical of the light, reliable cars popular in the early years of the 20th century.

1903 DE DION BOUTON MODEL Q

Coach-type leaf-spring suspension

Wooden spoked wheels inherited from the horse cart

Propeller shaft carrying drive from gear box to final-drive

Solid rubber tyre

Folding hood

Folding windscreen for rear-seat passenger

1909 ROLLS-ROYCE SILVER GHOST
Demand for more luxurious cars led to the manufacture of quality vehicles such as the Rolls-Royce Silver Ghost.

"Spirit of Ecstasy" mascot added in 1911

1909 ROLLS-ROYCE SILVER GHOST

Air-filled "pneumatic" tyres

1957
MERCEDES-
BENZ 300SL GULL WING
The futuristic design
of the 300SL
sports car
features
upward-
swinging
doors that
resemble
the wings
of a seagull.

"Gull wing"
doors

• The Aston Martin
Lagonda was the first
car with all-electronic
instruments.
• The jet-engined
car Thrust 2 holds
the Land Speed
Record, reaching
1,019.2 km/h
(633.5 mph) in 1983.

Rear wing
forces wheels
onto ground

Ferrari
Boxer 312
12-cylinder
engine

Light
fibreglass
body shell

Driver's
cockpit

1979 FERRARI 312T4
Powerful engines and road-gripping
wide tyres allow Formula One
racing cars to travel
at over 300 km/h
(190 mph).

CONTEMPORARY CARS
Modern cars are designed to cater
to specific driving requirements.

FOUR-WHEEL-DRIVE OFF-ROAD
VEHICLE, SUZUKI VITARA

MULTI-PURPOSE
VEHICLE (MPV),
FIAT ULYSSES

COMPACT CITY CAR,
RENAULT TWINGO

FOUR-WHEEL-DRIVE,
LUXURY SEDAN,
AUDI A8

BICYCLES

APART FROM WALKING there is no simpler and cheaper way to travel than on a bicycle. Bicycles were invented in Europe little more than 200 years ago, but today they are popular worldwide for both transport and leisure.

MODERN RACING BIKE · Air-filled tyres, an efficient gearing system, and a cushioned saddle make modern bicycles more comfortable and easier to ride than their predecessors.

Saddle

Crossbar

Front derailleur

Brake block

Spoke

Tyre

Rim

Chainrings

Rear derailleur (gear changer)

Sprockets or cogs

TYPES OF BICYCLE

RACING BIKE FOR ROAD RACES

BMX FOR ROUGH TERRAIN

MOUNTAIN BIKE

TANDEM FOR TWO PEOPLE

1790 THE COMTE DE SIVRAC BUILDS THE *CELERIFERE*

1813 CARL VON DRAIS BUILDS THE *DRAISIENNE*

1839 "BONESHAKER" IS FIRST BIKE WITH PEDAL-DRIVEN BACK WHEEL

1861 FIRST BIKE WITH PEDAL-DRIVEN FRONT WHEEL

TOUR DE FRANCE
Cycle races range from track sprints held over 1,000 m (1,094 yd) to multi-stage events lasting several weeks. One of the most famous road races is the 24-day Tour de France.

BICYCLE FACTS

• The longest bicycle, ridden by four people for a short distance in 1988, is 22.24 m (72.97 ft) long.

• There are 800 million bicycles in the world. They outnumber cars two to one.

Brake cable

Handlebar

Brake lever

Stem

Gear lever

Fork blade

Pedal

Large cogs allow fast travel downhill or on flat ground

Small cogs used for climbing uphill

Chain

Pedal

Hub axle or spindle

Valve

GEAR SYSTEMS
Many bicycles have gear systems that enable the cyclist to travel quickly or slowly while pedalling at a comfortable rate. By moving the gear lever, the cyclist lifts the chain from one cog to another.

C.1870 THE "PENNY FARTHING" FIRST APPEARS

1839 THE "BICYCLETTE" IS THE FIRST COMMERCIAL BICYCLE

1959 THE "MOULTON" IS FIRST NEW BIKE DESIGN FOR 50 YEARS

1990s "HPV" HUMAN-POWERED VEHICLE

MOTORCYCLES

THE SMALLEST and lightest form of motorized transport, motorcycles range from small-engined commuter mopeds to racing motorcycles that can reach speeds of more than 500 km/h (311 mph).

TYPES OF MOTORCYCLE

TRAIL BIKE FOR ROUGH TERRAIN

PERSONALLY ADAPTED "CUSTOM" MOTORCYCLE

LOW-POWER 50 CC MOPED

SMALL-WHEELED MOTOR SCOOTER

PARTS OF A MOTORCYCLE
A motorcycle is essentially a bicycle powered by an engine. Motorcycle engine sizes range from 50 cc (cubic capacity) through to more than 1,000 cc.

Saddle

Exhaust

Brake disc

Drive chain

Four-cylinder 1,002 cc engine

1885 MAYBACH AND DAIMLER'S WOODEN MOTORCYCLE

1892 FIRST COMMERCIALLY PRODUCED MOTORCYCLE

1901 WERNER COMPANY PRODUCES ONE OF FIRST PRACTICAL MOTORCYCLES

1904 FIRST HARLEY-DAVIDSON MOTORCYCLE, THE SILENT GREY FELLOW, PRODUCED

CORNERING
Motorcyclists lean over on bends to prevent the motorcycle's momentum throwing the bike over.

Mirror

Fuel tank

1992 YAMAHA FZR 1000 EXUP

Windscreen

Throttle connected to handlebar grip

Brake levers

Fairing (front enclosure)

Telescopic suspension forks

Side fairing removed to show engine

Radiator

Three-spoke wheels

Exhaust port

TWO-STROKE ENGINE
Smaller motorcycles often use valveless two-stroke engines. Fuel enters and exhaust is ejected through cylinder openings called ports. The moving piston opens and closes the ports.

1910 FIRST POPULAR MOTORCYCLE SIDECARS

1959 TRIUMPH COMPANY INTRODUCES THE HIGH PERFORMANCE BONNEVILLE

1978 MOTORCYCLE SPEED RECORD OF 512 KM/H (318 MPH) SET BY DONALD VESCO

1990s BMW COMPANY LAUNCHES COMPUTERIZED R1100

SHIPS AND BOATS

BOATS AND SHIPS have been used to transport people and goods across rivers, lakes and oceans for thousands of years. From the first dugout canoes to ocean liners, boats have played a major role in world trade.

Bipod or "double" mast

Lugsail made from reed

TITICACA RAFT
The elegant rafts made by the people of Lake Titicaca in the Andes mountains are built from reeds that grow in the lake.

ALGONQUIN TRANSPORT
Birchbark canoes were used by the native Canadian Algonquin to traverse the St. Lawrence River, in what is now called Ontario. The boats ranged in length from 3 m (10 ft) vessels to 10.5 m (35 ft) war canoes.

Yard   Mast

Battens keep sail straight

Four-sided sail

Cross-strut strengthens canoe

Birchbark hull

CHINESE JUNK
Traditional Chinese vessels or "junks" have four-sided sails which hang from a yard that crosses the mast at an angle.

OCEAN LINER
From the early 1900s to the 1950s, huge, luxurious liners carried many passengers across the oceans. Cheap, fast air travel caused their popularity to decline.

CUNARD LINE MAURETANIA   Bridge

Funnels expel exhaust fumes from boiler rooms

Verandah café

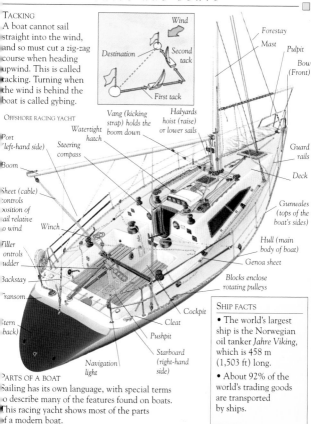

TACKING

A boat cannot sail straight into the wind, and so must cut a zig-zag course when heading upwind. This is called tacking. Turning when the wind is behind the boat is called gybing.

Wind

Destination

Second tack

First tack

OFFSHORE RACING YACHT

Vang (kicking strap) holds the boom down

Halyards hoist (raise) or lower sails

Watertight hatch

Port (left-hand side)

Steering compass

Boom

Sheet (cable) controls position of sail relative to wind

Winch

Tiller controls rudder

Backstay

Transom

Stern (back)

Navigation light

Cleat

Pushpit

Starboard (right-hand side)

Cockpit

Forestay

Mast

Pulpit

Bow (Front)

Guard rails

Deck

Gunwales (tops of the boat's sides)

Hull (main body of boat)

Genoa sheet

Blocks enclose rotating pulleys

PARTS OF A BOAT

Sailing has its own language, with special terms to describe many of the features found on boats. This racing yacht shows most of the parts of a modern boat.

SHIP FACTS

• The world's largest ship is the Norwegian oil tanker *Jahre Viking*, which is 458 m (1,503 ft) long.

• About 92% of the world's trading goods are transported by ships.

WARSHIPS AND SUBMARINES

THERE ARE MANY types of fighting vessel, from light, speedy destroyers to huge aircraft carriers and nuclear submarines.

1700s "MAN-OF-WAR"
By the 18th century, sailing ships had become floating fortresses. Rival northern European powers built heavily armed fighting ships called "men-of-war".

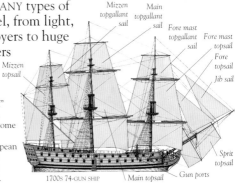

Mizzen topgallant sail

Main topgallant sail

Fore mast topgallant sail

Fore mast topsail

Fore topsail

Jib sail

Mizzen topsail

Sprit topsail

1700s 74-GUN SHIP

Main topsail

Gun ports

TYPES OF WARSHIP

AIRCRAFT CARRIER
The largest warship, a carrier houses 100 aircraft and a crew of over 2,000.

DESTROYER
Armed with guided missiles, the destroyer's role is to defend the fleet.

CRUISER
The cruiser is designed for speed and endurance at sea.

MINESWEEPER
This small vessel carries special equipment for locating and destroying mines.

BATTLESHIP
Most heavily armed battleships have been replaced by carriers.

PARTS OF A WARSHIP

Modern warships are armed with guns
and guided missiles for attack and
defence. Most vessels are also equipped
with advanced electronic equipment for
tracking and hitting targets.

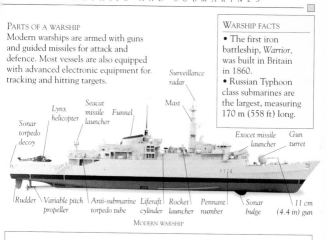

Surveillance
radar

Mast

Lynx
helicopter

Seacat
missile
launcher

Funnel

Sonar
torpedo
decoy

Exocet missile
launcher

Gun
turret

Rudder

Variable pitch
propeller

Anti-submarine
torpedo tube

Liferaft
cylinder

Rocket
launcher

Pennant
number

Sonar
bulge

11 cm
(4.4 in) gun

MODERN WARSHIP

MILITARY SUBMARINES

There are two main types of underwater warship.
Patrol submarines seek and destroy other vessels, while
missile-carrying submarines are equipped with nuclear
warheads aimed at enemy cities and military targets.

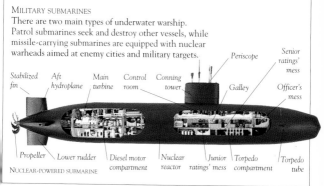

Periscope

Senior
ratings'
mess

Stabilized
fin

Aft
hydroplane

Main
turbine

Control
room

Conning
tower

Galley

Officer's
mess

Propeller

Lower rudder

Diesel motor
compartment

Nuclear
reactor

Junior
ratings' mess

Torpedo
compartment

Torpedo
tube

NUCLEAR-POWERED SUBMARINE

AIRCRAFT

THE FIRST PLANE flew
in only 1903, yet today
millions of people fly
each year. Aeroplanes are
heavier-than-air aircraft
with fixed wings, usually
powered by propellers
or jet turbines.

Lift (upward force)

Drag (backward force)

HOW A WING WORKS

Air passing over the curved
upper surface of a wing, or aerofoil,
travels faster than the air passing
beneath the flatter underside. The lower
pressure of the fast air above the wing in
relation to the slower air
beneath it creates lift.

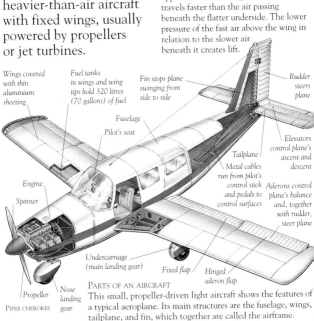

Wings covered with thin aluminium sheeting

Fuel tanks in wings and wing tips hold 320 litres (70 gallons) of fuel

Fin stops plane swinging from side to side

Rudder steers plane

Fuselage

Pilot's seat

Elevators control plane's ascent and descent

Engine

Tailplane

Metal cables run from pilot's control stick and pedals to control surfaces

Spinner

Ailerons control plane's balance and, together with rudder, steer plane

Undercarriage (main landing gear)

Fixed flap

Hinged aileron flap

Propeller

Nose landing gear

PIPER CHEROKEE

PARTS OF AN AIRCRAFT

This small, propeller-driven light aircraft shows the features of
a typical aeroplane. Its main structures are the fuselage, wings,
tailplane, and fin, which together are called the airframe.

FUSELAGE OF AN AIRLINER

The airframe of a jet airliner has to be capable of withstanding the stresses of high-speed flight and pressurization and depressurization of the passenger cabin. Airliners are built from light, strong materials such as aluminium alloys, titanium, and carbon fibre.

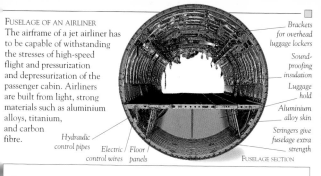

Brackets for overhead luggage lockers

Sound-proofing insulation

Luggage hold

Aluminium alloy skin

Stringers give fuselage extra strength

Hydraulic control pipes

Electric control wires

Floor panels

FUSELAGE SECTION

CONTROLLING THE PLANE

The wings and tail of an aeroplane are equipped with hinged flaps, or control surfaces, that allow it to pitch up or down, roll from side to side, or yaw left and right. To turn, the plane is banked, rolling and yawing at the same time.

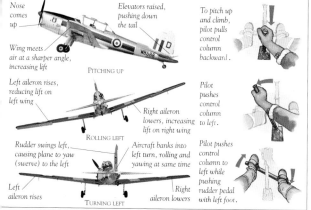

Nose comes up

Elevators raised, pushing down the tail

Wing meets air at a sharper angle, increasing lift

PITCHING UP

To pitch up and climb, pilot pulls control column backward.

Left aileron rises, reducing lift on left wing

Right aileron lowers, increasing lift on right wing

ROLLING LEFT

Pilot pushes control column to left.

Rudder swings left, causing plane to yaw (swerve) to the left

Aircraft banks into left turn, rolling and yawing at same time

Left aileron rises

Right aileron lowers

TURNING LEFT

Pilot pushes control column to left while pushing rudder pedal with left foot.

Types of aircraft

An aircraft is essentially any machine that enables people to fly.
Powered aeroplanes and helicopters, hot-air balloons, gas-filled
airships, and unpowered gliders are all different types of aircraft.
There are many different types of aircraft for different uses,
including transport, warfare, and recreation.

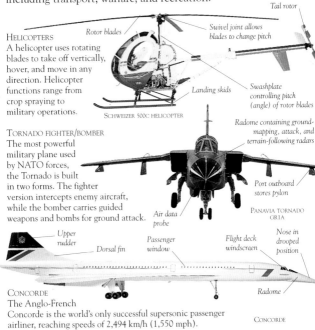

HELICOPTERS

A helicopter uses rotating
blades to take off vertically,
hover, and move in any
direction. Helicopter
functions range from
crop spraying to
military operations.

Rotor blades

Tail rotor

*Swivel joint allows
blades to change pitch*

Landing skids

*Swashplate
controlling pitch
(angle) of rotor blades*

SCHWEIZER 500C HELICOPTER

TORNADO FIGHTER/BOMBER

The most powerful
military plane used
by NATO forces,
the Tornado is built
in two forms. The fighter
version intercepts enemy aircraft,
while the bomber carries guided
weapons and bombs for ground attack.

*Radome containing ground-
mapping, attack, and
terrain-following radars*

*Port outboard
stores pylon*

*Air data
probe*

PANAVIA TORNADO
GR1A

CONCORDE

The Anglo-French
Concorde is the world's only successful supersonic passenger
airliner, reaching speeds of 2,494 km/h (1,550 mph).

*Upper
rudder*

Dorsal fin

*Passenger
window*

*Flight deck
windscreen*

*Nose in
drooped
position*

Radome

CONCORDE

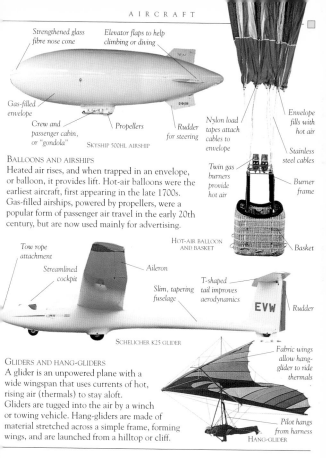

Strengthened glass fibre nose cone

Elevator flaps to help climbing or diving

Gas-filled envelope

Crew and passenger cabin, or "gondola"

Propellers

Rudder for steering

SKYSHIP 500HL AIRSHIP

Nylon load tapes attach cables to envelope

Envelope fills with hot air

Stainless steel cables

Twin gas burners provide hot air

Burner frame

Basket

HOT-AIR BALLOON AND BASKET

BALLOONS AND AIRSHIPS

Heated air rises, and when trapped in an envelope, or balloon, it provides lift. Hot-air balloons were the earliest aircraft, first appearing in the late 1700s. Gas-filled airships, powered by propellers, were a popular form of passenger air travel in the early 20th century, but are now used mainly for advertising.

Tow rope attachment

Streamlined cockpit

Aileron

Slim, tapering fuselage

T-shaped tail improves aerodynamics

EVW

Rudder

SCHELICHER K25 GLIDER

GLIDERS AND HANG-GLIDERS

A glider is an unpowered plane with a wide wingspan that uses currents of hot, rising air (thermals) to stay aloft. Gliders are tugged into the air by a winch or towing vehicle. Hang-gliders are made of material stretched across a simple frame, forming wings, and are launched from a hilltop or cliff.

Fabric wings allow hang-glider to ride thermals

Pilot hangs from harness

HANG-GLIDER

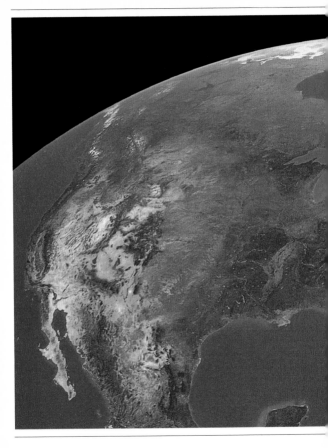

THE WORLD

HOW TO USE THIS SECTION

THESE PAGES SHOW YOU how to use the World
section of the encyclopedia. The maps are organized
by continent: North America, Central and South
America, Europe, Africa, North and West Asia,
South and East Asia, and Australasia. Information-
packed country fact pages separate the maps.

KEY TO ICONS
All the icons used on the
maps are listed below.

🎵 THE ARTS

☁ CLIMATE

🏛 COMMUNICATIONS

⚔ ENVIRONMENT

🦋 FLORA AND FAUNA

🏛 HISTORY

🏭 INDUSTRY

🏔 NATURAL
FEATURES

👪 PEOPLE

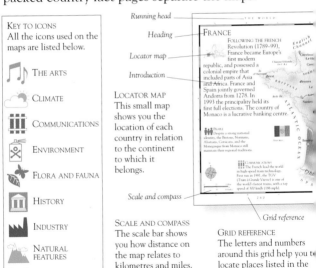

Running head
Heading
Locator map
Introduction
Scale and compass
Grid reference

LOCATOR MAP
This small map
shows you the
location of each
country in relation
to the continent
to which it
belongs.

SCALE AND COMPASS
The scale bar shows
you how distance on
the map relates to
kilometres and miles.
The compass points
show you north,
south, east, and west.

GRID REFERENCE
The letters and numbers
around this grid help you to
locate places listed in the
gazetteer index. See page
470 for an explanation
on how to use this grid.

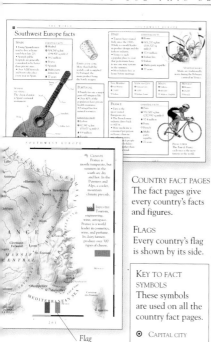

Flag

COUNTRY FACT PAGES
The fact pages give
every country's facts
and figures.

FLAGS
Every country's flag
is shown by its side.

KEY TO FACT
SYMBOLS
These symbols
are used on all the
country fact pages.

⊙ CAPITAL CITY

♠ AREA

♦ POPULATION

☙ CURRENCY

♀ MAIN LANGUAGE

▲ GOVERNMENT

● LIFE EXPECTANCY

GAZETTEER INDEX
A gazetteer index at the
back of the book lists major
towns, cities, rivers, lakes,
and mountain ranges that
appear on the map pages.

KEY TO MAPS

INTERNATIONAL BORDER	
DISPUTED BORDER	
STATE BORDER	
CAPITAL CITY	□ SHING' D.C.
STATE OR ADMINISTRATIVE CAPITAL	LANTA
MAJOR TOWN	○ arlesto
AIRPORT	⊕
SEAPORT	⊚
RIVER	
CANAL	
WADI	
LAKE	
SEASONAL LAKE	

GUIDE TO MAP PAGES

EUROPE
pp. 246–289

NORTH AND
WEST ASIA
pp. 314–329

SOUTH AND
EAST ASIA
pp. 330–349

AFRICA
pp. 290–313

INDIAN
OCEAN

AUSTRALASIA
AND OCEANIA
pp. 350–359

ATLANTIC
OCEAN

SOUTHERN
OCEAN

ARCTIC
OCEAN

Arctic Circle

ATLANTIC
OCEAN

NORTH AMERICA
pp. 204–227

PACIFIC
OCEAN

Tropic of Capricorn

Equator

**CENTRAL AND
SOUTH AMERICA**
pp. 228–245

PACIFIC
OCEAN

Tropic of Cancer

ATLANTIC
OCEAN

NORTH AMERICA

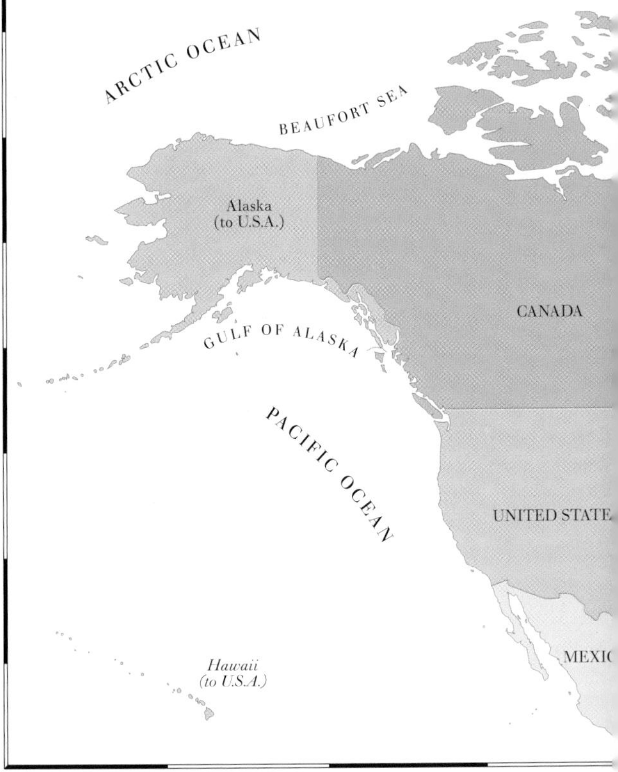

ARCTIC OCEAN

BEAUFORT SEA

Alaska
(to U.S.A.)

CANADA

GULF OF ALASKA

PACIFIC OCEAN

UNITED STATE

Hawaii
(to U.S.A.)

MEXIC

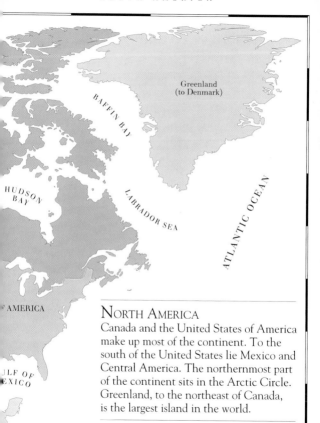

Greenland
(to Denmark)

BAFFIN BAY

HUDSON
BAY

LABRADOR SEA

ATLANTIC OCEAN

AMERICA

ULF OF
EXICO

NORTH AMERICA
Canada and the United States of America
make up most of the continent. To the
south of the United States lie Mexico and
Central America. The northernmost part
of the continent sits in the Arctic Circle.
Greenland, to the northeast of Canada,
is the largest island in the world.

ALASKA AND WESTERN CANADA

AT THE END OF the last ice age, people travelled from Asia into North America over the Bering landbridge, which connected the continents at present-day Alaska.

ALASKA
♦ 550,043
♡ English

INDUSTRY
Fishing, oil, minerals, timber. Railways were the key to the development of farming in western Canada. The USA's biggest oil field is at Prudhoe Bay, Alaska.

CLIMATE
A polar climate prevails in the north; the south is warmer. The Pacific coast, near Vancouver, has the warmest winters, and temperatures rarely fall below freezing.

HISTORY
The USA bought Alaska from Russia in 1867 for $7.2 million. Many Americans thought this was a waste of money until gold was discovered there in 1896 and oil in 1968.

ARCTIC OCEAN
Bering Strait
St. Lawrence I.
Nunivak I.
St. Matthew I.
Prudhoe Bay
BROOKS RANGE
BEAUFORT
ALEUTIAN Islands
BERING SEA
Umnak I.
Unalaska I.
Unimak I.
Bristol Bay
ALASKA (U.S.A.)
Yukon
Porcupine
Fairbanks
Dawson
Anchorage
ALASKA RANGE
Kodiak I.
Gulf of Alaska
WHITEHORSE
JUNEAU
YUKON TERRITORY
ROCKY MOUNTAINS
PACIFIC OCEAN
Queen Charlotte Is.
BRITISH COLUMBIA
Vancouver I.
Vancouver
VICTORIA

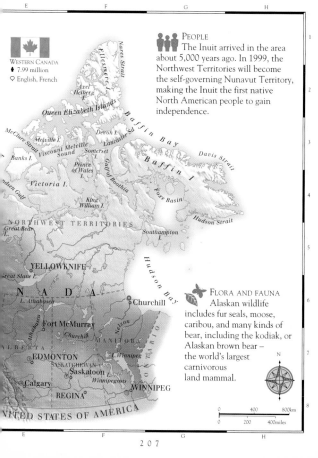

WESTERN CANADA
♦ 7.99 million
♀ English, French

Nares Strait

Ellesmere I.

Axel
Heiberg
I.

Queen Elizabeth Islands

McClure Strait
Melville I.
Viscount Melville
Sound
Devon I.
Lancaster Sd
Somerset
I.
Prince
of Wales
I.

Baffin Bay

Banks I.

Baffin I.

Davis Strait

udsen Gulf

Victoria I.

Gulf of Boothia

King
William I.

Foxe Basin

NORTHWEST TERRITORIES

Great Bear
L.

Southampton
I.

Hudson Strait

YELLOWKNIFE

eat Slave L.

N   A   D   A

Hudson Bay

Churchill

Fort McMurray

Nelson

Churchill

MANITOBA

ONTARIO

ALBERTA

EDMONTON

SASKATCHEWAN

L. Winnipeg

Saskatoon

Winnipegosis

Calgary

REGINA

WINNIPEG

ITED STATES OF AMERICA

PEOPLE
The Inuit arrived in the area about 5,000 years ago. In 1999, the Northwest Territories will become the self-governing Nunavut Territory, making the Inuit the first native North American people to gain independence.

FLORA AND FAUNA
Alaskan wildlife includes fur seals, moose, caribou, and many kinds of bear, including the kodiak, or Alaskan brown bear – the world's largest carnivorous land mammal.

N

0   400   800km
0   200   400miles

A   B   C   D

EASTERN CANADA

ALTHOUGH IT IS the second largest country in the world, Canada has a relatively small population. Most people live within 160 km (100 miles) of the US border. Snowbound for most of the year, the Hudson Bay area is a wilderness of forests, rivers, and lakes.

PEOPLE
The Vikings were the first Europeans to visit eastern Canada in about 986 BC. They settled for only a short time before the Native Americans drove them away.

INDUSTRY
Wood industries, oil, zinc, nickel, hydro-electricity, uranium. The area off the east coast called the Grand Banks is one of the world's richest fishing areas. Newsprint, made from wood pulp, is a major export from the Atlantic provinces.

Salisbur
Nottingham I.
Mansel I.

Inukjuak

Hudson Bay

Belcher Is.

C. Henrietta
Maria

MANITOBA

Severn

Winsk

James Bay

Attawapiskat
Attawapiskat
Albany

ONTARIO

CAN

Lake of the
Woods

L. Nipigon

Thunder Bay

UNITED

Lake Superior

STATES OF

Timmins

Sault
Sainte Marie

Sudbury

AMERICA

Lake Michigan

Lake Huron

Ottawa

TORONTO

La

Hamilton

Ont

London

Windsor

Niaga
Falls

L. Erie

UNIT

A   B   C

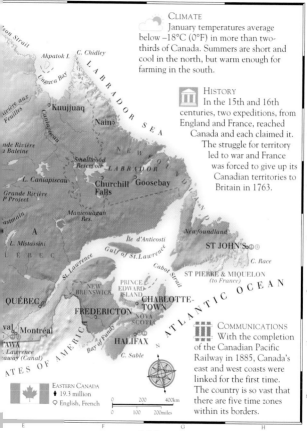

CLIMATE
January temperatures average below –18°C (0°F) in more than two-thirds of Canada. Summers are short and cool in the north, but warm enough for farming in the south.

HISTORY
In the 15th and 16th centuries, two expeditions, from England and France, reached Canada and each claimed it. The struggle for territory led to war and France was forced to give up its Canadian territories to Britain in 1763.

COMMUNICATIONS
With the completion of the Canadian Pacific Railway in 1885, Canada's east and west coasts were linked for the first time. The country is so vast that there are five time zones within its borders.

Map labels:

son Strait

Akpatok I. C. Chidley

Ungava Bay

LABRADOR

vière aux Feuilles

Kuujjuaq

Nain

Caniapiscau

nde Rivière a Baleine

NEWFOUNDLAND

Smallwood Reservoir

LABRADOR

L. Caniapiscau

LABRADOR SEA

Churchill Falls

Goosebay

Grande Rivière P Project

astmain

Manicouagan Res.

A

L. Mistassini

Ile d'Anticosti

Newfoundland

ST JOHN'S

QUÉBEC

C. Race

Gulf of St.Lawrence

St. Lawrence

Cabot Strait

ST PIERRE & MIQUELON (to France)

PRINCE EDWARD ISLAND

NEW BRUNSWICK

CHARLOTTE-TOWN

ATLANTIC OCEAN

QUÉBEC

FREDERICTON

NOVA SCOTIA

val Montréal

HALIFAX

AWA

Bay of Fundy

C. Sable

Lawrence away (Canal)

away (Canal)

STATES OF AMERICA

N

EASTERN CANADA
♦ 19.3 million
♢ English, French

0   200   400km
0   100   200miles

NORTHEASTERN STATES

WITH ITS RICH MINERAL resources and safe harbours, northeast America was the first area on the continent to be colonized by Europeans. In 1620, English pilgrims sailed on the *Mayflower* to settle in a region that is still called New England. During the mid-19th century, European immigrants settled in New York City and in other East Coast cities. Today, this region is the most densely populated and heavily industrialized area of the USA.

CLIMATE

This area of the USA has a temperate climate, with warm and humid summers. However, the northeastern region, in particular, can experience very heavy snowfall from November to April.

NORTHEASTERN STATES
♦ 51.5 million
♡ English

PEOPLE

Northeastern Native American tribes, such as the Wampanoag, the Algonquin, and the tribes of the Iroquois League, were the first to come into contact with European settlers and explorers.

INDUSTRY

Oil, iron, steel, chemicals, maple sugar, blueberries, cranberries, fishing, tourism. Vermont is the main producer of maple syrup in the USA. The stock exchange on Wall Street, New York City, is the largest in the world.

Lake Erie Bu

Erie

PENNSYLVA

Pittsburg

WEST VIRGINIA

APPALAC

Nia

NATURAL FEATURES
Lying on the border
between the USA and Canada,
Niagara Falls were formed about
10,000 years ago. About 180,000
tonnes (tons) of water go over
the falls every minute.

C A N A D A

M A I N E

Moosehead L.

L. Champlain

WHITE
ADIRONDACK
MTS.
MONTPELIER MTS.   **AUGUSTA**

Ontario
chester

VERMONT

NEW HAMPSHIRE

Syracuse   *Mohawk*
er Lakes
ALBANY   **CONCORD**
NEW YORK

CATSKILL
MTS.   **MASSACHUSETTS** **BOSTON**
Springfield Worcester *Cape Cod*
CONNECTICUT **PROVIDENCE**
Waterbury **HARTFORD**   RHODE
New Haven   ISLAND   *Nantucket I.*
Bridgeport   *Martha's Vineyard*
Paterson
Allentown Newark **New York City**
Long I.
HARRISBURG **TRENTON**
Wilmington Philadelphia
RYLAND Newark NEW JERSEY
DOVER
DELAWARE

Susquehanna
Delaware
Hudson
Connecticut
Kennebec
Penobscot

A T L A N T I C   O C E A N

HISTORY
In 1621, the
Mayflower pilgrims
celebrated their first
successful harvest.
Thanksgiving is now
an annual holiday,
observed on the
last Thursday
in November.

FLORA AND FAUNA
The Appalachian
Mountains are home to the
opossum, North America's
only species of marsupial,
or pouched mammal.

N

0   100   200km
0   50   100miles

SOUTHERN STATES

BY THE 19TH CENTURY, the wealth of the South was based on crops like tobacco, indigo, rice, and especially cotton, which was grown on large plantations by African slaves. The area is known today for New Orleans' jazz, Florida's Disney World, and the Kentucky Derby. The city of Washington, in the District of Columbia, was made the US capital in 1800.

Mississippi Delta

CLIMATE
Summers are long and hot; winters are mild, but temperatures are generally warmer on the coast than inland. Southern Florida is tropical.

INDUSTRY
Soya beans, coal, peanuts, cotton, citrus fruits, tobacco, oil, tourism. Georgia grows half of the USA's peanuts – most are used to make peanut butter.

THE ARTS
The French brought Mardi Gras to America in the early 1700. Celebrated in many of the souther states, the most famous festival is held in New Orleans. Here parade last for a week before Mardi Gras Day, the day before Lent starts.

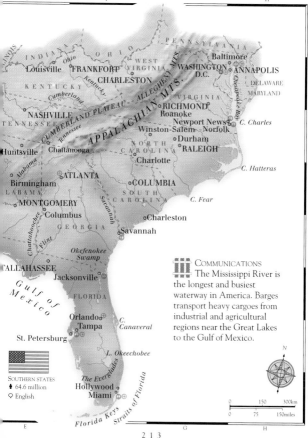

Louisville
FRANKFORT
CHARLESTON
Baltimore
WASHINGTON D.C.
ANNAPOLIS
DELAWARE
MARYLAND
NASHVILLE
RICHMOND
Roanoke
Newport News
Norfolk
C. Charles
Winston-Salem
Durham
Huntsville
Chattanooga
RALEIGH
Charlotte
C. Hatteras
ATLANTA
Birmingham
COLUMBIA
MONTGOMERY
C. Fear
Columbus
Charleston
Savannah
Okefenokee Swamp
TALLAHASSEE
Jacksonville
FLORIDA
Gulf of Mexico
Orlando
Tampa
C. Canaveral
St. Petersburg
L. Okeechobee
The Everglades
Hollywood
Miami
Florida Keys
Straits of Florida

INDIANA
OHIO
PENNSYLVANIA
Ohio
WEST VIRGINIA
ILLINOIS
KENTUCKY
Kentucky
Cumberland
Chesapeake Bay
ALLEGHENY MTS.
VIRGINIA
CUMBERLAND PLATEAU
TENNESSEE
Tennessee
APPALACHIAN MTS.
NORTH CAROLINA
ALABAMA
Alabama
SOUTH CAROLINA
Chattahoochee
GEORGIA
Flint
Savannah

COMMUNICATIONS

The Mississippi River is the longest and busiest waterway in America. Barges transport heavy cargoes from industrial and agricultural regions near the Great Lakes to the Gulf of Mexico.

SOUTHERN STATES
♠ 64.6 million
♀ English

N

0   150   300km
0   75   150miles

E   F   G   H

Lake of
the Woods

Upper Red L.

Lower
Red L.

Leech L.

MINNESOTA

Mississippi

Minneapolis

ST PAU

NORTH DAKOTA

SOUTH DAKOTA

GREAT LAKES

THE STATES OF
Indiana, Illinois,
Michigan, Ohio,
Wisconsin, and
Minnesota, which
all border on one or more of the
five Great Lakes, are often
called the industrial and
agricultural heartland of the
United States. The region is
rich in natural resources, with
large areas of fertile farmland
on flat plains called prairies.

CLIMATE
The region around the Great
Lakes has warm summers but quite
severe winters, and parts of the lakes can
freeze over. Minnesota, in particular,
suffers from heavy snowstorms.

ENVIRONMENT

The Great Lakes – Ontario, Huron,
Superior, Michigan, and Erie – together
form the largest area of fresh water in the
world. Heavy industry has caused severe
water pollution, and in some areas it is
dangerous to eat the fish or swim.

GREAT LAKES STATES
⚡ 46.4 million
♡ English

INDUSTRY
Vehicles, coal, iron,
grain, maize, cherries.
Nearly half of the world's maize
crop and a third of the cherry
crop are grown in the Great
Lakes region. Detroit is known
as "motor city" because it is the
centre of the US car industry.

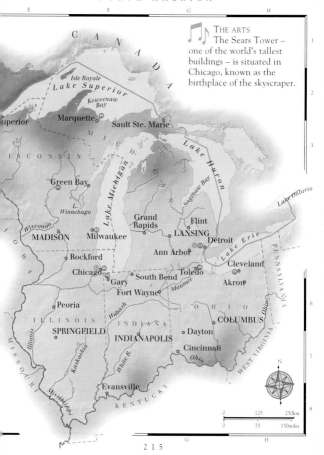

1

C   A   N   A   D   A

Isle Royale
Lake Superior

2

Superior

Keweenaw Bay

Marquette

Sault Ste. Marie

♪♪ THE ARTS
The Sears Tower –
one of the world's tallest
buildings – is situated in
Chicago, known as the
birthplace of the skyscraper.

M

3

WISCONSIN

Lake Huron

Green Bay

L. Winnebago

Lake Michigan

Saginaw Bay

Lake Ontario

4

Wisconsin

MADISON

Milwaukee

Grand
Rapids

Flint

LANSING

Detroit

Lake Erie

PENNSYLVANIA

IOWA

Rockford

Ann Arbor

5

Chicago

Gary

South Bend

Toledo

Cleveland

Akron

Fort Wayne

Maumee

Peoria

ILLINOIS

INDIANA

Wabash

OHIO

COLUMBUS

Ohio

6

MISSOURI

Illinois

SPRINGFIELD

INDIANAPOLIS

Dayton

Cincinnati

WEST VIRGINIA

White R.

Kaskaskia

Ohio

7

N

Evansville

Mississippi

KENTUCKY

0   125   250km

0   75   150miles

8

CENTRAL AND MOUNTAIN STATES

THE GREAT Plains, the Rocky Mountains, and the Mississippi lowlands dominate the landscape of the Midwest. Once home to Native Americans and herds of bison, the Great Plains were settled in the 19th century by Europeans, who forced the Native Americans onto reservations and slaughtered the bison to near extinction.

HISTORY
Pioneers travelling to the West had to cross the Great Plains, which were known as the "Great American Desert". The last area to be settled, it is now a wealthy agricultural region.

CLIMATE
West of the Rockies, the summers are cooler and the winters are warmer. States on the Great Plains have an extreme climate, which can change quite suddenly and violently – blizzards, hail, thunderstorms, and tornadoes may occur.

CENTRAL AND
MOUNTAIN STATES
♦ 18.7 million
♀ English

NATURAL FEATURES
The Rocky Mountains extend through Canada and the USA for more than 4,800 km (3,000 miles). They divide North America and separate the rivers flowing west to the Pacific from those flowing east to the Atlantic.

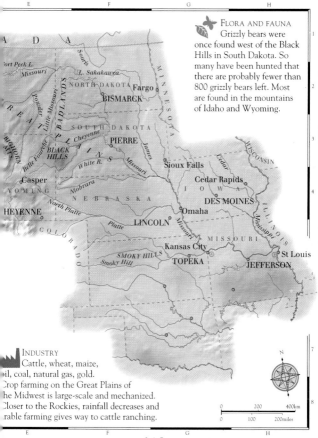

FLORA AND FAUNA
Grizzly bears were
once found west of the Black
Hills in South Dakota. So
many have been hunted that
there are probably fewer than
800 grizzly bears left. Most
are found in the mountains
of Idaho and Wyoming.

Fort Peck L.
Missouri
Powder
Little Missouri
Souris
L. Sakakawea
NORTH DAKOTA   Fargo
BISMARCK
BADLANDS
GREAT
BIGHORN Mts
SOUTH DAKOTA
Cheyenne
PLAINS
Belle Fourche
BLACK
HILLS
PIERRE
White R.
James
Missouri
Sioux Falls
WISCONSIN
Casper
Niobrara
Cedar
Cedar Rapids
WYOMING
NEBRASKA
IOWA
DES MOINES
North Platte
HEYENNE
Platte
LINCOLN
Omaha
ILLINOIS
COLORADO
Missouri
MISSOURI
Mississippi
Kansas City
SMOKY HILLS
Smoky Hill
TOPEKA
JEFFERSON
St Louis

INDUSTRY
Cattle, wheat, maize,
il, coal, natural gas, gold.
Crop farming on the Great Plains of
he Midwest is large-scale and mechanized.
Closer to the Rockies, rainfall decreases and
rable farming gives way to cattle ranching.

N

0   200   400km
0   100   200miles

SOUTHWESTERN STATES

THE FIRST Europeans in the Southwest were the Spanish, who travelled north from Mexico. This resulted in a mingling of Spanish and Native American cultures in the region. Gold and silver mining and cattle-ranching attracted other settlers in the late 19th century, when this area became part of the USA after the Mexican War.

NATURAL FEATURES

The Colorado plateau has some unusual landforms, including natural bridges and arches of solid rock. Over the past million years, the Colorado River has cut away the plateau, forming the world's largest river gorge – the Grand Canyon.

HISTORY

At the end of the Mexican War (1846–48), the USA acquired Utah, Nevada, California, and parts of Arizona, New Mexico, Colorado, and Wyoming. One of the causes of the war was a border dispute between Texas and Mexico.

SOUTHWESTERN STATES
♦ 28.4 million
♡ English

PEOPLE

Some of the earliest Native Americans lived in the Nevada area. Bones and ashes discovered near Las Vegas indicate that people may have lived there more than 20,000 years ago. Today, the region has the largest concentration of Native Americans in the country.

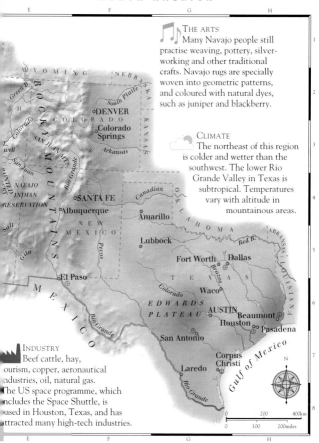

♪♫ THE ARTS
Many Navajo people still practise weaving, pottery, silver-working and other traditional crafts. Navajo rugs are specially woven into geometric patterns, and coloured with natural dyes, such as juniper and blackberry.

☁ CLIMATE
The northeast of this region is colder and wetter than the southwest. The lower Rio Grande Valley in Texas is subtropical. Temperatures vary with altitude in mountainous areas.

🏭 INDUSTRY
Beef cattle, hay, tourism, copper, aeronautical industries, oil, natural gas. The US space programme, which includes the Space Shuttle, is based in Houston, Texas, and has attracted many high-tech industries.

PACIFIC STATES

ALL THREE STATES on the West Coast are major agricultural producers – Washington and Oregon supply one-third of the USA's softwood timber, and California produces half of the country's fruit and vegetables. Situated where two of the Earth's plates meet, the area suffers from earthquakes and volcanic activity. Mount St. Helens, dormant since 1857, erupted in 1980, losing 400 m (1,300 ft) off its height.

NATURAL FEATURES
The lowest point in the western hemisphere is in Death Valley, 86 m (282 ft) below sea level. One of the driest, hottest places on Earth, the highest temperature, 57°C (135°F), was recorded there in 1913, and its average rainfall is only 38 mm (1.5 in) per year.

CLIMATE
Climate varies from the moderate coast to the snow-capped Sierra Nevada mountains. Much of California is arid desert.

INDUSTRY
Timber, aerospace industries, wine. The Santa Clara Valley, or Silicon Valley, specializes in hi-tech industry. Hollywood is considered the centre of the US film industry, although many major studios are no longer located there.

FLORA AND FAUNA
Redwoods are believed to be the tallest and oldest trees in the world. They are found along the West Coast from central California to southern Oregon and rarely occur more than 80 km (50 miles) inland.

PACIFIC STATES
37.5 million
★ English

Map labels:

NORTH AMERICA

ARIZONA
Colorado
MEXICO

MOJAVE DESERT
Salton Sea
San Bernardino
Pasadena
Glendale
Riverside
San Diego
Santa Ana
Oxnard
Los Angeles
Long Beach
Santa Barbara

Death Valley
NEVADA
SIERRA NEVADA
Fresno
Bakersfield

Klamath Falls
Goose L.
Eureka
Redding
Chico
Clear L.
Sacramento
C. Mendocino
SACRAMENTO
Concord
San Francisco
Oakland
San Jose
Stockton
San Joaquin

COAST RANGES

CALIFORNIA

PACIFIC

N

0   125   250km
0   75   150miles

MEXICO

THE ANCIENT empires of the Maya and Aztec flourished for centuries before the Spanish invaded Mexico in 1519, lured there by legends of hoards of gold and silver. Mexico gained its independence in 1836, after 300 years of Spanish rule. Today, most Mexicans are *mestizo*, a mix of Spanish and Native American. Although Spanish is the official language, Native American languages such as Maya, Nahuatl, and Zapotec are also widely spoken.

UNITED STATES

Tijuana Mexicali

Nogales

Ángel de la Guarda I.
Cedros I. Hermosillo

Tiburón I.

BAJA CALIFORNIA

Gulf of California

SIERRA MADRE

Culiacán

La Paz

CLIMATE
The Mexican plateau and mountains are warm for most of the year. The Pacific coast has a tropical climate.

MEXICO

FLORA AND FAUNA
The Mexican beaded lizard and the gila monster are the only two poisonous lizards known. The largest of all cacti is the giant saguaro, which grows in the Sonora Desert to a height of more than 18 m (60 ft).

NATURAL FEATURES
The plateau of Mexico is enclosed to the west and east by the Sierra Madre mountain ranges, which occupy 75 per cent of the total land area. Mexico is so mountainous and arid in parts that only 12 per cent of the land is arable.

E   F   G   H

AFRICA

Ciudad
Juárez

AMERICA

SIERRA MADRE ORIENTAL

Brazo del Norte

Chihuahua

Conchos

Rio Grande

M E X I C O

OCCIDENTAL

Monterrey

San Luis Potosí

Rio Grande de Santiago

Aguascalientes

rias

León   Ciudad
Madero

L. Chapala

Guadalajara   Poza Rica

PACIFIC

MEXICO CITY   L. Texcoco

Puebla

Balsas

SIERRA MADRE DEL SUR

Acapulco

OCEAN

N

Mérida

Gulf of Mexico

Campeche   Cozumel
I.

YUCATÁN
PENINSULA

Bay of Campeche

Villahermosa

Coatzacoalcos
Oaxaca   Tuxtla
Gutiérrez

GUATEMALA

BELIZE

Gulf of
Tehuantepec

Tapachula

ENVIRONMENT
Poor air quality is a problem in
Mexico City because it is surrounded by
mountains, which stop fumes from cars
and factories from escaping.

HISTORY
The remains of Mayan and
Aztec cities are found all over Mexico
and Central America. Mexico City is
built on the ruins of the Aztec
capital, Tenochtitlán.

INDUSTRY
Oil, natural gas, tourism,
minerals, brewing, agriculture.
Tourism employs nine per cent of
the workforce. Mexico is one of the
largest oil producers and supplies
one-sixth of the world's silver.

200   400km

100   200miles

North America facts

UNITED STATES OF AMERICA

- The US economy is the largest in the world.
- The nation is made up of 50 states plus the District of Columbia.
- The world's leading computer software is produced in the USA.

ESSENTIAL FACTS

- ⊙ Washington, DC
- ⌀ 9,372,610 sq km (3,618,760 sq miles)
- ♦ 257.8 million
- 💲 US dollar
- ♀ English
- ▲ Multi-party republic
- ♦ 76 years

WISE OLD BIRD
The USA's national symbol is the bald eagle.

WYOMING LANDSCAPE
The varied US scenery ranges from arid desert in Arizona through to mountainous lakeland in Wyoming.

SOUTHWESTERN STATES

ARIZONA
- ⊙ Phoenix
- ♦ 3.6 million

NEVADA
- ⊙ Carson City
- ♦ 1.1 million

TEXAS
- ⊙ Austin
- ♦ 17 million

COLORADO
- ⊙ Denver
- ♦ 3.3 million

NEW MEXICO
- ⊙ Santa Fe
- ♦ 1.5 million

UTAH
- ⊙ Salt Lake City
- ♦ 1.7 million

COWBOYS
Cattle-ranching is still big business in Texas today.

NORTHEASTERN STATES

CONNECTICUT
⊙ Hartford
♦ 3.2 million

NEW JERSEY
⊙ Trenton
♦ 7.7 million

DELAWARE
⊙ Dover
♦ 673,000

NEW YORK
⊙ Albany
♦ 18 million

MAINE
⊙ Augusta
♦ 1.2 million

PENNSYLVANIA
⊙ Harrisburg
♦ 12 million

MASSACHUSETTS
⊙ Boston
♦ 6 million

RHODE ISLAND
⊙ Providence
♦ 998,000

NEW HAMPSHIRE
⊙ Concord
♦ 1.1 million

VERMONT
⊙ Montpelier
♦ 567,000

PACIFIC STATES

CALIFORNIA
⊙ Sacramento
♦ 29.1 million

WASHINGTON
⊙ Olympia
♦ 4.8 million

OREGON
⊙ Salem
♦ 2.8 million

BASEBALL IS THE
NATIONAL SPORT
OF THE USA

THE STATUE
OF LIBERTY
New York's
famous statue
was given to
the USA by
France in 1884.

OUTLYING STATES

ALASKA
⊙ Juneau
♦ 527,000

HAWAII
⊙ Honolulu
♦ 1.1 million

GREAT LAKES

ILLINOIS
⊙ Springfield
♦ 11.7 million

MICHIGAN
⊙ Lansing
♦ 9.3 milllion

OHIO
⊙ Columbus
♦ 10.9 million

INDIANA
⊙ Indianapolis
♦ 5.6 million

MINNESOTA
⊙ St. Paul
♦ 4.4 million

WISCONSIN
⊙ Madison
♦ 4.9 million

NORTH
AMERICAN
MOOSE

DETROIT,
MICHIGAN, IS
THE CENTRE
OF THE
US CAR
INDUSTRY

CENTRAL AND MOUNTAIN STATES

IDAHO
- ⊙ Boise
- ♦ 1 million

IOWA
- ⊙ Des Moines
- ♦ 2.8 million

KANSAS
- ⊙ Topeka
- ♦ 2.5 million

MISSOURI
- ⊙ Jefferson City
- ♦ 5.2 million

MONTANA
- ⊙ Helena
- ♦ 806,000

NEBRASKA
- ⊙ Lincoln
- ♦ 1.6 million

NORTH DAKOTA
- ⊙ Bismarck
- ♦ 660,000

OKLAHOMA
- ⊙ Oklahoma City
- ♦ 3.2 million

SOUTH DAKOTA
- ⊙ Pierre
- ♦ 715,000

WYOMING
- ⊙ Cheyenne
- ♦ 475,000

Popcorn is roasted, puffed-up maize

POPCORN
Maize products are an export of the midwestern states.

SOUTHERN STATES

MALABAMA
- ⊙ Montgomery
- ♦ 4.1 million

ARKANSAS
- ⊙ Little Rock
- ♦ 2.4 million

FLORIDA
- ⊙ Tallahassee
- ♦ 12.7 million

GEORGIA
- ⊙ Atlanta
- ♦ 6.4 million

KENTUCKY
- ⊙ Frankfort
- ♦ 3.7 million

LOUISIANA
- ⊙ Baton Rouge
- ♦ 4.4 million

MARYLAND
- ⊙ Annapolis
- ♦ 4.7 million

MISSISSIPPI
- ⊙ Jackson
- ♦ 2.6 million

NORTH CAROLINA
- ⊙ Raleigh
- ♦ 6.6 million

TENNESSEE
- ⊙ Nashville
- ♦ 4.9 million

SOUTH CAROLINA
- ⊙ Columbia
- ♦ 3.5 million

VIRGINIA
- ⊙ Richmond
- ♦ 6.1 million

WEST VIRGINIA
- ⊙ Charleston
- ♦ 1.9 million

Peanut butter

Peanut

GEORGIA GROWS NEARLY HALF THE TOTAL PEANUT CROP OF THE USA

CANADA

- The CN Tower in Toronto is the tallest free-standing structure in the world.
- French-speaking Québec's claim for independence from the rest of the country is a key constitutional issue.
- Forests and lakes cover 40% of Canada.

ESSENTIAL FACTS

- ⊙ Ottawa
- ◑ 9,976,140 sq km (3,851,788 sq miles)
- ♦ 27.8 million
- ♙ Canadian dollar
- ♢ English, French
- ▲ Multi-party democracy
- ♦ 77 years

NATIVE CANADIANS Kwakiutls displayed their status on posts carved with animal and human figures.

SWEET SYMBOL The leaf of the sugar maple tree is Canada's national symbol.

SPOOKY FESTIVAL Celebrating skeletons are seen everywhere during Mexico's Day of the Dead.

MEXICO

- The Mexican landscape ranges from snow-capped mountains to tropical rainforests.
- Mexico City is the world's largest city.
- More people emigrate from Mexico than any other country in the world.

ESSENTIAL FACTS

- ⊙ Mexico City
- ◑ 1,958,200 sq km (756,061 sq miles)
- ♦ 90 million
- ♙ Mexican new peso
- ♢ Spanish
- ▲ Multi-party republic
- ♦ 70 years

CENTRAL AND SOUTH AMERICA

BRAZIL

ANTIGUA & BARBUDA

DOMINICA

ST. LUCIA

BARBADOS

ST. VINCENT & THE GRENADINES

GRENADA

TRINIDAD & TOBAGO

SURINAM

French Guiana (to France)

Puerto Rico (to U.S.A.)

GUYANA

VENEZUELA

ST. KITTS & NEVIS

DOMINICAN REPUBLIC

HAITI

BAHAMAS

CUBA

JAMAICA

CARIBBEAN SEA

COLOMBIA

PERU

ECUADOR

BELIZE

GUATEMALA

HONDURAS

EL SALVADOR

NICARAGUA

COSTA RICA

PANAMA

Galapagos Islands (to Ecuador)

PACIFIC

ATLANTIC OCEAN

URUGUAY

PARAGUAY

ARGENTINA

CHILE

Falkland Islands
(to U.K.)

OCEAN

CENTRAL AND SOUTH AMERICA

Until three million years ago, South America was an island with its own unique flora and fauna. The narrow Isthmus of Panama is the continent's only link to North America. South America's southernmost tip, Cape Horn, is only 970 km (600 miles) from Antarctica.

CENTRAL AMERICA AND THE CARIBBEAN

CENTRAL AMERICA FORMS a narrow land bridge joining North and South America. To the east lie the Caribbean islands, many of which are uninhabited.

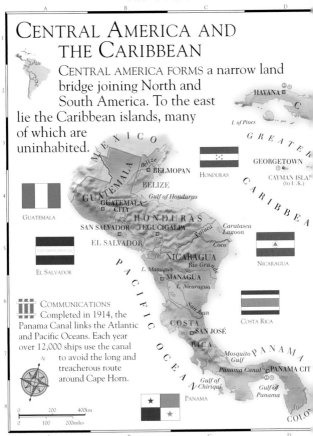

HAVANA

I. of Pines

GREATER

GEORGETOWN

CAYMAN ISLA
(to U.K.)

CARIBBEA

HONDURAS

MEXICO

Belize • BELMOPAN

BELIZE

GUATEMALA

GUATEMALA
CITY

GUATEMALA

Gulf of Honduras

HONDURAS

SAN SALVADOR • TEGUCIGALPA

Patuca

Caratasca
Lagoon

EL SALVADOR

EL SALVADOR

NICARAGUA

Coco

NICARAGUA

Rio Grande

L. Managua

MANAGUA

L. Nicaragua

PACIFIC

COSTA RICA

San Juan

COSTA
RICA

SAN JOSÉ

Mosquito
Gulf

PANAMA

Panama Canal • PANAMA CIT

OCEAN

Gulf of
Chiriqui

Gulf of
Panama

PANAMA

COLO

COMMUNICATIONS

Completed in 1914, the Panama Canal links the Atlantic and Pacific Oceans. Each year over 12,000 ships use the canal to avoid the long and treacherous route around Cape Horn.

N

| 0 | 200 | 400km |
| 0 | 100 | 200miles |

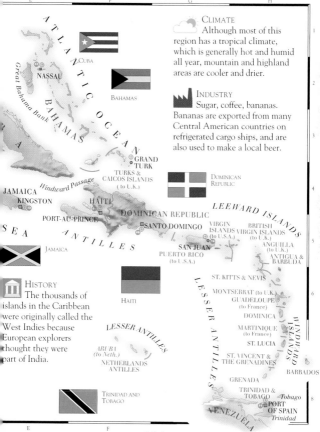

ATLANTIC OCEAN

CUBA

NASSAU

BAHAMAS

Great Bahama Bank

BAHAMAS

GRAND TURK

TURKS & CAICOS ISLANDS (to U.K.)

DOMINICAN REPUBLIC

JAMAICA

KINGSTON

Windward Passage

HAITI

PORT-AU-PRINCE

DOMINICAN REPUBLIC

SANTO DOMINGO

SEA

ANTILLES

JAMAICA

HAITI

LEEWARD ISLANDS

VIRGIN ISLANDS (to U.S.A.)

BRITISH VIRGIN ISLANDS (to U.K.)

ANGUILLA (to U.K.)

ANTIGUA & BARBUDA

SAN JUAN

PUERTO RICO (to U.S.A.)

ST. KITTS & NEVIS

MONTSERRAT (to U.K.)

GUADELOUPE (to France)

DOMINICA

MARTINIQUE (to France)

ST. LUCIA

LESSER ANTILLES

ARUBA (to Neth.)

NETHERLANDS ANTILLES

LESSER ANTILLES

ST. VINCENT & THE GRENADINES

GRENADA

TRINIDAD & TOBAGO

Tobago

PORT OF SPAIN

Trinidad

WINDWARD ISLANDS

BARBADOS

TRINIDAD AND TOBAGO

VENEZUELA

☁ **CLIMATE**
Although most of this region has a tropical climate, which is generally hot and humid all year, mountain and highland areas are cooler and drier.

🏭 **INDUSTRY**
Sugar, coffee, bananas. Bananas are exported from many Central American countries on refrigerated cargo ships, and are also used to make a local beer.

🏛 **HISTORY**
The thousands of islands in the Caribbean were originally called the West Indies because European explorers thought they were part of India.

Central America facts

NICARAGUA

• Lake Nicaragua is the only freshwater lake in the world to contain ocean animals.

ESSENTIAL FACTS

⊙ Managua

◔ 130, 000 sq km (50,193 sq miles)

♦ 4.1 million

⚍ New córdoba

♡ Spanish

HONDURAS

• The swampy Caribbean shoreline of Honduras is known as the Mosquito Coast.

ESSENTIAL FACTS

⊙ Tegucigalpa

◔ 112,090 sq km (43,278 sq miles)

♦ 5.6 million

⚍ Lempira

♡ Spanish

QUETZAL
Inca headdresses were decorated with the colourful tail feathers of the quetzal bird.

COTTON
The export of cotton is a major Nicaraguan industry.

BANANAS
Honduras has huge banana plantations. The work is hard and the pay is low.

GUATEMALA

• The ruined remains of temples and pyramids built by the ancient Mayans can still be seen in the forests of Guatemala.

ESSENTIAL FACTS

⊙ Guatemala City

◔ 108,890 sq km (42,043 sq miles)

♦ 10 million

⚍ Quetzal

♡ Spanish

EL SALVADOR

• Coffee accounts for 90% of the country's exported goods.
• El Salvador means "the saviour", referring to Christ.

ESSENTIAL FACTS

⊙ San Salvador

◔ 21,040 sq km (8,124 sq miles)

♦ 5.4 million

⚍ Salvadorean colón

♡ Spanish

COSTA RICA

- The constitution of Costa Rica is the only one in the world to ban National Armies.
- The name Costa Rica means "rich coast" in Spanish.

ESSENTIAL FACTS

- ⊙ San José
- ◔ 51,100 sq km (19,730 sq miles)
- ♠ 3.3 million
- ⚱ Costa Rican colón
- ♡ Spanish

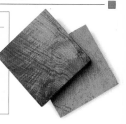

CUBAN BEE HUMMINGBIRD

CUBA

- As a result of fuel shortages, the main form of public transport is the bicycle.
- Cuba is the only communist country in the Americas.

ESSENTIAL FACTS

- ⊙ Havana
- ◔ 110,860 sq km (42,803 sq miles)
- ♠ 10.9 million
- ⚱ Cuban peso
- ♡ Spanish

PANAMA

- Many rare bird and animal species are threatened by the wholesale destruction of Panama's rainforests.

ESSENTIAL FACTS

- ⊙ Panama City
- ◔ 77,080 sq km (29,761 sq miles)
- ♠ 2.6 million
- ⚱ Balboa
- ♡ Spanish

EXPORTS
Belize exports grapefruit. Sugar is made from cane, which grows in Panama.

MAHOGANY
Costa Rica's forests have been devastated by excessive felling of trees, such as mahogany and cedar, for timber. Today, much forestland is protected.

BELIZE

- The Belizean barrier reef is the second largest in the world.
- Belize was formerly known as British Honduras, gaining independence in 1981.

ESSENTIAL FACTS

- ⊙ Belmopan
- ◔ 22,960 sq km (8,865 sq miles)
- ♠ 200,000
- ⚱ Belizean dollar
- ♡ English

Caribbean facts

DOMINICAN REPUBLIC

• Founded in 1496 by Christopher Columbus' brother, Santo Domingo is the oldest American city.

ESSENTIAL FACTS

⊙ Santo Domingo

◔ 48,730 sq km (18,815 sq miles)

♦ 7.6 million

☒ Dominican Republic peso

♡ Spanish

HAITI

• Many Haitians still practise the folk religion of voodoo.
• Haiti became the first independent black republic in 1804.

ESSENTIAL FACTS

⊙ Port-au-Prince

◔ 27,750 sq km (10,714 sq miles)

♦ 6.9 million

☒ Gourde

♡ French, Creole

Molasses

Rum, made from cane juice

Sugar cane

CANE PRODUCTS
Sugar cane thrives in the tropical Caribbean.

JAMAICA

• Reggae music originated in Jamaica.
• The Rastafarians of Jamaica worship Haile Selassie, the late emperor of Ethiopia.
• Large areas of Kingston are ruled by gang leaders, or *Dons*.

ESSENTIAL FACTS

⊙ Kingston

◔ 10,990 sq km (4,243 sq miles)

♦ 2.5 million

☒ Jamaican dollar

♡ English

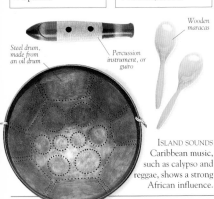

Wooden maracas

Steel drum, made from an oil drum

Percussion instrument, or guiro

ISLAND SOUNDS
Caribbean music, such as calypso and reggae, shows a strong African influence.

GRENADA

- ⊙ St. George's
- ♦ 91,000
- ♡ English, Creole

ST. LUCIA

- ⊙ Castries
- ♦ 156,000
- ♡ English, French

THE BAHAMAS

- ⊙ Nassau
- ♦ 300,000
- ♡ English, Creole

DOMINICA

- ⊙ Roseau
- ♦ 72,000
- ♡ English, French

ISLE OF SPICES
Many varieties
of spice are
grown on the
island of
Grenada.

Cloves

Mace

Bay leaf

Saffron

Cinnamon
stick

Ground
cinnamon

ST. KITTS & NEVIS

- ⊙ Basseterre
- ♦ 44,000
- ♡ English, Creole

ST. VINCENT & THE GRENADINES

- ⊙ Kingstown
- ♦ 109,000
- ♡ English, Creole

BARBADOS

- ⊙ Bridgetown
- ♦ 260,000
- ♡ English, Creole

TRINIDAD & TOBAGO

- ⊙ Port-of-Spain
- ♦ 1.3 million
- ♡ English

ANTIGUA & BARBUDA

- ⊙ St. John's
- ♦ 200,000
- ♡ English, Creole

STORMY WEATHER
The Caribbean
islands are often
subject to extreme
weather, such
as hurricanes
and typhoons.

Northern South America

THE INCAS RULED MUCH of this area in the 15th century, and today large numbers of their descendants live in Peru, Ecuador, and Bolivia. In 1533, the last Incan emperor was executed by the Spanish, who colonized this region. The French, Dutch, and British later settled in the countries east of Venezuela, although all but French Guiana are now independent.

VENEZUELA

GUYANA

SURINAM

CARIBBEAN SEA

Margarita I.

Gulf of Venezuela

Santa Marta · Maracaibo · Cumaná · Maturín
Barranquilla · L. Maracaibo · CARACAS · Ciudad Guayana
Cartagena · Barquisimeto · Valencia · Ciudad Bolívar
Gulf of Darién · Mérida · Barinas · Orinoco
PANAMA · Medellín · Apure · VENEZUELA · GUYANA
COLOMBIA · Meta · Villavicencio · GEORGETOWN
BOGOTÁ · Guaviare · New Amsterdam
Buenaventura · Cali · Magdalena · Cauca

Essequibo

Berbice · Corantyne

GEORGETOWN
New Amsterdam

PARAMARIBO

SURINAM

CAYENNE

FRENCH GUIANA
(to France)

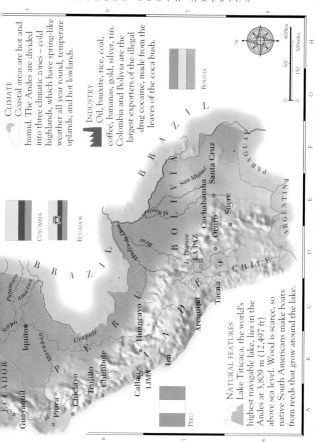

CLIMATE

Coastal areas are hot and humid. The Andes are divided into three climatic zones – cold highlands, which have spring-like weather all year round, temperate uplands, and hot lowlands.

INDUSTRY

Oil, bauxite, rice, coal, coffee, bananas, gold, silver, tin. Colombia and Bolivia are the largest exporters of the illegal drug cocaine, made from the leaves of the coca bush.

BOLIVIA

COLOMBIA

ECUADOR

NATURAL FEATURES

Lake Titicaca, the world's highest navigable lake, lies in the Andes at 3,809 m (12,497 ft) above sea level. Wood is scarce, so native South Americans make boats from the reeds that grow around the lake.

PERU

BRAZIL

BOLIVIA

PERU

ANDES

CHILE

ARGENTINA

PARAGUAY

ECUADOR

Guayaquil

Iquitos

Piura

Chiclayo

Trujillo

Chimbote

Callao · LIMA

Ica

Arequipa

Tacna

Huancayo

La Paz

Oruro

Cochabamba

Sucre

Santa Cruz

San Miguel

Mamoré

Beni

Madre de Dios

L. Titicaca

Amazon

Napo

Putumayo

Ucayali

Marañón

Northern South America facts

SURINAM

- Jaguars, pumas, ocelots, and iguanas live wild in Surinam.

ESSENTIAL FACTS

- ⊙ Paramaribo
- ◔ 163,270 sq km (63,039 sq miles)
- ✚ 400,000 million
- 🐚 Surinam guilder
- ♡ Dutch

Uncut gem

Rock

COLOMBIAN EMERALD

COLOMBIA

- The country of Colombia produces two-thirds of the world's emeralds.

ESSENTIAL FACTS

- ⊙ Bogotá
- ◔ 1,138,910 sq km (439,620 sq miles)
- ✚ 34 million
- 🐚 Colombian peso
- ♡ Spanish
- ▲ Multi-party republic
  - ● 69 years

PERU

- The Morochocha railway in Peru has the world's highest section of railway track.
- Peru is a strongly patriarchal, or male-dominated, society.

ESSENTIAL FACTS

- ⊙ Lima
- ◔ 1,285,220 sq km (496,223 sq miles)
- ✚ 22.9 million
- 🐚 New sol
- ♡ Spanish, Quechua, and Aymará

ECUADOR AND THE GALÁPAGOS

- Charles Darwin's studies on the Galápagos Islands in 1856 helped formulate his theories on the evolution of species.
- Ecuador's landscape features low coastal regions, high Andean peaks, and dense jungle.

ESSENTIAL FACTS

- ⊙ Quito
- ◔ 283,560 sq km (109,483 sq miles)
- ✚ 11.3 million
- 🐚 Sucre
- ♡ Spanish, Quechua

GALÁPAGOS TORTOISE

THE GALÁPAGOS
These islands lie 970 km (603 miles) west of Ecuador. Many of the islands' animals are unique.

Wing span of more than 3m (10ft)

ANDEAN CONDOR
The heaviest bird of prey in the world, the condor lives in the highest parts of the Andes.

GUYANA

• The Guyanese nation is the only English-speaking country in South America.
• Guyana means "land of many waters".

ESSENTIAL FACTS

⊙ Georgetown
◔ 214,970 sq km (83,000 sq miles)
♦ 800,000
⚇ Guyana dollar
♀ English, Creole

VENEZUELA

• Many Venezuelan people live in poverty.
• Venezuela is the most urbanized country in South America.
• Angel Falls, the highest waterfall in the world, lies in southern Venezuela.

ESSENTIAL FACTS

⊙ Caracas
◔ 912,050 sq km (352,143 sq miles)
♦ 20.6 million
⚇ Bolívar
♀ Spanish

BOLIVIA

• La Paz is the highest capital city in the world.
• Many Bolivian farmers are very poor, growing just enough food for their families to live on.
• Bolivia has the world's highest golf course and ski run.

ESSENTIAL FACTS

⊙ La Paz
◔ 1,098,580 sq km (424,162 sq miles)
♦ 7.8 million
⚇ Boliviano
♀ Spanish, Quechua, and Aymará

FRENCH GUIANA

• The European Space Agency conducts its rocket launches from French Guiana.
• The territory of French Guiana is the last remaining colony in South America.

ESSENTIAL FACTS

⊙ Cayenne
◔ 90,996 sq km (35,135 sq miles)
♦ 114,800
⚇ French franc
♀ French

CAYENNE PEPPER
Crushed South American chillies are used to make cayenne pepper.

BRAZIL

OCCUPYING NEARLY HALF of South America, Brazil has the largest river basin in the world. Many Brazilians are descendants of Portuguese, who colonized Brazil in the 16th century, and Africans, who were brought to work on sugar plantations. Brazil's Native American tribes have little contact with the outside world. In 1992, the United Nations held its first Earth Summit in Rio, partly to highlight the destruction of the Amazon rainforest, the largest rainforest in the world.

PEOPLE

There were once about two million indigenous people living in Amazonia. Today only 50,000 remain. The survival of many tribes and their way of life is threatened by the destruction of the Amazon rainforest.

ATLANTIC OCEAN

Natal

Fortaleza

Teresina

Parnaíba

São Luís

SERRA PELADA

Belém

FRENCH
GUIANA
(to France)

Xingu

Santarém

SURINAM

Amazon

GUYANA

Balbina
Res.

Manaus

Madeira

Tapajós

VENEZUELA

Negro

Amazon

Purus

B

R

AMAZON

BASIN

COLOMBIA

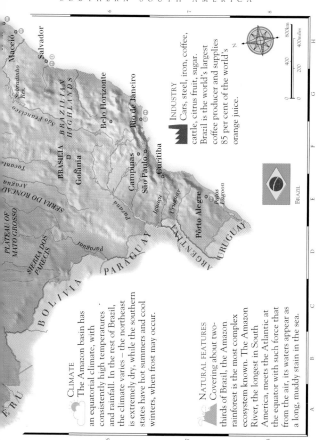

CLIMATE

The Amazon basin has an equatorial climate, with consistently high temperatures and rainfall. In the rest of Brazil, the climate varies – the northeast is extremely dry, while the southern states have hot summers and cool winters, when frost may occur.

NATURAL FEATURES

Covering about two-thirds of Brazil, the Amazon rainforest is the most complex ecosystem known. The Amazon River, the longest in South America, meets the Atlantic at the equator with such force that from the air, its waters appear as a long, muddy stain in the sea.

INDUSTRY

Cars, steel, iron, coffee, cattle, citrus fruit, sugar. Brazil is the world's largest coffee producer and supplies 85 per cent of the world's orange juice.

BRAZIL

N

| 0 | 200 | 400 | 800km |
| 0 | | 400 | 400miles |

PERU

BOLIVIA

PLATEAU OF
MATO GROSSO

SERRA DO RONCADO

SIERRA DOS
PARECIS

Paraguay

PARAGUAY

ARGENTINA

URUGUAY

Tocantins

BRASÍLIA

Goiânia

Paraná

Campinas

São Paulo

Curitiba

Uruguay

Iguaçu

Pôrto Alegre

Patos
Lagoon

BRAZILIAN
HIGHLANDS

São Francisco

Belo Horizonte

Rio de Janeiro

Sobradinho
Res.

Salvador

Maceió

SOUTHERN SOUTH AMERICA

THE LANDSCAPE OF this region of South America varies from snow-capped volcanoes in the Andes to the wastelands of Patagonia. In the heart of Argentina lie the Pampas, fertile grasslands where vast herds of cattle graze. In parts, grasses grow up to 3 m (10 ft) high. Chile is separated from the rest of the region by the Andes, which run the length of the continent.

CLIMATE

Paraguay is subtropical; farther south is temperate. The Andes have year-round snow, while parts of the Atacama desert in Chile have had no rain for 400 years.

URUGUAY

PARAGUAY

INDUSTRY

Copper, wool, beef, wheat. Chile is the world's largest copper producer, and Uruguay is the second-largest wool exporter.

ARGENTINA

HISTORY

Before the discovery of Cape Horn at the tip of the continent in 1616, ships used the dangerous Straits of Magellan to travel between the Atlantic and the Pacific Oceans. Today, ships use the Panama Canal.

NATURAL FEATURES

The longest chain of mountains in the world, the Andes extend for 7,240 km (4,500 miles). They are the most recently formed mountains on Earth, and the area suffers from earthquakes and volcanic activity. Glaciers, fjords, lakes, and deep-sea channels are features of the southern Andes.

MONTEVIDEO

Plate

BUENOS AIRES

Mar del Plata

Bahía Blanca

ATLANTIC OCEAN

Colorado

Negro

Gulf of San Matías

Valdés Peninsula

PAMPAS

Godoy Cruz

SANTIAGO

San Bernardo

L. Nahuel Huapi

Chubut

Comodoro Rivadavia

Deseado

Puerto Santa Cruz

Río Grande

Viña del Mar

Valparaíso

Chillán

Concepción

Los Ángeles

Bío-Bío

Temuco

Valdivia

Osorno

Puerto Montt

Chiloé I.

Chaitén

L. Colhué Huapi

L. Buenos Aires

L. Viedma

L. Argentino

PATAGONIA

ANDES

CHILE

TORRES DEL PAINE

Punta Arenas

Strait of Magellan

TIERRA DEL FUEGO

Cape Horn

CHILE

N

0   300   600 km

0   150   300 miles

Southern South America Facts

CHILE

- Democracy was restored in Chile in 1989 after 12 years of military rule under General Pinochet.
- The Atacama Desert in northern Chile is the driest place on Earth.

ESSENTIAL FACTS

- ⊙ Santiago
- ◐ 756,950 sq km (292,258 sq miles)
- ♦ 13.8 million
- ☙ Chilean peso
- ♀ Spanish
- ▲ Multi-party republic
- ♦ 72 years

TREE OF MYSTERY
The Chile pine, also known as the monkey puzzle tree, is native to the Andes, the world's longest mountain range.

URUGUAY

- The country of Uruguay is the smallest in South America.
- Almost half of the population lives in Montevideo.
- Hydroelectric power generates 86% of the country's electricity.
- Uruguay is tolerant of all forms of religion.

ESSENTIAL FACTS

- ⊙ Montevideo
- ◐ 177,410 sq km (68,498 sq miles)
- ♦ 3.1 million
- ☙ Uruguayan peso
- ♀ Spanish

PARAGUAY

- The majority of Paraguayans are *mestizo* – a mixture of native Guaraní Indian and Spanish blood.
- Half the work force is employed in agriculture.

ESSENTIAL FACTS

- ⊙ Asunción
- ◐ 406,750 sq km (157,046 sq miles)
- ♦ 4.5 million
- ☙ Guaraní
- ♀ Spanish, Guaraní

WOOLLEN SCARF

TEXTILES
Uruguay is a major exporter of handmade wool products.

GAUCHO
Argentinian cowboys are known as gauchos.

ARGENTINA

- Crop production and cattle and sheep rearing produces three-quarters of the nation's income.
- The Argentinian daily drink is a tea called *maté*.
- The tango dance originated in Buenos Aires in the late 19th century.

ESSENTIAL FACTS

- ⊙ Buenos Aires
- 2,766,890 sq km (1,068,296 sq miles)
- 33.5 million
- Argentinian peso
- Spanish
- ▲ Multi-party republic
- 71 years

PUDU
Southern Argentina's Patagonia region is home to the pudu, the world's smallest deer.

BRAZILIAN SOCCER
Football is Brazil's favourite sport, with over 20,000 soccer teams.

BRAZIL

- São Paulo is the world's second largest city, with 17 million inhabitants.
- Rio de Janeiro's *Mardi Gras* carnival is a major tourist attraction.
- Brazil has rich gold and diamond reserves.
- Many Brazilians live in poverty, despite the country's resources.

ESSENTIAL FACTS

- ⊙ Brasília
- 8,511,970 sq km (3,286,472 sq miles)
- 156.6 million
- Reál
- Portuguese
- ▲ Multi-party republic
- 66 years

EUROPE

*Jan Mayen I.
(to Norway)*

NORWEGIAN SEA

ICELAND

*Faeroe Islands
(to Denmark)*

NORWAY

SWEDEN

NORTH
SEA

DENMARK

UNITED KINGDOM

REPUBLIC OF
IRELAND

GERMANY

CZECH
RE

FRANCE

AUST

ITAL

PORTUGAL

SPAIN

*Gibraltar
(to U.K.)*

MALT

MEDITER

EUROPE

The Alps and the Pyrenees roughly divide the continent into north and south, forming a barrier that protects warm southern countries, such as Spain and Italy, from cold northern winds. Parts of Europe are moderated by the Gulf Stream, which circulates warm waters from the Caribbean, and even seas in the Arctic Circle stay ice-free in winter.

BARENTS SEA

FINLAND

BALTIC SEA

ESTONIA

LATVIA

LITHUANIA

RUSSIAN FEDERATION

BELORUSSIA

POLAND

SLOVAKIA

HUNGARY

UKRAINE

16

ROMANIA

13

BLACK SEA

BULGARIA

GEORGIA

14

AZERBAIJAN

ARMENIA

15

GREECE

MEDITERRANEAN SEA

1 NETHERLANDS
2 BELGIUM
3 LUXEMBOURG
4 LIECHTENSTEIN
5 SWITZERLAND
6 ANDORRA
7 MONACO
8 VATICAN CITY
9 SAN MARINO
10 SLOVENIA
11 CROATIA
12 BOSNIA/HERZEGOVINA
13 YUGOSLAVIA
14 MACEDONIA
15 ALBANIA
16 MOLDAVIA

SCANDINAVIA AND FINLAND

DURING PAST ICE AGES, much of Scandinavia and Finland were covered in glaciers that carved out the land, leaving steep-sided valleys, fjords, and lakes. The Finnish, originally from the east via Russia, differ from Scandinavians in culture and language.

FINLAND

CLIMATE

Norway's west coast is warmed by the Gulf Stream. Northern temperatures fall to –30°C (–22°F) during the six-month winter; the south is milder.

INDUSTRY

Fishing, timber, wood-pulp, paper, oil, gas, car manufacture. Norway is western Europe's largest producer of oil.

NORWAY

ARCTIC OCEAN

RUSSIAN FEDERATION

North Cape

Hammerfest

L. Inari

Ivalo

F I N L

Ounas

Tana

Oulu

Oulu

Muonio

Tornio

Tromso

Torne

Ume

L. Uddjaur

SVE

NORWEGIAN SEA

Lofoten

Vesteralen

N

W

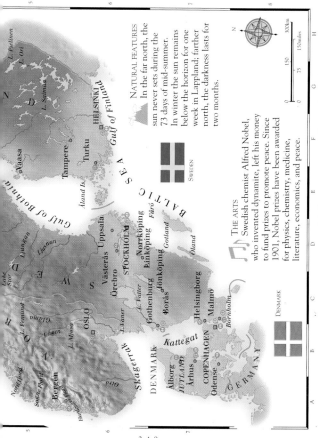

NATURAL FEATURES
In the far north, the sun never sets during the 73 days of mid-summer. In winter the sun remains below the horizon for one week in Lapland; farther north, the darkness lasts for two months.

SWEDEN

THE ARTS
Swedish chemist Alfred Nobel, who invented dynamite, left his money to fund prizes to promote peace. Since 1901, Nobel prizes have been awarded for physics, chemistry, medicine, literature, economics, and peace.

DENMARK

N

0   75   150   300km
0   150   150miles

BALTIC SEA

Gulf of Finland

HELSINKI
Turku
Tampere
Vaasa
Åland Is.
Fårö
Gotland
Öland
Norrköping
Linköping
Jönköping
Uppsala
Västerås
Örebro
STOCKHOLM
L. Vätter
L. Väner
Gothenburg
Borås
Helsingborg
Malmö
Bornholm
OSLO
Bergen
Nordfjord
Sogne Fjord
Hardanger
Oro
Kattegat
Skagerrak
DENMARK
JUTLAND
Ålborg
Århus
Odense
COPENHAGEN
GERMANY

Gulf of Bothnia

L. Pielinen
L. Ori
L. Saimaa

Lake Stor
Ljungan
Ljusnan
Indals
Lake Fæmund
Glåma
Lågen
L. Mjøsa

Northern Europe facts

ICELAND

- The remote interior of Iceland can only be reached by special vehicle, pony, or small plane.
- Iceland has the lowest population in Europe.
- Heating is provided by geothermal power.

ESSENTIAL FACTS

⊙ Reykjavik

◑ 103,000 sq km (39,770 sq miles)

♦ 300,000

☙ New Icelandic krona

♡ Icelandic

▲ Multi-party republic

♦ 78 years

ICELANDIC COD
More than a third of the world's cod-liver oil is produced in Iceland.

NORWAY

- According to Norway's constitution, the government's duty is to create conditions enabling every person to find work.

ESSENTIAL FACTS

⊙ Oslo

◑ 323,900 sq km (125,060 sq miles)

♦ 4.2 million

☙ Norwegian krone

♡ Norwegian

▲ Multi-party democracy

♦ 77 years

GRASS ROOFS
Some Norwegian holiday homes have turf-covered roofs.

LAND OF LEGO
Lego building bricks, known by children worldwide, were invented in Denmark.

DENMARK

- Single parents and cohabiting couples raise 40% of Danish children.
- Denmark is Europe's oldest monarchy, dating back to the 1100s.

ESSENTIAL FACTS

⊙ Copenhagen

◑ 43,069 sq km (16,629 sq miles)

♦ 5.2 million

☙ Danish krone

♡ Danish

▲ Multi-party democracy

♦ 75 years

SWEDEN

- Over 50% of Swedish women go out to work.
- Sweden has maintained a position of armed neutrality since 1815.
- Swedish law requires cars to travel with their headlights on at all times.
- Many Swedes invest in overseas property.

ESSENTIAL FACTS

- ☉ Stockholm
- ◓ 449,960 sq km (173,730 sq miles)
- ♦ 8.7 million
- ⚑ Swedish krona
- ♡ Swedish
- ▲ Multi-party democracy
- ♦ 78 years

SMÖRGÅSBORD
A Swedish smörgåsbord, meaning "sandwich table", is a spread of local delicacies served cold.

GREENLAND

Dependency of Denmark
(*Atlantic Ocean, pp.360–361*)

- ☉ Nuuk
- ♦ 55,385
- ♡ Inuit, Danish

FINNISH TIMBER
Most of Finland's wealth is provided by its timber exports.

Ladle

Sauna bucket

STEAM CLEANING
The Finns invented the steam bath, or sauna, over 1,000 years ago.

FINLAND

- Over half of Finland's population lives in the five districts around Helsinki.
- Finland was the first country to allow women to run for parliament.
- Finland's inland waterway system is the largest in Europe.

ESSENTIAL FACTS

- ☉ Helsinki
- ◓ 338,130 sq km (130,552 sq miles)
- ♦ 5 million
- ⚑ Markka
- ♡ Finnish, Swedish
- ▲ Multi-party republic
- ♦ 75 years

BRITISH ISLES

LYING OFF THE COAST of mainland Europe, the British Isles consist of two main islands, Ireland and Great Britain, and many smaller islands. England, Scotland, Wales, and Northern Ireland form the United Kingdom (UK). The Republic of Ireland became independent of the UK in 1921.

NATURAL FEATURES
The highest point in the British Isles is Ben Nevis in Scotland at a height of 1,343 m (4,406 ft).

UNITED KINGDOM

NORTH SEA

ATLANTIC OCEAN

Shetland Is.
Orkney Is.
Outer Hebrides
Lewis
North Uist
South Uist
Barra
Skye
Coll
Tiree
Mull
Colonsay
Jura
Islay
Arran
Kintyre
Londonderry
Aberdeen
Edinburgh
Glasgow
SCOTLAND
GRAMPIAN
SOUTHERN UPLANDS

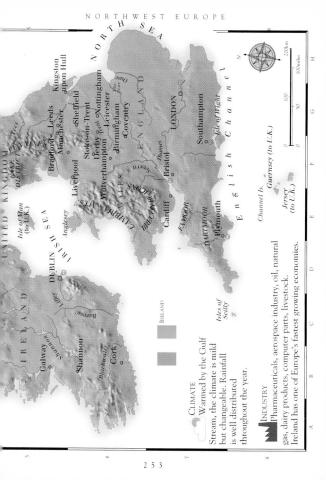

NORTH SEA

NORTH SEA

UNITED KINGDOM

LAKE DISTRICT

PENNINES

Isle of Man
(to U.K.)

IRISH SEA

Anglesey

Kingston
upon Hull

Bradford
Leeds

Manchester

Sheffield

Liverpool

Stoke-on-Trent

Nottingham

Derby

Leicester

Wolverhampton

Birmingham

Coventry

CAMBRIAN MTS.

WALES

BRECON
BEACONS

Cardiff

Bristol

ENGLAND

Ouse

LONDON

Thames

Southampton

Isle of Wight

English Channel

Severn

EXMOOR

Plymouth

DARTMOOR

Channel Is.

Guernsey (to U.K.)

Jersey
(to U.K.)

Isles of
Scilly

IRELAND

DUBLIN

Galway

Shannon

Cork

Liffey

Barrow

Blackwater

Suir

Shannon

IRELAND

CLIMATE
Warmed by the Gulf
Stream, the climate is mild
but changeable. Rainfall
is well distributed
throughout the year.

INDUSTRY
Pharmaceuticals, aerospace industry, oil, natural
gas, dairy products, computer parts, livestock.
Ireland has one of Europe's fastest growing economies.

N

200km

100

100miles

50

0

0

A   B   C   D   E   F   G   H

5   6   7   8

2 5 3

THE LOW COUNTRIES

BELGIUM, THE NETHERLANDS, and Luxembourg are known as the "Low Countries" because they are flat and low-lying. Much of the Netherlands lies below sea level and has been reclaimed from the sea. The Low Countries, also called "Benelux", are Europe's most densely populated countries.

NETHERLANDS

Map labels

GERMANY

Groningen

Assen

Leeuwarden

West Frisian Is.

Waddenzee

Zwolle

Flevoland

IJsselmeer

Enschede

Apeldoorn

Arnhem

Rhine

Utrecht

Nijmegen

AMSTERDAM

Haarlem

The Hague

Rotterdam

Dordrecht

Breda

's-Hertogenbosch

Bergen op Zoom

Middelburg

Maas

NORTH SEA

CLIMATE

The region is mostly temperate. Coastal areas are mildest, warmed by the Gulf Stream. Luxembourg's winters are cold and snowy.

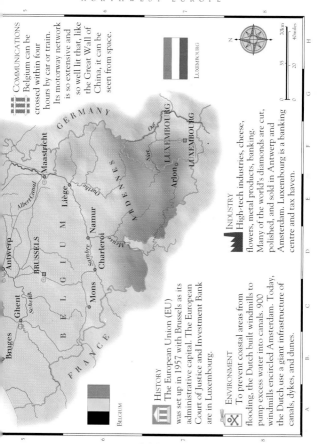

COMMUNICATIONS
Belgium can be crossed within four hours by car or train. Its motorway network is so extensive and so well lit that, like the Great Wall of China, it can be seen from space.

LUXEMBOURG

HISTORY
The European Union (EU) was set up in 1957 with Brussels as its administrative capital. The European Court of Justice and Investment Bank are in Luxembourg.

ENVIRONMENT
To prevent coastal areas from flooding, the Dutch built windmills to pump excess water into canals. 900 windmills encircled Amsterdam. Today, the Dutch use a giant infrastructure of canals, dykes, and dunes.

INDUSTRY
High-tech industries, cheese, flowers, metal products, banking. Many of the world's diamonds are cut, polished, and sold in Antwerp and Amsterdam. Luxembourg is a banking centre and tax haven.

BELGIUM

Northwest Europe facts

UNITED KINGDOM

• London's theatres, art galleries and historical buildings are a major tourist attraction.
• British people meet to talk and drink in public houses (pubs).
• Scotland retains a distinct educational and legal system that differs from the rest of the UK.

ESSENTIAL FACTS

⊙ London
◔ 244,880 sq km (94,550 sq miles)
⬩ 57.8 million
💷 Pound sterling
♀ English
▲ Multi-party democracy
⬩ 76 years

TALL BOY
Big Ben, the Houses of Parliament's clock, is one of London's major landmarks.

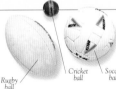

SPORTING EXPORTS
Many sports invented in the UK are now played worldwide.

Rugby ball

Cricket ball

Soccer ball

IRISH HARP
An instrument used in traditional Irish music, the harp has been played in Ireland since the 1100s.

REPUBLIC OF IRELAND

• The nation gained full sovereignty from the UK in 1937.
• Ireland has the lowest consumption of alcohol per person in the European Union.
• Irish Gaelic is used as an everyday language by around 20,000 people.

ESSENTIAL FACTS

⊙ Dublin
◔ 70,280 sq km (27,135 sq miles)
⬩ 3.5 million
💷 Irish punt (pound)
♀ Irish, English
▲ Multi-party republic
⬩ 75 years

BELGIUM

- The cultural mix of French-speaking Walloons and Flemings forms the national identity of Belgium.
- Belgium's motorway network is so extensive and well lit that it can be seen from space.
- The country is the world's third largest producer of chocolate.

ESSENTIAL FACTS

- ⊙ Brussels
- ◔ 33,100 sq km (12,780 sq miles)
- ✚ 10 million
- ☙ Belgian franc
- ♥ French, Dutch, Flemish
- ▲ Multi-party democracy
- ◖ 76 years

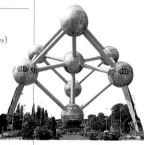

SPACE-AGE STRUCTURE
The design of Belgium's futuristic Atomium building is based on the molecular structure of an iron crystal.

NETHERLANDS

- Dutch laws on sexuality and drugs are less strict than in other parts of Europe.
- Rotterdam is the world's largest port.

ESSENTIAL FACTS

- ⊙ Amsterdam, The Hague
- ◔ 37,330 sq km (14,410 sq miles)
- ✚ 15.3 million
- ☙ Guilder
- ♥ Dutch
- ▲ Multi-party democracy
- ◖ 77 years

DUTCH TULIPS
The Netherlands is Europe's largest producer of flowers. The cultivation of bulbs such as daffodils and tulips is a speciality.

LUXEMBOURG

- ⊙ Luxembourg City
- ✚ 400,000
- ♥ Letzeburgish

LUXEMBOURG BANKING
The nation of Luxembourg is a centre of international banking and finance.

SPAIN AND PORTUGAL

SUPREME SKILL IN shipbuilding and navigation enabled both Spain and Portugal to become the most powerful empires of the 16th century. Both have a seafaring history; Christopher Columbus sailed to America in 1492, and Vasco da Gama, the Portuguese explorer, was the first to sail around Africa to India in 1497.

INDUSTRY
Fishing, car manufacture, olives, cork, ship building, citrus fruit, tourism. Spain and Portugal are famous for fortified wines. Sherry is named after Jerez de la Frontera, Spain, and Port after Porto, Portugal.

CLIMATE
Spain's coastal areas are milder than the central plateau, which has a more extreme temperature range. Almeria, Spain, contains Europe's only desert. Portugal's Mediterranean climate is moderated by the Atlantic.

PORTUGAL

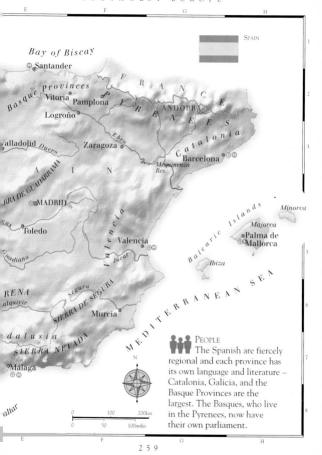

SPAIN

Bay of Biscay

⊕ Santander

Basque provinces

Vitoria Pamplona

Logroño

Valladolid *Duero*

F R A N C E

P Y R E N E E S

ANDORRA

Ebro

Zaragoza

Catalonia

Barcelona ⊕Ⓜ

S P A I N

SIERRA DE GUADARRAMA

⊡MADRID

Toledo

Tajus

Guadiana

Mequinenza Res.

Valencia

Valencia ⊕Ⓜ

Júcar

Balearic Islands

Minorca

Majorca

● Palma de Mallorca

Ibiza

RENA

Guadalquivir

Segura

SIERRA DE SEGURA

Murcia

M E D I T E R R A N E A N   S E A

Andalusia

SIERRA NEVADA

● Málaga

Gibraltar

N

PEOPLE

The Spanish are fiercely regional and each province has its own language and literature – Catalonia, Galicia, and the Basque Provinces are the largest. The Basques, who live in the Pyrenees, now have their own parliament.

0	100	200km
0	50	100miles

FRANCE

FOLLOWING THE FRENCH Revolution (1789–99), France became Europe's first modern republic, and possessed a colonial empire that included parts of Asia and Africa. France and Spain jointly governed Andorra from 1278. In 1993 the principality held its first full elections. The country of Monaco is a lucrative banking centre.

PEOPLE
Despite a strong national identity, the Bretons, Normans, Alsatians, Corsicans, and the Monegasque from Monaco still maintain their regional traditions.

ANDORRA

COMMUNICATIONS
The French lead the world in high-speed train technology. First run in 1981, the TGV (*Train à Grande Vitesse*) is one of the world's fastest trains, with a top speed of 300 km/h (186 mph).

| 0 | 75 | 150km |
| 0 | 50 | 100miles |

English Channel

Cherbourg
Le Havre

Channel Islands
(to U.K.)

Caen

Île d'Ouessant

Brest

NORMAND

BRITTANY

Rennes

Le Mar

Belle Île

Loire

Nantes

ATLANTIC

Poiti

Bordeaux

OCEAN

Garo

PYRENE

SPAI

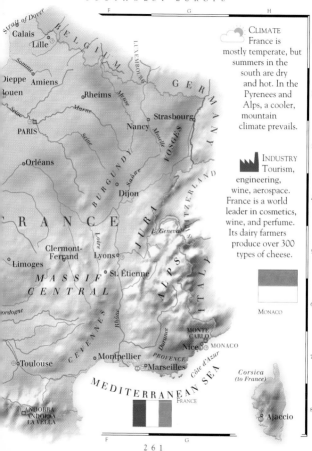

CLIMATE
France is mostly temperate, but summers in the south are dry and hot. In the Pyrenees and Alps, a cooler, mountain climate prevails.

INDUSTRY
Tourism, engineering, wine, aerospace. France is a world leader in cosmetics, wine, and perfume. Its dairy farmers produce over 300 types of cheese.

MONACO

FRANCE

Corsica
(to France)

Strait of Dover
Calais
Lille
BELGIUM
LUXEMBOURG
Dieppe Amiens
Rouen
Somme
GERMANY
Seine
Rheims
Marne
Meuse
Strasbourg
Nancy
Moselle
PARIS
Seine
VOSGES
Orléans
BURGUNDY
JURA
Dijon
Saône
SWITZERLAND
L. Geneva
Clermont-Ferrand Lyons
Loire
Limoges
St. Étienne
ALPS
MASSIF
CENTRAL
ITALY
Dordogne
CÉVENNES
Rhône
MONTE CARLO
Durance
Nice MONACO
Toulouse
Montpellier
PROVENCE
Marseilles
Côte d'Azur
ANDORRA
ANDORRA
LA VELLA
MEDITERRANEAN SEA
Ajaccio

ITALY AND MALTA

THE BOOT-SHAPED PENINSULA of Italy stretches from the Alps to the Ionian Sea and includes Sardinia, Sicily, and other small, offshore islands. Italy also contains two independent enclaves – the Vatican City in Rome and the Republic of San Marino near Rimini. The Romans, Arabs, French, Turks, Spanish, and British have all fought for or colonized Malta, which has been independent since 1964.

PEOPLE

The Venetians were a seafaring people, whose ships carried silks and spices from Asia. The Venetian trader and explorer Marco Polo is said to have brought the recipe for pasta from China.

HISTORY

Italy was once a collection of small kingdoms and city-states, which were vulnerable to internal wars. It was united in 1870, through the efforts of the soldier Giuseppe Garibaldi and the politician Count Camillo di Cavour.

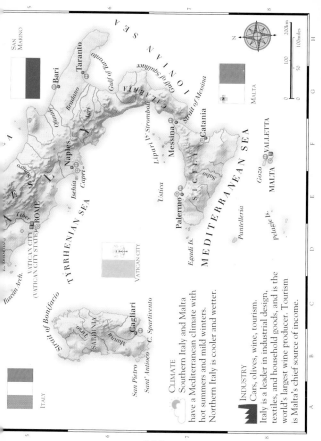

CLIMATE
Southern Italy and Malta have a Mediterranean climate with hot summers and mild winters. Northern Italy is cooler and wetter.

INDUSTRY
Cars, olives, wine, tourism. Italy is a leader in industrial design, textiles, and household goods, and is the world's largest wine producer. Tourism is Malta's chief source of income.

Southwest Europe facts

SPAIN

• Young Spanish men tend to live at home until their late 20s.
• Spanish public hospitals are generally considered to be better than private ones.
• Over 3,000 festivals and feasts take place every year in Spain.

ESSENTIAL FACTS

⊙ Madrid
◑ 504,780 sq km (194,900 sq miles)
♦ 39.2 million
🏛 Peseta
♡ Spanish
▲ Multi-party democracy
♦ 77 years

PORTUGUESE CORK
More than half the world's cork is supplied by Portugal, the main product being the bottle stopper.

SPANISH SIX-STRING

The classical guitar is Spain's national instrument.

Tuning pegs

Nut

Neck

Frets

Soundhole

Bridge

Hollow body

Strings

PORTUGAL

• Family ties are a major part of Portuguese life.
• Over 40% of the population have private health insurance.
• Portugal has few natural resources.

ESSENTIAL FACTS

⊙ Lisbon
◑ 92,390 sq km (35,670 sq miles)
♦ 9.9 million
🏛 Escudo
♡ Portuguese
▲ Multi-party republic
♦ 74 years

ANDORRA

⊙ Andorra la Vella
♦ 58,000
♡ Catalan

ITALY

- Tourists have visited Italy since the 1500s.
- Italy is a world leader in product design and the fashion industry.
- Venice is such a popular place to visit that pedestrians have to use one-way systems in the summer.
- Most Italians live at home before marriage.

ESSENTIAL FACTS

⊙ Rome

◔ 301,270 sq km (116,320 sq miles)

♦ 57.8 million

♙ Italian lira

♀ Italian

▲ Multi-party republic

● 77 years

VENETIAN MASKS
Masks are traditionally worn during the February carnival in Venice.

SAN MARINO	VATICAN CITY	MALTA	MONACO
⊙ San Marino	⊙ Vatican City	⊙ Valletta	⊙ Monaco
♦ 23,000	♦ 1,000	♦ 400,000	♦ 28,000
♀ Italian	♀ Italian, Latin	♀ Maltese, English	♀ French

FRANCE

- Paris is the most visited European city.
- The French wine industry dates back to 600 BC.
- More medicine is consumed per person in France than in any other country.
- Most French people spend their holidays in France, rather than travelling abroad.

ESSENTIAL FACTS

⊙ Paris

◔ 551,500 sq km (212,930 sq miles)

♦ 57.4 million

♙ Franc

♀ French

▲ Multi-party republic

● 77 years

PEDAL POWER
The *Tour de France* cycle race is the most famous in the world.

CENTRAL EUROPE

HISTORICALLY ONE OF the least stable parts of the continent, central Europe became part of the Eastern Bloc after World War II. Czechoslovakia, Poland, and Hungary all had communist governments with strong ties with the former USSR. In 1989, they broke away from communism and in 1993 Czechoslovakia split into the Czech Republic and Slovakia.

BELORUSSIA

LITHUANIA

RUSSIAN FEDERATION (KALININGRAD OBLAST)

L. Mamry

L. Śniardwy

PODLASIE

Lublin

BALTIC   SEA

L. Jeziorak

Bug

Narew

Vistula

WARSAW

Łódź

Gdańsk

POMERANIA

Bydgoszcz

L. Włocławskie

POLAND

Warta

Pomeranian Baš

Noteć

Poznań

Odra

Prosna

Wrocław

GERMANY

POLAND

CZECH REPUBLIC

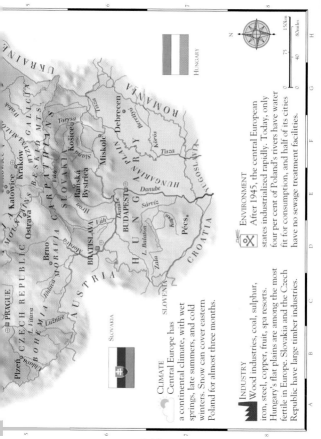

HUNGARY

SLOVAKIA

CLIMATE
Central Europe has a continental climate, with wet springs, late summers, and cold winters. Snow can cover eastern Poland for almost three months.

INDUSTRY
Wood industries, coal, sulphur, iron, steel, copper, fruit, spa resorts. Hungary's flat plains are among the most fertile in Europe. Slovakia and the Czech Republic have large timber industries.

ENVIRONMENT
After 1945, the central European states industrialized rapidly. Today, only four per cent of Poland's rivers have water fit for consumption, and half of its cities have no sewage treatment facilities.

GERMANY

IT WAS NOT UNTIL 1871 that many small independent states were united under Prussia to form Germany. After 1945, the country was divided again, into a democratic West Germany and a Soviet-dominated East Germany.

Reunified in 1990, Germany is, with France, a leading member of the European Union and is currently Europe's strongest economic power.

INDUSTRY
Cars, heavy and precision engineering, electronics, chemicals. Germany has a strong industrial sector and is Europe's main car producer.

POLAND

Rügen

Oder

BERLIN
Potsdam

Elbe

BALTIC SEA

Mecklenburg Bay

Rostock

Schwerin

Magdeburg

Elbe

Kiel

Lübeck

Hamburg

SAXONY

Brunswick

Mittelland Canal

HARZ MTS

NORTH SEA

DENMARK

Kiel Canal

Bremen

Hanover

Bielefeld

Weser

Helgoland

North Frisian Is.

East Frisian Is.

Dortmund-Ems Canal

Münster

Ems

NETHERLANDS

Essen

L. Müritz

Ruhr

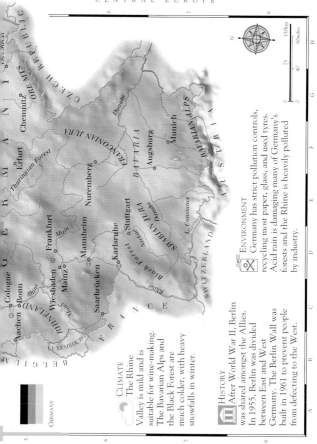

GERMANY

CLIMATE
The Rhine Valley is mild and is suitable for wine-making. The Bavarian Alps and the Black Forest are much colder, with heavy snowfalls in winter.

HISTORY
After World War II, Berlin was shared amongst the Allies. In 1955, Berlin was divided between East and West Germany. The Berlin Wall was built in 1961 to prevent people from defecting to the West.

ENVIRONMENT
Germany has strict pollution controls, recycling most paper, glass, and used tyres. Acid rain is damaging many of Germany's forests and the Rhine is heavily polluted by industry.

CZECH REPUBLIC
ORE MTS.
Chemnitz
Erfurt
Thuringian Forest
GERMANY
FRANCONIAN JURA
Nuremberg
Donube
Augsburg
Munich
BAVARIA
BAVARIAN ALPS
AUSTRIA
Cologne
Aachen Bonn
RHINELAND
Rhine
Mosel
Wiesbaden
Mainz
Frankfurt
Main
Mannheim
Neckar
Karlsruhe
Saarbrücken
Stuttgart
SWABIAN JURA
Black Forest
Danube
L. Constance
SWITZERLAND
FRANCE
LUXEMBOURG
BELGIUM

SWITZERLAND AND AUSTRIA

ONCE THE CENTRE OF the vast Hapsburg Empire, Austria became an independent country in 1918. Switzerland has been a neutral country since 1815, and many international organizations, such as the Red Cross, have their headquarters there. Liechtenstein is closely allied to Switzerland, which handles its foreign relations.

LIECHTENST

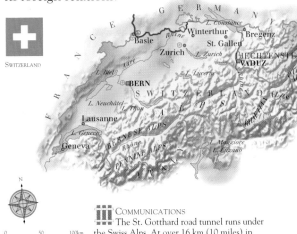

SWITZERLAND

GERMANY

FRANCE

L. Constance
Winterthur
Basle Rhine Bregenz
Zurich St. Gallen
Aare L. Zurich LIECHTENSTE
VADUZ
L. Biel L. Lucerne
BERN
S W I T Z E R L A N D ALPS
L. Neuchâtel L. Thun
Lausanne
L. Geneva BERNESE ALPS Rhône L. Maggiore
Geneva Rhône L. Lugano
PENNINE ALPS

N

0   50   100km
0   25   50miles

III COMMUNICATIONS
The St. Gotthard road tunnel runs under the Swiss Alps. At over 16 km (10 miles) in length, it is the world's longest road tunnel.

CLIMATE
Altitude determines climate, with alpine areas experiencing colder temperatures and more rainfall. South of the Alps is considerably warmer and sunnier.

AUSTRIA

THE ARTS
Many famous musicians, such as Beethoven, Mozart, Schubert, and Brahms, lived and worked in Vienna.

NATURAL FEATURES
The Alps form part of an almost continuous mountain-belt, stretching from the Pyrenees in France to the Himalayas in Asia. They are also the source of Europe's largest rivers – the Rhine, Rhône, and Danube.

INDUSTRY
Pharmaceuticals, financial services, tourism, chemicals, electrical engineering. Liechtenstein is the centre of world dental manufacture. False teeth and dental materials are exported to over 100 countries.

Central Europe facts

SWITZERLAND

- Three-quarters of Switzerland consists of mountains, forests, and ice.
- Swiss inventions include baby food and condensed milk.
- The banks of Switzerland attract investors worldwide.

ESSENTIAL FACTS

- ⊙ Bern
- ◔ 41,290 sq km (15,940 sq miles)
- ♦ 6.9 million
- ⚱ Swiss franc
- ♡ German, French, Italian
- ▲ Multi-party republic
- ♦ 78 years

QUALITY TIME Swiss watchmakers are famous for the quality and craftmanship of their products.

GERMANY

- The rivers and canals of Germany carry as much freight as its roads.
- The best-known beer festival in Europe, the *Oktoberfest*, is held annually in the city of Munich.

ESSENTIAL FACTS

- ⊙ Berlin
- ◔ 356,910 sq km 137,800 sq miles)
- ♦ 80.6 million
- ⚱ Deutschmark
- ♡ German
- ▲ Multi-party republic
- ♦ 76 years

AUSTRIA

- University degrees take six years or more to complete in Austria.
- Salzburg's summer music festival is a major tourist attraction.

ESSENTIAL FACTS

- ⊙ Vienna
- ◔ 83,850 sq km (32,375 sq miles)
- ♦ 7.8 million
- ⚱ Austrian schilling
- ♡ German
- ▲ Multi-party republic
- ♦ 76 years

GERMAN BEER STEIN

VIENNESE WHIRL Austrian composer Johann Strauss (1825–1899) composed the famous Viennese *Blue Danube* waltz.

CZECH REPUBLIC

• The Czech homeland was originally called Bohemia.
• Prague's gilded church roofs gave the city the name *zlata Praha*, or "golden Prague".
• The Czech Republic is the most polluted country in Europe.

ESSENTIAL FACTS

⊙ Prague
◒ 78,370 sq km
 (30,260 sq miles)
♦ 10.4 million
♒ Czech koruna
♡ Czech
▲ Multi-party republic
♦ 71 years

SLOVAKIA

• Separation from the Czech Republic in 1993 resulted in full independence for Slovakia for the first time in over 1,000 years.

ESSENTIAL FACTS

⊙ Bratislava
◒ 49,500 sq km
 (19,100 sq miles)
♦ 5.3 million
♒ Slovak koruna
♡ Slovak

LIECHTENSTEIN

⊙ Vaduz
♦ 29,000
♡ German, Alemannish

POLAND

• The largest remaining herds of European bison are found in the eastern forests of Poland.
• Poland has seven international borders.
• Polish women hold prominent policy-making posts in politics and business.

ESSENTIAL FACTS

⊙ Warsaw
◒ 312,680 sq km
 (120,720 sq miles)
♦ 38.5 million
♒ Zloty
♡ Polish
▲ Multi-party republic
♦ 72 years

HUNGARY

• The Hungarian language has features not found in any other western language.
• The city of Budapest was originally Buda and Pest, two towns located on either side of the River Danube.

ESSENTIAL FACTS

⊙ Budapest
◒ 93,030 sq km
 (35,919 sq miles)
♦ 10.5 million
♒ Forint
♡ Hungarian
▲ Multi-party republic
♦ 70 years

BUDAPEST, HUNGARY
The beautiful city of Budapest is famous for its healing spa waters.

THE WESTERN BALKANS

THE COUNTRIES OF Slovenia, Croatia, Dalmatia, Serbia, Montenegro, and Bosnia and Herzegovina were first united in 1918 and were named Yugoslavia in 1929. In 1991, civil war broke out between the main ethnic groups (Serbs, Muslims, Croats) resulting in the dissolution of communist Yugoslavia in 1992. Serbia and Montenegro have since formed the Federal Republic of Yugoslavia, but warfare continues in Bosnia.

INDUSTRY
Coal, chromium, mercury ore.
UN sanctions against Yugoslavia and war in Bosnia have taken a toll on their economies.

YUGOSLAVIA

SLOVENIA

CROATIA

CLIMATE
The interior has a continental climate, with warm summers and bitterly cold winters. Coastal areas have a Mediterranean climate.

HISTORY
Albania is now emerging from 50 years of isolation. Under communism, free speech and religion were banned, and even beards were forbidden.

PEOPLE
Aid has been crucial to the survival of many Bosnians. By 1993, one million people had been made homeless and an additional million had fled the country.

BOSNIA–HERZEGOVINA

ALBANIA

MACEDONIA

ROMANIA AND BULGARIA

AFTER A LONG history of invasion and occupation, Romania and Bulgaria became part of the Soviet bloc after World War II. In the early 1990s, Romania and Bulgaria rose up against their repressive communist governments – Bulgaria's president was imprisoned and Romania's was executed.

ROMANIA

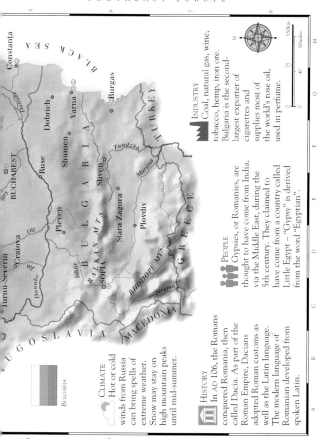

B L A C K   S E A

Constanta

Danube

Dobrich

Burgas

Varna

Ruse

Shumen

TURKEY

BUCHAREST

Iași

Tundzha

Craiova

Pleven

BULGARIA

Sliven

Turnu-Severin

Danube

Olt

Marisa

Stara Zagora

Plovdiv

BALKAN MTS.

Iskür

GREECE

SOFIA

RHODOPE MTS.

Struma

YUGOSLAVIA

MACEDONIA

BULGARIA

INDUSTRY

Coal, natural gas, wine, tobacco, hemp, iron ore. Bulgaria is the second-largest exporter of cigarettes and supplies most of the world's rose oil, used in perfume.

PEOPLE

Gypsies, or Romanies, are thought to have come from India, via the Middle East, during the 5th century. They claimed to have come from a country called Little Egypt – "Gypsy" is derived from the word "Egyptian".

CLIMATE

Hot or cold winds from Russia can bring spells of extreme weather. Snow may stay on high mountain peaks until mid-summer.

HISTORY

In AD 106, the Romans conquered Romania, then called Dacia. As part of the Roman Empire, Dacians adopted Roman customs as well as the Latin language. The modern language of Romanian developed from spoken Latin.

N

150km

80miles

0   40   75

GREECE

SURROUNDED BY THE Aegean, Ionian, and Cretan seas, no part of Greece is more than 137 km (85 miles) from the coast. Its territory includes the mainland on the Balkan peninsula, and more than 1,400 islands. The country is mountainous and less than one-third of the land is cultivated. Greece gained its independence in 1830 after a long and fierce war, ending 400 years of Turkish rule.

MACE
L. Prespa
ALBANIA
Aliakmon
Corfu
Corfu
PINDUS MTS.
IONIAN SEA
Levkas
Akheloos
L. Trikhonis
Kefallinia
Gulf of Patrai
IONIAN IS.
Zakinthos

GREECE

CLIMATE

Northwestern Greece is alpine, while parts of Crete are almost subtropical. The islands and the large central plain of the mainland have a Mediterranean climate, with high summer temperatures and mild winters.

ENVIRONMENT

Athens suffers from smog, known as *nefos*, which damages its ancient monuments. The Parthenon, part of the Acropolis, has suffered more erosion in the previous two decades than in the past two thousand years.

HISTORY

Regarded as the founders of democracy, the ancient Greeks were advanced for their time. They were the first to study medicine, geometry, and physics (on a scientific basis), and Greece was home to great thinkers such as Plato, Aristotle, and Socrates.

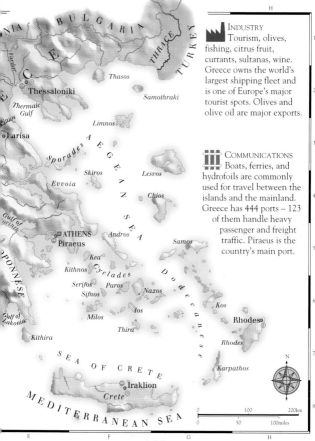

INDUSTRY
Tourism, olives, fishing, citrus fruit, currants, sultanas, wine. Greece owns the world's largest shipping fleet and is one of Europe's major tourist spots. Olives and olive oil are major exports.

COMMUNICATIONS
Boats, ferries, and hydrofoils are commonly used for travel between the islands and the mainland. Greece has 444 ports – 123 of them handle heavy passenger and freight traffic. Piraeus is the country's main port.

BULGARIA

THRACE

TURKEY

Vardar

Thasos

Thessaloniki

Samothraki

Thermaic
Gulf

Limnos

Larisa

Sporades

AEGEAN SEA

Skiros

Lesvos

Evvoia

Chios

Gulf of
Corinth

ATHENS
Piraeus

Andros

Samos

PONNESE

Kea

Dodecanese

Kithnos

Cyclades

Serifos   Paros

Sifnos

Naxos

Kos

Gulf of
Lakonia

Milos

Ios

Rhodes

Thira

Rhodes

Kithira

SEA OF CRETE

Karpathos

N

Iraklion

Crete

MEDITERRANEAN SEA

| 0 | | 100 | | 200km |
| 0 | 50 | | 100miles | |

279

Southeast Europe facts

CROATIA

- One-third of Croatia is held by the Serbs.
- The Adriatic coastline of Croatia was a popular tourist destination before the recent civil war.

ESSENTIAL FACTS
- ⊙ Zagreb
- ◔ 56,540 sq km (21,830 sq miles)
- ♦ 4.9 million
- ✿ Kuna
- ♡ Croatian

DALMATIANS
The Dalmatian dog is named after its first known home, the Dalmatian coastal region of Croatia.

YUGOSLAVIA

- Settlers have lived on the site of present-day Belgrade for 7,000 years.

ESSENTIAL FACTS
- ⊙ Belgrade
- ◔ 25,715 sq km (9,929 sq miles)
- ♦ 10.6 million
- ✿ New Yugoslav dinar
- ♡ Serbian

SLOVENIA

- The average wage in Slovenia is the highest among the former Yugoslav republics.

ESSENTIAL FACTS
- ⊙ Ljubljana
- ◔ 20,250 sq km (7,820 sq miles)
- ♦ 2 million
- ✿ Tolar
- ♡ Slovene

SLOVENIA IS A MAJOR PRODUCER OF MERCURY, WHICH IS USED IN THERMOMETERS

BOSNIA AND HERZEGOVINA

- The Bosnian civil war made over two million people homeless by the year 1995.

ESSENTIAL FACTS
- ⊙ Sarajevo
- ◔ 51,130 sq km (19,741 sq miles)
- ♦ 4.5 million
- ✿ Bosnian dinar
- ♡ Serbo-Croat

ALBANIA

- The Albanian's name for their nation is Shqipërisë, which means "land of the eagle".

ESSENTIAL FACTS
- ⊙ Tirana
- ◔ 28,750 sq km (11,100 sq miles)
- ♦ 3.3 million
- ✿ New lek
- ♡ Albanian

ROMANIA

- The tuberculosis rate in Romania is the highest in Europe.
- The Romanian Danube delta is to be used as a site for a biosphere reserve.

ESSENTIAL FACTS

- ☉ Bucharest
- ◔ 237,500 sq km (91,700 sq miles)
- ♦ 23.4 million
- ⚖ Leu
- ♥ Romanian

DRACULA
Romania's Transylvania region is the mythical home of vampire Count Dracula.

GREECE

- People in the Greek Islands use the flat roofs of their houses to dry fruit in summer and collect rain in winter.

ESSENTIAL FACTS

- ☉ Athens
- ◔ 131,990 sq km (50,961 sq miles)
- ♦ 10.2 million
- ⚖ Drachma
- ♥ Greek
- ▲ Multi-party republic
- ♦ 77 years

MACEDONIA

- Lake Ohrid in Macedonia is the deepest lake in Europe.

MACEDONIA FACTS

- ☉ Skopje
- ◔ 25,715 sq km (9,929 sq miles)
- ♦ 1.9 million
- ⚖ Denar
- ♥ Macedonian

BULGARIA

- In Bulgaria there is a national museum devoted entirely to humour and satire.
- Bulgarians nod for "no" and shake their heads for "yes".

ESSENTIAL FACTS

- ☉ Sofia
- ◔ 110,910 sq km (42,822 sq miles)
- ♦ 8.9 million
- ⚖ Lev
- ♥ Bulgarian
- ▲ Multi-party republic
- ♦ 72 years

GREEK MUSIC
The stringed bouzouki is an important instrument in traditional Greek music.

ROSE PETALS
Much of the rose oil used in the world's perfume industry is supplied by Bulgaria.

THE BALTIC STATES AND BELORUSSIA

LITHUANIA, ESTONIA, AND LATVIA – the three Baltic States – were the first republics to declare their independence from the Soviet Union in 1990-91. Economic reform has been slow and problems such as food shortages still remain. Many areas of Belorussia are still affected by the 1986 Chernobyl nuclear disaster. The clean-up will take decades, and is a major drain on the nation's finances.

PEOPLE

Russians, Belorussians, and Ukrainians resettled in Latvia when it was part of the USSR. Today Latvians make up only about half of the whole population, and they are a minority in the capital

ESTONIA

LATVIA

BELORUSSIA

LITHUANIA

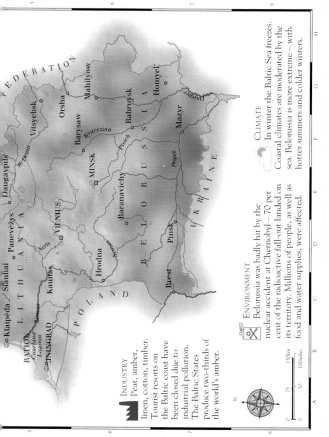

RUSSIAN
FEDERATION

Klaipėda · Šiauliai · Panevežys · Daugavpils

Vitsyebsk

Orsha

Mahilyow

W. Dzvina

LITHUANIA

Neris

VILNIUS

Kaunas

Nemon

Hrodna

Neman

POLAND

Barysaw

Byarezina

MINSK

BELORUSSIA

Baranavichy

Pinsk

Brest

Pripet

Babruysk

Ptsich

Homyel'

Mazyr

Dnipro

UKRAINE

KALININGRAD
(RUSSIAN
FEDERATION)

Courland
Lagoon

CLIMATE

In winter the Baltic Sea freezes.
Coastal climates are moderated by the
sea. Belorussia is more extreme – with
hotter summers and colder winters.

ENVIRONMENT

Belorussia was badly hit by the
nuclear accident at Chernobyl – 70 per
cent of the radioactive fall-out landed on
its territory. Millions of people, as well as
food and water supplies, were affected.

INDUSTRY

Peat, amber,
linen, cotton, timber.
Tourist resorts on
the Baltic coast have
been closed due to
industrial pollution.
The Baltic States
produce two-thirds of
the world's amber.

N

0   75   150km
0   50   100miles

EUROPEAN RUSSIA

SPANNING THE TWO continents of Europe and Asia, the Russian Federation is the world's largest country. In 1917, the world's first communist government took power and in 1923, Russia became the USSR, which included many territories that were once part of the Russian Empire. Economic reforms in the 1980s led to changes resulting in the fall of communism in 1991.

INDUSTRY
Oil, gas, gold, diamonds, hydrocarbons, precious metals. Russia has large reserves of iron, coal, and nickel. Huge factories, which have grown without environmental controls, are causing pollution problems.

Novaya Zemlya

KARA SEA

Kara Strait

Kara Vaygach I.

Yorkuta

Usa

BARENTS SEA

Pechora

Kolguyev I.

Murmansk

L. Imandra

KOLA PENINSULA

Arkhangel'sk

WHITE SEA

L. Pyaozero

L. Topozero

L. Segozero

Dvina

L. Onega

L. Ladoga

FINLAND

R U S S I A N

St. Petersburg

ESTONIA

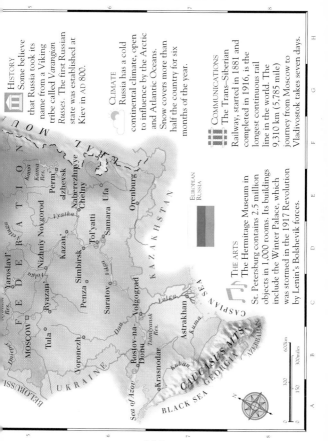

HISTORY
Some believe that Russia took its name from a Viking tribe called *Varangian Russes*. The first Russian state was established at Kiev in AD 800.

CLIMATE
Russia has a cold continental climate, open to influence by the Arctic and Atlantic Oceans. Snow covers more than half the country for six months of the year.

COMMUNICATIONS
The Trans–Siberian Railway, started in 1881 and completed in 1916, is the longest continuous rail line in the world. The 9,310 km (5,785 mile) journey from Moscow to Vladivostok takes seven days.

THE ARTS
The Hermitage Museum in St. Petersburg contains 2.5 million objects in 1,000 rooms. Its buildings include the Winter Palace, which was stormed in the 1917 Revolution by Lenin's Bolshevik forces.

EUROPEAN RUSSIA

RUSSIAN FEDERATION

MOSCOW

Yaroslavl'
Nizhniy Novgorod
Perm'
Naberezhnyye Chelny
Izhevsk
Kazan'
Ufa
Orenburg
KAZAKHSTAN
Tol'yatti
Samara
Simbirsk
Penza
Saratov
Ryazan'
Tula
Voronezh
Volgograd
Rostov-na-Donu
Krasnodar
Astrakhan
CASPIAN SEA
CAUCASUS MTS.
GEORGIA
AZERBAIJAN
BLACK SEA
Sea of Azov
UKRAINE
BELORUSSIA
Volga
Don
Kuban
Kama
URAL MOUNTAINS
Lyatka
Tsimlyansk Res.
Kama Res.

0   150   300 miles
0   300   600 km

N

UKRAINE AND THE CAUCASUS

SEPARATED FROM the Russian Federation by the Caucasus mountains, the newly independent Caucasian Republics – Armenia, Azerbaijan, and Georgia – are rich in natural resources. The Ukraine, Europe's largest country, is dominated by a flat and fertile plain.

ENVIRONMENT
As a result of the 1986 Chernobyl nuclear disaster, 4 million Ukrainians live in radioactive areas. In 1994, reactors from the Chernobyl plant were still being used to provide nuclear power.

CLIMATE
Ukraine and Moldavia have a continental climate, with distinctive seasons. Armenia, Azerbaijan, and Georgia are protected from cold air from the north by the Caucasus mountains.

INDUSTRY
Coal, iron, cars, wine, citrus fruit, cotton, minerals. The Ukraine was known as the "breadbasket" of the Soviet Union as its steppes were extensively cultivated. Georgia's known oil reserves are as yet unexploited.

MOLDAVIA

N

0   150   300km
0   75   150miles

Map labels: BELORUSSIA, POLAND, SLOVAKIA, HUNGARY, Euts'k, Sluch, Styr, Chernihi, Chernobyl, Kiev Res., Rivne, Zhytomyr, KIEV, L'viv, Ternopil', Khmel'nyts'kyy, Bila Tserkva, Vinnytsya, Ivano-Frankivs'k, Dniester, UKRA, Chernivtsi, MOLDAVIA, ROMANA, CHISINAU, Mykola, Odesa

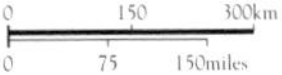

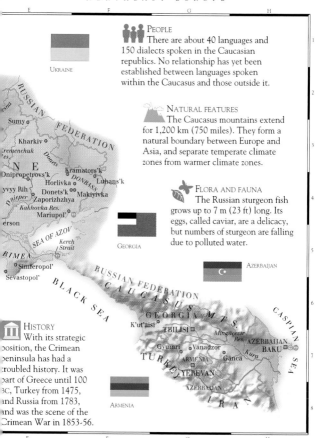

UKRAINE

PEOPLE
There are about 40 languages and 150 dialects spoken in the Caucasian republics. No relationship has yet been established between languages spoken within the Caucasus and those outside it.

NATURAL FEATURES
The Caucasus mountains extend for 1,200 km (750 miles). They form a natural boundary between Europe and Asia, and separate temperate climate zones from warmer climate zones.

FLORA AND FAUNA
The Russian sturgeon fish grows up to 7 m (23 ft) long. Its eggs, called caviar, are a delicacy, but numbers of sturgeon are falling due to polluted water.

GEORGIA

AZERBAIJAN

HISTORY
With its strategic position, the Crimean peninsula has had a troubled history. It was part of Greece until 100 BC, Turkey from 1475, and Russia from 1783, and was the scene of the Crimean War in 1853-56.

ARMENIA

Northeast Europe facts

EUROPEAN RUSSIA

(See **Russian Federation** ESSENTIAL FACTS, p.329)

• Many Russians now have satellite dishes and tune in to Western TV channels for news and entertainment.
• Hospital food is normally provided by patients' families due to lack of funds.

ST. BASIL'S CATHEDRAL
This 16th-century Russian building, with its nine great domes, is situated within Moscow's Kremlin fortress.

LATVIA

• The national flag is said to represent a sheet stained with the blood of a 13th-century Latvian hero.
• Latvia is the most built-up Baltic State.

ESSENTIAL FACTS

⊙ Riga

◒ 64,589 sq km (24,938 sq miles)

♦ 2.7 million

⚒ Lats

♡ Latvian

ESTONIA

• The standard of living in Estonia is higher than in any former Soviet republic.

ESSENTIAL FACTS

⊙ Tallinn

◒ 45,125 sq km (17,423 sq miles)

♦ 1.6 million

⚒ Kroon

♡ Estonian

LITHUANIA

• Most of the Baltic States' amber is found on Lithuania's Amber Coast.

ESSENTIAL FACTS

⊙ Vilnius

◒ 65,200 sq km (25,174 sq miles)

♦ 3.8 million

⚒ Litas

♡ Lithuanian

BELORUSSIA

• Cancer cases have increased dramatically since the Chernobyl nuclear disaster in 1986.

ESSENTIAL FACTS

⊙ Minsk

◒ 207,600 sq km (80,154 sq miles)

♦ 10.3 million

⚒ Belorussian rouble

♡ Belorussian

GEORGIA

• Most Georgians live in poverty.
• In Greek mythology, the legendary Golden Fleece was found in Western Georgia.

ESSENTIAL FACTS

⊙ Tbilisi
◍ 69,700 sq km (26,911 sq miles)
♦ 5.5 million
🏛 Coupon
♡ Georgian

ARMENIA

• In the fourth century, Armenia became the first country in the world to adopt Christianity as its state religion.

ESSENTIAL FACTS

⊙ Yerevan
◍ 29,000 sq km (11,505 sq miles)
♦ 3.6 million
🏛 Armenian dram
♡ Armenian

AZERBAIJAN

• The nation of Azerbaijan became the first of the former Soviet republics to declare independence from Moscow in 1991.

ESSENTIAL FACTS

⊙ Baku
◍ 86,600 sq km (33,436 sq miles)
♦ 7.3 million
🏛 Manat
♡ Azerbaijani

UKRAINE

• Western Ukrainians oppose their eastern counterparts' proposed closer ties with Russia.
• The name Ukraine means "frontier".

ESSENTIAL FACTS

⊙ Kiev
◍ 603,700 sq km (233,090 sq miles)
♦ 52.2 million
🏛 Karbovanets (coupons)
♡ Ukrainian
▲ Multi-party republic
♦ 70 years

Borscht

Sour cream

Piroshki (savoury pastries)

BORSCHT
Russia's famous beetroot soup, *borscht*, comes from the Ukraine.

MOLDAVIA

• The underground wine vaults of Moldavia contain entire "streets" of bottles built into rock quarries.
• Moldavia was part of Romania until Soviet incorporation in 1940.

ESSENTIAL FACTS

⊙ Kishinev
◍ 33,700 sq km (13,000 sq miles)
♦ 4.4 million
🏛 Moldavian leu
♡ Romanian

AFRICA

MEDITERRANEAN SEA

RED SEA

TUNISIA

ALGERIA

MOROCCO

WESTERN SAHARA

MAURITANIA

SENEGAL

GAMBIA

GUINEA-BISSAU

GUINEA

SIERRA LEONE

MALI

BURKINA

IVORY COAST

GHANA

TOGO

BENIN

NIGER

NIGERIA

CAMEROON

LIBYA

EGYPT

CHAD

SUDAN

CENTRAL AFRICAN

ERITREA

DJIBOUTI

ETHIOPIA

YE

Madeira
(to Portugal)

Canary Islands
(to Spain)

SEYCHELLES

COMOROS

MADAGASCAR

KENYA

BURUNDI

TANZANIA

RWANDA

MALAWI

MOZAMBIQUE

ZAIRE

ZAMBIA

ZIMBABWE

SWAZILAND

CONGO

ANGOLA

BOTSWANA

LESOTHO

SOUTH
AFRICA

GABON

NAMIBIA

SAO TOME & PRINCIPE

ATLANTIC OCEAN

AFRICA

Both tropics and the equator
run through Africa, the
warmest of all the continents.
The land around the tropics
is starved of rain creating great
deserts such as the Sahara
and the Kalahari. In contrast,
high rainfall around the
equator has produced lush
tropical rainforests.

WEST AFRICA

BY 1914, MANY European countries, such as France, Britain, and Portugal, had divided up most of Africa between them. Despite independence, foreign companies still own many of the coffee and cocoa plantations in the region.

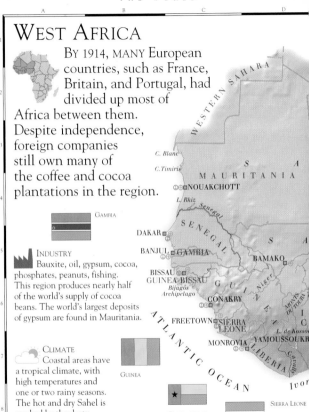

GAMBIA

INDUSTRY
Bauxite, oil, gypsum, cocoa, phosphates, peanuts, fishing. This region produces nearly half of the world's supply of cocoa beans. The world's largest deposits of gypsum are found in Mauritania.

GUINEA

CLIMATE
Coastal areas have a tropical climate, with high temperatures and one or two rainy seasons. The hot and dry Sahel is marked by the dusty *harmattan* wind.

GUINEA-BISSAU

SIERRA LEONE

WESTERN SAHARA

C. Blanc
C. Timiris

MAURITANIA

NOUAKCHOTT

L. Rkiz

Senegal

SENEGAL

DAKAR

BANJUL
GAMBIA

BAMAKO

BISSAU
GUINEA-BISSAU

Bijagós
Archipelago

CONAKRY

G U I N E

Niger

FREETOWN
SIERRA
LEONE

L. de Kossou

MONROVIA
YAMOUSSOUKR

LIBERIA

Ivor

ATLANTIC OCEAN

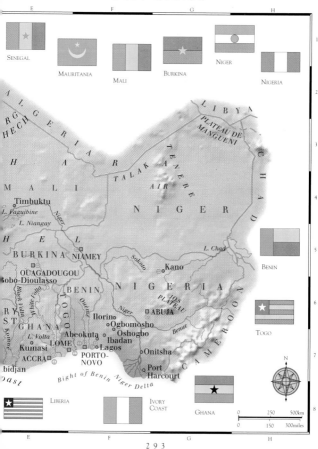

SENEGAL

MAURITANIA

MALI

BURKINA

NIGER

NIGERIA

ALGERIA

HECH

RG

HA

MALI

Timbuktu

L. Faguibine

L. Niangay

HEL

L

BURKINA

NIAMEY

OUAGADOUGOU

Bobo-Dioulasso

BENIN

Black Volta

RY

White Volta

GHANA

TOGO

L. Volta

Kumasi

LOME

ACCRA

bidjan

oast

LIBYA

PLATEAU DE
MANGUENI

TALAK

TÉNÉRÉ

AIR

NIGER

CHAD

L. Chad

Sokoto

Kano

BENIN

NIGERIA

JOS
PLATEAU

Oueme

Niger

ABUJA

Ilorin

Ogbomosho

Oshogbo

Abeokuta

Ibadan

Lagos

Onitsha

PORTO-
NOVO

Port
Harcourt

Benue

CAMEROON

TOGO

Bight of Benin

Niger Delta

LIBERIA

IVORY
COAST

GHANA

N

0   250   500km

0   150   300miles

NORTHWEST AFRICA

SPANNING THE continent of Africa, from the Atlantic to the Red Sea, the Sahara covers 9 million sq km (3.5 million sq miles) and is the world's largest desert. Droughts and the over-use of land for farming are causing the Sahara to spread into the Sahel (semi-arid grasslands). Italy, the UK, Spain, and France have all had colonies in this region.

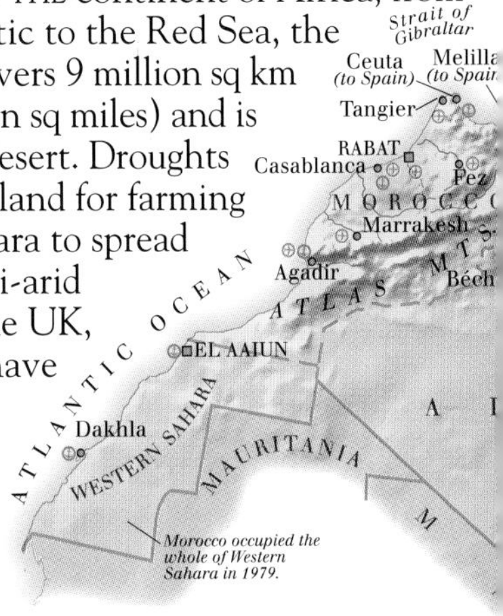

Morocco occupied the whole of Western Sahara in 1979.

MOROCCO

INDUSTRY
Oil, gas, phosphates, tourism, olives, dates, fruit. Morocco and Tunisia attract millions of tourists every year. They are also leading phosphate producers. Algeria and Libya have significant oil reserves.

CLIMATE
Coastal areas have a temperate climate with hot, dry summers and wet winters. Mountain areas are cooler. Most areas are affected by the many different kinds of Sahara wind, such as the *sirocco*, the *chergui*, and the *chili*.

NATURAL FEATURES
The Atlas Mountains extend over 2,410 km (1,500 miles) from the Canary Islands in the Atlantic to Tunisia. Like the Alps, the Atlas Mountains were formed when the continental plates of Europe and Africa pushed together.

Map labels: Strait of Gibraltar, Ceuta (to Spain), Melilla (to Spain), Tangier, RABAT, Casablanca, Fez, MOROCCO, Marrakesh, Agadir, Béch, ATLAS, EL AAIUN, Dakhla, WESTERN SAHARA, MAURITANIA, ATLANTIC OCEAN

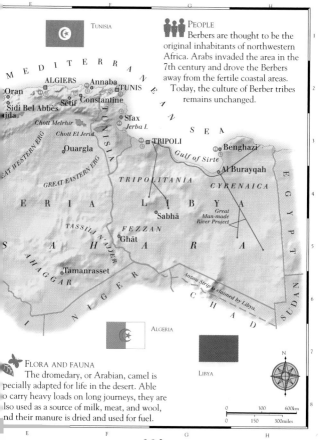

TUNISIA

MEDITERRA...

ALGIERS Annaba
Oran   TUNIS
Sidi Bel Abbès Sétif Constantine
jda   *Sfax*
        Chott Melrhir   *Jerba I.*
        Chott El Jerid
        Ouargla   □ TRIPOLI
REAT WESTERN ERG   Gulf of Sirte
                                    Al Burayqah
        GREAT EASTERN ERG
                    TRIPOLITANIA   CYRENAICA
E R I A   L I B Y A
        TASSILI N'AJJER   FEZZAN   Great
                        Sabhā   Man-made
                                   River Project
        Ghāt
A H A G G A R   S A H A R A
        Tamanrasset
        N I G E R   Aozou Strip is claimed by Libya.
                        C H A D   S U D A N

SEA

Benghazi

E
G
Y
P
T

People

Berbers are thought to be the original inhabitants of northwestern Africa. Arabs invaded the area in the 7th century and drove the Berbers away from the fertile coastal areas. Today, the culture of Berber tribes remains unchanged.

ALGERIA

LIBYA

Flora and Fauna

The dromedary, or Arabian, camel is pecially adapted for life in the desert. Able o carry heavy loads on long journeys, they are lso used as a source of milk, meat, and wool, nd their manure is dried and used for fuel.

N

0   300   600km
0   150   300miles

West Africa facts

IVORY COAST

- Yamoussoukro's giant Christian basilica is the second largest church in the world.
- The Ivory Coast is home to 66 different West African tribes.
- Most people live on the sandy coastal strip.

ESSENTIAL FACTS

- ☉ Yamoussoukro
- ◔ 322,463 sq km (124,503 sq miles)
- ♦ 13.4 million
- ☷ CFA franc
- ♡ French, Akran

Peanut pod ripens underground

GROUNDNUT PLANT
Peanuts, or groundnuts, are a major crop in West Africa.

LIBERIA

- The country of Liberia was founded in 1847 as a home for freed slaves from the USA.
- Human rights have have frequently been abused in Liberia, with citizens being massacred or forced to flee to neighbouring states.

ESSENTIAL FACTS

- ☉ Monrovia
- ◔ 111,370 sq km (43,000 sq miles)
- ♦ 2.8 million
- ☷ Liberian dollar
- ♡ English

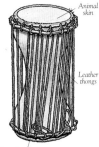

Animal skin

Leather thongs

Squeezing the "waist" changes the drum's sound

WEST AFRICAN KALUNGU, OR "TALKING DRUM"

SENEGAL

- The name Senegal comes from the Islamic Zenegar Berbers, who invaded the region in the 1300s.
- Senegal produced the first satirical journal in Africa with the founding of the publication *Le Politicien* in 1978.

ESSENTIAL FACTS

- ☉ Dakar
- ◔ 196,720 sq km (75,950 sq miles)
- ♦ 7.9 million
- ☷ CFA franc
- ♡ French

WESTERN SAHARA

- ☉ No capital
- ♦ 200,000
- ♡ Varied Arab dialects

GHANA

• Mining has polluted the environment and destroyed areas of land.
• Ghana was the first British colony in Africa to gain independence.

ESSENTIAL FACTS

⊙ Accra

◔ 238,540 sq km
(92,100 sq miles)

♦ 16.4 million

☷ Cedi

♢ English

SIERRA LEONE

• The citizens of Freetown are largely descended from slaves freed from Britain and the USA.
• Sierra Leone is one of the world's poorest nations.

ESSENTIAL FACTS

⊙ Freetown

◔ 71,740 sq km
(27,699 sq miles)

♦ 4.5 million

☷ Leone

♢ English

BENIN

• Positions of power in Benin's retail trade are often held by women.

ESSENTIAL FACTS

⊙ Porto-Novo

◔ 112,620 sq km
(43,480 sq miles)

♦ 5.1 million

☷ CFA franc

♢ French

MAURITANIA

• Slavery, although officially illegal, still persists in Mauritania.

ESSENTIAL FACTS

⊙ Nouakchott

◔ 1,025,520 sq km
(395,953 sq miles)

♦ 2.2 million

☷ Ouguiya

♢ French

COCOA
West Africa grows half the world's cocoa.

BURKINA

• Poor soils and droughts in Burkina force many men to migrate seasonally to Ghana and the Ivory Coast for work.

ESSENTIAL FACTS

⊙ Ouagadougou

◔ 274,200 sq km
(105,870 sq miles)

♦ 9.8 million

☷ CFA franc

♢ French

MALI

• The Malian town of Timbuktu was the centre of the huge Malinke empire in the 14th century.
• Malians strongly disapprove of flaunted wealth.

ESSENTIAL FACTS

⊙ Bamako

◔ 1,240,190 sq km
(478,837 sq miles)

♦ 10.1 million

☷ CFA franc

♢ French

West Africa facts

NIGER

• The threat of drought and desertification is Niger's primary concern.

ESSENTIAL FACTS

⊙ Niamey
◔ 1,267,000 sq km (489,188 sq miles)
✦ 8.5 million
✿ CFA franc
♀ French

CAPE VERDE

(*Atlantic Ocean,* pp.360–361)

⊙ Praia
✦ 400,000
♀ Portuguese, Creole

GAMBIA

⊙ Banjul
✦ 900,000
♀ English

GUINEA

• The three bright colours of Guinea's flag represent the national motto of "work, justice, solidarity".

ESSENTIAL FACTS

⊙ Conakry
◔ 245,860 sq km (94,926 sq miles)
✦ 6.3 million
✿ Guinea franc
♀ French

TOGO

• The retail trade in Togo is dominated by the "Nana Benz", or market-women, of Lomé.

ESSENTIAL FACTS

⊙ Lomé
◔ 56,290 sq km (21,927 sq miles)
✦ 3.9 million
✿ CFA franc
♀ French, Kabye, Ewe

GUINEA-BISSAU

⊙ Bissau
✦ 1 million
♀ Portuguese

NIGERIA

• Modern medicine is not available in rural Nigeria as the health service is concentrated in urban areas.
• Nigeria is the most heavily populated country in Africa.

ESSENTIAL FACTS

⊙ Abuja
◔ 923,770 sq km (356,668 sq miles)
✦ 119 million
✿ Naira
♀ English
▲ Military regime
❧ 52 years

NIGERIAN TWINS

All twins in Nigeria, boys and girls, are given the same names. The firstborn is called Taiwo, the second Kehinde.

Northwest Africa facts

TUNISIA

• The Berber village of Matmata was a location for the planet Tatooine in the 1977 film *Star Wars*.
• Esparto grass grown on the plains of Tunisia is used to make quality paper.
• Tunisians use falcons to hunt partridge, quail, and hare in the summer.

ESSENTIAL FACTS

⊙ Tunis
⬤ 163,610 sq km (63,170 sq miles)
♦ 8.6 million
🏛 Tunisian dinar
♀ Arabic

ALGERIA

• The Algerian population is mainly Arab, under 30 years of age, and urban-based.
• The highest sand dunes in the world are found in east central Algeria.
• More than 80% of Algeria lies within the Sahara desert.

ESSENTIAL FACTS

⊙ Algiers
⬤ 2,381,740 sq km (919,590 sq miles)
♦ 27.1 million
🏛 Dinar
♀ Arabic

PATTERNED LEATHER BAG

LEATHER GOODS Morocco and Tunisia produce quality leather goods for tourists to buy.

MOROCCO

• The Karueein University at Fès, which was founded in AD 859, is the world's oldest existing educational institution.

ESSENTIAL FACTS

⊙ Rabat
⬤ 698,670 sq km (269,757 sq miles)
♦ 27 million
🏛 Moroccan dirham
♀ Arabic

LIBYA

• The West has ignored Libya due to its past links with terrorist groups.
• Libyan oil contains no sulphur, resulting in little pollution when it is burned.

ESSENTIAL FACTS

⊙ Tripoli
⬤ 1,759,540 sq km (679,358 sq miles)
♦ 5.5 million
🏛 Libyan dinar
♀ Arabic

NORTHEAST AFRICA

THE NILE, THE LONGEST river in the world, carries rich mud from the highlands of Sudan into Egypt, creating some of the most fertile land in the world. About 99 per cent of Egypt's population live on the river's banks. Ethiopia, Somalia, and Sudan have been beset by drought, famine, and war and about half of Africa's 4.5 million refugees come from this area.

EGYPT

HISTORY

Hieroglyphs were a set of mysterious symbols until the discovery of the Rosetta Stone in 1799. The Stone is inscribed in three different scripts: ancient Greek, demotic, and hieroglyphs. By comparing the royal names in the scripts, hieroglyphs were finally deciphered 25 years later.

ERITREA

MEDITERRANEAN SEA

ISRAEL

Gulf of Aqaba
Gulf of Suez

RED SEA

Port Said
El Mansûra
Ismâ'ilîya
Alexandria
Suez
SINAI
CAIRO
Giza
Helwân
El Faiyûm
Nile
El Minya
Asyût
Sohâg
Qena
Luxor
Valley of the Kings
Philae
Aswân
L. Nasser

Qattâra Depression

NUBIAN DESERT

E G Y P T

LIBYAN DESERT

Abu Simbel

LIBYA

DJIBOUTI

SOMALIA

ETHIOPIA

SUDAN

COMMUNICATIONS
Opened in 1869, the Suez Canal connects the Mediterranean and the Red Sea, shortening the route from Europe to the Far East. Nearly 17,500 ships use it each year.

Gulf of Aden

HORN OF AFRICA

INDIAN OCEAN

SOMALIA

Berbera
Hargeysa

DJIBOUTI
DJIBOUTI

ERITREA
Dahlak Archipelago

ASMARA

Port Sudan

Gonder
L. Tana

ETHIOPIA

Dire Dawa

Awash

ETHIOPIAN HIGHLANDS

ADDIS ABABA

Shebeli

Genale

MOGADISHU

Juba

Kismaayo

Atbara

Omdurman
KHARTOUM

Khartoum North

Blue Nile

Wad Medani

SUDAN

White Nile

El Obeid

Nile

Omo

L. Abaya

L. Turkana

Southeast Sudan is administered by Kenya

KENYA

UGANDA

ZAIRE

CENTRAL AFRICAN REPUBLIC

CHAD

500km

300miles

N

CENTRAL AFRICA

MUCH OF THIS region is covered in dense tropical rainforest, drained by the Congo (Zaire) River, which forms a huge arc on its way to the Atlantic. In the 16th century Portugal and Spain set up trading posts on the west coast as part of the slave trade. Millions of Africans from this region were sent as slaves to the New World. Many people in coastal areas still speak Spanish and Portuguese.

CHAD

INDUSTRY
Timber, oil, iron, cocoa, coffee, copper. Bélinga, Gabon, contains the world's largest iron ore deposits. Many central African countries have unexploited oil and gas reserves.

CENTRAL AFRICAN REPUBLIC

CAMEROON

EQUATORIAL GUINEA

LIBYA

Aozou Strip claimed by Libya

TIBESTI

CHAD

NIGER

L. Chad

Kousseri

N'DJAMENA

Maroua

Ergueig

Garoua

Logone

Chari

Moundou

Sarh

NIGERIA

CLIMATE

Central Africa covers three climatic zones. Equatorial areas are hot and humid with little distinction between seasons. Farther north lies the semi-arid Sahelian belt, and the far north lies within the Sahara desert.

CENTRAL EAST AFRICA

LARGE AREAS OF savannah, or grassland, in central Africa provide grazing for both domestic and wild animals. Industry is poorly developed in the region – Zambia, Rwanda, Burundi, and Uganda suffer from having no sea ports. Lake Victoria is the largest lake in Africa, and a source of the River Nile.

FLORA AND FAUNA
Poaching remains a major problem in this area. To combat this, all the countries in this region have set up wildlife parks to protect animals such as elephants and zebra.

INDUSTRY
Tobacco, coffee, tea, tourism, cloves, copper. Zambia is the world's fifth-largest producer of copper. Wildlife parks in this region attract thousands of tourists.

UGANDA

RWANDA

KENYA

SOMALIA

ETHIOPIA

CHALBI DESERT

L. Turkana

Tana

K E N Y A

ABERDARE RANGE

NAIROBI

Galana

Mombasa

L. Manyara

L. Eyasi

GREAT RIFT VALLEY

Southeast Sudan is administered by Kenya

S U D A N

Albert Nile

Victoria Nile

L. Albert

L. Kyoga

UGANDA

KAMPALA

Lake Victoria

Mwanza

L. Edward

T A N Z A N I A

RWANDA

KIGALI

BURUNDI

BUJUMBURA

ZAIRE

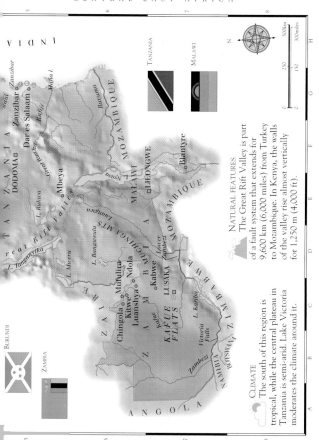

NATURAL FEATURES

The Great Rift Valley is part of a fault system that extends for 9,600 km (6,000 miles) from Turkey to Mozambique. In Kenya, the walls of the valley rise almost vertically for 1,250 m (4,000 ft).

CLIMATE

The south of this region is tropical, while the central plateau in Tanzania is semi-arid. Lake Victoria moderates the climate around it.

Northeast Africa facts

EGYPT

- Overpopulation is a major problem in Eygpt, where it is estimated a baby is born every 24 seconds.
- The ancient pyramids were built to house the mummified bodies of Egyptian kings.

ESSENTIAL FACTS

- ⊙ Cairo
- ⬠ 1,001,450 sq km (386,660 sq miles)
- ♦ 56.1 million
- ⚱ Egyptian pound
- ♀ Arabic
- ▲ Multi-party republic

GREAT PYRAMIDS AT GIZA, EGYPT

ETHIOPIA

- Famines are a regular occurrence in Ethiopia.

ESSENTIAL FACTS

- ⊙ Addis Ababa
- ⬠ 1,228,221 sq km (435,605 sq miles)
- ♦ 51 million
- ⚱ Ethiopian birr
- ♀ Amharic, English

DJIBOUTI

- ⊙ Djibouti
- ♦ 500,000
- ♀ Arabic, French

SUDAN

- The Sudd plain in Sudan contains the world's largest swamp.

ESSENTIAL FACTS

- ⊙ Khartoum
- ⬠ 2,505,815 sq km (967,493 sq miles)
- ♦ 27.4 million
- ⚱ Sudanese dinar
- ♀ Arabic

ERITREA

- Three-quarters of Eritrea's people are dependent on food aid.

ESSENTIAL FACTS

- ⊙ Asmara
- ⬠ 93,680 sq km (36,170 sq miles)
- ♦ 3.5 million
- ⚱ Ethiopian birr
- ♀ Tigrinya, Arabic

SOMALIA

- In 1992, civil war in Somalia led to the UN's worst refugee crisis.

ESSENTIAL FACTS

- ⊙ Mogadishu
- ⬠ 637,660 sq km (246,200 sq miles)
- ♦ 9.5 million
- ⚱ Somali shilling
- ♀ Somali, Arabic

Central East Africa facts

KENYA

- Ethnic violence is the main political issue.
- Kenya has over 40 national parks and game reserves, and two marine parks in the Indian ocean.

ESSENTIAL FACTS

- ⊙ Nairobi
- ◔ 580,370 sq km (224,081 sq miles)
- ♦ 26.1 million
- ♛ Kenya shilling
- ♀ Swahili

MASAI WARRIORS
The Masai are a tribe of nomadic herders who live on the borders of Kenya and Tanzania.

RWANDA

- ⊙ Kigali
- ♦ 7.5 million
- ♀ Kinyarwanda, French

GORILLAS OF RWANDA
Rwanda is one of the last remaining sanctuaries of the mountain gorilla.

BURUNDI

- ⊙ Bujumbura
- ♦ 5.8 million
- ♀ Kirundi, French

UGANDA

- The rugged Ruwenzori mountain range of Uganda is also known as the "Mountains of the Moon".

ESSENTIAL FACTS

- ⊙ Kampala
- ◔ 235,880 sq km (91,073 sq miles)
- ♦ 19.2 million
- ♛ New Uganda shilling
- ♀ English

TANZANIA

- One-third of Tanzania is national park or game reserve.
- The use of Swahili as a universal language has reduced ethnic rivalries.

ESSENTIAL FACTS

- ⊙ Dodoma
- ◔ 945,090 sq km (364,900 sq miles)
- ♦ 28.8 million
- ♛ Tanzanian shilling
- ♀ English, Swahili

Central Africa facts

ZAMBIA

• Victoria Falls in Zambia is called *Musi-o-Tunyi* by African people, which means "the smoke that thunders".

ESSENTIAL FACTS

⊙ Lusaka

⊘ 752,610 sq km (290,563 sq miles)

🕴 8.9 million

🐚 Zambian kwacha

♢ English, Bemba, Tonga

CHAD

• The tropical, cotton-producing south is Chad's most heavily populated region.
• The Tibesti plateau is a site of prehistoric rock painting.

ESSENTIAL FACTS

⊙ N'Djamena

⊘ 1,284,000 sq km (495,752 sq miles)

🕴 6 million

🐚 CFA franc

♢ French, Sara, Maba

FISH FOOD
Lake Chad's fish, such as this *tilapia*, are a major source of food for people who live in the region.

EQUATORIAL GUINEA

⊙ Malabo

🕴 400,000

♢ Spanish, Fang

Alluvial diamond

LITTLE GEMS
Zaire is the world's largest producer of diamonds used in industry.

ZAIRE

• The rainforests of Zaire comprise almost 50% of Africa's remaining woodlands.

ESSENTIAL FACTS

⊙ Kinshasa

⊘ 2,345,410 sq km (905,563 sq miles)

🕴 41.2 million

🐚 New zaire

♢ French

CENTRAL AFRICAN REPUBLIC

• Hunting of elephants in the CAR was finally banned in 1985.

ESSENTIAL FACTS

⊙ Bangui

⊘ 622,980 sq km (240,530 sq miles)

🕴 3.3 million

🐚 CFA franc

♢ French

CONGO

• In 1970, Congo became the first declared communist state in Africa.
• Congo has been used in the past as a dump for Western toxic waste.

ESSENTIAL FACTS

⊙ Brazzaville

◔ 342,000 sq km (132,040 sq miles)

♦ 2.4 million

☗ CFA franc

♡ French

CAMEROON

• The Portuguese explorers who colonized Cameroon fished for prawns called *camaroes*, from which the country derived its name.

ESSENTIAL FACTS

⊙ Yaoundé

◔ 475,440 sq km (183,570 sq miles)

♦ 12.5 million

☗ CFA franc

♡ English, French

RESPECT FOR THE DEAD
This wooden figure from Cameroon was made to honour an ancestor.

SÃO TOMÉ & PRÍNCIPE

⊙ São Tomé

♦ 121,000

♡ Portuguese

SPIRITED FIGURE
Central African folk religions believe fetish figures like this are inhabited by spirits.

GABON

• Libreville was founded as a settlement for freed French slaves in 1849.
• Menial jobs in Gabon are done by immigrant workers.

ESSENTIAL FACTS

⊙ Libreville

◔ 267,670 sq km (103,347 sq miles)

♦ 1.3 million

☗ CFA franc

♡ French

MALAWI

• Lake Malawi contains at least 500 species of fish.
• Malawi's name means "the land where the sun is reflected in the water like fire".

ESSENTIAL FACTS

⊙ Lilongwe

◔ 118,480 sq km (45,745 sq miles)

♦ 10.7 million

☗ Kwacha

♡ English, Chewa

SOUTHERN AFRICA

THE RICHEST DEPOSITS of valuable minerals in Africa, such as gold and diamonds, are found in its southern region. Many surrounding countries rely on South Africa for work and trade. Racial segregation under apartheid operated from 1948 until 1994 when South Africa's first multi-racial elections were held. Namibia won its independence from South Africa in 1990, but neighbouring Angola has been in a state of civil war since 1975.

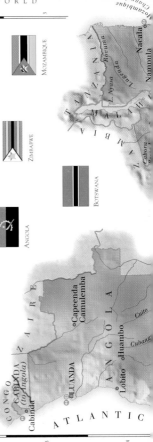

MOZAMBIQUE

ZIMBABWE

BOTSWANA

ANGOLA

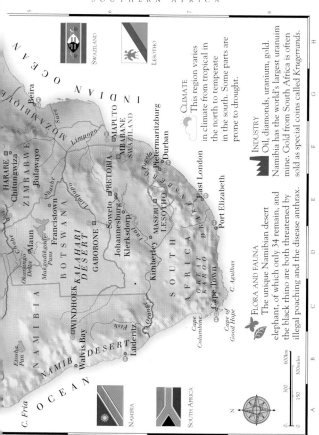

SWAZILAND

LESOTHO

CLIMATE
This region varies in climate from tropical in the north to temperate in the south. Some parts are prone to drought.

INDUSTRY
Oil, diamonds, uranium, gold. Namibia has the world's largest uranium mine. Gold from South Africa is often sold as special coins called *Krugerrands*.

FLORA AND FAUNA
The unique Namibian desert elephant, of which only 34 remain, and the black rhino are both threatened by illegal poaching and the disease anthrax.

NAMIBIA

SOUTH AFRICA

N

0   300   600km

0   150   300miles

Southern Africa facts

ZIMBABWE

• Most people in Zimbabwe belong to the Shona or Ndebele tribes.
• Zimbabwe was formerly known as Southern Rhodesia.

ESSENTIAL FACTS

⊙ Harare
◔ 390,580 sq km (150,800 sq miles)
♦ 10.9 million
💰 Zimbabwe dollar
♡ English

COLOURFUL DECOR
Ndebele women decorate their homes with bright geometric patterns.

MOZAMBIQUE

• Over 90% of the citizens of Mozambique live in poverty.
• Polygamous marriages are common among those wealthy enough to take second wives.

ESSENTIAL FACTS

⊙ Maputo
◔ 801,590 sq km (309,493 sq miles)
♦ 15.3 million
💰 Metical
♡ Portuguese

BOTSWANA

• The people of Botswana place such value on rain as a resource that their currency, the pula, is named in its honour.

ESSENTIAL FACTS

⊙ Gaborone
◔ 581,730 sq km (224,600 sq miles)
♦ 1.4 million
💰 Pula
♡ English

SWAZILAND

⊙ Mbabane
♦ 800,000
♡ Siswati, English

ANGOLA

• Injuries caused by exploding mines have led to the nation of Angola having the highest number of amputees in the world.

ESSENTIAL FACTS

⊙ Luanda
◔ 1,246,700 sq km (481,351 sq miles)
♦ 10.3 million
💰 New kwanza
♡ Portuguese

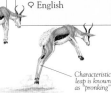

SPRINGBOKS
These small antelopes live in the grasslands of South Africa.

Characteristic leap is known as "pronking"

MADAGASCAR

(*Indian Ocean*,
   pp.362–363)
• This country is
the world's largest
producer of vanilla.
• Madagascar is a
unique environment;
80% of its plants and
animal species are
found nowhere else.

ESSENTIAL FACTS

⊙ Antananarivo

◑ 587,040 sq km
   (226,660 sq miles)

♦ 13.3 million

☷ Malagasy franc

♡ Malagasy, French

LESOTHO

⊙ Maseru

♦ 1.9 million

♡ English, Sesotho

LARGEST LEMUR
Madagascar is home to
the Indri, the largest of
the world's lemurs.

COMOROS

⊙ Moroni

♦ 600,000

♡ Arabic, French

NAMIBIA

• The Namib is the
Earth's oldest, and one
of its driest, deserts.

ESSENTIAL FACTS

⊙ Windhoek

◑ 824,290 sq km
   (318,260 sq miles)

♦ 1.6 million

☷ South African rand

♡ English

SOUTH AFRICA

• President Nelson
Mandela and former
president F. W. De Klerk
were awarded the Nobel
Peace Prize in 1994 for
their work dismantling
apartheid.
• Tourists are
increasingly attracted to
South Africa's beaches,
stunning scenery, and
prize-winning vineyards.

ESSENTIAL FACTS

⊙ Pretoria, Cape Town,
   Bloemfontein

◑ 1,221,040 sq km
   (471,443 sq miles)

♦ 37.4 million

☷ Rand

♡ Afrikaans, English,
   9 African languages

▲ Multi-party republic

♦ 62 years

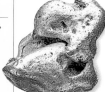

BURIED TREASURE
South Africa has the
world's deepest goldmine,
descending 3,777 m
(12,392 ft) underground.

NORTH AND WEST ASIA

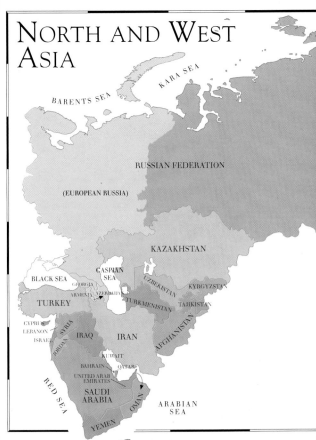

BARENTS SEA

KARA SEA

RUSSIAN FEDERATION

(EUROPEAN RUSSIA)

KAZAKHSTAN

BLACK SEA

CASPIAN SEA

GEORGIA

UZBEKISTAN

KYRGYZSTAN

ARMENIA AZERBAIJAN

TURKEY

TURKMENISTAN

TAJIKISTAN

CYPRUS

LEBANON

ISRAEL

SYRIA

JORDAN

IRAQ

IRAN

AFGHANISTAN

KUWAIT

BAHRAIN QATAR

UNITED ARAB EMIRATES

RED SEA

SAUDI ARABIA

OMAN

ARABIAN SEA

YEMEN

NORTH AND WEST ASIA

Asia is the largest continent in the world, occupying nearly one-third of the world's total land area. In the south, the Arabian Peninsula is mostly hot, dry desert. In the north lie cold deserts, treeless plains called steppes, and the largest needleleaf forest in the world, which stretches from Siberia to northern Europe.

NEAR EAST

AT THE JUNCTION of Africa, Asia, and Europe, the Near East is a mosaic of deserts, mountains, and fertile valleys. After centuries of conflict, there are now hopes for peace in the region. Lebanon is beginning to emerge from a civil war that began in 1975 and the disputes over territories in Israel, such as the West Bank and the Gaza Strip, are starting to be resolved.

LEBANON

INDUSTRY

Oil, potash, cotton, fruit. Water is in short supply in this region and special irrigation techniques are used in order to avoid waste. Syria's main cash crop is cotton.

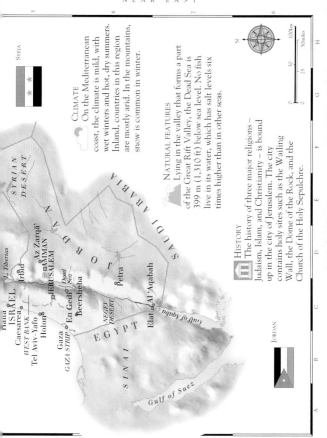

SYRIA

CLIMATE
On the Mediterranean coast, the climate is mild, with wet winters and hot, dry summers. Inland, countries in this region are mostly arid. In the mountains, snow is common in winter.

NATURAL FEATURES
Lying in the valley that forms a part of the Great Rift Valley, the Dead Sea is 399 m (1,310 ft) below sea level. No fish live in its water, which has salt levels six times higher than in other seas.

HISTORY
The history of three major religions – Judaism, Islam, and Christianity – is bound up in the city of Jerusalem. The city contains holy sites such as the Wailing Wall, the Dome of the Rock, and the Church of the Holy Sepulchre.

JORDAN

N

100 km
50
50 miles
25
0
0

SYRIA

SYRIAN DESERT

Hula
Caesarea
Tel Aviv-Yafo
Holon
Gaza
GAZA STRIP

ISRAEL
WEST BANK
En Gedi
Beersheba
NEGEV DESERT

M. Tiberias
Irbid
Az Zarqā'
AMMAN
JERUSALEM
Dead Sea

JORDAN

SAUDI ARABIA

Petra

Elat Al 'Aqabah
Gulf of Aqaba

EGYPT

SINAI

Gulf of Suez

TURKEY

BRIDGING THE CONTINENTS of Europe and Asia, Turkey was once the centre of the Ottoman Empire, which controlled a quarter of Europe. Cyprus became independent from the UK in 1960, but was invaded by Turkey in 1974. Southern Cyprus is Greek; Turkish Northern Cyprus is recognized by only Turkey.

TURKEY

INDUSTRY
Wheat, corn, sugar beets, nuts, fruit, cotton, tobacco, tourism. Carpet-weaving is a centuries-old tradition. Figs and peaches are grown on the coast of the Mediterranean.

ENVIRONMENT
Turkey's dam-building projects on the Tigris and Euphrates Rivers have met with disapproval from Syria and Iraq, whose own rivers will have reduced flow as a result.

PEOPLE
The Kurds are Turkey's main minority group and one of the largest groups of stateless people in the world. Their homeland, Kurdistan, straddles three countries: Turkey, Iraq, and Iran. Kurds are fighting for the recognition of their rights within Turkey.

E   F   G   H

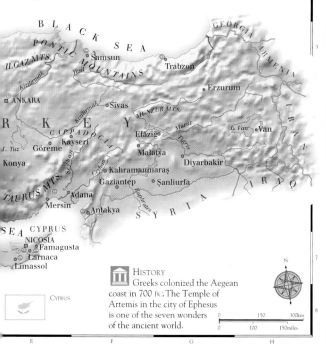

NATURAL FEATURES
Turkey lies within the Alpine-Himalayan mountain belt. The Arabian, African, Eurasian, Aegean, and Turkish plates all converge within its borders, resulting in severe seismic activity.

CLIMATE
Coastal regions of Turkey and Cyprus have a Mediterranean climate. The Turkish interior has cold, snowy winters and hot, dry summers.

HISTORY
Greeks colonized the Aegean coast in 700 BC. The Temple of Artemis in the city of Ephesus is one of the seven wonders of the ancient world.

BLACK SEA

PONTIC MOUNTAINS

ILGAZ MTS.

GEORGIA

ARMENIA

Samsun

Trabzon

Yeşil

Kızılırmak

Erzurum

ANKARA

Sivas

MUNZUR MTS.

Murat

L. Van

Van

IRAN

CAPPADOCIA

Kızılırmak

Elâziğ

Tigris

L. Tuz

Göreme

Kayseri

Malatya

Diyarbakir

Konya

Seyhan

Ceyhan

Kahramanmaraş

Gaziantep

Şanlıurfa

IRAQ

TAURUS MTS.

Adana

Mersin

Antakya

Euphrates

SYRIA

SEA

CYPRUS

NICOSIA

Famagusta

Larnaca

Limassol

CYPRUS

N

0   150   300km
0   100   150miles

E   F   G   H

MIDDLE EAST

ISLAM WAS FOUNDED in AD 570 in Mecca, Saudi Arabia, and spread throughout the Middle East, where today it is the main religion. Oil has brought wealth to the region but in 1991, the area was devastated by the Gulf War.

IRAQ

INDUSTRY
Oil, natural gas, fishing, carpet-weaving, offshore banking. Saudi Arabia has the world's largest oil reserves. Over 60 per cent of the world's desalination plants are used in this region to make sea water drinkable.

SAUDI ARABIA

KUWAIT

CLIMATE
Most of the countries in this region are semi-arid, with low rainfall. Inland, summer temperatures can reach 48°C (119°F) with winter temperatures falling to freezing.

BAHRAIN

QATAR

HISTORY
Ancient civilizations developed about 5,500 years ago in Mesopotamia, between the Tigris and Euphrates Rivers. The Sumerian civilization had advanced methods of irrigation, sophisticated architecture, and a form of writing called cuneiform.

UNITED ARAB EMIRATES

YEMEN

Gulf of Aqaba

H E J A Z

R E D

S E A

Mecca
⊕ ⊙ ◉ ◔
Jedda

Abh

Hodeid
Al Mukhā
Bab el Mand

Near East facts

ISRAEL

• The average age in Israel is only 25.6 years.
• Israeli citizenship is the right of all Jews.

ESSENTIAL FACTS

⊙ Jerusalem

⌀ 20,700 sq km
(7,992 sq miles)

♦ 5.4 million

💰 New shekel

♥ Hebrew, Arabic

▲ Multi-party republic

♦ 76 years

WAILING
WALL,
JERUSALEM

CYPRUS

⊙ Nicosia

♦ 700,000

♥ Greek, Turkish

JORDAN

• King Hussein, the longest-reigning Arab ruler, has led Jordan since 1952.

ESSENTIAL FACTS

⊙ Amman

⌀ 89,210 sq km
(34,440 sq miles)

♦ 4.4 million

💰 Jordanian dinar

♥ Arabic

TURKEY

• Grapes, one of the world's oldest crops, were first grown in Anatolia, Turkey.

ESSENTIAL FACTS

⊙ Ankara

⌀ 779,450 sq km
(300,950 sq miles)

♦ 59.6 million

💰 Turkish lira

♥ Turkish

▲ Multi-party republic

♦ 67 years

LEBANON

• The press has greater freedom in Lebanon than in any other Arab country.

ESSENTIAL FACTS

⊙ Beirut

⌀ 10,400 sq km
(4,015 sq miles)

♦ 2.9 million

💰 Lebanese pound

♥ Arabic

SYRIA

• The world's first alphabet was found in the ancient Syrian city of Ugarit.

ESSENTIAL FACTS

⊙ Damascus

⌀ 185,180 sq km
(71,498 sq miles)

♦ 13.8 million

💰 Syrian pound

♥ Arabic

Middle East facts

IRAN

ESSENTIAL FACTS

⊙ Tehran

◔ 1,648,000 sq km
(636,293 sq miles)

♦ 63.2 million

🖩 Iranian rial

♡ Farsi

▲ Islamic republic

♦ 67 years

SAUDI ARABIA

ESSENTIAL FACTS

⊙ Riyadh

◔ 2,149,690 sq km
(829,995 sq miles)

♦ 16.5 million

🖩 Saudi riyal

♡ Arabic

▲ Absolute monarchy

♦ 69 years

QATAR	BAHRAIN
⊙ Doha	⊙ Manama
♦ 500,000	♦ 500,000
♡ Arabic	♡ Arabic

IRAQ

ESSENTIAL FACTS

⊙ Baghdad

◔ 438,320 sq km
(169,235 sq miles)

♦ 19.9 million

🖩 Iraqi dinar

♡ Arabic

▲ Single-party republic

♦ 66 years

ARAB HEADDRESSES
Men and women wear
headcloths to protect
them from the sun.

UNITED ARAB EMIRATES

ESSENTIAL FACTS

⊙ Abu Dhabi

◔ 83,600 sq km
(32,278 sq miles)

♦ 1.7 million

🖩 UAE dirham

♡ Arabic

KUWAIT

ESSENTIAL FACTS

⊙ Kuwait City

◔ 17,820 sq km
(6,880 sq miles)

♦ 1.8 million

🖩 Kuwaiti dinar

♡ Arabic

OMAN

ESSENTIAL FACTS

⊙ Muscat

◔ 212,460 sq km
(82,030 sq miles)

♦ 1.7 million

🖩 Omani rial

♡ Arabic

YEMEN

ESSENTIAL FACTS

⊙ Sana

◔ 527,970 sq km
(203,849 sq miles)

♦ 13 million

🖩 Yemen riyal

♡ Arabic

CENTRAL ASIA

FOR CENTURIES, many people in central Asia lived in mountains as nomads, or in cities that sprung up along the Silk Road. When the region came under Soviet rule, industry was developed and irrigation schemes made farming possible.

INDUSTRY
Cotton, gold, gas, sulphur, mercury, opium, hydroelectricity. Uzbekistan has the largest single gold mine in the world. Tajikistan has 14 per cent of the world's known uranium resources.

HISTORY
In the early 1900s, most of this region, except for Afghanistan, came under Soviet rule, which restricted the use of local languages and Islam. Today, these newly independent countries are resuming the religions, languages, and traditions of their past.

ENVIRONMENT
Crop irrigation draws water from the Amu Darya river, reducing the amount of water flowing into the Aral Sea. By the year 2000, the Sea will have shrunk to an estimated third of its original size.

TURKMENISTAN

USTYURT PLATEAU

ARAL SEA

TURAN LOWLAND

L. Sarykamysh

Nukus

UZBI

Zaliv Kara-Bogaz-Gol

Tashauz

Urgench

C A S P I A N   S E A

Krasnovodsk

Nebit Dag

TURKMENISTAN

ASHKABAD

I R A N

Kopet-dag

Murgab

Tedzhen

Herā

AF

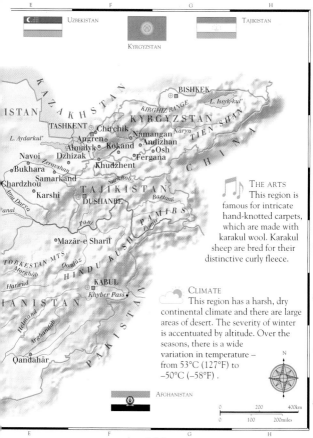

E F G H

UZBEKISTAN

KYRGYZSTAN

TAJIKISTAN

KAZAKHSTAN

BISHKEK

KIRGHIZ RANGE

L. Issyk-kul'

KYRGYZSTAN

TIEN SHAN

TASHKENT Chirchik

Naryn

L. Aydarkul'

Angren Namangan Andizhan

Almalyk Kokand Osh

Navoi Dzhizak Fergana

C H I N A

Bukhara Zeravshan Khudzhent

Chardzhou Samarkand

Karshi TAJIKISTAN

DUSHANBE Surkhob

Bartang

PAMIRS

anal

Vanj Pamir

THE ARTS

This region is famous for intricate hand-knotted carpets, which are made with karakul wool. Karakul sheep are bred for their distinctive curly fleece.

Mazār-e Sharif

TURKESTAN MTS. Morghāb Qonduz

Harīrūd

HINDU KUSH

CLIMATE

This region has a harsh, dry continental climate and there are large areas of desert. The severity of winter is accentuated by altitude. Over the seasons, there is a wide variation in temperature – from 53°C (127°F) to –50°C (–58°F).

KABUL

NISTAN Khyber Pass

PAKISTAN

Helmand

Arghandāb

N

Qandahār

AFGHANISTAN

0 200 400km

0 100 200miles

E F G H

RUSSIAN FEDERATION AND KAZAKHSTAN

THE URAL mountains separate European and Asian Russia, which extends from the frozen Arctic lands in the north to the central Asian deserts in the south. In 1991, Kazakhstan became the last Soviet republic to gain independence.

CLIMATE
Kazakhstan has a continental climate. Winter temperatures in Russia vary little from north to south, but fall sharply in the east, especially in Siberia.

PEOPLE
There are 57 nationalities with their own territories within the Russian Federation. A further 95 groups have no territories of their own, although these groups make up only six per cent of the population.

Murmansk
BARENTS SEA

FINLAND
ESTONIA
LATVIA
BELORUSSIA
Pskov
Novgorod
St. Petersburg
Arkhangel'sk
Smolensk
MOSCOW
Yaroslavl'
UKRAINE
Tula
Voronezh
Ryazan'
Kirov
Perm'
URAL MOUNTAINS
Penza
Kazan'
Izhevsk
Rostov-na-Donu
Simbirsk
Naberezhnyye Chelny
Saratov
Samara
Krasnodar
Tol'yatti
Ufa
Yekaterinburg
GEORGIA
Volgograd
Ural
Ural'sk
Orenburg
Chelyabinsk
Astrakhan
Grozny
Atyrau
Aktyubinsk
Kustanai
Omsk
CASPIAN SEA
Emba
Tselinograd
Ishim
KIRGHIZ STEPPE
L. Tengiz
Karaganda
UZBEKISTAN
ARAL SEA
KAZAKHSTAN
Kzyl-Orda
L. Balkhash
TURKMENISTAN
Syr Darya
Chu
UZBEKISTAN
Shymkent
ALMA-ATA
KIRGHIZIA

KAZAKHSTAN

HISTORY

Kazakhstan was absorbed by Russia in the 19th century, when Russians began to settle the land used by nomadic Kazakhs. Settlement and industrial development increased after 1917.

Bering St.

Wrangel I.

EAST SIBERIAN SEA

CHURCHI SEA

Ayon Is.

Anadyr'

C. Navarin

BERING SEA

Bear Is.

New Siberian Is.

LAPTEV SEA

C. Chelyuskin

Severnaya Zemlya

Bolshevik I.

ovaya emlya

Karkodan

KORYAK RANGE

Cape Olyutorskiy

Karaginskiy Is.

Belyy Is.

TAYMYR PENINSULA

Pyasino

L. Taymyr

Olenëk Bay

Anabar

Olenëk

KAMCHATKA

GYDA PENINSULA

Khatanga

CENTRAL SIBERIAN PLATEAU

Vilyuy

Petropavlovsk-Kamchatskiy

Noril'sk

PUTORANA MTS.

RUSSIAN

Lower Tunguska

Vilyuy

Yakutsk

KOLYMA RANGE

Magadan

C. Lopatka

Paramushir Is.

Nakhodka BERIAN

Yenisey

FEDERATION

Lena

Aldan

Maya

SEA OF OKHOTSK

C. Yelizavety

Vakh

SIBERIA

Stony Tunguska

Lena

Vitim

Amga

Uchur

DZHUGDZHUR RANGE

Ob'

Ket'

Angara

STANOVOY RANGE

Olëkma

Oleder

Sakhalin

Tomsk

Krasnoyarsk

L. Baikal

Shilka

Zeya Res.

Blagoveshchensk

Amur

Khabarovsk

Yuzhno-Sakhalinsk

Novosibirsk

Novokuznetsk

Abakan

Angarsk

Ulan-Ude

arnaul

Biysk

Kyzyl

Irkutsk

CHINA

SEA OF JAPAN

emipalatinsk

MONGOLIA

Vladivostok

NORTH KOREA

L. Zaysan

RUSSIAN FEDERATION

INDUSTRY

Oil, gas, coal, gold, diamonds. Mineral-rich Kazakhstan has the world's largest chromium mine. Siberia has large gas, coal, and oil fields.

| 0 | 600 | 1200km |

| 0 | 300 | 600miles |

Central Asia facts

UZBEKISTAN

- Many young Uzbeks are sent to Turkey to study business practice.
- Arranged marriages are still the custom in rural areas.

ESSENTIAL FACTS

- ⊙ Tashkent
- ◔ 1,138,910 sq km (439,733 sq miles)
- ♦ 21.1 million
- 🎩 Som
- ♀ Uzbek

UZBEK HEADWEAR
Velvet hats like this one are commonly worn in Uzbekistan.

KYRGYZSTAN

- The nation of Kyrgyzstan is the most rural ex-Soviet republic.

ESSENTIAL FACTS

- ⊙ Bishkek
- ◔ 198,500 sq km (76,640 sq miles)
- ♦ 4.6 million
- 🎩 Som
- ♀ Kyrgyz

TURKMENISTAN

- Ashgabat is a breeding centre for the Akhal-Teke, a breed of racehorse able to maintain its speed in desert conditions.
- Most Turkmen live around desert oases.

ESSENTIAL FACTS

- ⊙ Ashgabat
- ◔ 488,100 sq km (188,455 sq miles)
- ♦ 4 million
- 🎩 Manat
- ♀ Turkmen

TAJIKISTAN

- The traditions and language of Tajikistan are similar to those of Iran.
- Violence perpetrated by armed gangs is a major problem in all but the most remote areas.

ESSENTIAL FACTS

- ⊙ Dushanbe
- ◔ 143,100 sq km (55,251 sq miles)
- ♦ 5.7 million
- 🎩 Rouble
- ♀ Tajik

AFGHANISTAN

- Most Afghans live in extreme poverty.

ESSENTIAL FACTS

- ⊙ Kabul
- ◔ 652,090 sq km (251,770 sq miles)
- ♦ 20.5 million
- 🎩 Afghani
- ♀ Persian, Pashtu

CARROTS WERE FIRST GROWN FOR FOOD IN AFGHANISTAN

Russian Federation and Kazakhstan facts

RUSSIAN FEDERATION

- Moscow and St. Petersburg are the most popular tourist destinations in the Commonwealth of Independent States (CIS).
- Russia still maintains a military presence in most of the former USSR.
- Organized crime bosses are Russia's wealthiest group.

ESSENTIAL FACTS

- ⊙ Moscow
- ◔ 17,075,400 sq km (6,592,800 sq miles)
- ♟ 149.2 million
- ☗ Rouble
- ♡ Russian
- ▲ Multi-party republic
- ♦ 70 years

(See also **European Russia**, p.288)

KAZAKHSTAN SPACE CENTRE
The Russian space programme is based at Baykonour in Kazakhstan.

The "Buran" unmanned Russian space shuttle

SIBERIAN HUSKIES
The husky is used for pulling sledges and hunting.

EAR OF WHEAT
Kazakhstan's steppes, or grasslands, were ploughed up to grow grain crops in the 1950's.

KAZAKHSTAN

- A large community of foreign business people now lives in Alma-Ata.
- Kazakhstan joined the International Monetary Fund (IMF) in 1992.
- The Kazakhs remain committed to Islam and loyal to the three clan federations, or Hordes.

ESSENTIAL FACTS

- ⊙ Alma-Ata
- ◔ 2,717,300 sq km (1,049,150 sq miles)
- ♟ 17.2 million
- ☗ Tenge
- ♡ Kazakh
- ▲ Multi-party republic
- ♦ 69 years

SOUTH AND EAST ASIA

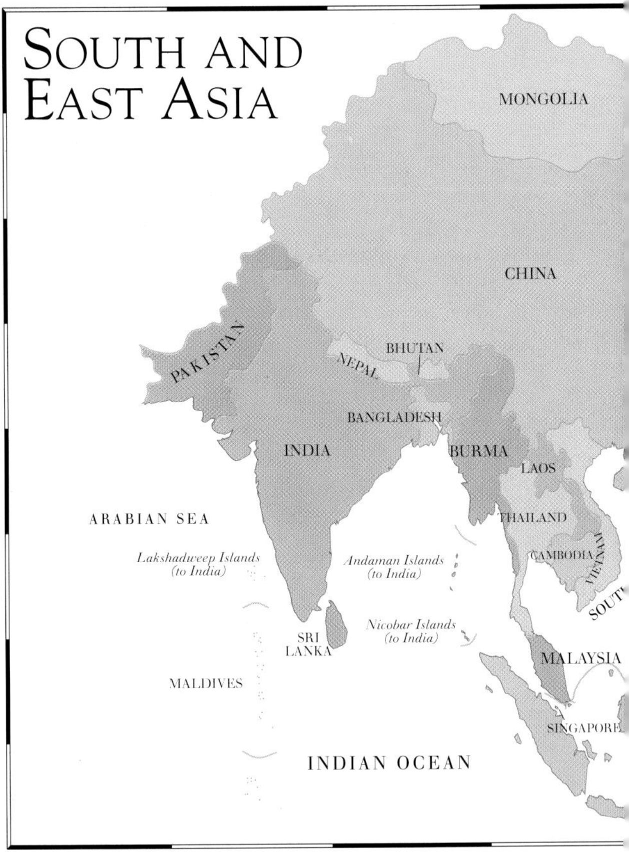

MONGOLIA

CHINA

PAKISTAN

BHUTAN

NEPAL

BANGLADESH

INDIA

BURMA

LAOS

THAILAND

CAMBODIA

VIETNAM

SOUTH

ARABIAN SEA

*Lakshadweep Islands
(to India)*

*Andaman Islands
(to India)*

SRI
LANKA

*Nicobar Islands
(to India)*

MALAYSIA

MALDIVES

SINGAPORE

INDIAN OCEAN

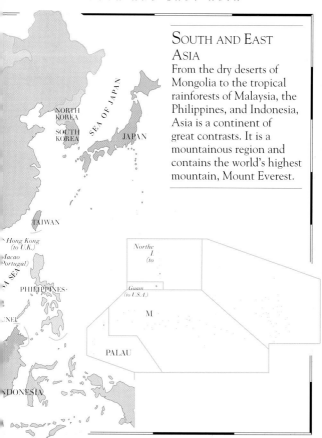

SOUTH AND EAST ASIA

From the dry deserts of Mongolia to the tropical rainforests of Malaysia, the Philippines, and Indonesia, Asia is a continent of great contrasts. It is a mountainous region and contains the world's highest mountain, Mount Everest.

NORTH KOREA

SEA OF JAPAN

SOUTH KOREA

JAPAN

TAIWAN

Hong Kong (to U.K.)

Macao (to Portugal)

A SEA

PHILIPPINES

NEL

Northe I (to

Guam (to U.S.A.)

M

PALAU

NDONESIA

INDIAN SUBCONTINENT

SEPARATED FROM THE rest of Asia by the Himalayas, India is the second most populated country after China. It is estimated that India's population will overtake that of China by 2030. To the north, Nepal and Bhutan lie nestled in the Himalayas between China and India. To the south lies Sri Lanka, once known as Ceylon.

INDUSTRY
Tea, jute, iron, cut diamonds, cotton, rice, sugar cane, textiles. Bangladesh exports 80 per cent of the world's jute fibre. Sri Lanka is the largest tea exporter in the world. Pakistan is a major exporter of rice.

HISTORY
In 1947, when India gained independence, religious differences led to the creation of two countries – Hindu India and Muslim Pakistan. In 1971, a short civil war broke out between East and West Pakistan and East Pakistan became Bangladesh.

INDIA

NATURAL FEATURES
The Himalayas were formed as a result of a violent crumpling of the Earth's crust. Frequent earthquakes indicate that the process is continuing. The highest peaks in the world, including Mount Everest, are in this mountain system.

| 0 | 350 | 700miles |
| 0 | 200 | 400kms |

1

PAKISTAN

NEPAL

BHUTAN

2

3

4

5

CLIMATE
Sri Lanka and southern
India are tropical, with little
seasonal variation in temperature.
The north has a cold alpine climate.
Cyclones regularly build up in the
Bay of Bengal, and Bangladesh is
often flooded during the monsoon.

6

7

8

BANGLADESH

SRI LANKA

Bay of Bengal

eshawar
•ISLAMABAD •Srinagar
•awalpindi
•Gujranwala
Lahore •Amritsar
•isalabad •Jalandhar
•ultan •Ludhiana Chandigarh
•Meerut
NEW •Bareilly
DELHI •Lucknow
Jaipur •Agra KATHMANDU •THIMPHU
Gwalior BHUTAN
•odhpur •Kota •Kanpur Varanasi •Guwahati
Gandi Res. Allahabad •Patna •Imphal
Ahmadabad •Bhopal Jabalpur Rajshahi BANGLADESH
•adodara •Indore Narmada Ranchi Dhanbad DACCA •Agartala
Surat •Nagpur Calcutta• Khulna
Nasik Tapti Chittagong
•Thane Godavari Mahanadi
Bombay •Pune DECCAN
•Sholapur Vishakhapatnam
•nagi PLATEAU •Hyderabad
•Dharwad Vijayawada

INDIA
CHINA
HIMALAYAS
Brahmaputra
BURMA
EASTERN GHATS
COROMANDEL COAST
MALABAR COAST

Krishna

•Mangalore
•Bangalore Madras
•Coimbatore
•Cochin •Jaffna
•Madurai
Trivandrum
SRI LANKA
•COLOMBO
•Galle

Indian Subcontinent facts

INDIA

- The Bombay film industry is the world's biggest producer of feature films.
- Nearly half of India's adults are illiterate.
- Cultural and religious pressures in India encourage people to have large families.

ESSENTIAL FACTS

- ⊙ New Delhi
- ◔ 3,287,590 sq km (1,289,338 sq miles)
- ♦ 896.6 million
- ♛ Rupee
- ♀ Hindi, English
- ▲ Multi-party republic
- ♦ 60 years

REGAL BEAST
The national symbol of India is the Royal Bengal tiger, which is a protected species.

THE SPICE OF LIFE
Indian cooking uses highly flavoured seasonings and subtle combinations of spices to flavour each dish.

Fresh coriander

Ground coriander

Fresh ginger

Ground turmeric

Cardamom pods

SRI LANKA

- In 1960, Sri Lanka became the first country in the world to elect a woman prime minister.
- Ethnic tension between the minority Tamils and majority Sinhalese led to civil war in 1983.

ESSENTIAL FACTS

- ⊙ Columbo
- ◔ 65,610 sq km (25,332 sq miles)
- ♦ 17.9 million
- ♛ Sri Lanka rupee
- ♀ Sinhalese, Tamil

BANGLADESH

- Most transportation in Bangladesh is via rivers and waterways.
- Destruction of crops by cyclones and flooding is a frequent problem.

ESSENTIAL FACTS

- ⊙ Dhaka
- ◔ 143,998 sq km (55,598 sq miles)
- ♦ 122.2 million
- ♛ Taka
- ♀ Bengali, Urdu

PAKISTAN

• The first woman ever to lead a Muslim country was Benazir Bhutto, elected prime minister of Pakistan in 1988.
• The Punjabi majority controls Pakistan's army and bureaucracy.

ESSENTIAL FACTS

⊙ Islamabad
⚲ 796,100 sq km
  (307,374 sq miles)
♦ 128.1 million
⛁ Pakistani rupee
♡ Urdu, Punjabi
▲ Multi-party republic
♦ 58 years

TOP TEAM
The nation of Pakistan has one of the world's best cricket teams.

EYES OF BUDDHA
The all-seeing eyes of Buddha adorn the walls of many temples in Nepal.

NEPAL

• Prince Siddhartha Gautama, the founder of Buddhism, was born in southern Nepal in 563 BC.
• Nepal's divorce laws are biased in favour of the male partner.

ESSENTIAL FACTS

⊙ Kathmandu
⚲ 140,800 sq km
  (54,363 sq miles)
♦ 21.1 million
⛁ Nepalese rupee
♡ Nepali

NEPALESE
WELCOME
A prayer-like gesture is the traditional greeting in Nepal.

SEYCHELLES
(*Indian Ocean*, pp.362–363)
⊙ Victoria
♦ 69,000
♡ Creole, English, French

BHUTANESE
SPORT
Archery is the national sport of Bhutan.

BHUTAN
⊙ Thimphu
♦ 1.7 million
♡ Dzongkha

MALDIVES
(*Indian Ocean*, pp.362–363)
⊙ Male'
♦ 200,000
♡ Dhivehi

MAURITIUS
(*Indian Ocean*, pp.362–363)
⊙ Port Louis
♦ 1.1 million
♡ English

CHINA AND MONGOLIA

ISOLATED FROM THE western world for centuries, the Chinese were the first to develop the compass, paper, gunpowder, porcelain, and silk. Three autonomous regions lie within western China – Inner Mongolia, Xinjiang, and Tibet. The Gobi desert in vast Mongolia is the world's most northern desert.

PEOPLE
Han Chinese make up 93 per cent of China's population. China has relaxed its 1979 one-child policy for minority groups, such as the Mongolians, Tibetans, and Muslim Uygurs, after some groups faced near extinction.

HISTORY
Tibet was invaded by China in 1950. The Chinese destroyed Tibet's traditional agricultural society and brutally repressed Buddhism. In 1959 there were more than 6,000 Buddhist monasteries – by 1980, only 179 remained.

Map labels

KAZAKHSTAN
L. Uvs
Har Us L.
ALTAI MTS.
XINJIANG UIGHUR
Ürümqi
AUTONOMOUS
TIEN MTS.
Tarim
L. Bosten
REGION
Tarim Basin
Lop Nur
TAKLA MAKAN
DESERT
C
KYRGYZSTAN
TAJIKISTAN
KARAKORAM
AFGHANISTAN
ALTUN MTS.
BAY
PAKISTAN
KUNLUN MTS.
Aksai
Chin
(Controlled by
China, claimed
by India)
TIBETAN
Demchok
(Claimed by both
China and India)
AUTONOMOUS
TANGGULA MTS.
GANGDISE RANGE
REGION
Brahmaputra (Yarlung Zangbo)
Lhasa
INDIA
NEPAL
HIMALAYAS
BHUTAN
IN

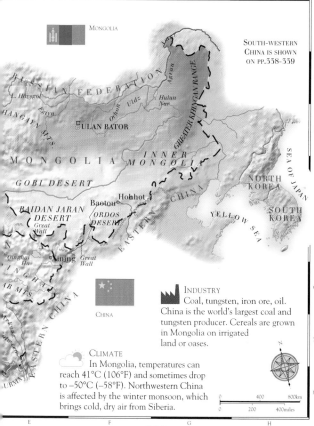

MONGOLIA

SOUTH-WESTERN
CHINA IS SHOWN
ON PP. 338–339

RUSSIAN FEDERATION

L. Hövsgöl

Egiyn

HANGAYN MTS.

Onon

Uldz

Hulun
Nur

ULAN BATOR

Argun

GREATER KHINGAN RANGE

M O N G O L I A   I N N E R   M O N G O L I A

GOBI DESERT

BADAIN JARAN
DESERT

Great
Wall

Baotou

Hohhot

ORDOS
DESERT

E A S T E R N   C H I N A

NORTH
KOREA

SEA OF JAPAN

SOUTH
KOREA

YELLOW SEA

Qinghai
Hu

Xining

Great
Wall

SHING

AR MTS.

ESTERN CHINA

URMA

CHINA

INDUSTRY
Coal, tungsten, iron ore, oil.
China is the world's largest coal and
tungsten producer. Cereals are grown
in Mongolia on irrigated
land or oases.

CLIMATE
In Mongolia, temperatures can
reach 41°C (106°F) and sometimes drop
to –50°C (–58°F). Northwestern China
is affected by the winter monsoon, which
brings cold, dry air from Siberia.

N

0   400   800km

0   200   400miles

E   F   G   H

CHINA AND KOREA

ONE-FIFTH of the world's population live in China – mostly in the eastern part of the country. Annexed to Japan in 1910, Korea was divided between the USA and Communist Russia after World War II. North and South Korea were formed in 1948.

NORTH-WESTERN CHINA IS SHOWN ON PP. 336–337

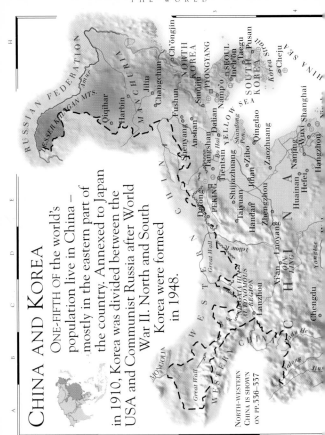

NORTH KOREA

SOUTH KOREA

TAIPEI

Kao-hsiung

TAIWAN

TAIWAN

Changsha

Fuzhou

Xiamen

GUANGXI-ZHUANG
REGION
Nanning
Canton
Dongguang
HONG KONG
MACAO
Kowloon
MACAO
(to Portugal)
(to U.K.)
Leizhou Pen.

SOUTH CHINA SEA

Guiyang

Haikou

Hainan

Gulf of
Tonking

Nanchang

Hongshui He

VIETNAM

LAOS

Kunming

Mekong

BURMA

CHINA

PEOPLE
Korea has been inhabited by one ethnic group for 2,000 years and even today those with the same surname group may not marry each other. Most Taiwanese are descendants of the Chinese supporters of the deposed Ming dynasty, who migrated in 1644.

CLIMATE

Southern South Korea and Taiwan have a tropical monsoon climate similar to that of south China. North Korea has a continental climate.

HISTORY
In 1949, the People's Republic of China was established as a communist state, and Taiwan became a separate country.

COMMUNICATIONS
South Korea has one of the world's best public transport systems. Buses, trains, boats, and planes are all integrated in one timetable.

INDUSTRY

Rice, electronics, wheat, finance, textiles. Hong Kong has the busiest container port in the world. Taiwan is the world's leading producer of watches, computers, televisions, and track shoes.

JAPAN

CONSISTING OF FOUR main islands and 4,000 smaller ones, Japan is the world's leading industrial nation. Since two-thirds of the land is mountainous, the majority of people live on the coast. Japan has about 1,500 minor earthquakes a year, but severe earthquakes, such as the one in Kobe in 1994, occur every few years. Underwater earthquakes sometimes cause huge surge waves, or *tsunami*, along Japan's Pacific coast.

INDUSTRY

Fishing, ship building, motor vehicles, computers, televisions, high-tech electronics. Motor vehicles are Japan's biggest export, and its stock exchange ranks second in the world. Japan excels at producing miniature electronic goods.

HISTORY

Japan was once ruled by warlords called shoguns, who discouraged contact with the outside world. In 1639, Japan cut ties with other nations and ordered all Europeans to leave, except the Dutch who were allowed one trading ship per year.

Aleutian Islands

Hidaka Is.

Nemuro Strait

La Pérouse Strait

SEA OF OKHOTSK

HIDAKA MTS.

ISHIKARI MTS.

Hokkaidō

Ishikari Bay

Sapporo

Ishikari Riv.

Tsugaru Strait

Hachinohe

Sendai

OU MTS.

Mogami

Honshū

Shinano

Toyama Bay

SEA OF JAPAN

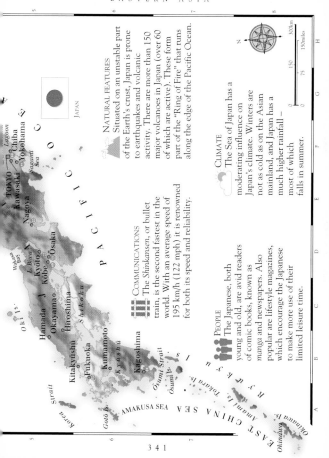

JAPAN

NATURAL FEATURES

Situated on an unstable part of the Earth's crust, Japan is prone to earthquakes and volcanic activity. There are more than 150 major volcanoes in Japan (over 60 of which are active). These form part of the "Ring of Fire" that runs along the edge of the Pacific Ocean.

CLIMATE

The Sea of Japan has a moderating influence on Japan's climate. Winters are not as cold as on the Asian mainland, and Japan has a much higher rainfall – most of which falls in summer.

COMMUNICATIONS

The *Shinkansen*, or bullet train, is the second fastest in the world. With an average speed of 195 km/h (122 mph) it is renowned for both its speed and reliability.

PEOPLE

The Japanese, both young and old, are avid readers of comic books, known as *manga* and newspapers. Also popular are lifestyle magazines, which encourage the Japanese to make more use of their limited leisure time.

PACIFIC OCEAN

Lagoon
Chiba
TOKYO Yokohama
Kawasaki Sagami
Nagoya Sea

Kyōto Osaka
Wakasa Bay Kōbe
Hamada Okayama Hiroshima
Okiis. Shikoku

Kitakyūshū
Fukuoka Kumamoto
Kyūshū Kagoshima
Gotō Is. Ōsumi Strait
Ōsumi Is.
Korea Strait Tokara Is.
AMAKUSA SEA Ryūkyū
EAST CHINA SEA Amami Is.
Okinawa Is.
Okinawa

N

0   150   300km
0   75   150miles

341

Eastern Asia facts

China

• China has the world's oldest continuous civilization; recorded history began 4,000 years ago.
• Mao Tse-tung founded and dominated communist China from 1949 until his death in 1976.

ESSENTIAL FACTS

⊙ Beijing

9,396,960 sq km (3,628,166 sq miles)

1.2 billion

Yuan

Mandarin

▲ Single-party republic

71 years

WONDERWALL
The Great Wall of China is the longest man-made structure in the world.

BAMBOO LUNCH
Pandas living in the forests of China's Sichuan mountains feed on bamboo shoots.

Mongolia

• The Mongolian press is strongly outspoken, with no slander or libel laws.
• Most Mongolians are nomadic, but some now live on state-run farms.
• The poorest people in Mongolia cannot even afford to buy bread.

ESSENTIAL FACTS

⊙ Ulan Bator

1,565,000 sq km (604,247 sq miles)

2.4 million

Tughrik

Khalkha Mongol

Macao

Chinese territory under Portuguese administration until 1999.

⊙ Macao

477,850

Chinese, Portuguese

Hong Kong

Chinese territory under UK administration until 1997.

⊙ Victoria

5.8 million

English, Cantonese

MONGOLIAN YAK
Yaks provide Mongolian herders with milk, butter, meat, wool, and leather.

SOUTH KOREA

- Over 60% of South Koreans are named Kim, Lee, or Pak.
- It is not considered respectable for married women to have jobs in South Korea.

ESSENTIAL FACTS

- ⊙ Seoul
- ◖ 99,020 sq km (38,232 sq miles)'
- ♦ 44.5 million
- ♕ Won
- ♀ Korean, Chinese
- ▲ Multi-party republic
- ● 70 years

NORTH KOREA

- The Korean Worker's Party is the only legal political party.
- Private telephones and cars are forbidden.

ESSENTIAL FACTS

- ⊙ Pyongyang
- ◖ 120,540 sq km (46,540 sq miles)
- ♦ 23.1 million
- ♕ Won
- ♀ Korean

KOREAN GINSENG ROOT IS WIDELY USED IN TRADITIONAL ASIAN MEDICINE

TAIWAN

- Taiwan is the world's biggest bicycle producer.
- China regards Taiwan as a province of the Chinese mainland.

ESSENTIAL FACTS

- ⊙ Taipei
- ◖ 36,179 sq km (13,969 sq miles)
- ♦ 20.8 million
- ♕ New Taiwan dollar
- ♀ Mandarin

JAPAN

- People in Japan define themselves by the company they work for, not the job they do.
- Japan is Hollywood's biggest export market.
- The Japanese constitution forbids the use of troops abroad except in self-defence.

ESSENTIAL FACTS

- ⊙ Tokyo
- ◖ 377,800 sq km (149,869 sq miles)
- ♦ 125 million
- ♕ Yen
- ♀ Japanese
- ▲ Multi-party democracy
- ● 79 years

HEAVYWEIGHTS Japanese sumo wrestlers eat a daily stew called *chanko-nabe*, made of seafood, meat, vegetables, and tofu, to maintain their bulk.

MAINLAND SOUTHEAST ASIA

FOR MOST OF its history, Thailand has been an independent kingdom. Malaysia includes 11 states on the mainland (Malaya), as well as Sabah and Sarawak in Borneo. Cambodia, Laos, and Vietnam have suffered from years of civil war. Burma has become more and more isolated from the world by its repressive government.

LAOS

BURMA
(MYANMAR)

L. Thac Ba
Thai Nguyen
Red R.
Viet Tri
Hong Gai
HANOI
Hai Phong
Nam Dinh
Black R.
Thanh
Hoa
Nam Ou
Luang
Phrabang
Vinh
Mekong
L A O S
Nam Pheuk
Chiang Mai

Gulf of Tongking

C H I N A

KAREN RANGE

Chindwin
Irrawaddy
Monywa
Mandalay
Saging
Sumarapura
Pakokku
Taunggyi
L. Inle
B U R M A
Minbu
Pyinmana
Prome
Sittang
Sandoway

CHIN HILLS

I N D I A

DESH

Bay of Bengal

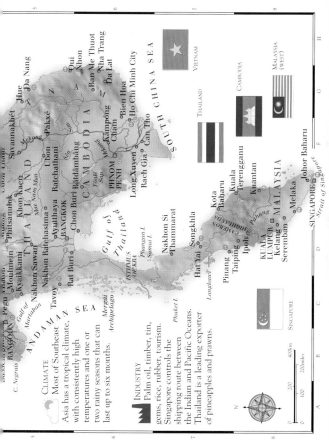

SOUTH CHINA SEA

VIETNAM

THAILAND

CAMBODIA

MALAYSIA
(WEST)

Da Nang
Hue
Savannakhét
Qui
Nhon
Pakxé
Ban Me Thuot
Nha Trang
Da Lat
Biên Hoa
Ho Chi Minh City
Kâmpong
Cham
PHNOM
PENH
Bătdâmbâng
Can Tho
Long Xuyen
Rach Gia

Ubon
Ratchathani
Khon Kaen
Kôrôt
Phitsanulok
Moulmein
Nakhon Sawan
Kwaikkami
Ayutthaya
BANGKOK
Chon Buri
Rat Buri
Nakhon Ratchasima

RANGOON
C. Negrais

Tavoy

ANDAMAN SEA

Gulf of
Martaban

Mergui
Archipelago

Gulf of
Thailand

ISTHMUS
OF KRA

Phuket I.

Phangan I.
Samui I.

Nakhon Si
Thammarat

Hat Yai
Songkhla

Langkawi

Kota
Baharu

Kuala
Terengganu

Kuantan

Pinang
Taiping
Ipoh
KUALA
LUMPUR
Kelang
Seremban
Melaka

CAMERON
HIGHLANDS

Pahang

MALAYSIA

Johor Baharu

SINGAPORE
Strait of Singapore

SINGAPORE

☁ **CLIMATE**

Most of Southeast
Asia has a tropical climate,
with consistently high
temperatures and one or
two rainy seasons that can
last up to six months.

🏭 **INDUSTRY**

Palm oil, timber, tin,
gems, rice, rubber, tourism.
Singapore controls the
shipping route between
the Indian and Pacific Oceans.
Thailand is a leading exporter
of pineapples and prawns.

N

400km

200miles

0   100   200

MARITIME SOUTHEAST ASIA

SCATTERED BETWEEN the Indian and
Pacific Oceans are thousands of tropical
mountainous islands. Once called the
East Indies, Indonesia was ruled by the
Dutch for 350 years. More than half of its 13,677
islands are still uninhabited. The Philippines lie on
the "Ring of Fire", and are subject to earthquakes
and volcanic activity. Borneo is shared
among Indonesia, Malaysia, and Brunei.

PHILI

BRUNEI

Balabac
Strait

SOUTH CHINA SEA

Kota
Kinabalu

BANDAR SERI
BEGAWAN

SABA

BRUNEI

Medan

MALAYSIA
(EAST)

Rajang

CRO

RANGE

Simeulue

L.Toba

Anambas Is.

Natuna Is.

Kuching

SARAWAK

Borneo

Nias

Strait of
Singapore

MULLER MTS.

Samarinda

Sumatra

Kapuas

Padang

Batanghari

Lingga

Pontianak

Balikpapan

Siberut

Singkep

Bangka

Jambi

BARISAN MTS.

Belitung

Banjarmasin

Palembang

JAVA
SEA

I
N

Tanjungkarang

D

N

JAKARTA

Cirebon

Semarang

Bogor

Surabaya

Bali

Bandung

Kediri

Jember

Yogyakarta

Malang

Denpasar

Java

Lombok

INDIAN

OCEAN

MALAYSIA (EAST)
SABAH AND SARAWAK

0   300   600km
0   150   300miles

Luzon Strait

Luzon

Baguio

Dagupan

Angeles Cabanatuan

MANILA

Lucena

Batangas

Mindoro Naga Legaspi

Mindoro Strait

Panay Calbayog

Cadiz Samar

Iloilo Tacloban

Palawan Bacolod Cebu

PPINES Negros Butuan

Cagayan de Oro

Iligan Mindanao

Zamboanga Davao

SULU SEA

Jolo General

Sulu Archipelago Santos

Talaud Is.

CELEBES SEA

PHILIPPINE SEA

PACIFIC OCEAN

PHILIPPINES

INDUSTRY
Palm oil, timber, rice, oil, natural gas, copper, chrome, tourism. Malaysia is the largest producer of palm oil and computer disk-drives. Indonesia is a major exporter of natural gas.

ENVIRONMENT
Logging, especially in Borneo and the Philippines, is a problem in the region. Forest communities, like the Malaysian Penan, are being destroyed. Some tree species are near extinction.

CLIMATE
Countries situated around the equator are hot and humid all year. Variations in climate are related to latitude.

Manado

Gulf of Tomini

Palu

Celebes

Makassar Strait

MOLUCCA SEA

Sula Is.

Moluccas

Halmahera

Supiori

Biak

Jayapura

Mamberamo

IRIAN JAYA

MAOKE MTS.

SERAM SEA

Kendari

Buru Seram

Ambon

Kai Is.

ARAFURA SEA

Aru Is.

Digul

Dolak

PAPUA NEW GUINEA

BANDA SEA

Ujung Pandang

O   N   E   S   I   A

FLORES SEA

Sumbawa

Flores

Lesser Sunda Islands

Kupang

TIMOR SEA

Sumba Roti

Timor

Tanimbar Is.

INDONESIA

F   G   H

Southeast Asia facts

BURMA

• The country of Burma is also called Myanmar.
• Burma is the world's biggest exporter of teak.

ESSENTIAL FACTS

⊙ Rangoon

◔ 676,550 sq km
  (261,200 sq miles)

♦ 44.6 million

🛢 Kyat

♡ Burmese (Myanmar)

LAOS

• In 1994, the Mekong River's "Friendship Bridge" became the first Thai–Laos road link.

LAOS FACTS

⊙ Vientiane

◔ 236,800 sq km
  (91,428 sq miles)

♦ 4.6 million

🛢 Kip

♡ Lao, Miao, Yao

SINGAPORE

• The nation is the world leader in new biotechnologies.
• Chewing gum is banned by law in Singapore.

SINGAPORE FACTS

⊙ Singapore City

◔ 620 sq km
  (239 sq miles)

♦ 2.8 million

🛢 Singapore dollar

♡ Malay, Chinese, Tamil, English

THAILAND

• Criticism of the Thai king, who is head of state, is not allowed.
• Thailand, meaning "land of the free", is the only Southeast Asian nation never to be colonized.

MOBILE SHOP
Floating markets are a common sight on the waterways of Southeast Asia.

THAILAND FACTS

⊙ Bangkok

◔ 513,120 sq km
  (198,116 sq miles)

♦ 56.9 million

🛢 Baht

♡ Thai

▲ Multi-party democracy

  ♦ 69 years

VIETNAM

• A new species of mammal, the Vu Quang Ox, was recently discovered in the forests of north Vietnam.
• The Vietnam war cost two million lives.

VIETNAM FACTS

⊙ Hanoi

◔ 329,560 sq km
  (127,243 sq miles)

♦ 70.9 million

🛢 New dong

♡ Vietnamese

KOMODO DRAGON
The "dragon" of Komodo
in Indonesia is the
world's largest lizard.

INDONESIA

• The world's biggest
island chain, Indonesia
is made up of 13,677
islands spread over
4,830 km (3,000 miles)
and three time zones.
• Indonesia was formerly
known as the Dutch
East Indies.
• Forest survival is
threatened by logging.

INDONESIA FACTS

⊙ Jakarta
◔ 1,904,570 sq km
   (735,355 sq miles)
✚ 194.6 million
💰 Rupiah
♡ Bahasa Indonesia
▲ Multi-party republic
● 62 years

BRUNEI

⊙ Bandar Seri Begawan
✚ 300,000
♡ Malay

PHILIPPINES

• The Filipino nation
is the only Christian
country in Asia.

PHILIPPINES FACTS

⊙ Manila
◔ 300,000 sq km
   (115,831 sq miles)
✚ 66.5 million
💰 Philippine peso
♡ Filipino, English
▲ Multi-party republic
● 65 years

CAMBODIA

• Over one million
Cambodians died
between 1975 and 1979
under Pol Pot's Marxist
Khmer Rouge regime.
• Cambodians are
descended from the
Khmers, who arrived
in Southeast Asia in
around 2,000 BC.
• Aid provides 70% of
government revenue.

CAMBODIA FACTS

⊙ Phnom Penh
◔ 181,040 sq km
   (69,000 sq miles)
✚ 9 million
💰 Riel
♡ Khmer

MALAYSIA

• The nation is the
world's leading producer
of natural rubber.

ESSENTIAL FACTS

⊙ Kuala Lumpur
◔ 329,750 sq km
   (127,317 sq miles)
✚ 19.2 million
💰 Ringgit
♡ Malay

MALAYSIAN
RUBBER
Workers extract
latex by cutting
rubber trees and
collecting the
sap that oozes
from the cut.

AUSTRALASIA AND
OCEANIA

NAURU

PAPUA NEW
GUINEA

SOLOMON
ISLANDS

Coral Sea Islands
(to Australia)

VANUATU

New Caledonia
(to France)

AUSTRALIA

TASMAN SEA

NEW ZEALAND

SOUTHERN OCEAN

Auckland Islands
(to N.Z.)

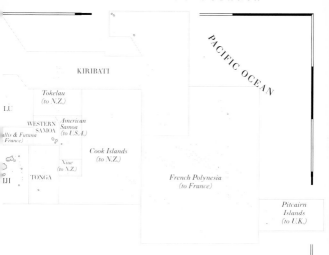

PACIFIC OCEAN

KIRIBATI

Tokelau
(to N.Z.)

LU

WESTERN
SAMOA
allis & Futuna
France)

American
Samoa
(to U.S.A.)

Cook Islands
(to N.Z.)

Niue
(to N.Z.)

TONGA

IJI

French Polynesia
(to France)

Pitcairn
Islands
(to U.K.)

Chatham Island
(to N.Z.)

AUSTRALASIA AND OCEANIA

Millions of years ago, the continent of
Australia and the islands of New Guinea
and New Zealand split away from the
other southern continents. These island
countries have many unique plants and
animals, such as Australia's marsupials,
or pouched mammals. The thousands of
islands scattered in the Pacific are either
volcanic islands or coral atolls.

PACIFIC OCEAN

THE LARGEST AND deepest
ocean, the Pacific covers a
greater area of the Earth's surface
than all the land areas together.
Its deepest point – 11,033 m
(36,197ft) – is deep enough
to cover Mount Everest.
Melanesia, Micronesia,
and Polynesia are the
main inner Pacific
island groups.

MICRONESIA

NAURU

NATURAL FEATURES

Some Pacific islands are
coral atolls – ring-shaped islands
or chains of islands surrounding
a lagoon. They are formed when
coral builds up on a sunken bank or
on a volcano crater in the open sea.

PALAU

SOLOMON
ISLANDS

ENVIRONMENT

Nuclear testing by
USA dangerously polluted
areas in the South Pacific.
Countries such as Japan,
Australia, and New Zealand
want the region made into a
nuclear-free zone.

VANUATU

FIJI

N

| 0 | 1500 | 3000km |
| 0 | 750 | 1500miles |

SEA OF
OKHOTSK

ASIA

Shanghai

Kobe

Yokohama

Hong Kong

Manila

SOUTH
EAST ASIA

NORTHERN
MARIANA IS.

GUAM

FEDERATED STATES
OF MICRONESIA

NAURU

ARAFURA
SEA

CORAL
SEA

Great
Barrier
Reef

AUSTRALIA

NEW
CALEDONIA

Sydney

TASMAN
SEA

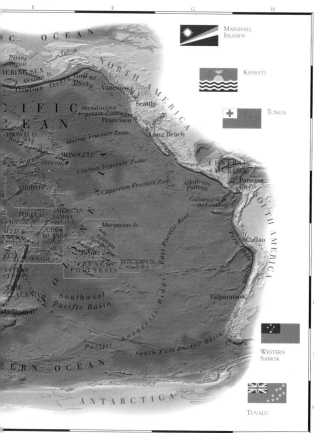

MARSHALL
ISLANDS

KIRIBATI

TONGA

WESTERN
SAMOA

TUVALU

E F G H

PACIFIC OCEAN
NORTH AMERICA

Bering
Strait
BERING SEA
Yukon
Aleutian Trench
Aleutian Is.
Gulf of
Alaska
Vancouver

Mendocino
Fracture Zone
Seattle
San
Francisco
Long Beach

MIDWAY IS.

Murray Fracture Zone

HONOLULU

Clarion Fracture Zone

CENTRAL
AMERICA
Panama
CITY

KIRIBATI

Clipperton Fracture Zone

Albatross
Plateau
Galápagos Is.
(to Ecuador)

FORD IS.
AMERICAN
SAMOA

Marquesas Is.

Callao

COOK
ISLANDS

Tahiti

East Pacific Rise

PITCAIRN IS.

WESTERN
SAMOA

FRENCH
POLYNESIA

NEW
ZEALAND
Southwest
Pacific Basin

Valparaíso

Wellington

Pacific
Antarctic Ridge

South East Pacific Basin
C. Horn

SOUTHERN OCEAN

ANTARCTICA

SOUTH AMERICA

E F G H

AUSTRALIA AND PAPUA NEW GUINEA

THE SMALLEST, flattest, and driest continent, Australia has a landscape that varies from tropical rainforest to arid desert. Lying to the north, Papua New Guinea (PNG) is so mountainous that its tribes are isolated from each other and from the outside world.

AUSTRALIA

TIMOR SEA

DARWIN
Joseph Bonaparte Gulf
ARNHEM LAND

INDIAN OCEAN

KIMBERLEY PLATEAU
KING LEOPOLD RANGES
Fitzroy

NORT
TERR

GREAT SANDY DESERT

North West C.
HAMERSLEY RANGE
L. Macleod

A U S
WESTERN
L. Mackay
L. Disappointment
Alice Sprin
MACDONNEL RANGES

GIBSON DESERT

AUSTRALIA

Dirk Hartog I.
L. Carnegie
GREAT VICTORIA DESERT

L. Barlee
L. Moore
PERTH

C. Naturaliste
C. Leeuwin
C. Pasley
NULLARBOR PLAIN
Great Australian Big

CLIMATE

Most people live in temperate zones that occur within 400 km (249 miles) of the coast in the east and southeast, and around Perth in the west. The interior, west, and south are arid; the north is tropical. PNG is tropical, yet snow falls on its highest mountains.

INDUSTRY

Coal, gold, uranium, cattle, tourism, wool, wine- and beer-making. Australia is a leading exporter of coal, iron ore, gold, bauxite, and copper, and has the largest known diamond deposits. PNG has the largest copper mine in the world and one of the largest gold mines.

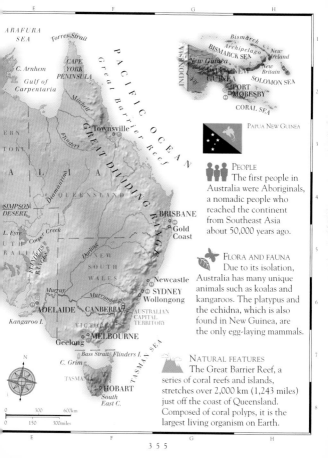

ARAFURA SEA

Torres Strait

C. Arnhem

CAPE YORK PENINSULA

Gulf of Carpentaria

PACIFIC OCEAN

Great Barrier Reef

Mitchell

Bismarck Archipelago

BISMARCK SEA

New Ireland

New Guinea

BISMARCK

PAPUA NEW GUINEA

New Britain

PORT MORESBY

SOLOMON SEA

CORAL SEA

PAPUA NEW GUINEA

PEOPLE
The first people in Australia were Aboriginals, a nomadic people who reached the continent from Southeast Asia about 50,000 years ago.

Townsville

GREAT DIVIDING RANGE

Flinders

Diamantina

QUEENSLAND

SIMPSON DESERT

L. Eyre

Cooper

Creek

FLINDERS RANGES

BRISBANE

Gold Coast

Darling

NEW SOUTH WALES

Murray

Murrumbidgee

Newcastle

SYDNEY

Wollongong

ADELAIDE

CANBERRA

AUSTRALIAN CAPITAL TERRITORY

Kangaroo I.

VICTORIA

MELBOURNE

Geelong

N

Bass Strait

Flinders I.

C. Grim

TASMAN SEA

TASMANIA

HOBART

South East C.

0   300   600km

0   150   300miles

FLORA AND FAUNA
Due to its isolation, Australia has many unique animals such as koalas and kangaroos. The platypus and the echidna, which is also found in New Guinea, are the only egg-laying mammals.

NATURAL FEATURES
The Great Barrier Reef, a series of coral reefs and islands, stretches over 2,000 km (1,243 miles) just off the coast of Queensland. Composed of coral polyps, it is the largest living organism on Earth.

NEW ZEALAND

ONE OF THE LAST places on Earth to be inhabited by people, New Zealand lies about halfway between the equator and the South Pole. It is made up of the main North and South Islands, separated by the Cook Strait, and numerous smaller islands. The first settlers were Maoris, who came from the Polynesian islands about 1,200 years ago.

NATURAL FEATURES

New Zealand lies on the "Ring of Fire", a band of volcanic activity that almost encircles the Pacific Ocean. New Zealand has about 400 earthquakes each year, although only about 100 are strong enough to be felt.

PEOPLE

In recent years, Maoris have protested the lack of observance of the Treaty of Waitangi, which protected their rights. About 10 per cent of the total population are Maori.

FLORA AND FAUNA

Many of New Zealand's animals have been introduced – two species of bat are the only native land mammals. New Zealand has no snakes.

Great Exhibition Bay

Kaipara Harbour

Auckland

North Island

Great Barrier I.

Bay of Plenty

Hamilton

L. Taupo

Hawke Bay

TASMAN SEA

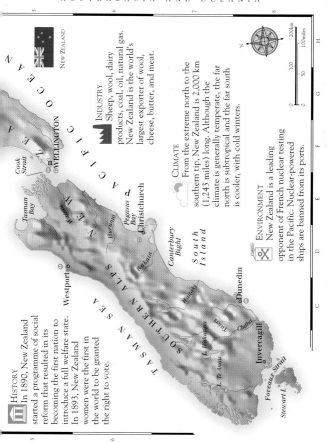

NEW ZEALAND

INDUSTRY

Sheep, wool, dairy products, coal, oil, natural gas. New Zealand is the world's largest exporter of wool, cheese, butter, and meat.

CLIMATE

From the extreme north to the southern tip, New Zealand is 2,000 km (1,243 miles) long. Although the climate is generally temperate, the far north is subtropical and the far south is cooler, with cold winters.

ENVIRONMENT

New Zealand is a leading opponent of French nuclear testing in the Pacific. Nuclear-powered ships are banned from its ports.

HISTORY

In 1890, New Zealand started a programme of social reform that resulted in its becoming the first nation to introduce a full welfare state. In 1893, New Zealand women were the first in the world to be granted the right to vote.

PACIFIC OCEAN

WELLINGTON

Cook Strait

Tasman Bay

Pegasus Bay

Christchurch

NEW ZEALAND

Westport

Waitaki

Rakaia

Buller

Canterbury Bight

South Island

Dunedin

Waitaki

L. Wakatipu

L. Te Anau

Taieri

Clutha

Invercagill

TASMAN SEA

SOUTHERN ALPS

Foveaux Strait

Stewart I.

Australasia and Oceania facts

AUSTRALIA

• The suburban area of the city of Sydney is the largest in the world; it is twice as large as Beijing and six times the size of Rome.

• Aboriginal land and civil rights claims are an increasingly important item on the political agenda.

ESSENTIAL FACTS

⊙ Canberra

◔ 7,686,850 sq km (2,967,893 sq miles)

♦ 17.8 million

⛆ Australian dollar

♀ English

▲ Multi-party democracy

♦ 77 years

LIFE'S A BEACH
Surfing and watersports are popular Australian leisure activities.

NEW ZEALAND

• The landscape of New Zealand is the most varied in the world relative to its size, offering mountains, fjords, lakes, glaciers, rainforests, beaches, mud pools, and geysers.

• Many of New Zealand's top jobs in business and politics are held by women.

ESSENTIAL FACTS

⊙ Wellington

◔ 268,680 sq km (103,730 sq miles)

♦ 3.5 million

⛆ New Zealand dollar

♀ English

▲ Multi-party democracy

♦ 75 years

PAPUA NEW GUINEA

• The feathers of certain unique bird species in Papua New Guinea produce a poison that causes painful blisters on contact with human skin.

ESSENTIAL FACTS

⊙ Port Moresby

◔ 462,840 sq km (178,700 sq miles)

♦ 4.1 million

⛆ Kina

♀ English

KIWI BIRD
The flightless kiwi is the most famous of New Zealand's creatures.

VANUATU
- ⊙ Port-Vila
- ♦ 155,000
- ♡ Bislama, English, French

FIJI
- ⊙ Suva
- ♦ 700,000
- ♡ English, Fijian

PALAU
- ⊙ Koror
- ♦ 16,000
- ♡ Palauan, English

KIRIBATI
- ⊙ Bairiki
- ♦ 66,000
- ♡ English, Kiribati

TONGA
- ⊙ Nuku'alofa
- ♦ 101,000
- ♡ Tongan, English

TUVALU
- ⊙ Fingafale
- ♦ 9,000
- ♡ Tuvaluan, Kiribati

WESTERN SAMOA
- ⊙ Apia
- ♦ 162,000
- ♡ Samoan, English

NAURU
- ⊙ No official capital
- ♦ 10,000
- ♡ Nauruan, English

MARSHALL ISLANDS
- ⊙ Majuro
- ♦ 48,000
- ♡ English, Marshallese

SOLOMON ISLANDS
- ⊙ Honiara
- ♦ 400,000
- ♡ English

Thatched roof made of palm fronds

Simple house

Wooden outrigger boat with main hull and twin floats

Home-produced food

MICRONESIA
- ⊙ Kolonia
- ♦ 101,000
- ♡ English

ISLAND LIFE
On the remoter islands of the Pacific, people live much as their ancestors did, fishing, keeping animals, and growing fruit and vegetables.

ATLANTIC OCEAN

BENEATH THE WATERS of the Atlantic Ocean lies the Mid-Atlantic Ridge, one of the world's longest mountain chains. Some of its peaks are so high they form islands, such as the Azores. Apart from a wide rift-valley in the centre of the ridge, the ocean consists of vast featureless plains and is 8 km (5 miles) at its deepest point.

ICELAND

CAPE VERDE

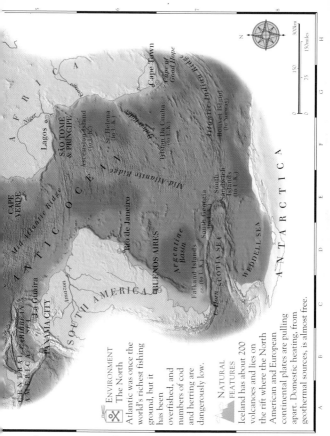

ATLANTIC OCEAN

ENVIRONMENT

The North Atlantic was once the world's richest fishing ground, but it has been overfished, and numbers of cod and herring are dangerously low.

NATURAL FEATURES

Iceland has about 200 volcanoes and lies on the rift where the North American and European continental plates are pulling apart. Domestic heating, from geothermal sources, is almost free.

361

INDIAN OCEAN

THE SMALLEST of the world's oceans, the Indian Ocean has some 5,000 islands scattered across its area. Beneath its surface, three great mountain ranges converge towards the ocean's centre – an area of strong seismic and volcanic activity. The ocean's greatest depth, 7,440 m (24,400 ft), is in the Java Trench.

CLIMATE
The monsoon winds blow over the Indian Ocean – from the southwest or from the northeast according to the season. The southwesterly monsoon brings heavy rains to southern Asia.

ENVIRONMENT
The Indian Ocean is at risk from oil pollution from tankers carrying oil from the Persian Gulf.

FLORA AND FAUNA
Owing to its position off the African coast, Madagascar is home to many unique animals, such as tenrecs, lemurs, and fossas.

COMOROS

MALDIVES

SEYCHELLES

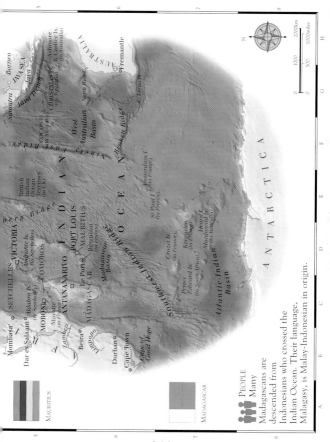

INDIAN OCEAN

Sumatra   Borneo
JAVA SEA
Java   Sumba   Timor
AUSTRALIA

Fremantle

N

0   1000   2000km
0   500   1000miles

Christmas I.
(to Australia)
Cocos Is.
(to Australia)   Ashmore
& Cartier Is.
(to Australia)

West
Australian
Basin

Broken Ridge

North Passat

A. Leeuwin

Ninety East Ridge

INDIAN

Amsterdam I.
(to France)

British
Indian
Ocean
Territory
(to UK)

St Paul I.
(to France)

OCEAN

ANTARCTICA

Mombasa

SEYCHELLES   VICTORIA

Aldabra Is.
(to Seychelles)
Indispute Is.
(to Seychelles)

Dar es Salaam

MORONI

COMOROS

Mayotte
(to France)

ANTANANARIVO

Le Port   PORT LOUIS
Réunion   MAURITIUS
(to France)

Mid-Indian Ridge

Madagascan
Basin

Crozet Is.
(to France)

Kerguelen
(to France)

Heard I.
McDonald Is.
(to Australia)

Amsterdam I.
(to France)

MADAGASCAR

Zambezi

Beira

Limpopo

Durban

Prince
Edward Is.
(to South Africa)

Atlantic-Indian
Basin

South-West Indian Ridge

Cape Town
Edge of
Good Hope

MAURITIUS

PEOPLE
Many
Madagascans are
descended from
Indonesians who crossed the
Indian Ocean. Their language,
Malagasy, is Malay-Indonesian in origin.

MADAGASCAR

ANTARCTICA

CONTAINING 80 PER CENT OF the world's fresh water, the continent of Antarctica lies buried under ice more than 2 km (1.2 miles) thick. The surrounding seas are partly frozen, and icebergs barricade over 90 per cent of the coastline.

ATLANTIC OCEAN

INDIAN OCEAN

South Orkney Is. (to U.K.)

SCOTIA SEA

Elephant I. (to U.K.)

Drake Passage

South Shetland Is. (to U.K.)

ANTARCTIC PENINSULA

Lützow-Holm Bay

QUEEN MAUD LAND

ENDERBY LAND

Anvers I. (to U.S.A.)

WEDDELL SEA

PALMER LAND

C. Darnley

Mackenzie Bay

BELLINGSHAUSEN SEA

SOUTH POLAR PLATEAU

Peter the First I. (to Norway)

ELLSWORTH MTS.

• South Pole

DAVIS SEA

MARIE BYRD LAND

AMUNDSEN SEA

TRANSANTARCTIC MTS.

Vincennes Bay

C. Colbeck

ROSS SEA

WILKES LAND

Porpoise Bay

PACIFIC OCEAN

C. Adare

Balleny Is.

FLORA AND FAUNA

Not many plants and animals can survive on land, although the surrounding seas teem with life. Despite the cold, few birds and sea creatures migrate to warmer waters.

CLIMATE

Powerful winds form a narrow storm belt that creates severe blizzards. Summer temperatures barely reach over freezing point, and in winter the temperature can fall to –80°C (–112°F).

ENVIRONMENT

Scientists estimate that the ozone hole emerged over Antarctica in 1980. Each spring, increased sunshine activates CFCs, leading to rapid ozone depletion.

THE ARCTIC

A FROZEN OCEAN surrounded by land, the Arctic is covered by ice up to 30 m (98 ft) thick. Most of the surrounding tundra, or vast treeless plains, are permanently frozen.

ALASKA
U.S.A.
RUSSIAN FEDERATION
CHUKCHI SEA
Pevek
Wrangel I.
(to Russian Fed.)
EAST SIBERIAN SEA
BEAUFORT SEA
Prudhoe Bay
Limit of Permanent Pack Ice
New Siberian Is.
(to Russian Fed.)
LAPTEV SEA
Tiksi
Banks I.
(to Canada)

Melville I.
(to Canada)
Queen Elizabeth
Islands
Resolute
Axel Heiberg I.
(to Canada)
Devon I.
(to Canada)
Ellesmere I.
(to Canada)
Thule

A R C T I C
O C E A N
· North Pole

Limit of Permanent Pack Ice

TAIMYR PENINSULA

Severnaya Zemlya
(to Russian Fed.)

KARA SEA

CANADA

Baffin I.
(to Canada)
Baffin Bay

KNUD RASMUSSEN
LAND

GREENLAND
(to Denmark)

Franz Josef Land
(to Russian Fed.)

BARENTS SEA

SVALBARD
(to Norway)

LONGYEARBYEN
Spitsbergen

Davis Strait
Godhavn

GREENLAND SEA

GODTHÅB
(NUUK)
Scoresbysund

Narsarsuaq
Denmark Strait
Jan Mayen
(to Norway)

ATLANTIC
OCEAN
C. Farvel

ICELAND

🏛 PEOPLE
Inuits have lived in the Arctic Circle since 2500 BC. Vikings arrived in AD 986.

WORLD TIME ZONES

IMAGINARY LINES are drawn around the globe, either parallel to the equator (latitude) or from pole to pole (longitude, or meridians). The Earth is divided into 24 time zones, one for each hour of the day. Greenwich is on 0° meridian and time advances by one hour for every 15° of longitude east of Greenwich.

TIME ZONES
The numbers on the map indicate the number of hours that must be subtracted or added to reach GMT. When it is noon at Greenwich, for example, it is 11 p.m. in Sydney, Australia. Time zones are adjusted to regional administrative boundaries.

KEY TO MAP

◐ MINUS HOURS

◐ PLUS HOURS

○ GREENWICH MEAN TIME

◐ DATE LINE

▦ TIME ZONES

GMT
Greenwich Mean Time (GMT) is the time in Greenwich, England. Clocks are set depending on whether they are east or west of Greenwich.

INTERNATIONAL DATE LINE
The International Date Line is an imaginary line that runs along the 180° meridian but deviates around countries.

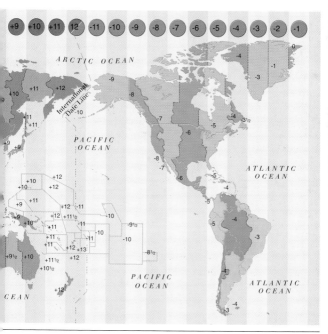

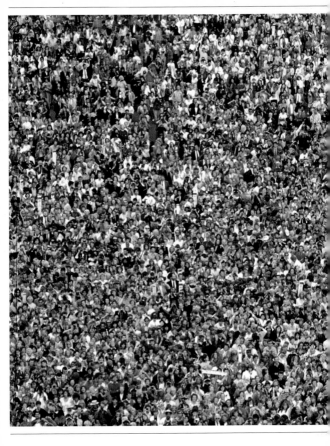

PEOPLE AND SOCIETY

MYTHS AND LEGENDS

ALMOST EVERY culture has stories, or myths, to explain the world around them. Legends are tales that have some basis in real events.

MYTHICAL BEASTS

Many myths are about fantastic beasts, such as the unicorn (a single-horned horse) and the phoenix (a bird that rises from its own ashes). The dragon is a winged serpent that breathes fire. It is an important symbol in cultures as far apart as Wales and China.

DRAGON'S BREATH

KING ARTHUR

One of Britain's most famous legendary figures is the hero King Arthur, who is thought to be based on a real 5th-century Celtic chieftain. One of the many stories about King Arthur tells how he was given the magic sword Excalibur by the Lady of the Lake, as shown in the above picture.

SACRED SITES

• Mt. Shasta, California, USA, is sacred to Native Americans.

• Uluru (Ayers Rock) in Australia is sacred to the Aboriginals.

• The Tor (mound) at Glastonbury, England, is said to be the resting place of the Holy Grail, the cup Christ drank from at the Last Supper.

This mask, made of turquoise mosaic, represents Quetzalcoatl, the chief god of the Aztecs.

AZTEC MYTHS

The mythical world of the Aztec people of Central Mexico, South America, was dominated by the figure of Quetzalcoatl. He was the chief god of the Aztecs, and took the form of a feathered serpent. According to myth, Quetzalcoatl created humans and gave them knowledge, then sailed away on a raft of serpents.

Greek myths

Many stories are told about ancient Greece. Legendary tales, such as those surrounding the Trojan War, have a basis in historical fact, while myths about figures like Perseus and Medusa are more fantastic.

Perseus

Gorgons have a head of snakes instead of hair

Theseus *Minotaur*

PERSEUS AND MEDUSA
One Greek myth tells the story of Perseus, who beheaded a gorgon called Medusa. The gorgon's head had the power to turn people to stone.

THESEUS AND THE MINOTAUR
The Minotaur was a mythical creature, half-man and half-bull, that lived in a labyrinth (maze) on the island of Crete. It was eventually slain by a Theban prince called Theseus.

Greek soldiers hid inside the huge wooden horse

MASK OF KING AGAMEMNON

TROJAN HORSE
According to legend, when the Greeks were fighting the Trojans, they beat them by a trick. They built a wooden horse, then hid in it, outside the gates of Troy. The Trojans dragged the wooden horse into the city to see what it was. At night, the Greek soldiers crept out and opened the city gates to let their army in.

TROJAN WARS
In *The Iliad*, Homer wrote about the Trojan Wars of c. 1200 BC. The legend tells how Agamemnon, King of Mycenae, Greece, led an army against the Trojans to rescue his brother's captured wife, Helen.

RELIGIONS

MOST PEOPLE HAVE some kind of belief or faith that helps to explain life and death. Many worship either one or several gods. The four major world religions are Christianity, Islam, Hinduism, and Buddhism.

CHRISTIANITY

Christians believe that Jesus Christ is the Son of God, and when Jesus was crucified (nailed to a cross), he rose from the dead to join God in Heaven. Christianity has more followers than any other religion.

The cross is the symbol of Christianity

ORIGIN
Christianity began in about AD 30 in Jerusalem, in present-day Israel.

THE BIBLE

This Christian holy book is made up of two parts called the Old and New Testaments. In the Old Testament are the sacred writings of the Jews. The New Testament tells the story of Christ's life and the origin of Christianity.

The first Bible was printed in 1455, by Johannes Gutenberg.

JESUS CHRIST

Jesus lived in the Holy Land (Israel) about 2,000 years ago. From the age of 30, he began to preach and heal the sick. He was tried and put to death for openly challenging Hebrew beliefs.

TEN COMMANDMENTS

Christians try to obey ten rules, which are adapted from the Jewish scriptures.

1 Worship one God.
2 Make no image of God.
3 Respect God's name.
4 Keep Sunday holy.
5 Honour your parents.
6 Do not kill.
7 Do not commit adultery.
8 Do not steal.
9 Do not tell lies.
10 Do not be envious.

ISLAM

A star and a crescent moon symbolize Islam.

The followers of Islam are Muslims, who believe in Allah. Islam means "submission", and Muslims believe they must obey Allah and live by the five pillars (rules) set out in their holy book, the *Koran.*

ORIGIN
Islam began in about AD 600 in Mecca, in present-day Saudi Arabia. It is now practised all over the world.

THE KORAN
In Islam's holy book, Allah shows the prophet Muhammad how people should live. Muslims treat this book with great respect and must wash before touching it.

KORAN (*Qur'an*)

MUHAMMAD
Born in Mecca, Muhammad (c. 570–632) was the last and the greatest of the 26 Islamic prophets.

Muhammad is Allah's messenger.

HINDUISM

The symbol of Hinduism is the sound "Om".

Hindus worship many gods and believe in *dharma*, the correct way to live. Like Buddhists, Hindus believe we have all lived before, as animals as well as people. By following the *dharma*, we may achieve a perfect state of *Moksha* and need never be reborn again.

ORIGIN
Hinduism began in India, in about 1750 BC. It has spread through much of Asia.

VEDAS
Early Hindu beliefs were written as songs and chants in the *Vedas* c. 1400 BC.

The Rig Veda is the most important book of the Vedas.

FOUNDERS
Hinduism has no single founder. The Aryans, who invaded India about 4,000 years ago, brought early Hindu gods, such as Shiva.

SHIVA

BUDDHISM

The symbol of Buddhism is an eight-spoked wheel.

The Buddhist faith is based on the teachings of Buddha, who believed that we must rid ourselves of desire in order to free ourselves from suffering. Buddhists believe that life is a sequence of birth, death, and rebirth, and that by following the Eightfold Path of Buddhism, we can reach a state of peace called *Nirvana*.

ORIGINS
Buddhism began in India in about 500 BC. It is now the religion of 300 million people.

BUDDHA
Prince Siddartha Gautama (Buddha) lived from 563–483 BC. He gave up his riches to preach and meditate.

Buddha means "enlightened one"

Extracts from the Pali Canon

THE PALI
The collected teachings of Buddha are called the *Pali Canon*. The best-known is the *Dhammapada*.

SIKHISM

The Khanda is the symbol of Sikhism.

This faith began in northern India. It is based on the worship of one God, the eternal Guru, and on the cycle of rebirth.

ORIGINS
Sikhism began in north India and Pakistan in about 1500. It has spread to North America and Britain.

This book is treated with great respect

GURU GRANTH SAHIB

GURU GRANTH
This sacred book contains hymns and poems written by the Gurus.

THE FIVE K'S
Sikhs must wear these five items: *Kesh* (uncut hair, under a turban, if a man); *Kara* (a steel bracelet); *Kangha* (a hair comb); *Kirpan* (a sword); and *Kaccha* (short trousers as an undergarment).

Sikh men wear a turban

JUDAISM

The Jewish symbol is the star of David.

Followers of Judaism are called Jews. They believe in one God whose law is written in the *Tanach*. Judaism began about 4,000 years ago in Canaan. Today this area is mainly Israel.

ORIGINS

Judaism originated in about 2000 BC. in Canaan, "the Promised Land". Today, Judaism has spread to most parts of the world.

Tallit, or prayer shawl

Menorah, or branched candlestick

Yarmulke, or skull cap

The Tanach

TANACH

The Jewish Bible, or *Tanach*, tells the history of the Jewish people. The *Torah* is the most important part, as it contains the laws that God revealed to Moses.

SHINTOISM

In Japan, Shintoists worship gods of nature, and there are Shinto shrines in parks, gardens, and on mountains. Shintoists worship alone, and their symbol is the outline of a temple gate.

According to Shinto faith, Mount Fuji is a Shinto god. People come to pray at a shrine on its summit.

CONFUCIANISM

This faith is based on the teachings of K'ung-Fu-tze (551–479 BC), or Confucius, who was known for his wise sayings. In the *Analects*, Confucius taught the wisdom of living in harmony with nature. He said "Never do to others what you would not like them to do to you".

K'UNG-FU-TZE

TAOISM

Lao-Tze founded the faith of Taoism in China 2,400 years ago. Taoists believe in many gods. Their symbol of *Yin Yang* represents the balance and harmony of opposites.

YIN YANG

The name Lao-Tze means "Old Master".

LAO-TZE

GODS AND GODDESSES

MANY OF THE ANCIENT civilizations, such as those in Greece, Rome, and Egypt, worshipped several gods and goddesses.

Ancient Egypt

The gods and goddesses of ancient Egypt often had the body of a human and the head of an animal, which represented that creature's power. The chief of the gods was the Sun-god Re, who had different names at different times of the day.

BASTET, THE CAT-GODDESS

HORUS' EYE
The symbol of the "wadjet" eye represents the vengeful eye of Horus, torn out in the struggle for Egypt.

"WADJET" EYE

BASTET
The goddess Bastet was the daughter of Re, the Sun-god. She represented the power of the Sun to ripen crops, and she took the form of a cat.

OSIRIS
The god of the under-world and judge of the dead was called Osiris. People believed he ruled over a world below ground that looked like Egypt. Osiris took the form of a mummified man.

OSIRIS

ANUBIS
The son of Osiris was the god Anubis, who had the head of a jackal. Anubis was said to guide the souls of the dead to Osiris for their judgement.

ANUBIS

Ancient Greece

The Greeks believed that all the gods were the descendants of Gaia (the earth) and Uranos (the sky), and that they behaved in the same way as humans.

ZEUS
The King of the gods was Zeus, who is represented as a strong, middle-aged man. He was noble, but easily angered.

HEPHAESTUS
The God of fire and the husband of Aphrodite, Hephaestus was lame.

Eros

Aphrodite

MIRROR CASE

APHRODITE
The Greek goddess of love was called Aphrodite.

Pan

APOLLO
The young god of the sun and of medicine was Apollo.

Ancient Rome

The Romans adopted many Greek gods and gave them new names. Aphrodite became Venus, Zeus became Jupiter, and Ares, the god of war, became Mars.

TEMPLES
Many emperors were made gods after their death. Temples such as this were built in their honour.

TEMPLE OF AUGUSTUS AND LIVIA

JUPITER
The king of the Roman gods, Jupiter was a sky-god whose symbols were the eagle and the thunderbolt. Jupiter was much like the Greek god Zeus.

MONEY AND TRADE

THE METAL COINS and paper
banknotes that we use to buy
things are called money, or currency.
Money also comes in the form of
credit cards, cheques, and the
computer records of a bank account.

Cowrie shells were used as money

EARLY MONEY
Before coins were
invented, people used to
exchange stones, shells,
beads, and furs for food
and other goods.

EARLY LYDIAN COIN

THE FIRST COINS
The earliest-known coins
were made in the kingdom
of Lydia (now Turkey)
more than 2,700 years ago.
These coins were weighed
lumps of electrum (a mix
of silver and gold), which
were stamped, or minted
to guarantee their weight.

14TH-CENTURY CHINESE
PAPER MONEY

THE FIRST PAPER MONEY
In 10th-century China, people
began to leave their coins with
merchants, in exchange for a
hand-written paper receipt.
In the 11th century, the Chinese
government fixed the value of
these receipts. This became
the first paper money.

Burnisher for smoothing

Sharp "burins" for engraving the design

The design for the banknote is hand-engraved back-to-front on to a steel plate

MAKING BANK NOTES
Banknotes have to be printed in a very
elaborate and secret way to reduce the
chances of forgery. The four stages of
making a banknote are designing, paper-
making, ink-mixing, and printing.
The design is engraved on a steel plate by
hand. This is called "intaglio" engraving.

PRINTING PLATE

PROOF FOR
BACKGROUND

PROOF FOR MAIN DESIGN

This design uses eight inks, printed in reds, yellows, blues, and buffs.

Every note is individually numbered

NUMBERING MACHINE

The finished specimen banknote is shown to customers all over the world.

FINISHED BANKNOTE

THE STOCK MARKET
People often raise money to start a business by selling "shares" in it. If the business make a profit, the shareholders receive a dividend (payment). The stock market is where shares, or stocks, are bought and sold by "stockbrokers".

IMPORTS AND EXPORTS

BALANCE OF TRADE
Countries measure their success at trading by their "balance of payments", which is the difference between the amount they sell abroad (exports) and the amount they buy in (imports).

TOKYO STOCK EXCHANGE, JAPAN

KEY STOCK EXCHANGES		
Country	City	Index
Japan	Tokyo	Nikkei Average
United States	New York	Dow-Jones
United Kingdom	London	FTSE-100 *
Germany	Frankfurt	DAX **

* Financial Times Stock Exchange 100
** Deutsche Aktien Index

GOVERNMENT AND LAW

ALL COUNTRIES are run by a government. Some are harsh dictatorships, and others are liberal democracies. Every government implements policies that affect the daily lives of the nation's people. The business of government is called politics.

DEMOCRACY

This system, in which a country is ruled by the people, or their elected representatives, began in Athens, Greece, 2,500 years ago. Many other countries are now governed in this way.

Pericles was leader of democratic Athens at the height of its power.

POLITICAL SYSTEMS

Most countries are "capitalist", and the land and businesses are owned by individuals or small groups. In "communist" countries, all businesses are state-run. "Socialists" believe that governments should grant everyone equal rights, a fair share of money, education, health, and housing.

COMMUNIST MAGAZINE

Abraham Lincoln was US president 1861–1865.

PARLIAMENT

In many countries, government policy is debated and the laws are agreed upon in an assembly called parliament. People elect members of parliament to act as their representatives.

HOUSE OF COMMONS, UK

REPUBLIC

Most countries are republics, which have no king or queen. The "head of state" is a president who is elected by the people. The government is also elected by the people. A country with a king or queen is called a monarchy. Kings were once thought to rule by God's will. Their power is now usually limited by a set of rules called a constitution.

BRANCHES OF GOVERNMENT

THE CAPITOL, HOME OF THE US CONGRESS, WASHINGTON, DC

LEGISLATURE
The legislature is an elected assembly, or "house", that amends and makes laws. In the USA, it is called Congress.

EXECUTIVE
The executive puts laws into effect and administers the country. It is headed by a president or a prime minister who appoints heads of different departments.

JUDICIARY
The judiciary makes sure that laws are applied fairly. In the USA, the highest legal body is the Supreme Court.

Law

Every country has rules, or laws, to help people live together and to keep them in order. Laws are decided by governments or religious leaders and they are enforced by the police and the courts.

CRIMINAL LAW
Criminal law covers crimes such as murder and theft.

CIVIL LAW
This kind of law deals with disputes, rather than crimes. Civil law also deals with day-to-day events such as buying a house and making a will.

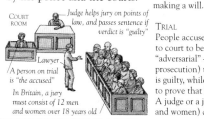

COURT ROOM

Judge helps jury on points of law, and passes sentence if verdict is "guilty"

Lawyer

A person on trial is "the accused"

In Britain, a jury must consist of 12 men and women over 18 years old

TRIAL
People accused of crimes are usually taken to court to be "tried". Typically, trials are "adversarial" – one set of lawyers (the prosecution) tries to prove that the accused is guilty, while another (the defence) tries to prove that he or she is innocent.
A judge or a jury (a group of ordinary men and women) decides who is right.

BUILDINGS

HOUSES, CHURCHES, and offices
are all buildings. The design and
construction of buildings is called
architecture.

*In Oceania, "longhouses" are built
on stilts in case of flooding.*

TRADITIONAL HOMES

People around
the world build
their homes from
the materials they
have available.
From houses of
timber or stone,
to huts of mud or
woven reeds,
every country
has its own style.

*In South Africa, the dome-
shaped kraals have grass roofs.*

*Swiss chalets are built
from wooden timbers.*

*Some Asian nomads live
in canvas or felt "yurts".*

*Algerian houses are close
together to keep out the sun.*

*Japanese houses have
sliding doors.*

*North American houses
have wooden "clapboards".*

CLASSICAL ARCHITECTURE

There are three styles, or
orders, of classical Greek
architecture: Doric,
Ionic, and Corinthian.
The columns of Greek
temples often have a
decorative head, or
capital, on the top.
Across the columns is a
broad lintel called the
entablature. This
consists of an architrave,
a frieze, and a cornice.

Entablature   *Frieze*

Decorative capital

CLASSICAL GREEK TEMPLE

ORDERS

These three
orders were used
in three different
periods of history.

*Doric was used
from 700 BC.*

*Ionic was used
from 600 BC.*

*Corinthian was
used from 500 BC.*

DOMES
Curved roofs, or domes, are a feature of many religious and state buildings around the world.

HEMISPHERICAL DOME

ONION DOME

POLYHEDRAL DOME

SAUCER DOME

VAULTS
Vaults are arched roofs or ceilings. The four main types of vault are shown here.

BARREL VAULT

GROIN VAULT

RIB VAULT

FAN VAULT

ARCHES
An arch is an opening that is curved or pointed at the top. These features are often used in large buildings to span openings and carry weight.

POINTED ARCH

HORSESHOE ARCH

LOBED ARCH

SKYSCRAPERS
The invention of reinforced concrete, plate glass, and steel in the mid 1800s enabled architects to design and build extremely tall constructions, or "skyscrapers". The first skyscrapers were built in Chicago. Giant buildings are now found in most major cities. At 452 m (1,482 ft), the Petronas Tower, in Kuala Lumpur, Malaysia, is the world's tallest building.

NEW YORK SKYSCRAPERS
Many of the skyscrapers in New York City were erected by Iroquois and Mohawk Indians, who showed no fear of heights.

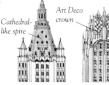

Cathedral-like spire

Art Deco crown

WOOLWORTH BUILDING 1913

GENERAL ELECTRIC BUILDING 1930s

WORLD TRADE CENTER 1971

6500 BC–301 BC

c. 6500 BC One the first known towns, Çatal Hüyük, is built in Turkey, using rectangular mud bricks.

c. 2650–2150 BC Pyramids are built in the lower Nile valley, in Egypt. The Step Pyramid at Saqqara is designed by a High Priest called Imhotep, who is the first known architect.

Massive stones arranged in a huge circle

STONEHENGE, ENGLAND

c. 2200 BC Stonehenge is built in England, using massive stones. It was probably built as a religious monument.

c. 2112–2095 BC The Sumerians build stepped temples called ziggurats in Mesopotamia, using mud bricks.

c. 1700–1200 BC Beehive tombs, or tholos are built by the Mycenaean civilization on the Greek mainland.

c. 1500 BC The Minoan Palace of Knossos is rebuilt on the Greek island of Crete.

800–200 BC Etruscans use arches in the construction of their buildings in what is now called Italy.

700–400 BC The ancient Greeks build temples of such perfect proportions that their style of building becomes known as "classical". This classical style of architecture is copied many times throughout history.

300 BC–AD 850

THE PARTHENON, ATHENS, GREECE

c. 300 BC Buddhists build stupas (mounds) in India and southeastern Asia to symbolize the dome of heaven.

c. 200 BC–AD 500 Roman architecture takes over the classical Greek style and the Etruscan arch. The Romans introduce concrete, which enables them to build huge vaults and arches.

AD 300–1540 Pre-Columbian civilizations in the Americas build stepped pyramids crowned with temples. One of these is the pyramid known as Giant Jaguar, at Tikal in Guatemala.

330–1453 The Byzantine style of architecture develops when the Roman Empire moves its capital to Byzantium, renaming it Constantinople (now Istanbul, Turkey). The largest dome of its time, the Hagia Sophia, is built there in AD 537.

607–670 The oldest surviving wooden building, the Horyuji Buddhist monastery, is built at Nara, in Japan.

618–782 The earliest Chinese timber building, the Nanchan Buddhist temple, is built on a holy mountain in Shaanxi province.

690–850 Early Islamic mosques and palaces are designed around courtyards.

900–1839	1840–TODAY

900–1150 The Romanesque style of architecture spreads across western Europe, featuring round-headed arches on top of cylindrical columns.

1100–1500 The Gothic style is used in Christian churches in northern Europe. It has pointed arches and flying buttresses, allowing very tall, light structures.

1113–1150 Angkor Wat, a vast stone city, is built by the Khmers in what is now Cambodia.

c. 1420 The Renaissance begins in Italy, reviving Roman and Greek building methods. Brunelleschi (1377–1446) and Alberti (1404–1472) are key figures.

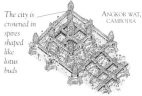

The city is crowned in spires shaped like lotus buds

ANGKOR WAT, CAMBODIA

c. 1650 The Baroque style is developed. Architects are commissioned by the Catholic Church to build very grand, ornate churches and palaces.

1750–1840 Neo-Classical architects return to plain, elegant Roman and Greek styles of building.

1830–1930s During a Gothic revival, architects build churches, public buildings, and even railway stations, in an attempt to recapture the style of medieval cathedrals.

1840–1890 The Industrial Revolution provides new materials, such as plate glass, steel, and reinforced concrete, which transform traditional building methods.

1890 After the invention of the lift, the first skyscrapers are built in Chicago.

1900–40s American architect Frank Lloyd Wright (1867–1959) promotes "organic" architecture, designing buildings that blend in with nature.

1919–33 Walter Gropius (1883–1969) leads a design team in Weimar, Germany (the Bauhaus school), creating designs based on modern industrial technology.

1920s The Swiss architect, Le Corbusier (1887–1965) leads the new style of International Modernism in building design.

1970s A "hi-tech" style, with much steel, glass, and exposed pipes, is led by Richard Rogers (b. 1933) and Norman Foster (b. 1935).

Late 1970s Post-modern design develops. New designs blend elements from the architectural styles of different eras and cultures.

1980s–1990s Architects begin to take environmental concerns into account, such as recycling and saving energy. Some new buildings use solar power.

EMPIRE STATE BUILDING, NEW YORK CITY, USA

ARTISTS' MATERIALS

ARTISTS paint pictures and create sculptures.
The main materials that an artist needs for painting
are sketching materials (for an initial drawing or a
finished work), paint and paintbrushes, and a surface
to paint on. This surface may be paper for watercolour
painting, canvas for oils, or wood for acrylics.

SCULPTURE
A sculptor can use almost
any material for sculpting,
but bronze, marble,
and clay are the most
popular for figurative
work (based on
the human
body).

*Early
sculptures, like
this figurine of a
woman, were made of clay.*

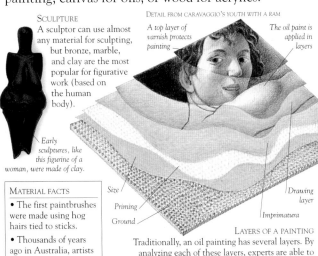

DETAIL FROM CARAVAGGIO'S YOUTH WITH A RAM

*A top layer of
varnish protects
painting*

*The oil paint is
applied in
layers*

Size

Priming

Ground

*Drawing
layer*

Imprimatura

MATERIAL FACTS
• The first paintbrushes
were made using hog
hairs tied to sticks.
• Thousands of years
ago in Australia, artists
mixed natural pigments
in their mouths to paint
cave walls.

LAYERS OF A PAINTING
Traditionally, an oil painting has several layers. By
analyzing each of these layers, experts are able to
date a picture accurately, and they can also tell if
it is a fake. This artwork, showing a section of
Caravaggio's *Youth with a Ram*, shows the layers
that were used in paintings of the 17th century.

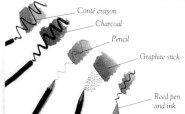

DRAWING TOOLS

Most drawings are sketches (quick drawings) done as a preparation for a finished work. But a drawing can also be a finished picture in itself. Artists usually draw with dry materials such as pencils, crayons, or charcoal.

Conté crayon

Charcoal

Pencil

Graphite stick

Reed pen and ink

PAINTS

The three main kinds of paint are oils, which were first used in the 1400s; watercolours, popular with 18th century landscape artists; and acrylics, popular in the 1960s.

Oil paints are a mixture of dry pigment and an oil such as linseed.

Watercolour paints are pigments bound with gum arabic. They are diluted with water.

Acrylic paints are either applied with a knife or diluted and used with a paintbrush.

PAINTBRUSHES

The two main kinds of paintbrush are soft-hair brushes for watercolours, and bristle brushes for oil paintings and acrylics. The length and shape of the hairs on a brush may be round, flat, or "filbert".

ROUND   FLAT   FILBERT

MONA LISA

The most famous painting is Leonardo da Vinci's *Mona Lisa*, painted in 1503. It is a portrait of Lisa, the wife of a nobleman named Francesco del Gioconda. That is why the painting is sometimes called *La Gioconda*.

MONA LISA, THE LOUVRE, PARIS

Malachite makes a green pigment.

Lapis lazuli makes a blue pigment.

PIGMENTS

Paint is made from powdered colours called pigments. These were originally natural colours from plants and rocks, but today most are made using chemicals.

2700 BC–AD 599

c. 27,000 BC Small clay statues of pregnant women, known as "Venus figurines" appear across Europe.

c. 15,000 BC Early artists use fingers, brushes, and hollow reeds to paint animals on the walls of the Lascaux caves, France.

VENUS FIGURINE, FRANCE C. 27,000 BC

c. 4000–1000 BC Egyptian art includes wall and scroll paintings, gold jewellery, and painted statues sculpted from limestone.

2000–1100 BC Minoans on the island of Crete, Greece decorate their palace walls with coloured murals.

1600–1027 BC The Shang dynasty in China discovers how to cast bronze and create bowls and jugs for food and wine.

c. 500 BC The Nok culture in Nigeria, West Africa, produces life-like terracotta figurines of humans.

c. 500–323 BC Greek sculptors produce elegant statues of gods and athletes made of marble, bronze, and clay.

AD 100–400 Gandharan sculpture develops in the Indus valley, Pakistan. It is influenced by Greek art, and shows scenes from the life of Buddha.

100–1000 Mayan carvings are created in Central America, combining ornate figures with hieroglyphs (picture writing).

400–1110 Medieval monks in Europe create illuminated manuscripts.

600–1839

600–1185 Icons (religious portraits) are painted in Eastern Europe.

618–907 Chinese artists of the T'ang dynasty paint stunning landscapes.

1000–1200 The Romanesque style develops in the church sculptures and murals of Europe.

1000–1600 Huge stone figures are made on Easter Island, Polynesia.

1368–1644 The Ming dynasty in China is famous for its blue-glazed porcelain bowls and vases.

1400–1500 The Renaissance begins in Florence, Italy. Masaccio (1401–1428) uses perspective in his paintings.

Late 1400s Islamic miniature painting flourishes in Persia.

1490–1520 The High Renaissance, exemplified in works by Leonardo da Vinci

THE ANNUNCIATION, LEONARDO DA VINCI

(1452–1519), Michelangelo (1475–1564), and Raphael (1483–1520).

1600s The golden age of Dutch painting, with pictures by Rembrandt (1606–1669) and Vermeer (1632–1675).

Late 1700s–mid 1800s The Romantic school, notably Turner (1775–1851) and Friedrich (1774–1840) focuses on human emotions and nature.

1840–1899

1840s Realism develops in France, with painters such as Courbet (1819–1877) depicting people in a more life-like way.

THE WINNOWERS, GUSTAVE COURBET 1855

1850s–70s Pre-Raphaelites in England, such as Millais (1829–1896), Burne-Jones (1833–1898), and Rossetti (1828–1882) are influenced by artists before Raphael, but develop their own style of painting.
1860s–90s Impressionism begins in France as painters try to capture their impressions of fleeting moments, especially Monet (1840–1926) and Manet (1832–1883).
1880–1905 Post-Impressionist artists such as Cézanne (1839–1906), Van Gogh (1853–1890), and Gauguin (1848–1903) develop their own style, using strong colours and shapes.
1880s–1890s Expressionism develops in Europe as artists such as Kirchner (1880–1938) use intense colour and free brushstrokes to express their feelings.
1880s–90s Symbolist artists such as Moreau (1826–1898) create images based on symbolic inner meanings.

1900–TODAY

1907–1920s Cubism develops in Paris with Picasso (1881–1973) and Braque (1882–1963) using bold geometric shapes.
1910–50 Artists of the Abstract movement, led by Kandinsky (1866–1944) begin to paint and sculpt ideas instead of realistic objects.
1916 The Dada movement, originally a protest against World War I, rejects traditional forms of art.
1920s Surrealist painters such as Dali (1904–1989) and Ernst (1891–1976) explore their dreams and Freud's psychoanalytic ideas in their painting.
1940s Abstract Expressionism appears in New York, where artists such as Jackson Pollock (1912–1956) experiment with the physical properties of paint.
1950s–60s Pop Art develops in the US and Britain as artists such as Warhol (1928–87) begin to use consumer goods and images from the media in their art.
1960s–90s Performance artists such as Gilbert (b. 1943) & George (b. 1942) combine music, theatre, film, and video in their work.
1970s–90s Video artists such as Korean-born Nam Jun Paik (b. 1932) feature video projection and computer technology in their exhibitions.

PLANTED, GILBERT AND GEORGE 1992

MUSICAL INSTRUMENTS

THERE ARE THOUSANDS of musical instruments, each making its own distinctive sound. They are usually grouped into percussion, strings, woodwind, brass, and keyboard.

HARP
Harps date back at least 6,000 years. Strings stretched over a frame are finger plucked to give a beautiful rippling sound. This harp is for traditional Irish music.

IRISH HARP

Strings

All stringed instruments consist of a series of stretched strings connected to a hollow box that amplifies (makes louder) the string's vibrations. The string is set in motion by being plucked, as with a harp; by the friction of a bow, as with a violin, or by being struck, as with a piano.

Strands of horse hair

VIOLIN AND BOW

Tuning pegs are turned to change pitch of each string

Thinnest string has highest pitch

VIOLIN
The violin family was invented in around 1550 and now consists of the violin, viola, cello and bass. The strings are usually played with a bow.

All members of the violin family have an F-shaped sound hole

Bridge supports strings

Magnetic pick-ups convert string vibrations into electrical signals

Screw for tightening bow

Machine heads for tuning strings

Frets

Neck

Tremolo arm

ELECTRIC GUITAR

Steel truss rod to strengthen neck

GUITAR
The electric guitar is a key instrument in rock and pop music. In an electric guitar, plucked strings are amplified electronically.

Crash cymbal

Tom-tom drums

Ride cymbal

DRUM KIT

Snare drum *Bass drum*

PERCUSSION

Instruments that are played by hitting them are called percussion. They include drums, cymbals, xylophones, gongs, and much more. Percussion underlines the rhythm of the music.

Heavy iron frame

Hammers strike strings to make sound

Tuning pins

88-note keyboard – pressing the keys swings hammers

KEYBOARD

Keyboards, including harpsichord, piano, organ, and synthesizer, are among the most versatile of all instruments. They are played by pressing levers or keys with the fingers.

WIND INSTRUMENTS

WOODWIND

Flutes, clarinets, oboes, and bassoons all have a reed in the mouthpiece to set up the vibrations that make the sound. They are called woodwind even though they are often made of brass.

Mouthpiece

Thumb keys

Neck

Pads change notes

SAXOPHONE

The saxophone is neither woodwind nor brass. It is shaped like a brass instrument but has a reed.

Bell projects sound

Blow hole

FLUTE

BRASS

Brass instruments include cornet, trumpet, horn, tuba, and trombone. The sound is made by the vibration of the player's lips against the mouthpiece.

Valve

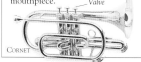

CORNET

MUSIC

ROCK, JAZZ, AND FOLK MUSIC are often played from
memory by small groups of talented musicians. Some
types of music, such as classical music, is written down
for orchestras of people playing different instruments.

THE ORCHESTRA
Orchestras range from small
string orchestras to
huge symphony
orchestras with
90 or more
players. Similar
instruments are
grouped together.

Vibraphone
Timpani
Drums
Gong
PERCUSSION
Tuba
Trombone
French horn
Trumpet
BRASS
Saxophone
Bassoon
WOODWIND
Piano
Clarinet
Oboe
Double bass
Flutes
Strings in small groups called desks
Piccolo
Cello
STRINGS
1st violins
Viola
Conductor
2nd violins
STRINGS
Harp

MUSICAL GROUPS
Musical groups range from duos with
two performers to symphony orchestras
with up to 120.

*A jazz quartet includes
drums and bass; a
string quartet is two
violins, viola, and cello.*

*A quintet usually
has five wind or
five brass
instruments.*

Violin *Viola* *Cello*

CELLO AND PIANO DUO   STRING TRIO   JAZZ QUARTET   MIXED QUINTET

PITCH

The pitch of each note is shown by how high it sits on the stave. Musical pitch is grouped into eight notes called an octave. The notes of each octave are named from low to high using the letters A to G, plus the A that begins the next octave.

ONE OCTAVE OF THE SCALE OF C MAJOR

C Major notes on stave correspond to white keys on piano keyboard

PIANO KEYBOARD

NOTE VALUES

Name	Sign	Rest
Semibreve (4 beats)	o	
Minim (2 beats)		
Crotchet (1 beat)		
Quaver (half-beat)		
Semiquaver (quarter-beat)		
Demiquaver (32nd-beat)		

Key signature shows which key music is in

More than two notes played together produces a chord

Natural sign cancels sharp or flat on next note

Rest shows length of pause in music

mf

sf

Treble clef. The bass stave has a bass clef

Time signature shows type and number of beats in a bar, or measure

Dot makes note last as long again

Quavers equal half a beat

Bar line marks end of bar, or measure

Sforzando means accent (emphasize) the note loudly

Dynamic markings indicate how loud or soft to play music – mf means mezzo-forte, or moderately loud

MUSICAL NOTATION

Composers write down music using an international code of signs and symbols that enables musicians to interpret and play a composition. The notes are written on two bands of five lines, called staves. The lower stave (bass) is for low notes; the upper stave (treble) is for higher notes. Music is divided into measures called bars, each with the same number of beats.

15,000 BC–AD 650	770–1750

Before 15,000 BC Stone-Age people played bone flutes.

c. 3000 BC Harps and lyres appear in Sumerian writing.

2600 BC Pa-Pab-Bi-gagir-gal of Ur in Mesopotamia is the first musician whose name is known.

c. 2500 BC Oldest-known harp placed in Queen Puabi's tomb at Ur.

EGYPTIAN TOMB PAINTING

2200 BC Groups of musicians appear in Egyptian tomb paintings.

605 BC King Nebuchadnezzar of Babylon has an orchestra play at the dedication ceremony of an image of himself made in gold.

c. 550 BC The ancient Greek philosopher Pythagoras (580–500 BC) creates the first mathematical theory of musical harmony.

408 BC The oldest fragment of written music is a chorus for a play called *Orestes*, by ancient Greek dramatist Euripides (c. 480–406 BC).

AD 650 School for church music founded in Rome by Pope Gregory (c. AD 540–604) develops Gregorian chant, a style of singing.

700s Orchestras play *gamelan* (gongs) in Indonesia, to accompany traditional puppet shows and dance.

750 The Court of Caliph Harun al-Rashid in Persia becomes famous for its music played by musicians, like Ishaq al-Mausili (767–850).

1100s Monks add a second or third tune to the simple "plainsong" of the Gregorian chant to create the first polyphonic music.

1300s Paris becomes focus of polyphonic music, and early French composer Guillaume de Machaut (1300–1377) writes ballads (songs) in this form.

1480 First printed music in Europe.

1500s Palestrina (1525–1594) and Monteverdi (1567–1643) write polyphonic vocal masses for church.

FIRST PRINTED MUSIC IN EUROPE

1500s Polyphonic music played on instruments such as viola and lutes, especially for dances such as the pavane.

1600s Opera developed by the Camerata, a group of poets and musicians in Florence, Italy.

1600–1750 Baroque-Era composers write in harmony, creating melody by combining notes from the major and minor scales. Baroque pieces contrast loud, soft, fast, and slow musical passages.

1650–1889

1650–1700
Composers like
J.S. Bach
(1685–1750),
Vivaldi
(1678–1741),
and Handel
(1685–1759) write
elaborate
instrumental works
called sonatas and
concerto grossos.

J.S. BACH

1750–1820 In the Classical Era,
instrumental pieces are clearly
structured and elegant.
Late 1700s Classical music is brought to
a peak by Mozart (1756–1791) and
Beethoven (1770–1827).
Early 1800s Beethoven writes
emotional, passionate pieces on a grand
scale, ushering in the Romantic Era.
1820–1900 The Romantic Era features
composers such as Schubert
(1797–1828), Berlioz (1803–1869), and
Wagner (1813–1883), who write great
piano and orchestral works.
1830s–1850s Liszt (1811–1886) and
Chopin (1810–1849) compose dazzling,
virtuoso piano music.
1870s–1880s Verdi (1813–1901) takes
opera to new heights.
1860s–1890s Composers like Dvořák
(1841–1904), Grieg (1843–1907), and
Tchaikovsky (1840–1893), are inspired
by the folk music of their countries.
1870s Wagner creates a new form
of music drama.

1890–TODAY

Late 1800s Blues played by black
Americans.
c. 1900 Jazz music appears in New
Orleans, USA, combining African
rhythms and Western harmony.
Early 1900s Composers, like Stravinsky
(1882–1971) and Bartók (1881–1945),
begin to write music in which dissonance
(clashing notes) creates a thrilling sound.
1910s onwards Schoenberg (1874–1951)
creates "atonal" music in which the key
shifts continually.
1930s Gershwin (1898–1937)
mixes jazz and classical music in
Rhapsody in Blue.
1950s Black Americans play rock and
roll, later taken up by white singers, such
as Buddy Holly and Elvis Presley.
1960s Rock and roll develops into
rock, with bands such as The Who and
The Rolling Stones, and pop, with groups
like The Beatles and The Beach Boys.
1970s Groups such as The Bee Gees and
Chic make disco music popular.
1980s Electronic
dance music emerges
from black American
neighbourhoods into
mainstream music.
1990s Energetic
dance beats, such as
house, techno, and
jungle, are popular.
Emergence of guitar-
based "alternative"
rock.

ROCK SINGER
CHUCK BERRY

DANCE

OVER THOUSANDS of years, varied styles of dance have developed all over the world.

DANCE TIMELINE

15,000 BC Stone-Age rock paintings show people dancing.

TANZANIAN ROCK PAINTING

3000–1000 BC Ancient Egyptians use ritual dance to worship gods such as Isis.

AD 400 First Kagura dances are performed at Shinto shrines in Japan.

1300–1500 Mass dances in Europe cause frenzy.

Late 1400s *Ballo*, Italian dance with a storyline, is the earliest form of ballet.

c. 1600 Kathakali dance emerges in India.

1830s–1840s Romantic ballet flourishes.

c. 1900 Isadora Duncan (1877–1927) develops freer forms of modern dance.

1930s Fred Astaire popularizes tap dancing.

1950s Rock-and-roll dancing.

1980s Break dancing and body-popping are born.

FRED ASTAIRE

1990s Companies design dances for TV and stage.

BALLET

The three main ballet styles are Romantic, Classical, and Modern, distinguished mainly by differences in clothing and music. All ballet dancers learn five basic positions for the arms and feet.

FIVE BASIC ARM POSITIONS

FIRST

SECOND

THIRD

FOURTH

FIFTH

FIVE BASIC FEET POSITIONS

FIRST

SECOND

THIRD

FOURTH

FIFTH

Arm movements are slow

Hand movements are complex

Traditional costume

TRADITIONAL DANCE

Nearly every country in the world has its own traditional form of dance. These dances have often developed from simple religious or tribal rituals into complex dance forms with set movements.

THAI CLASSICAL DANCER

THEATRE

MODERN THEATRE originated in ancient Greece, where actors wearing masks were used to tell a story or demonstrate a theme.

THEATRE BUILDING

The ancient Greeks saw theatre in vast open-air stadiums; modern theatres are smaller and indoors, and take many forms.

Several exits for complex plays

ENGLISH 16TH-CENTURY THEATRE

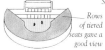

Rows of tiered seats gave a good view

ANCIENT GREEK AMPHITHEATRE

Seats

MODERN THEATRE

SHAKESPEARE

William Shakespeare (1564–1616) was born in Stratford-upon-Avon, England. In about 1590, he moved to London, where he wrote at least 37 plays, including *Hamlet* and *Romeo and Juliet*.

KABUKI THEATRE

The performers of Kabuki theatre are men who wear elaborate make-up to play a particular role.

WICKED MALE   CRAB   NOBLE MALE

THEATRE TIMELINE

c. 3000 BC Religious rituals involve music and drama.

c. 1000 BC Chinese and Indian dance-dramas become formalized.

c. 500 BC Thousands of ancient Greeks see dramas by Aeschylus (525–456 BC), Sophocles (496–406 BC), and Euripides (484–406 BC).

AD 1–100 "Pantomimus" popular in Rome.

c. 1500 Commedia dell'Arte, mimed comedy, spreads from Italy.

1603 Okuni, a young Japanese woman, creates Kabuki theatre.

Early 1600s Theatre flourishes in England and Spain with writers like Shakespeare and Lope de Vega (1562–1635).

COMMEDIA DELL'ARTE

c. 1800 Peking Opera begins in China.

1870s–90s New form of realistic drama created by Ibsen (1828–1906).

PEKING OPERA

3500 BC–AD 1380	1380–1840s

c. 3500 BC The oldest known writing of marks on clay tablets are made at the Sumerian city of Uruk.

3300 BC Egyptians write in hieroglyphs (picture writing).

c. 2000 BC The Sumerian epic *Gilgamesh* is recorded on clay tablets.

c. 800 BC The Greek writer Homer writes *The Iliad*.

600 BC The Greek writer Aesop writes his fables, which include the story of *The Boy Who Cried Wolf* and *The Crow and Pitcher*.

AESOP'S FABLES

500 BC Hindu *Bhagavadgita* written.

200 BC Greeks invent parchment.

c. 30–19 BC Roman writer Virgil writes *The Aeneid*.

AD 105 Chinese invent paper.

868 Earliest printed book, the Chinese *Diamond Sutra*.

1007 In Japan, Murasaki Shikibu (973–1014) writes *The Tale of Genji*, the world's first novel.

1048–1123 Persian poet Omar Khayyam writes *The Rubáiyát*.

1190–1320 Icelandic saga (oral tales) written down.

1321 Dante (1265–1321) writes his *Divine Comedy* in Ravenna, Italy.

c. 1350 Boccaccio (1313–1375) writes *The Decameron* in Florence.

c. 1387 Chaucer (1343–1400) writes *The Canterbury Tales* in Windsor Castle.

GUTENBERG'S BIBLE

c. 1450 Johannes Gutenberg (1390–1468) invents printing by movable type in Germany.

1605 Cervantes (1547–1616) writes *Don Quixote*, a satire about an elderly Spanish knight.

1667 English poet Milton (1608–1674) writes *Paradise Lost*.

1697 French author Charles Perrault (1628–1703) writes *Tales of Mother Goose*.

1719 English writer Daniel Defoe (1660–1731) writes *Robinson Crusoe*.

1808 German poet Goethe (1749–1832) writes *Faust*.

1811–1817 Jane Austen (1775–1817) writes *Pride and Prejudice*, *Emma*, and other novels.

1818 Mary Shelley (1797–1851) writes *Frankenstein*.

1830s French novelist Balzac (1799–1850) writes *Père Goriot*.

1841 American writer Edgar Allen Poe (1809–1849) writes *Murders in the Rue Morgue*, the first detective story.

1840–70 Charles Dickens (1812–1870) writes *Great Expectations*, *Oliver Twist*, and other novels, often in parts that were serialized in magazines of the time.

1840s–1869

1840s Charlotte Brontë (1816–1855) writes *Jane Eyre*, her sister Emily (1818–1848) *Wuthering Heights*.

CHARLOTTE BRONTË

1851 American writer Herman Melville (1819–1891) writes *Moby Dick*.

1852 American writer Harriet Beecher Stowe (1811–1896) writes *Uncle Tom's Cabin* about the injustice of slavery.

1857 French author Gustave Flaubert (1821–1880) writes *Madame Bovary*.

1862 French author Victor Hugo (1802–1885) writes *Les Misérables*.

1864 French author Jules Verne (1828–1905) writes *Journey to the Centre of the Earth*.

1865–72 Russian writer Tolstoy (1828–1910) writes *War and Peace*.

1866 Russian writer Dostoyevsky (1821–1881) writes *Crime and Punishment*.

1867 French writer Émile Zola (1840–1902) writes *Thérèse Raquin*.

1873 The first typewriter is made in the USA by the Remington company.

1881 American author Henry James (1843–1916) writes *Portrait of a Lady*.

1883 Robert Louis Stevenson (1850–1894) writes *Treasure Island*.

1894 Rudyard Kipling (1865–1936) writes *The Jungle Book*.

1900–TODAY

1926 A.A. Milne (1882–1956) writes *Winnie-the-Pooh*.

1870–1900 Thomas Hardy (1840–1928) writes many novels and poems.

1913 Indian poet Rabindranath Tagore (1861–1941) writes *Gitanjali*.

1913 D. H. Lawrence (1885–1930) writes *Sons and Lovers*.

1917 Czech writer Franz Kafka (1883–1924) writes *The Trial*.

1922 Publication of French writer Marcel Proust's (1871–1922) *Remembrance of Things Past*; Irish writer James Joyce's (1882–1941) *Ulysses*.

1925 American writer F. Scott Fitzgerald (1896–1940) writes *The Great Gatsby*.

1929 Ernest Hemingway (1899–1961) writes *Farewell to Arms*.

EARLY PAPERBACKS

1935 The first paperback books go on sale.

1943 Dutch Jewish girl Anne Frank (1929–1945) writes her diary.

1970s Desktop publishing arrives.

1986 The first CD-ROM book.

A CD-ROM holds text, sound, and moving images, and many books can be stored on one disc.

PHOTOGRAPHY

MILLIONS OF TIMES a day, a camera
shutter clicks somewhere in the
world to take a photograph, making
an instant visual record of a scene,
whether it is just a family snapshot
or a dramatic news picture.

35-MM
ROLL FILM

INSIDE AN SLR CAMERA
The most popular type of camera with serious
amateurs and many professional photographers is
the SLR, or Single Lens Reflex. The SLR has a
prism that reflects light from the lens to the
eyepiece, allowing the photographer to see
directly through the camera lens.
It also has interchangeable lenses.

FILM FORMATS
Cameras are built to suit
particular film formats
(sizes). The most popular
format is 35 mm, which is
used in most compacts and
SLRs. Studio photographers
often use a medium format
for extra quality.

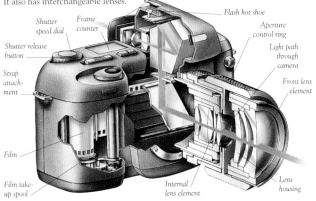

*Rear
viewfinder*

*Shutter
speed dial*

*Frame
counter*

Flash hot shoe

*Aperture
control ring*

*Shutter release
button*

*Light path
through
camera*

*Strap
attach-
ment*

*Front lens
element*

Film

*Film take-
up spool*

*Internal
lens element*

*Lens
housing*

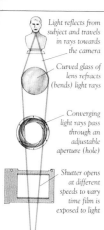

Light reflects from subject and travels in rays towards the camera

Curved glass of lens refracts (bends) light rays

Converging light rays pass through an adjustable aperture (hole)

Shutter opens at different speeds to vary time film is exposed to light

When lens is focused, light rays focus on the film to create a sharp image

LIGHT INSIDE A CAMERA
A camera is essentially a lightproof box with a hole at the front holding a glass lens. The lens projects a bright, sharp picture of the world into the camera where it is recorded on film, or, in electronic cameras (such as videos), on light-sensitive cells.

PHOTOGRAPHY TIMELINE

400 BC Chinese scholar uses a pinhole in silk to project an image in a darkened room.

18TH-CENTURY CAMERA OBSCURA

AD 1020 Arab scholar Alhazen describes how a pinhole in a camera obscura (dark room) can be used to view solar eclipses.

1558 Battista della Porta fits a lens in the pinhole to sharpen the image.

1560–1860 Camera obscuras become common in public buildings.

1700s Portable camera obscuras made for artists.

1727 Johann Schulze (1687–1744) shows how silver nitrate darkens when exposed to light.

c. 1800 Tom Wedgwood makes images by exposing paper coated with silver salts to the light.

1826 First photo made by Joseph Niepce (1765–1833) on a pewter plate in a camera obscura.

1839 Daguerreotype, first practical photographic process, invented by Frenchman Louis Daguerre (1800–1877).

1839 Fox Talbot (1800–1877) creates negatives using Calotype process, enabling copies of photos to be made.

1851 Archer's (1813–1857) Collodion allows paper prints to be made from glass negatives.

1861 Maxwell (1831–1879) makes first colour photo.

1888 First Kodak camera, using roll film.

1906 First practical colour photo process invented by French Lumière brothers.

EARLY COLOUR FILM

1913 35-mm film invented.

1924 The Leica, the first successful 35-mm camera.

1935 Kodachrome colour transparency film.

1947 First instant camera invented by Land (1909–1991) marketed as Polaroid.

1994 First electronic still and video camera launched.

CINEMA

CINEMA IS a multi-million-dollar business, with people all over the world visiting the cinema to see feature films. Many high-budget films use complex special effects, as well as "movie stars", to attract audiences.

ARNOLD SCHWARZENEGGER IN *TERMINATOR 2*

FILM
Most films are now recorded on 35-mm film. All the pictures on the film are still, but they are run through the projector so quickly – eight frames, or pictures, a second – that we see only continuous movement on the screen. One full-length feature uses 2.5 km (1.5 miles) of film.

9.5-mm film introduced by French Pathé company in 1922 for amateur films

Sound track

35-MM FILM

FILM GENRES
Most feature films fall into one of a several categories or "genres", including comedy (*Four Weddings and a Funeral*), romance (*Tin Cup*), science fiction (*Terminator 2*), action (*Die Hard*), or horror (*Interview with the Vampire*).

SPECIAL EFFECTS
Computer technology has dramatically increased the scope of special effects, allowing techniques such as morphing.

The points of both the hand and the spider are plotted on the computer. When the two sets of points coincide, the transformation is complete.

Morphing is used to transform one thing into another or to create animation in a live-action film.

The outline of the spider is just visible.

The mid-point of the morphing process.

The spider is almost complete.

ANIMATION

By filming drawings or models in different positions, animators can bring them to life. Computer-generated animation can produce very sophisticated animation sequences, such as those seen in *Toy Story*.

Bugs Bunny is one of the oldest cartoon characters.

Plasticine models can be moved to animate them, like this gorilla from Creature Comforts.

CINEMA TIMELINE

1879 The Zoogyroscope is developed by English photographer Eadweard Muybridge (1830–1914). It projects images of photographic sequences onto a screen in quick succession, creating an illusion of movement.

1881 Frenchman Étienne Marey (1830–1904) invents a camera that takes pictures on a revolving plate.

1894 Kinetograph (film camera) and Kinetoscope (film viewer) marketed by Americans Thomas Edison (1847–1931) and W.K Dickson (1860–1933).

1895 French Lumière brothers show the first real film in a theatre in Paris.

1895 The world's first cinema opens in Atlanta, Georgia, USA.

1913 Hollywood's first feature film, *Squaw Man*, made by Jesse Lasky (1880–1958), Cecil B. de Mille (1881–1959), and Samuel Goldwyn (1882–1974). Early films are in black and white and silent.

1920–1930s Picture palaces reach the peak of their popularity.

1927 *The Jazz Singer* is the first "talkie" (movie with sound).

JAZZ SINGER POSTER

1929 The first Oscars.

1932 Technicolor invented.

1953 Wide-screen image created by Cinemascope.

1970 Steadicam allows camera operator to move while holding camera steady.

OSCAR

1990s Computer graphics used to make animations.

THE OLYMPIC GAMES

HELD EVERY FOUR YEARS, the modern Games began in 1896 as the brainchild of French scholar Pierre de Coubertin, who was inspired by stories of the ancient Greek games. Separate Winter Olympics have been staged since 1924, and Paralympics for the disabled since 1960.

OLYMPIC FLAME
Following ancient Greek tradition, the Olympics are still started by a torch, which is lit on Mount Olympus in Greece and carried by runners in relays to the Olympic stadium.

OLYMPIC SYMBOL
The five Olympic rings represent the five continents of the world. Some 200 nations send more than 10,000 entrants to compete in nearly 30 different sports.

OLIVE WREATH
In the ancient Greek games, 2,000 years ago, winners were crowned with a sacred olive wreath.

PARALYMPICS
Like the Olympics, the Paralympic Games for disabled people are held every four years.

OLYMPIC MEDALS
In the modern Olympics, individuals and teams compete for gold (first), silver (second), and bronze (third) medals.

GOLD MEDAL FROM THE 1984 GAMES

WINTER OLYMPICS
The Winter Games, held two years after the Summer Olympics, include skiing, figure and speed skating, and ice-hockey.

CLASSIFICATION OF SPORTS

The many different types of sport can be classified into three basic groups, which can then be subdivided further.

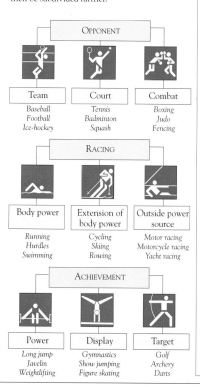

OPPONENT

Team	Court	Combat
Baseball	*Tennis*	*Boxing*
Football	*Badminton*	*Judo*
Ice-hockey	*Squash*	*Fencing*

RACING

Body power	Extension of body power	Outside power source
Running	*Cycling*	*Motor racing*
Hurdles	*Skiing*	*Motorcycle racing*
Swimming	*Rowing*	*Yacht racing*

ACHIEVEMENT

Power	Display	Target
Long jump	*Gymnastics*	*Golf*
Javelin	*Show jumping*	*Archery*
Weightlifting	*Figure skating*	*Darts*

SUMMER OLYMPIC VENUES

Year	Venue
1896	Athens, Greece
1900	Paris, France
1904	St Louis, USA
1908	London, UK
1912	Stockholm, Sweden
1920	Antwerp, Belgium
1924	Paris, France
1928	Amsterdam, Holland
1932	Los Angeles, USA
1936	Berlin, Germany
1948	London, UK
1952	Helsinki, Finland
1956	Melbourne, Australia
1960	Rome, Italy
1964	Tokyo, Japan
1968	Mexico City, Mexico
1972	Munich, Germany
1976	Montreal, Canada
1980	Moscow, USSR
1984	Los Angeles, USA
1988	Seoul, South Korea
1992	Barcelona, Spain
1996	Atlanta, USA
2000	Sydney, Australia

BALL GAMES

MANY TEAM GAMES are played with a large, inflated ball. Soccer, volleyball, and basketball are played with a round ball. Other forms of football use an oval ball.

AMERICAN FOOTBALL

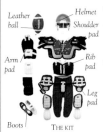

Leather ball

Helmet

Shoulder pad

Arm pad

Rib pad

Leg pad

Boots

THE KIT

THE GAME
American football is a tough game of running, passing, and body-tackling. The field is divided into strips. When a team has the ball it tries to advance the ball strip by strip in a series of "downs".

THE SNAP
Each down starts with a snap, as the centre passes the ball back to the quarterback, who sets up a play by throwing a pass or slipping the ball to a running back.

SOCCER

Team colours on shirt

SOCCER PLAYER

Round leather ball

THE GAME
Soccer is the world's most widely played game, and attracts more spectators than any other sport. A match is played by two teams of 11 players each, and the aim is to score by kicking or heading the ball into the opponent's goal.

45–90 m wide

Penalty area

90–120 m long

Centre circle

Halfway line

Penalty spot

Goal area

THE PITCH
Soccer pitches are almost always of grass and vary in size, but penalty areas are always the same.

VOLLEYBALL

Two teams of six players use their hands and arms to knock a ball over a net. A point is won if the ball lands in the opposition's court or if they fail to return it. The high net means players must jump high.

OVERHAND SERVE

Forearms or fingers are used to knock the ball up, ready for the spike.

UNDERHAND SERVE

PREPARING TO SPIKE (SMASH)

A team may touch the ball up to three times before returning it.

FOREARM PASS (DIG)

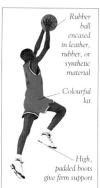

Rubber ball encased in leather, rubber, or synthetic material

Colourful kit

High, padded boots give firm support

BASKETBALL

In this fast, popular game, teams of five dribble the ball with their hands or pass and compete to throw the ball into the opponent's net.

RUGBY

Rugby Union has teams of 15 players; Rugby League has 13. Both games involve running, passing, and body-tackling. In Union, play often restarts with a scrum in which forwards interlock and try to push each other over the ball.

Scrum breaks when ball is cleared.

RUGBY UNION SCRUM

AUSTRALIAN RULES

This 18-a-side game, developed in Melbourne c. 1858, is played on an oval field in four quarters of 25 minutes each. Players kick, handpass, and run with the oval ball.

Goalposts

AUSTRALIAN RULES PITCH

BALL AND STICK GAMES

MANY OF THE WORLD'S
most popular games involve
hitting a small ball with a
stick, a bat, or a racket.

BASEBALL

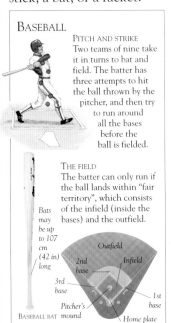

PITCH AND STRIKE
Two teams of nine take
it in turns to bat and
field. The batter has
three attempts to hit
the ball thrown by the
pitcher, and then try
to run around
all the bases
before the
ball is fielded.

THE FIELD
The batter can only run if
the ball lands within "fair
territory", which consists
of the infield (inside the
bases) and the outfield.

*Bats
may
be up
to 107
cm
(42 in)
long*

Outfield

*2nd
base*   *Infield*

*3rd
base*

*1st
base*

*Pitcher's
mound*

Home plate

BASEBALL BAT

CRICKET

BATTING
Cricket is an
11-a-side game.
Two batsmen are
in at any one time.
The batsman
stands at the crease
and defends the
wicket with the
bat as the ball is
bowled. He must
try to hit the ball
to score runs.

DISMISSING THE BATSMAN

BOWLED
The ball hits the wicket.
If the batsman blocks
a ball with his body
he is "leg before
wicket".

Wicket

Crease

RUN OUT
The fielding
team "break"
the wicket before
the batsman returns.

STUMPED
The batsman
leaves the crease,
and the fielders
hit the wicket.

*Batsman tries
to hit ball*

HOCKEY AND LACROSSE

HOCKEY
Two teams of 11 use a stick to drive the ball into their opponent's goal. Goalkeepers have to be protected from the ball, which can travel at 160 km/h (100 mph).

GOALKEEPER

HOCKEY OUTDOOR STICK

Helmet

Gauntlet

Kicker enables keeper to use his or her feet

Side shooting

Men's lacrosse teams have 10 players, women's have 12.

Cradling the ball

Throwing the ball

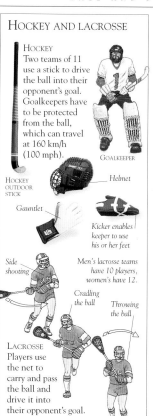

LACROSSE
Players use the net to carry and pass the ball and drive it into their opponent's goal.

RACKET GAMES

TENNIS
Players use a racket to hit a ball over a net so that it lands in the opposite court and cannot be returned. Matches are played in sets of games, with a maximum of five sets for men and three for women. The court may be grass or clay. A doubles court is larger than a singles court.

TENNIS RACKET

Singles sideline

Net

Doubles sideline

TENNIS COURT

SQUASH
A squash game is played in an enclosed court. Players aim to hit the ball onto one or more walls so their opponent cannot hit it before it bounces twice on the floor. Games are played to nine points, matches to the best of three or five games.

SQUASH

COMPETITION SPORTS

ATHLETICS and sports such as weightlifting and gymnastics are based on individual prowess.

TRACK EVENTS
Most running events take place on the track.

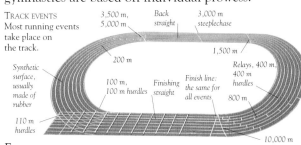

3,500 m, 5,000 m

Back straight

3,000 m steeplechase

200 m

1,500 m

Synthetic surface, usually made of rubber

100 m, 100 m hurdles

Finishing straight

Finish line: the same for all events

Relays, 400 m, 400 m hurdles

800 m

110 m hurdles

10,000 m

FIELD EVENTS

These include jumping events, such as long jump, triple jump, high jump, and pole vault, and throwing events, such as the shot, discus, hammer, and javelin. Women do not take part in the pole vault or hammer in the Olympics.

THE SHOT
The athlete puts (throws) from the shoulder and must not step out of the circle.

THE DISCUS
Usually thrown after a couple of wind-up swings and a full turn.

THE JAVELIN
The throw is measured to where the point first touches the ground.

THE HAMMER
This metal ball on a wire is hurled after 3 or 4 full turns.

TRIPLE JUMP
This consists of a hop, step, and jump, starting with a run-up and ending in a sandpit.

Hop

COMBINED EVENTS

First day	Second day
Decathlon (men)	
100 m race	110 m hurdle
Long jump	Discus
Shot put	Pole vault
High jump	Javelin
400 m race	1500 m race
Heptathlon (women)	
100 m hurdle	Long jump
High jump	Javelin
Shot put	800 m race
200 m race	

WEIGHTLIFTING

There are two categories: snatch, and clean and jerk.

Bar is lifted first to the shoulders, then to full arm's length overhead as the lifter stands up.

SNATCH

Bar is lifted to full arm's length overhead in a single movement. The lifter then stands up.

CLEAN AND JERK

Gymnast must change handholds and direction constantly

Points are given for good continuity and rhythm

GYMNASTICS

Gymnastics consists of exercises on the floor, beam, rings, asymmetric, parallel, and horizontal bars, vaulting horse, and pommel horse. Judges award marks out of ten for the gymnast's performance at the exercise. Rhythmic gymnastics for women is performed to music with ribbons, balls, ropes, clubs, or hoops.

ASYMMETRIC BARS

Beam is 10 cm (4 ins) wide and 5 m (16 ft) long

Female gymnasts walk, run, leap, and somersault along a beam for 70–90 seconds

THE BEAM

Athlete throws arms forwards, ready for landing

STEP

JUMP

WINTER SPORTS

THE SLIPPERINESS of snow and ice
has inspired a range of winter sports,
from the grace of figure skating to
the thrill of downhill skiing.

ICE HOCKEY
PLAYER

SPEED SKATING

In long-track racing, two
skaters race against the
clock on an outdoor 400-m
track. In short-track
racing, four or six skaters
race each other round a
111.12-m indoor track.

SPEED SKATER

ICE HOCKEY

Ice hockey is a fast and
furious six-a-side game in
three 20-minute periods.
The aim is to shoot the
hard rubber puck into the
opposition's goal.

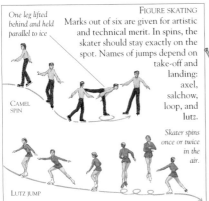

*One leg lifted
behind and held
parallel to ice*

FIGURE SKATING

Marks out of six are given for artistic
and technical merit. In spins, the
skater should stay exactly on the
spot. Names of jumps depend on
take-off and
landing:
axel,
salchow,
loop, and
lutz.

CAMEL
SPIN

*Skater spins
once or twice
in the
air.*

LUTZ JUMP

*Blocking
pad*

*Catch
glove*

*Leg
pad*

THE GOALKEEPER

Goalkeepers need a lot
of extra protection from
the puck, which travels
at high speed.

Jumpers speed down a ramp and leap into the air for a distance of 70–90 m.

SKI JUMPER

Skier adopts a streamlined shape for speed and distance through the air

Points are awarded for style as well as distance.

NORDIC SKIING

This includes ski-jumping and cross-country skiing, which involves short uphill sections. The biathlon involves cross-country skiing and rifle shooting at targets.

CROSS-COUNTRY SKIER

Skiers use freestyle (like a skater) or classical (diagonal stride)

Bindings allow heel to lift off ski

Narrower, shorter ski than Alpine skis

ALPINE SKIING

This type of skiing involves slalom and downhill races, which are all run against the clock, and freestyle, which is judged on style and technique. In downhill racing, each skier races once; slalom and giant slalom are decided on the combined time for two runs.

In downhill, skiers hurtle down a set route at speeds of up to 140 km/h (86 mph).

In slalom, skiers zig-zag between red and blue flags without missing any out.

Freestyle skiers perform acrobatics by jumping off "moguls" (snow bumps) and ramps.

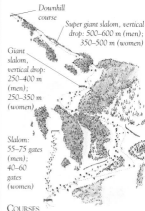

Downhill course

Super giant slalom, vertical drop: 500–600 m (men); 350–500 m (women)

Giant slalom, vertical drop: 250–400 m (men); 250–350 m (women)

Slalom: 55–75 gates (men); 40–60 gates (women)

COURSES AND GATES

Flags marking the course are set on single poles for slalom gates, double poles for giant, and super giant slalom.

WATER SPORTS

THE POPULARITY of water sports, both indoors in pools and outdoors on rivers, lakes, and the sea, has increased greatly in recent years.

WINDSURFING
Also called board sailing, windsurfing uses a sailboard with a swivelling sail that propels and steers the board. The windsurfer holds the boom which surrounds and supports the sail.

Mast

Sail

Window

Boom

Board

Universal joint swivels in all directions

Wet suits protect against cold

SURFING
Surfing is a spectacular sport in which surfers paddle out to sea on boards and ride big breakers back to shore. In competition, surfers are judged for style, grace, and timing.

Boards are usually made of fibreglass

YACHT TYPES

ONE-PERSON DINGHY
Simple one-person dinghys, such as the Topper class, are designed as training boats but are also raced.

TWO-PERSON BOAT WITH TRAPEZE
A two-person boat, such as the 470 class, is used in Olympic racing.

CATAMARAN
Twin-hulled, two-person catamarans, such as the Tornado class, also sail in Olympic races.

TWO-PERSON DINGHY
A two-person dinghy, such as the Flying Dutchman class, is used for training and racing.

OCEAN-GOING YACHT
An ocean-going yacht, such as the 12 m class, sail heavy seas in offshore racing.

SWIMMING STROKES

FRONT CRAWL
This is the
fastest stroke
and is used in
freestyle races.

Legs move up and down from the hips

Arms and legs move alternately

Body kept straight and flat

BREASTSTROKE
This is the slowest
stroke. Arms and legs
stay underwater.

Arms move together, circling from outstretched position

Legs kick out like a frog

BACKSTROKE
This is the only
stroke that
swimmers start
in the water.

Legs paddle

Arms pull alternately in windmill motion

Body kept straight and flat

BUTTERFLY
Like the breaststroke,
this is a symmetrical
stroke, but it is
very energetic.

Strong double-arm pull

Dolphin-like double leg kick

DIVING TYPES
In diving, marks
are awarded for
springboard
(3 m above the
water) and
highboard
(10 m). There
are over 80
standard dives.
Shown here are
three of the best
known dives.

Twisting in mid air

Arms spread wide

Body straight for entry

TWIST DIVE

Pike position

Hands touch toes

Feet lift up for straight entry

INWARD DIVE PIKED

Pike position

Shoulders fall back for vertical entry

REVERSE DIVE PIKED

COMBAT SPORTS

BOXING AND WRESTLING are combat sports, as are fencing, archery, and shooting, and the martial arts of East Asia.

RED BELT
9TH–10TH DAN

BLACK BELT
1ST–5TH DAN

BROWN BELT
1ST KYU

BLUE BELT
2ND KYU

ORANGE BELT
3RD KYU

GREEN BELT
4TH KYU

YELLOW BELT
5TH KYU

MARTIAL ARTS

KARATE

Strikes and kicks are used in karate, which means "empty hands".

AIKIDO

Meaning "the way of all harmony", aikido uses only defensive techniques.

JU JITSU

This is the ancient Japanese fighting art from which judo and aikido developed.

KENDO

Japanese sword-fighting, or kendo, is practised in armour.

JUDO

Competitors in the martial art of Judo, which means "the gentle way", use throws and holds to defeat their opponent. Grades or "belts" range from "kyu" (student) to "dan" (advanced).

BOXING

Governed by strict protective rules, competitors wear gloves. Professional fights are up to 12 three-minute rounds. Amateurs go three rounds.

BOXING WEIGHTS	PROFESSIONAL	AMATEUR
Flyweight	49–50.8 kg	48–51 kg
Featherweight	55.3–57.2 kg	54–57 kg
Lightweight	59–61.2 kg	57–6 1 kg
Middleweight	70–72.6 kg	71–75 kg
Heavyweight	over 86.2 kg	81–91 kg

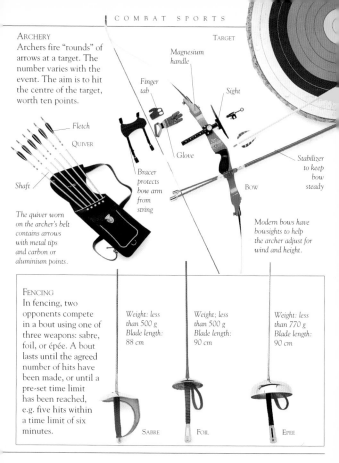

ARCHERY
Archers fire "rounds" of arrows at a target. The number varies with the event. The aim is to hit the centre of the target, worth ten points.

TARGET

Magnesium handle

Finger tab

Sight

Fletch

QUIVER

Glove

Shaft

Bracer protects bow arm from string

Stabilizer to keep bow steady

BOW

The quiver worn on the archer's belt contains arrows with metal tips and carbon or aluminium points.

Modern bows have bowsights to help the archer adjust for wind and height.

FENCING
In fencing, two opponents compete in a bout using one of three weapons: sabre, foil, or épée. A bout lasts until the agreed number of hits have been made, or until a pre-set time limit has been reached, e.g. five hits within a time limit of six minutes.

*Weight: less than 500 g
Blade length: 88 cm*

*Weight; less than 500 g
Blade length: 90 cm*

*Weight: less than 770 g
Blade length: 90 cm*

SABRE

FOIL

EPEE

EQUESTRIAN EVENTS

COMPETITIONS ON HORSEBACK are known as equestrian events. They include racing, show-jumping, and eventing. In eventing, the riders' skill is tested as they take their horses through three disciplines over three days: show jumping, speed and endurance, and dressage.

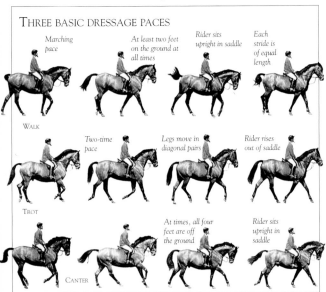

THREE BASIC DRESSAGE PACES

Marching pace

At least two feet on the ground at all times

Rider sits upright in saddle

Each stride is of equal length

WALK

Two-time pace

Legs move in diagonal pairs

Rider rises out of saddle

TROT

At times, all four feet are off the ground

Rider sits upright in saddle

CANTER

Show jumping

If the horse clips an obstacle, the rider incurs a fault. Riders with fewest faults compete against each other against the clock.

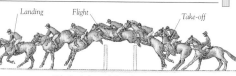

Landing   Flight   Take-off

Rider bends forwards from the hip and straightens on landing.

Show jumping course

Start   Gate   Triple bars   Wall

Finish

Obstacles

Obstacles must be jumped in a set order between start and finish.

SHOW JUMPING FAULTS	
ERROR	FAULT
Fence (or part of) down	4
Foot in water	4
Refusal	3
2nd refusal	6
3rd refusal	Elimination
Fall (horse or rider)	8
Exceeding time allowance	¼ per sec
Jumps taken out of sequence	Elimination

Horse racing

There are two kinds of horse racing: steeplechase, which includes jumps over fences, ditches, and water jumps, and hurdles, which are 3.2–5.6 km races for three-year-olds and older. The horses are almost always Thoroughbreds.

Jockey's helmet

A jockey wears a crash helmet under his or her cap, and carries a whip.

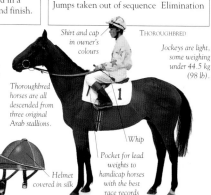

Shirt and cap in owner's colours

THOROUGHBRED

Jockeys are light, some weighing under 44.5 kg (98 lb)

Thoroughbred horses are all descended from three original Arab stallions.

Whip

Pocket for lead weights to handicap horses with the best race records

Helmet covered in silk

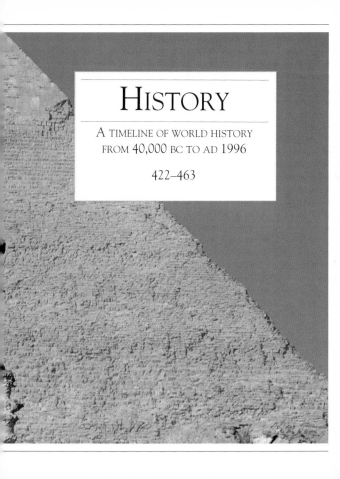

History

A TIMELINE OF WORLD HISTORY
FROM 40,000 BC TO AD 1996

422–463

40,000–32,501 BC	32,500–25,001 BC

AFRICA

c. 34,000 Hunter-gatherers occupy areas of present-day Lesotho and Zambia.

30,000 Disappearance of Neanderthals.

Ostrich
Wild ostriches formed part of the ancient African diet.

ASIA

40,000 Cro-Magnon humans living in Palestine at Skhūl and Kafzel.

27,000–19,000 Female statuettes called "Venus" figurines, thought to have been used in worship, are made at various sites in Russia, France, and Italy.

"Venus" figurines
These rounded statuettes of female figures may have been symbols of fertility.

EUROPE

40,000 Neanderthals active in France, at La Chapelle-Aux-Saints, La Ferassie, and La Quina. Cro-Magnons start to spread to Europe.
35,000 Start of Upper Paleolithic Period. Use of flaked stone tools, and bone and horn implements.

AMERICAS

35,000 First humans arrive in North America from Asia.

27,000–19,000 Probable date of earliest figurative art in Dordogne, France.

Early flint tool

OCEANIA

40,000 Probable arrival of Aboriginals in Australia.

25,000–17,501 BC | 17,500–10,001 BC

20,000 The Ice Age causes the world's average temperature to drop and sea levels to lower. Humans have to adapt and work together to survive.

Mammoth hunt
*Ice-Age people
hunted in groups
and shared the kill.*

15,000 Last rainy period in northern Africa.

16,000 Coldest point in glaciation.
14,000–11,000 El-Kebarch culture in Israel builds free-standing round huts.
11,000 Natufian culture in Palestine becomes one of the first groups to form permanent settlements.
10,500 Earliest-known pottery produced, Fukui cave, Japan.

Natufian huts
*The mud, reed, and timber
huts of the Natufians were
often used to store grain.*

15,000 Wall paintings made in caves at Lascaux, France.
15,000–10,000 High point of art produced by Magdalenian culture.
12,500 Magdalenian toolmakers make the first bone and antler harpoons and fishing spears.

The origins of art
*Early artists painted images of animals
and humans on the walls of caves.*

25,000 Cave dwellers present in Brazil. | **15,000** First Brazilian cave art.

24,000 Earliest-known cremation at Lake Mungo, New South Wales, Australia. | **16,000** Cave art, north coast of Australia.

	10,000–8501 BC	8500–7001 BC
AFRICA	**10,000** Hunting camps established in Sahara region after Ice Age ends.	**8500** Earliest Saharan rock paintings. **8000** Pottery made in Sahara region.
ASIA	**9000–8000** Wheat and barley grown in Jordan and Syria. Pottery produced at Mureybet, Syria. Goats and sheep domesticated in Iran and Jordan.	**8000** Jericho, the first town, appears. Ice Age ends in Far East. **7500** Pigs domesticated in Crimea.
EUROPE	**10,000** Ice cap retreats.	**8300** Retreat of glaciers.
AMERICAS	**10,000** First people reach southern tip of South America. **9000** Clovis hunter-gatherers in the Great Plains of North America begin to hunt bison.	**8500** Cultivation of wild grasses and beans in Peru. **8000** Semi-permanent settlements established in North America.
OCEANIA		

Early farming
Cereal crops were first cultivated in the Middle East in 8000 BC.

Domesticated pig
The modern pig evolved from the wild boar domesticated by early farmers.

Jericho Tower
The ancient town of Jericho was strongly built, with a stone wall, tower, and defensive ditch.

North American bison

7000–5501 BC	5500–4001 BC

6500 Cattle domesticated.
7000–6000 Discovery that heating certain rocks (ores) releases pure metal that can then be shaped or moulded.

Early metal-workers

7000–6500 Domestication of oxen in eastern Mediterranean.
6500–5700 Important early town at Çatal Hüyük, Turkey. Its houses are built of mud brick and share walls.
6200 Copper smelted in Turkey.

5000 Irrigation in Mesopotamia. Rice farming in China. Ubaid culture in Mesopotamia.
4500 Farming around River Ganges in India.
4400 Horses domesticated in Russia.

5000 Farming begins in western Europe. Gold and copper used in Balkans.
4500 First megalithic chamber tombs built in Portugal and in Brittany, France. Their remains (dolmens) show a great knowledge of engineering.

Çatal Hüyük

Dolmens at Carnac
Upright stones placed in a row and roofed to form a covered walk can be seen at Carnac, Brittany.

6500 Britain separated from mainland as ice melts.
6500 First farming communities established in southeastern Europe.

6500 Potatoes cultivated in Peru.

c. 4000–5000 First settlements at Anåhuac, Mexico. Maize grown in Mexico. Pyramid temples built in Peru.

5000 New Guinea and Tasmania separated from Australia as sea level rises.

4000–3376 BC	3375–2751 BC

AFRICA

3750 Earliest-known production of bronze alloy. The process is also developed in Sumer, southern Babylonia.
3500 First sailing vessels built in Egypt.

3100 Pharaoh Menes the Fighter unites Upper and Lower Egypt.
3000 Development of hieroglyphic writing in Eygpt.

Egyptian mummy
Preserving the bodies of important people was an ancient Egyptian custom.

ASIA

4000 Beginning of bronze casting in the Middle East.
3500 Earliest Chinese city at Liang-ch'eng chen. Sumerians invent the wheel and plough.

Mesopotamian wheel

3500 Ancient Egyptians establish one of the world's longest-lasting civilizations.

EUROPE

3250 Earliest picture-writing by Sumerians in Mesopotamia.
3000 Development of Sumerian cities. First use of the plough in China.
2850 Legendary reign of the Chinese Xia dynasty.

AMERICAS

c. 4000 Domestication of llama and alpaca in Andes, South America.

Inca llama figurine
The Incas of South America used llamas as pack animals and also for meat.

3200 Beginnings of early Cycladic civilization in Aegean islands.
3000 Spread of copper use.
2900 Danubian culture in central Europe.

OCEANIA

3200 Maize farmed in South America.
3000 First pottery in Americas.

Maize

3000 Probable introduction of dogs into Australia.

2750–2126 BC

2686 Beginning of ancient Egyptian Old Kingdom.
2646 Pyramid of Zoser built at Saqqara.
2590 Building of Great Pyramid of Khufu at Giza.
2500 Sahara region begins to dry out.
2150 Decline of ancient Egyptian Old Kingdom.
2133 Rise of ancient Egyptian Middle Kingdom.

2750 The legendary King Gilgamesh reigns in Uruk, Mesopotamia.
2500 Birth of Indus Valley civilization in Pakistan. Horse domesticated in Central Asia.
2371 Semite people establish Mesopotamia's greatest empire.

Indus Valley sculpture
This sculpture of a priest or divine king was made by people in the Indus Valley city of Mohenjo-Daro.

2500 Earliest barrow burials in Britain. Beginnings of Dolmen period of Scandinavian Neolithic age.
2200 The first Stonehenge is built in England.

2500 First large settlements and building of temple mounds in Andes area.

2125–1501 BC

1786 Egyptian Middle Kingdom ends.
1652 War between Egypt and Asian Hyksos people.
1550 Rise of Egyptian New Kingdom.

2000 Hittites begin invasions of Anatolia.
1900 Fall of Indus civilization.
1800 Beginnings of Assyrian Empire.
1792 Birth of Hammurabi, founder of Babylonian Empire.

Lotus-design tile
This tile dates from the reign of King Akhenaten in the Egyptian New Kingdom.

2000 Rise of the prosperous Minoan sea-trading civilization in Crete.
1600 Origins of Mycenean civilization.
1500 Linear B script in use on Crete.

Minoan wall painting
The wealthy Minoan people decorated the walls of their palaces with colourful murals.

2000 Earliest Peruvian metalworking. Inuits reach northern Greenland.

2000 Beginnings of settlement of Melanesia in the South Pacific.

	1500–1276 BC	1275–1051 BC
AFRICA	**1300** Temple of Abu Simbel built in Nubia for Rameses II. **Hittite soldier**	**1218** Egypt invaded by Sea Peoples from the Aegean. **1182** Second invasion of Egypt by Aegean Sea Peoples.
ASIA	**1500** Phrygia established by people moving from Thrace in the Balkans to Asia Minor. Composition of hymns of Rig Veda. **1400** Chinese capital moved to Anyang, in present-day South Korea.	**c. 1375** First alphabet script devised by Phoenicians. **1294** Egyptians fight Hittites at Qadesh for control of Palestine. **1200** Collapse of Hittite Empire. Jews settle in Palestine. **1100** Phoenician traders begin to spread out from eastern Mediterranean.
EUROPE	**1500** Beginning of Bronze Age in Scandinavia. **1450** Decline of Minoan civilization in Crete.	**1200** Decline of Mycenean culture in Greece. **c. 1120** City of Mycenae destroyed.  **Mycenean bull's head** *This clay bull's head has small holes in its mouth and was used as a ritual sprinkler at religious ceremonies.*
AMERICAS	**1300** Rise of Olmec civilization in Mexico. **Olmec stone carving** *This colossal stone head of an Olmec king was carved from basalt.*	
OCEANIA	**1300** Settlers reach Western Polynesia (Fiji).	

1050–826 BC	825–601 BC

900 Foundation of kingdom of Kushin Nubia.

814 Phoenicians found the city state of Carthage in northern Africa.

1027 Zhou warriors overthrow the Shang dynasty in China.
1000 Kingdom of Israel under King David.

Shang Fang Ding
This four-legged food vessel was made in China during the Shang dynasty (c. 1600–1027 BC).

800 Aryans from present-day Iran spread into southern India.
771 Zhou dynasty collapses in China.
721–05 Assyrian Empire at height of its powers.
660 Reign of Jimmu, legendary first Japanese emperor.
650 Chinese begin to use iron.
612 Decline of Assyrian power.
c. 604–562 Nebuchadnezzar II rules Neo-Babylonian (Chaldean) Empire. Hanging Gardens built in city of Babylon, Mesopotamia.

Sentry at the Ishtar Gate, Babylon

1000 Etruscans arrive in Italy and begin building a loosely connected alliance of city states.

Etruscan warrior figurine
The Etruscans produced unique, high-quality sculpture and bronzework.

776 First recorded Olympic Games in Greece.
753 Foundation of Rome.
750 Greek city-states establish settlements around Mediterranean.
700 Iron Age culture of Halstatt, Austria, spreads through central and western Europe.
650 Earliest surviving Latin inscriptions.
621 The Laws of Dracon become the first written laws of Athens, Greece.

900 Height of Chavin farming civilization in Andes, South America.
800 Zapotec civilization of Central America produces first writing in Americas.

1000 Most of Polynesian Islands settled.

600–451 BC	450–301 BC

AFRICA

600 Phoenicians sail around Africa.
600 Building of Temple of the Sun at Meroë, Sudan.
500 Iron-working Nok culture begins in Nigeria.

304 Egypt independent under Ptolemy I.

ASIA

560 Lao–Tze writes his philosophical work, Tao Te Ching, in China.
550 King Cyrus II of Persia founds Persian Empire.
486 Death of Siddhartha Gautama, founder of Buddhist religion.

403 Start of "Warring States" period in China.
334–26 Alexander the Great conquers Asia Minor, Persia, and parts of India.
323 Death of Alexander the Great and division of his empire.
322 Chandragupta founds Mauryan Empire in India.

Alexander the Great
The Macedonian warrior-king Alexander the Great built an empire that helped spread Greek culture in western Asia.

EUROPE

510 Origins of Roman Republic.
505 Establishment of democracy in Athens.
500 Celtic people flourish in central Europe.
490 Greeks defeat Persians at Battle of Marathon.

Buddhist stupa at Sanchi, India
Mauryan emperor Asoka became a Buddhist and set up thousands of monuments (stupas) around the empire. Each is said to contain a part of Buddha's body.

AMERICAS

Decorative Celtic horned helmet

450 Iron Age culture firmly established in central and western Europe.
431–04 Sparta defeats Athens in Peloponnesian Wars.
338 Macedonians gain control of Greece at Battle of Chaeronea.

OCEANIA

500 Trading contacts established in South Pacific islands.

400 Decline of Olmec civilization.

300–151 BC

290 Foundation of library at Alexandria, Egypt.

262 Mauryan emperor Asoka converts to Buddhism.
240 Beginning of Parthian dynasty in northern Persia.
221 Chinese unity brought about by the first emperor, Qin Shi Huangdi.
207 Disintegration of unity in China.
202 China reunited under Han dynasty.

290 Rome gains control of central Italy.
264–41 Rome victorious against Carthage in First Punic War and wins control of Sicily.
218–01 Carthaginians, led by Hannibal, defeated in Second Punic War by Roman general Scipio.

Roman sword

300 Mound-building cultures flourish in North America. Beginning of early Mayan civilization in Central America.
200 Rise of Nazca civilization in Peru, South America.

150–1 BC

149–6 Rome destroys Carthage in Third Punic War and founds province of Africa.
100 Camels introduced into Sahara region.
30 Egypt becomes Roman province on death of Mark Antony and Cleopatra.

112 Opening up of "Silk Road" trade route gives the West some access to China.
64 Roman general Pompey conquers Syria.
53 Parthia halts eastward expansion of Rome.

49 Rome under Julius Caesar invades Gaul.
45 Julius Caesar becomes sole ruler of Rome after civil war.
31 Battle of Actium gives Octavian power over Rome.
27 Roman Empire replaces Republic. Octavian becomes Augustus, the first emperor.

100 Emergence of Anasazi, Hohokam, and Mogollon peoples as they begin farming in southwestern North America. Okvik hunters settle in northern Alaska.

Nazca pottery
The Nazca produced decorative textiles, metalworks, and pottery.

AD 1–149	AD 150–299

AFRICA

c. 17–24 Tacfarinas leads Numidian people in revolt against Roman government in northern Africa.
50 Kingdom of Axum begins to expand in Ethiopia.
61–63 Roman forces move into Sudan.

150 Berber and Mandingo barbarians start to dominate Sudan area.
250 Axum (Ethiopia) controls trade in Red Sea.

Circular Sassanian city at Firuzbad, Persia (Iraq)

ASIA

9 Overthrow of Han dynasty in China.
25 Han dynasty restored.
c. 33 Jesus Christ crucified in Jerusalem.
60 Beginning of Kushan Empire in India.
70 Romans seize control of Jerusalem in Israel and destroy Jewish temple.
105 Paper first used in China.
132 Jewish revolt against Roman rule.

200 Mishnah, the book of Jewish law, completed. Indian epics of Ramayana and Mahabharata composed.
Creation of the Hindu scripture, Bhagavad Gita.

EUROPE

43 Romans invade Britain.
79 Mount Vesuvius erupts and destroys the town of Pompeii in southern Italy.
117 Height of Roman Empire.

The four tetrarchs
In AD 293, Emperor Diocletian divided the Roman Empire in two, appointing an emperor and deputy to rule each half. This sculpture represents the Empire's four leaders (tetrarchs).

AMERICAS

1 Beginning of Moche civilization in northern Peru.
50 Nazca people create vast lines and patterns in the desert.

Bust of Augustus, the first Roman emperor

OCEANIA

1–100 Hindu-Buddhists from Southeast Asia colonize Sumatra and Java in Indonesia.

AD 300–449

325 Axum destroys kingdom of Meroë.
400 Adoption of Christianity in Axum.
439 Vandals establish kingdom in
northern Africa.

304 Invasion of Huns creates
further division of China.
320 Chandragupta I founds
Gupta Empire in northern India.

**The symbol of
Christianity**
*The teachings of the Jewish
preacher Jesus Christ, who
was crucified
c. AD 33, spread
around the world
after his death.
The faith gained
widespread
acceptance after
the Roman emperor
Constantine converted
to Christianity in AD 313.
Christ's death on the cross
led to its use as a symbol
of the faith.*

313 Edict of Milan leads to toleration of
Christianity throughout Roman Empire.
330 Emperor Constantine moves capital
of Roman Empire to Constantinople, at
site of present-day Istanbul, Turkey.
410 Invading Visigoths sack Rome.

300 Rise of great Monte Alban and
Teotihuacán civilizations in Mexico.

300 Eastern Polynesia settled.

AD 450–599

533 Emperor Justinian wins back
northern Africa for Rome.

480 End of Indian
Gupta Empire.
520 Rise of
mathematics in
India with
invention of
decimal number
system.
531 Height of
Sassanian Empire
in Persia.
550 Buddhism
introduced into
Japan.
589 Reunification
of China under
Sui dynasty.

Japanese carving of
a sleeping Buddha

450 Angles, Jutes,
and Saxons settle
in Britain.
476 Overthrow of
Romulus Augustulus, the last
western Roman emperor.
486 Clovis people establish Frankish
kingdom in present-day northern France,
Belgium, and parts of western Germany.
493 Ostrogoths gain power in Italy.
552 Emperor Justinian restores Italy
to Roman control.
568 Lombards take over northern Italy.

c. 450–600 Population of city of
Tiahuanaco in Bolivia reaches 50,000.

AD 600–724 | AD 725–849

AFRICA

c.700 Trans-Saharan trade brings prosperity to Kingdom of Ghana. Bantu Africans cross River Limpopo and take iron-working technology to the south.

751 Muslims defeat Mongols at Samarkand in central Asia.
794 Kyoto, ancient capital of Japan, established.
802 Khmers found empire in Cambodia and Laos.

ASIA

618 Reunification of China under T'ang dynasty.
622 Year One of the Islamic calendar.
637 Followers of Islam (Muslims) seize Jerusalem.

Muslim at prayer
The Arab merchant Muhammad founded the Islamic religion in AD 610. His teachings inspired the Arab peoples, and by AD 750 had gained control of land stretching from Spain to Afghanistan.

EUROPE

c. 675 Nomadic Bulgar people settle in lands south of the Danube.
711 Islamic Moors invade Spain.

732 Defeat of Moors by Frankish leader Charles Martel halts advance of Muslims through Europe.
768 Charlemagne crowned King of the Franks.
844 Defeat of Picts unites Scotland.

King Charlemagne
The Holy Roman Empire was founded by King Charlemagne of the Franks in AD 800 after he conquered most of the Christian lands of western Europe.

AMERICAS

600 Mayan civilization in Central America flourishes. Mayans build great pyramidal temples and develop writing and advanced mathematics.

Temple at Palenque
This Mayan temple contained the funeral chamber of the lord Pacal, who died in AD 683 after ruling for 68 years.

OCEANIA

AD 850–974

900 Hausa kingdom of Daura founded in northern Nigeria.
920 The Kingdom of Ghana in western Africa begins a prosperous golden age.

888 Chola dynasty of Tamil kings replaces the Pallavas in southern India and Sri Lanka.
935–41 Civil war in Japan.
960 Sung dynasty begins rule in China.
1007 Japanese noblewoman Murasaki Shikubu writes the first novel.

911 The Viking leader Rollo is granted land in Normandy by the King of France.
930 Córdoba becomes the seat of Arab learning in Spain.
966 Conversion of Poles to Christianity.

Viking longship
Late in the eighth century the Viking people of present-day Scandinavia went in search of treasure to plunder and new lands to settle. Their golden age of trade, exploration, and colonization lasted until AD 1100.

900 Beginnings of Mixtec civilization in Mexico.

950 Polynesian navigator Kupe discovers New Zealand, and Maori settlers arrive.

AD 975–1099

980 Arab traders settle on eastern coast of Africa.
1054 Ghana conquered by Muslim Almoravid dynasty.

Japanese literature
Over 600,000 words long, The Tale of Genji, a prince in search of love and wisdom, was the first novel.

1044 Gunpowder invented in China.

982 The Viking warrior Erik the Red settles in Greenland.
1000 Leif Eriksson, son of Erik the Red, sails down North American coast and names it "Vinland".
1066 William of Normandy defeats King Harold of England at Battle of Hastings.
1096 First Crusades begin.

980 Toltec people build their capital city at Tula in Mexico.
1000 Foundation of Chima civilization in Peru.

Maori hek tiki
This hek tiki, or neck pendant, was worn by the first Maori settlers to bring good luck or ward off evil spirits.

1100–1149

1150–1199

AFRICA

c. 1100 First Iron Age settlement in Zimbabwe, Southern Africa.

1169 Saladin, a Muslim warrior and commander in the Egyptian army, becomes ruler of Egypt.
1190 Lalibela rules as Emperor of Ethiopia.

ASIA

1104 Acre in Israel captured by Crusaders. Their name comes from the Latin *crux*, or cross, the symbol of Christ.

Knights of Christ
European Christians sent armed expeditions called Crusades to recapture the holy lands from Saracen Muslims.

1156 Civil war between rival clans in Japan leads to domination of the country by its Samurai warlords.
1187 Saladin captures Jerusalem from Crusaders.
1191 Zen Buddhism introduced to Japan.

EUROPE

1115 French philosopher Peter Abelard begins teaching in Paris, France. St. Bernard establishes important monastery at Clairvaux, France.
1119 Foundation of Bologna University in Italy.
1142 Alfonso Henriques becomes first King of Portugal.

Zen Buddhist monks in meditation
The practice of Zen Buddhism is unlike other faiths in its belief that the path to self-knowledge lies in personal instruction by a master rather than the study of scriptures.

AMERICAS

c. 1100 Chimu civilization flourishes in Peru on northwest coast.

1170 Murder of Thomas à Becket, Archbishop of Canterbury, England.
1174 Building of Old London Bridge in England and the "Leaning Tower" in Pisa, Italy.

"Leaning Tower" of Pisa

OCEANIA

1100s Giant statues built on Easter Island, South Pacific.

Chimu ear ornament

1170s Chichimec nomads overthrow Toltec capital city of Tula in Mexico, leading to fall of Toltec Empire.

1200–1249

1234 Sun Diata founds the Mali Empire in West Africa.

Genghis Khan
The Mongol chieftain Temujin was proclaimed Genghis Khan, or "Universal Ruler".

1206 Genghis Khan establishes the Mongol Empire. The Islamic faith takes root in new Kingdom of Delhi, India.

1229 Sixth Crusaders recapture Jerusalem.

1232 Explosive rockets used in war between Chinese and Mongols.

1237 Mongol army begins conquest of Russia.

1244 Egyptians retake Jerusalem.

1204 Constantinople sacked and looted by Fourth Crusaders.

1209 Franciscan order founded by St. Francis of Assisi, Italy.

1215 St. Dominic establishes Dominican Order in Spain. King John of England grants political rights to barons by signing the Magna Carta.

1240s Foundations laid in Germany for commercial and defensive Hanseatic League of northern European trade towns.

c.1200 Incas in Peru centred around settlement at Cuzco. First maize farmers by Mississippi River in North America.

1200 First settlers from Indonesia and Philippines arrive in Fiji and spread throughout Polynesia.

1250–1299

1250 Mamluk rebel slave-soldiers become the rulers of Egypt.

1250 The Japanese monk Nicherin proclaims *Lotus Sutra* the supreme Buddhist scripture.

1260 Mamluks halt Mongol advance at Battle of Ain Jalut in Palestine.

1291 Saracens capture Acre, ending the Crusades.

1281 Mongol invaders' fleet driven from Japan by the Kamikaze, or "Divine Wind".

c.1294 Persians convert to Islam.

Marco Polo and fellow travellers in the Far East

1271 Aged only 16, Marco Polo begins his journeys around the Far East, travelling from Venice, Italy to China.

1273 Rudolf Hapsburg becomes ruler of Germany and founds the powerful Hapsburg dynasty.

c. 1250 Restoration of Mayan Empire and building of a new capital at Mayapan in Mexico. Incas expand their capital at Chan-chan in northern Peru.

c. 1250 Stone platforms later used to erect religious statues built in Polynesia.

	1300–1339	**1340–1379**
AFRICA	**1300** Origins of Benin kingdom in Nigeria. **1324** Mansa Musa makes pilgrimage to Mecca.	**1348** Population of Egypt devastated by the Black Death plague. **1352** Moroccan scholar Ibn Battuta makes his great journey across the Sahara to Mali.
ASIA	**c. 1300** Osman I establishes Ottoman dynasty in Turkey. **1321** Tughluq dynasty founded in Delhi, India.	**1340** Indian Hindu empire of Vijayanagar becomes centre of resistance to Islam. **1350** Majapahit Empire founded in Java. **1368** Mongols driven from China by Tai Tsu, founder of the Ming dynasty.
EUROPE	**1309** The Pope moves from Rome, Italy, to Avignon in France, creating a rift in the Western Church.	**1346** The 100 Years War between England and France begins with the Battle of Crécy. **1347** The Black Death reaches Europe. **1358** Peasant revolt near Paris, France.
AMERICAS	**c.1300** Major expansion of Incas through Andes. **1325** Aztecs found capital at Tenochtitlán.	**1350** Acamapitchli becomes Aztec ruler and begins expansion of the empire.
OCEANIA		**1350** Maoris create rock art in New Zealand.

Mansa Musa, Emperor of Mali
The West African Mali Empire under Mansa Musa was famed for its size and wealth.

Plague carriers
Fleas on rats carried and transmitted the Black Death, a combination of bubonic and pneumonic plague, which killed a quarter of the European population.

Human sacrifice
Aztec and Inca civilizations believed their angry gods could only be soothed by blood sacrifice.

1380–1419	1420–1459

c.1400 Kingdom of Zimbabwe thrives on gold trade.

1398 Mongol leader Tamerlane sacks Indian city of Delhi.
1404–33 Chinese navigator Chang Ho explores India and East Africa.
1405 Death of Tamerlane leads to fall of Mongol Empire.
1411 Ahmad Shah founds Ahmadabad, an important commercial city in India.

The murder of Wat Tyler
Peasant revolts in the years following the Plague were ruthlessly put down.

1381 Wat Tyler and John Ball lead Peasants' Revolt in England against high taxes and low pay. The uprising is crushed and the leaders killed.
1389 Ottoman Turks crush Christian Serbs at Kossovo, Serbia.
1415 French defeated by the English at the Battle of Agincourt in France.

c. 1400 Viracocha becomes first Inca empire builder, establishing permanent rule over conquered neighbouring lands.

1432 Portuguese explorers reach the Azores Islands.

1448 Major reforms begin in Thailand under King Traillok.

Thai bronze Buddha
The dominant religion in 15th-century Thailand was Buddhism.

1429 Joan of Arc leads French forces and lifts the Siege of Orléans.
1450 Italian cities of Florence, Milan, and Naples form an alliance.
1450s German craftsman Johannes Gutenberg produces the first printed books in Europe.
1453 Constantinople falls to Ottoman sultan Muhammad II, ending the centuries-old Byzantine Empire.

Muhammad II
Ottoman leader Muhammad II dragged 70 ships overland to avoid a huge iron chain protecting the waterway into Byzantium when he invaded the city.

1438 Inca overlord Pachacuti greatly enlarges the Inca Empire.

1460–1479

1480–1499

AFRICA

1464 Sonni Ali becomes ruler of Songhai people in West Africa.

1482 First Portuguese settlements established on Gold Coast of West Africa.
1488 Sea route from Europe to Asia opened by Portuguese navigator Bartolomeu Diaz, sailing around the Cape of Good Hope, South Africa.

ASIA

1467 Beginning of the Onin War in Japan, which continues for over 10 years. It leads to the end of the feudal system and the rise of large territories.

Battling warriors in the Onin civil war

1497–98 Portuguese explorer Vasco da Gama sails to India via Africa.

Portuguese caravel
The caravel ships used by Portuguese explorers were longer, narrower, and easier to manoeuvre than earlier craft.

EUROPE

1463–79 Ottoman Turks and Venetians from Italy fight for control of the Mediterranean. The Turks are the eventual victors.
1479 Kingdoms of Aragon and Castille in Spain united by the marriage of King Ferdinand and Queen Isabella.

1492 Christian conquest of Granada ends Islamic regional control in Spain and results in expulsion of Jews.
1494 Treaty of Tordesillas leads Spain and Portugal to agree to divide the unexplored world between their two nations.

AMERICAS

1470s Collapse of Chimu culture in Northern Peru.
1473 Aztec capital Tenochtitlán absorbs neighbouring city of Tlatelolco.

The Renaissance
The rediscovery or "renaissance" of Greek and Roman ideas on art, literature, and science spreads through Europe from Italy during the 14–1500s.

OCEANIA

1450–1500 Widespread cultivation of wet taro, a starchy root vegetable, in the Hawaiian islands.

1492 Italian explorer Christopher Columbus reaches the Caribbean islands of the Americas.
1497 John Cabot of Italy discovers Newfoundland, present-day Canada.

1500–1519

1500s Southern African Bantus trade with Europeans. Hausa states develop in West Africa.
1517 Ottomans conquer Eygpt.

1502 Safavid dynasty begins in Persia.

c. 1503 Italian artist Leonardo da Vinci begins painting the Mona Lisa.
1512 Michelangelo paints ceiling of the Sistine Chapel, Italy.
1517 European Reformation begins.

The Reformation
Protestant (protesting) churches were formed after Martin Luther called for reform of the corrupt Catholic Church in a list he nailed to his church door in 1517.

1501–02 Amerigo Vespucci of Italy explores the coast of Brazil. First African slaves taken to the West Indies.
1519 Portuguese explorer Ferdinand Magellan sails across the Pacific Ocean.
1520 Spaniard Hernando Cortés brings down the Aztec Empire.

Moctezuma's headdress
This is a replica of a headdress said to have belonged to the last Aztec ruler Moctezuma, who was murdered by Cortés of Spain in 1520.

1520–1539

1520–21 Portuguese traders reach China.
1526 Babur I becomes first Moghul Emperor of India.

Babur I of India
A descendant of Genghis Khan, Babur I was a brilliant military leader who also took an interest in art and poetry.

1529 Ottoman Turks besiege Vienna.
1533 Ivan the Terrible comes to the throne in Russia.

1532 Francisco Pizarro of Spain overthrows Incas in South America by kidnapping and murdering their Emperor, Atahualpa. The leaderless Inca Empire then crumbles.
1534 French explorer Jacques Cartier sails along the St. Lawrence River in Canada.

Inca knife

1526 Portuguese begin landings in Polynesia.

1540–1564	1565–1589

AFRICA

c. 1540s Portuguese begin organization of the transatlantic slave trade.

1566 Sulayman I, ruler of the Ottoman Empire, dies as his empire reaches its peak.
1577 Akbar the Great completes unification of northern India, providing a structured system of government.

Akbar the Great in religious discussion
The Islamic Moghul emperor Akbar was renowned for his tolerance of other religions.

ASIA

1542 Traders from Portugal reach Japan.
1546 King Tabinshweti unites Burma.
1556 Akbar the Great becomes Moghul emperor of India.

EUROPE

1541 French Protestant reformer John Calvin sets up Puritan state in Geneva, Switzerland.
1545 Meeting of Catholic leaders at Council of Trent in northern Italy begins Catholic Counter-Reformation.
1564 Birth of English playwright William Shakespeare.

1571 European alliance defeats Ottoman Turkish fleet at Battle of Lepanto, Greece.
1572 St. Bartholomew's Day Massacre of Protestants (Huguenots) in France.
1588 English navy defeats the Armada, Spain's huge invasion fleet.

St. Bartholomew's Day Massacre

AMERICAS

1540's Spanish arrive in California on the west coast of North America.

1567 Portuguese establish Rio de Janeiro in Brazil.
1579 Francis Drake claims the west coast of North America for England.

OCEANIA

1550 Maoris sail from North Island, New Zealand, to settle on South Island.

Maori migration

1567 Spanish explorer Mendaña becomes first European to reach Solomon Islands.

1590–1614	1615–1639

1591 Moroccans and European mercenaries destroy Songhai Empire.
1600s Trading posts set up on African coast by all major European powers.

1620s Queen Nzinga of Ndongo defeats the Portuguese in Angola.

1590 Shah Abbas of Persia makes peace with Ottoman Turkey.
1592 Japan invades Korea under commander Hideyoshi.
1603 Ieyasu of Tokugawa clan becomes ruler of Japan. English East India Company established.
1602 Dutch East India Company founded.

Gatehouse of Edo Castle, Japan
The Tokugawa shogun (ruler) Ieyasu built a heavily fortified castle at the capital city of Edo, now modern Tokyo.

1620s Formation of Japanese national policy restricting contact with the outside world.

1598 Edict of Nantes ends civil war in France, giving Catholics and Huguenots equal rights.
1604 Russians settle in Siberia.
1605 Failure of Gunpowder Plot in London, England, and arrest of ringleader Guy Fawkes.
1610 French King Henry IV assassinated.
1613 Michael Romanov becomes first Russian Romanov Tsar (king).

1618 Beginning of Thirty Years' War in Europe between Catholic and Protestant powers.

1620 *Mayflower* pilgrims set sail from England for North America.
1625 French begin to settle West Indies.
1626 Dutch found New Amsterdam on site of present-day New York.
1630 Dutch East India Company seizes part of Brazil for its sugar and silver.

1607 John Smith establishes a colony in Virginia at Jamestown.
1608 Foundation of Quebec in Canada.
1609 Henry Hudson sails up the Hudson River on the east coast of North America.

1595 Mendaña lands on Marquesas Islands in the central South Pacific.
1606 Spanish explorer Luis Vaez de Torres sails between Australia and New Guinea. Portuguese arrive at Tahiti.

Building Manhattan
The first brick house on the site of present-day Manhattan, New York, was built on The Strand in New Amsterdam, now Whitehall Street.

1640–1669

1670–1699

AFRICA

1652 Dutch found colony at Cape Town in southern Africa.
1663 Death of Queen Nzinga of Ndongo in Angola.

1670s French colonists settle in Senegal.
1690s Asante kingdom established on Gold Coast of West Africa.

Manchu lord with Chinese subjects, pigtailed to show inferiority

ASIA

1644 Manchus invade China, replacing Ming dynasty.
1657 City of Edo on site of present-day Tokyo, Japan, is destroyed by fire.

1683 K'ang Hsi of China conquers Formosa, now modern Taiwan.
1690 Job Caharnock of the English East India Company founds city of Calcutta.

1672 Third Anglo-Dutch trade war begins.
1677 Ottoman Empire at war with Russia.
1682 Peter the Great of Russia starts reign.
1685 Louis XIV of France abolishes Edict of Nantes' protection of the rights of Huguenot protestants. Many flee to England as a result.

EUROPE

1642 Civil War in England.
1643 Louis XIV of France begins reign.
1648 End of the Thirty Years' War in Europe.
1649 Oliver Cromwell executes Charles I of England and sets up Commonwealth.

1688 Protestant William of Orange defeats Catholic James II at the Battle of the Boyne and becomes king of England.

Louis XIV of France in classical costume

AMERICAS

1642 French explorer De Maisonneuve founds Ville-Marie (Montreal) in Canada.
1664 English forces seize New Amsterdam from Dutch and rename it New York.

1670 Colony founded in South Carolina. English Hudson's Bay Company established.
1675 War between colonists and Native Americans devastates New England.
1680 French explorer Robert Cavalier de la Salle claims Mississippi valley for France.
1692 Salem witch trials begin in New England.

OCEANIA

1642 Dutch explorer Abel Tasman becomes first European to reach Van Dieman's Land, Tasmania.

1680 The dodo becomes extinct.

Dodo

1700–1729

1702 French win "Asiento", or monopoly, on shipping of African slaves to Spanish colonies.
1712 Rise of Futa Jalon kingdom in West Africa.

1707 Death of Moghul leader Aurangzeb leads to break-up of the empire and new opportunities for European traders.
1727 Border fixed between China and Russia.

1700 Death of Charles II of Spain, leaving a French heir, leads to War of Spanish Succession.
1703 Russian Tsar Peter the Great founds St. Petersburg.
1707 Act of Union joins England and Scotland.

1709 Abraham Darby's use of coke instead of charcoal to extract metal from iron ore (smelting) starts English Industrial Revolution.

Peter the Great forced nobles to shave

1709 Mass emigration of Germans to America begins.
1710 South Sea Company increases British trade with South America.
1720–22 Spanish occupation of Texas. Collapse of English South Sea and French Mississippi Companies.

1722 Dutch navigator Roggeveen reaches Samoa and Easter Island.

1730–1759

1739 Nadir Shah of Persia defeats the Moghuls and captures city of Delhi, India.
1740s Anglo/French rivalry in India.
1750 China conquers Tibet.
1757 Bengali army defeated by the British at the Battle of Plassey.

1746 Victory of English at Battle of Culloden, Scotland, ends Scottish revolt.
1748 Marie Theresa becomes Empress of Austria.
1755 Earthquake at Lisbon in Portugal.
1756–1763 Seven Years War between Britain and France.

Captured slaves assembled for sale
Slaves transported from Africa to the Americas were often worked to death on plantations owned by European settlers.

1733 England passes the Molasses Act, forbidding trade between American and West Indian colonies. Colony of Georgia founded.
1739 Slave uprising in South Carolina.
1759 English forces defeat French on Plains of Abraham in Quebec, Canada.

1760–1779	1780–1799

AFRICA

1764 Osei Kwadwo becomes Asante ruler in West Africa.
1768 Independent Eygpt under Ali Bey.

Asante gold weight

1794 Beginning of Qaja dynasty's rule in Persia.

ASIA

1761 Marathas defeated by Afghans at Battle of Panipat.
1763 Treaty of Paris makes Britain dominant power in India.

ENCYCLOPEDIE,
OU
DICTIONNAIRE RAISONNÉ
DES SCIENCES,
DES ARTS ET DES MÉTIERS,

Inspirational reading
L'Encyclopedie expressed the ideals of justice, equality, and rational thought proposed by followers of the Enlightenment movement.

1789 French Revolution begins in Paris.
1795 Formation of France's Directoire government.
1796 Edward Jenner introduces smallpox vaccine in England. French general Napoleon Bonaparte begins Italian campaigns.

EUROPE

1762 Catherine the Great begins reign over Russia.
1751–1786 Ideas of Enlightenment thinkers published in L'Encyclopedie.

Storming the Bastille
The Bastille prison in Paris was a symbol of aristocratic tyranny. Its overthrow by the people in 1789 launched the French Revolution.

AMERICAS

1773 Rebel colonists throw English tea into the harbour at the Boston Tea Party.
1775–83 American colonists fight against British rule in Revolutionary War.
1776 Signing of US Declaration of Independence.

1780 Tupac Amara leads Incas of Peru in revolt against Spain.
1787–9 US Constitution and Bill of Rights written and ratified.
1791 Revolution in Haiti led by former slave Toussaint L' Ouverture.
1793 City of York founded on site of present-day Toronto in Canada.

OCEANIA

1770 Captain James Cook reaches Australia.

Captain Cook trades with Islanders
English navigator James Cook explored the South Pacific and was renowned for taking great care of his crews.

1788 Foundation of British colony of New South Wales in Australia.

1800–1819

1804 British win control of Cape of Good Hope.
1816 Shaka becomes leader of the Zulu warriors.

1815 Java restored to Dutch by the British.
1819 Singapore founded by Stamford Raffles.

Zulu warrior

1805 English admiral Horatio Nelson dies victorious against the French at the Battle of Trafalgar.
1812 French rule under Emperor Napoleon Bonaparte in almost all of Europe.
1815 Napoleon finally defeated at Battle of Waterloo.

Napoleon Bonaparte

1811 Paraguay and Venezuela gain independence from Spain.
1812–1815 British Canada resists invasion from the USA.

1806 First white women arrive in New Zealand.
1817 First European emigrants settle Australian grasslands.

1820–1839

1822 Liberian republic for freed slaves founded in West Africa.
1830 French invade Algeria. British and Dutch South Africans (Boers) clash in South Africa.
1836 Start of Great Trek of the Boer farmers to establish independent republics in Transvaal and the Orange Free State.

1824 Britain and Burma at war.
1839–42 China seizes opium imports from India, starting First Opium War.

1821–9 Greek War of Independence from Ottoman Turkey.
1825 First passenger railway opens in England.
1830 French King Charles X overthrown in July Revolution.
1832 First Reform Act extends voting rights in Britain.
1837 Queen Victoria begins reign in England.

The Rocket
English engineer George Stephenson built this early steam-powered locomotive in 1829.

1821 Mexico wins independence from Spain. Mexicans rule Texas until 1836.
1822 Brazil gains independence from Portuguese.
1832 Samuel Morse invents electric telegraph in USA.

S. O. S.
Morse code

1825 Charles Darwin begins a five-year voyage to the Pacific for scientific research.

1840–1844

1845–1849

AFRICA

1840 Iman Sayid Said, ruler of Oman, makes the island of Zanzibar off the east African coast his capital.
1843 British take over Boer colony in northeastern province of Natal.

1847 Bantus defeated by British in southern Africa.

1845–9 Anglo/Sikh war ends in defeat for Sikhs and the beginning of British rule over their homeland, the Punjab.
1848 Nasir ud-Din begins reign as Shah (ruler) of Persia.

ASIA

1842 Treaty of Nanking gives Hong Kong to Britain and opens trading links with China.

Penny Black stamp

1845–46 Failure of potato crop in Ireland leads to severe famine.
1848 Year of Revolution in Europe.
1849 Collapse of revolutionary movements.

EUROPE

1840 The introduction of the Penny postage stamp leads to a low-cost, universally priced British postal service.

1845 Texas and Florida become US states.
1846 USA and Mexico at war over Texas.
1848 California Gold Rush leads to rapid population growth in western United States.
First US women's rights convention in New York State.

AMERICAS

1840 First general anaesthetic used in America by C.W. Long.
Upper and Lower Canada form self-governing union.

Native Americans defend their land
Increased numbers of European settlers threatened Native American territories.

OCEANIA

1840 Treaty of Waitangi signed in New Zealand.
Last convict-settlers arrive in Australia.

British and Maoris at Waitangi
The Treaty of Waitangi gave Britain possession of New Zealand in return for recognizing ancient Maori land rights.

1850–1854

1854 Independent Orange Free State set up in South Africa.

1850–64 Taiping revolt in China.
1852–53 Second war between England and Burma.
1853–54 US Navy forces Japan to open up to Western trade.

1851 Great Exhibition celebrating the industrial age held at the Crystal Palace in London.
1853–56 Crimean War between Russia, Britain, and France.

Crystal Palace

1850 California becomes a US state.
1851 First pedal-powered sewing machine made by I.S. Singer.
1853 Completion of railroad from New York to Chicago.

1850 Australian Colonies Act enables New South Wales, Tasmania, and South Australia to have virtual self-government.
1851 Australian Gold Rush begins.

Gold panners

1855–1859

1855 Discovery of Victoria Falls by English explorer Livingstone leads to European exploration of African interior.

1856–57 Persia's seizure of Herat, Afghanistan, leads to war with Britain.

Uprising in India
The refusal of Hindu and Muslim soldiers to comply with an order on religious grounds led to a major protest against British rule in 1857.

1857 Britain governs India directly after "Indian Mutiny".
1858 Treaty of Tientsin forces China to trade with the West.

1856 Henry Bessemer invents industrial steel-making process in England.
1859–61 Giuseppe Garibaldi leads the "red shirts" in the War of Italian Unification, capturing Sicily and southern Italy to form a new Italian state.

Garibaldi

1858 Reformer Benito Juarez becomes president of Mexico.
1856 Formation of anti-slavery Republican party in USA.

1856 Major Australian colonies achieve self-government.

1860–1869	1870–1879

AFRICA

1860s Britain, France, Belgium, Germany, and Portugal begin to explore and colonize inner Africa.
1869 Opening of the Suez Canal in Egypt links the Mediterranean Sea with the Indian Ocean.

1879 British defeat Zulu uprising led by King Cetshwayo at Ulundi, South Africa.
1881 Boers rebel against British rule in South Africa, leading to First Boer War.

Zulu shield
The South African Zulu people fought the British and Boer settlers to protect their land.

ASIA

1861 Empress Tze Hsi begins her 47-year rule of China.
1862 French occupation of Indo-China in Southeast Asia.

1870s Japan begins industrialization.
1872 Feudal control of Japan ends. Compulsory education is introduced.

EUROPE

1864–66 Prussian forces defeat Denmark and Austria.
1866 Swedish chemist Alfred Nobel invents dynamite.

Empire-builder
Chief minister of the Prussian state in Germany, Otto von Bismarck united the country and founded the German Empire in 1871 with Prussian King William I as emperor.

1870s Most Western European countries start industrialization.
1871 Otto von Bismarck invades and defeats France. Britain legalizes trade unions.
1876 French build refrigerated cargo ships.

Key innovations
The late 19th century saw dramatic advances in technology with the development of new inventions like electric light and telephones.

AMERICAS

1861 US Civil War begins.
1865 Union victory in Civil War. President Abraham Lincoln assassinated.
1867 British North America Act creates Dominion of Canada.

North vs South
The split of 11 Southern states from the Union in 1861 led to civil war in the USA.

1876 Sioux and Cheyenne tribes defeat Custer at the Battle of Little Bighorn.
1876–1911 Porfirio Diaz begins rule as President of Mexico.
1879–84 Chile defeats Peru and Bolivia in the War of the Pacific.
1883 Thomas Edison invents the light bulb.

OCEANIA

1860–70 War between Maoris and white settlers in New Zealand.

1876 Tahiti becomes a French colony.

1880–1889

1882 British rule of Egypt begins. **1886** Gold discovered in South Africa.

Chinese revolt against Western power

1880s Britain and France move into Burma and Vietnam. **1885** Indian National Congress Party formed.

1884 Berlin Conference decides colonial divisions in Africa. First deep underground railway built in London. **1885** Karl Benz builds first car driven by internal combustion engine in Germany. **1888** Scottish surgeon John Dunlop patents pneumatic (air-filled) tyre. Kaiser (Emperor) William II starts German reign.

Benz Motorwagen

1882 Thomas Edison designs the first hydroelectric power station. **1884** First skyscraper built in Chicago. **1889** King Pedro II deposed by army revolt and Brazil declared a republic.

1884 Volcano erupts on island of Krakatoa in Indonesia. **1885-86** Opening up of goldfields in New Guinea.

1890–1899

1896 Ethiopians defeat Italian army. **1899** Second Boer War begins in South Africa.

1899-1901 Chinese government supports peasant revolt by the Society of Harmonious Fists to rid China of all foreigners. This so-called "Boxer Rebellion" is crushed by Western forces.

1896 Modern Olympic Games introduced in Greece. **1897** Greece and Turkey at war.

1890 Last massacre of Native Americans in USA at Battle of Wounded Knee in Dakota. First moving picture (film) shows appear in New York. **1895** Cuban revolt against Spanish rule. **1896** Gold struck in Klondike, Canada. **1898** USA wins Spanish-American War and takes over the Philippines. Cuban independence from Spain.

Sioux warrior
Around 300 members of the Sioux tribe were slaughtered at the Battle of Wounded Knee.

1893 New Zealand Prime Minister Richard Seddon introduces advanced social reforms, including granting women the vote.

	1900–1904	1905–1909
AFRICA	**1902** Ovimbundu people of Angola revolt against Portuguese rule. **1904** Federation of French West Africa created.	**1905** Independent Union of former Boer republics founded in South Africa.
ASIA	**1904-5** Russo-Japanese war in Manchuria, ending in defeat for Russia and the total destruction of its fleet. **Russians fight the Japanese at the Battle of Liaio-Yang**	**1907** Discovery of oil in Persia, now modern Iran. **1909** Conflict between China and Tibet.
EUROPE	**1900** Expansion of German navy begins arms race with Britain. **1903** Votes for Women Movement formed in Britain by suffragette Emmeline Pankhurst. First Tour de France cycle race. **1904** French and British empires agree to Entente Cordiale (friendly understanding).	**1905** Tsar of Russia forced to grant democratic rights in October Manifesto. Physicist Albert Einstein formulates his Special Theory of Relativity. **1908** The AEG turbine factory in Berlin, Germany, becomes the world's first steel and glass building.
AMERICAS	**1900** Coca-Cola first produced in USA. **1901** Theodore Roosevelt becomes youngest-ever US president after assassination of President McKinley. **1902** Plastic invented in USA. **1903** Orville and Wilbur Wright build the first aeroplane and make a successful powered flight.	**1906** US forces occupy Cuba. Major earthquake damage in San Francisco. **1907** First comic strips appear in USA. **1908** Henry Ford manufactures first Model T motor car.
OCEANIA	**1900** Australia becomes a Commonwealth. New Zealand takes over the Cook Islands. **Wright Flyer**	**1907** New Zealand becomes a dominion. Minimum basic wage law set in Australia.

1910–1914

1911 Lamogi people of Uganda rebel against British rule.
1912 African National Congress formed to fight for black people's rights.

1910 Japan takes over Korea.
1911 Chinese revolution overthrows Manchu dynasty.

The sinking of the *Titanic*

1910 Halley's Comet appears.
1911 Norwegian explorer Roald Amundsen reaches South Pole.
1912 The *Titanic*, the world's largest ocean liner, strikes an iceberg on her maiden voyage, sinking with the loss of 1,513 lives.
1912–13 Greece, Serbia, Bulgaria, and Montenegro unite to defeat Ottoman Turkey in the Balkan War.
1914 European alliances break down with the assassination of Archduke Ferdinand, heir to the Austro-Hungarian Empire. World War I begins.

German soldiers, World War I

1911 Mexican dictator Diaz overthrown in revolution.
1912–33 US troops occupy Nicaragua.
1914 Opening of Panama Canal.

1914 Australia and New Zealand join the Allies in World War I.

1915–1919

1917 Ras (Prince) Tafari takes power in Ethiopia.

1915 Mohandas Gandhi becomes leader of the Indian National Congress Party.
1919 British troops fire on peaceful Indian protest in Amritsar Massacre, killing 379 people.

1915 Bulgaria aligns with Central Powers (Germany, Austro-Hungary) and Italy joins Allies (Britain, France, Russia, Serbia) in World War I.
1916 Irish revolt against British rule in Easter Rising.
1917 Communists take over from Tsar in Russian Revolution, leading to civil war. Greece joins the Allies.
1918 World War I ends with Allied victory.

Comrades in arms
Russian workers inspired by Vladimir Lenin of the Communist Bolshevik Party overthrew the tyrannical Tsar Nicholas II in 1917.

1915–16 Unrest in Haiti and Dominican Republic put down by US troops.
1917 USA enters World War I.

1919 Australia acquires former German colonies in the Pacific.

1920–1924

1925–1929

AFRICA

1922 Egypt under King Faud wins conditional independence from Britain.
1923 Ethiopia joins League of Nations.

1926 End of Berber and Arab revolt against Europeans in North Africa.

1927 Communists led by Mao Tse-tung attempt to overthrow Chinese government.
1929 Arabs attack Jews in Jerusalem, Palestine in a conflict over the Wailing Wall.

ASIA

1923 Major earthquake in Tokyo, Japan. End of Ottoman Empire as Mustafa Kemal becomes president of new Republic of Turkey.

Dictator of Italy
Fascist leader Benito Mussolini led Italy into World War II on Germany's side in 1940. He was captured and executed in 1945.

1925 Mussolini, Fascist leader of Italy, rules the country as a dictator.
1926 Police and army defeat general strike in Britain.

EUROPE

1920 Communist Red Army under Leon Trotsky wins Russian Civil War.
1922 Benito Mussolini becomes prime minister of Italian government.
1923 Partial Irish independence from Britain with creation of Irish Free State.
1924 Russian leader Vladimir Lenin dies and is succeeded by Josef Stalin.

1927 *The Jazz Singer*, starring Al Jolson, is released in the USA. It is the first "talkie", or film including a synchronized speech and music soundtrack.
1929 Prices of shares on American stock exchange fall rapidly in Wall Street Crash.

AMERICAS

1920 Prohibition (banning) of the manufacture and sale of alcohol begins in USA.
1924 US military planes make first airborne trip around the world.

The Great Depression
In October 1929, panicking share dealers on Wall Street, New York, sold 13 million shares in one day. This led to the worldwide economic crisis called the Great Depression, in which millions of people lost their jobs, businesses, savings, and homes.

OCEANIA

1923 Ross area of Antarctica becomes New Zealand dependency.

1927 Canberra becomes capital of Australia.

1930–1934

1930 Ras Tafari crowned as
Haile Selassie I in Ethiopia.
1934 Lagos Youth Movement formed,
demanding self-government of Nigeria.

1930s Indian leader Gandhi leads
non-violent opposition to
British rule in India.
1934–35 Long March of
Communists across China
to find sanctuary in the
Shaanxi province.
Troops supporting
the Nationalist leader
Chiang Kai-shek pursue them daily.

**Chinese communist troops
on the Long March**

1933 Adolf Hitler, Führer (leader)
of the Nazi Party, becomes
German Chancellor.

Führer of the Nazis
*Adolf Hitler's dream of German
world domination resulted in
World War II and ended with the
failure of his Russian invasion.
He committed suicide at the end of
the war to avoid capture and trial.*

1931 British Parliament grants
Canada full independence.
1933 Franklin D. Roosevelt
becomes US President, ending
prohibition of alcohol.

1931 First solo trans-Tasmanian flight.
1934 Airmail service from Australia
to Britain introduced.

1935–1939

1935 Italian forces invade Ethiopia.

1936 Signing of
alliance between
Japan and Germany.
1937 Japan occupies
much of Chinese
coast, leading to war
between the nations.

The rise of Japan
*Military rule of Japan in the late 1930s
led to displays of the nation's strength
in warfare and empire-building.*

1936 Olympic Games in Berlin, Germany.
1936–39 Spanish Civil War ends in
victory for Fascists and defeat
for Communists.
1937 Frank Whittle invents
the jet engine in Britain.
1938 Czechoslovakia taken
over by German forces.
1939 Britain and France
declare war on Germany
after Hitler invades Poland.
Beginning of World War II.

1935 US National Labour
Relations Act comes into force.

1937 Formation of Royal New Zealand
Air Force.
1939 Australia and New Zealand
join Allied forces against Germany.

	1940–1941	1942–1943
AFRICA	**1940** British Navy sinks French fleet at Oran to prevent its capture by Germany. **1941** Allied troops overrun Italy's African colonies. German forces led by Erwin Rommel arrive in Libya to help Italy.	**1942** Allied troops land in Morocco and force Rommel's troops to retreat from El Alamein.
ASIA	**1941** French colonies in Southeast Asia taken over by Japanese. **1941–42** Japan captures the Philippines, Malaya, Hong Kong, Singapore, Burma, and Indonesia.	**1942** US Navy defeats Japan in Coral Sea of New Guinea and at Midway Island. **1943–44** Series of victories by USA in Pacific islands pushes back Japanese forces. **Winston Churchill** *The many rousing speeches given on the radio by Britain's wartime leader Winston Churchill helped inspire the Allies to victory.*
EUROPE	**1940** Germany occupies Denmark, Norway, France, Belgium, and the Netherlands. Winston Churchill becomes Prime Minister of Britain. British air force prevents German invasion in the Battle of Britain. **1941** Hungary, Bulgaria, Greece, and parts of Yugoslavia and Russia under Germans.	**1943** Allied troops take over Sicily, then invade Italian mainland. **1943** German forces driven out of Russia.
AMERICAS	**1940** Xerox photocopying machine invented. Development of penicillin and other early antibiotics. **1941** USA joins Allies in World War II after Japanese attack on US Navy at Pearl Harbor in Hawaii.	**1942** Enrico Fermi builds first US nuclear reactor. Mexico and Brazil join Allies. Nylon used for hosiery and parachutes first produced in USA. **Nylon stockings** **Attack on Pearl Harbor** *The surprise assault by Japanese forces on the US Navy fleet at Pearl Harbor, Hawaii, in 1941 sank or damaged 18 ships and destroyed 200 aircraft.*
OCEANIA	**1940s** Australia prepares for the eventuality of a Japanese invasion.	**1942** Japanese bomb Darwin, Australia, and invade New Guinea and part of Papua.

1944–1945

1946–1947

1944 Japan attacks India but is defeated at Kohima.
1945 USA drops first atomic bombs on Japanese cities of Hiroshima and Nagasaki. Emperor Hirohito authorizes Japanese surrender.

Emperor Hirohito of Japan
Japanese pilots thought of Emperor Hirohito as a god and considered it an honour to die for him on "kamikaze" missions, which involved crash-diving explosive-packed planes into Allied ships.

1944 Allies invade France and drive back Germans.
1945 German forces surrender.

1945 USA tests first atomic bomb in New Mexico.

Dawn of the Nuclear Age
The first atomic bomb was dropped on Hiroshima, Japan, in 1945, instantly killing about 80,000 people. A second bomb was dropped on the city of Nagasaki three days later, leading to the surrender of Japan and the end of World War II.

1944 Mass breakout of Japanese prisoners of war in Australia.
1945 Australia recovers New Guinea and Papua territory from Japan.

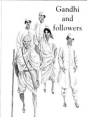
Gandhi and followers

1947 India gains independence from Great Britain amid riots that kill 500,000 people. Indian leader Gandhi begins a protest fast against the continuing violence.

1947 Marshall Plan offers US aid to help European countries rebuild their economies after World War II.

United Nations flag
The United Nations (UN) was established in 1945 to foster friendly relations between nations and to try to solve international disputes without war.

1947 US government promises to aid any country resisting communism.

1947 South Pacific Commission formed to discuss economic and health issues of South Pacific islands.

1948–1950

1951–1953

AFRICA

1950 Group Areas Act enforcing racial segregation (apartheid) passed in South Africa.

Jewish nation
In 1948, the United Nations established the state of Israel in the ancient Jewish homeland of Palestine. The resulting conflict over territory between Israelis and Arab Palestinians has continued ever since.

1951 Libyan independence from Italy sanctioned by USA.
1953 Military coup in Egypt ends anarchy and establishes a republic.

ASIA

1948 Gandhi assassinated in India. State of Israel created in Palestine.
1949 Founding of Mao Tse-tung's new Communist Republic in China.

1950-53 War between communist North Korea and US-occupied South Korea.
1953 Edmund Hillary and Sherpa Tenzing Norgay are first people to reach summit of Mount Everest.

Hillary and Tensing

EUROPE

1948 Berlin Airlift of supplies defeats USSR's blockade of West Berlin.
1949 Germany divided in two, with USA, France, and Britain running the West, and USSR controlling the East. Western Europe and USA form defensive NATO alliance against attack by USSR.

1952 Greece and Turkey join NATO.

1950s Black Americans intensify their campaign for civil rights.
1953 Link between smoking and lung cancer first established in USA.

AMERICAS

1948 Harry Truman wins Presidential election in USA.
1950 Senator Joseph McCarthy begins anti-communist "witch-hunts" in USA.

Post-war Europe
After World War II, Europe was divided into the USSR-controlled East and the US-backed West. The uneasy peace between each side, known as the Cold War, led to an arms race between the USA and USSR in which both superpowers began to stockpile nuclear weapons.

OCEANIA

1951 Australia, New Zealand, and USA sign ANZUS Pact defence alliance.

1954–1956

1954 National Liberation Front formed in Algeria to fight French rule.
1955 African National Congress (ANC) pressure group in South Africa adopts anti-racist Freedom Charter.
1956 Eygptian leader Nasser captures the Suez Canal.

1954 French defeated by communist forces at Dien Bien Phu, North Vietnam. Vietnam divided into communist North and US-backed South.
1956 Israel captures Sinai peninsula from Arab forces in eight days.

Symbol of Soviet Communism

1955 Warsaw Pact defence treaty signed by communist nations, allowing Soviet (USSR) troops to be stationed in any communist Eastern European country. West Germany joins NATO, and East Germany becomes part of Warsaw Pact.
1957 USSR launches Sputnik I, the world's first artificial satellite.

1955 Military coup in Argentina overthrows President Juan Perón.

1957–1959

1957 Ghana becomes first country in sub-Saharan Africa to gain independence.

1958 King Faisal II of Iraq is removed by a military revolt and a new republic founded.
1959 Tibetan uprising against Chinese occupation crushed. The Dalai Lama, Tibet's spiritual leader, is forced to flee the country.

The Dalai Lama

1958 Charles de Gaulle begins strong presidential rule in France.

1958 USA's first atomic-powered submarine, *USS Nautilus*, makes undersea crossing of North Pole.
1959 Revolution in Cuba brings communist Fidel Castro to power, strengthening Cuban ties with the Soviets.

Sputnik I satellite

1959 Olympics held in Melbourne, Australia. Antarctic Treaty preserves the area for research.

	1960–1963	1964–1967
AFRICA	**1960** Independence gained by 17 African colonies. A peaceful demonstration in Sharpeville against white rule in South Africa ends in the death of 69 protestors and banning of the ANC.	**1964** ANC leader Nelson Mandela jailed in South Africa. **1965** White-ruled Rhodesia declares independence from Britain. **1967** Dr. Christiaan Barnard completes first heart transplant in South Africa.
ASIA	**1963** Diem, leader of South Vietnam, is assassinated in a military coup.	**Cultural revolution in China** *Mao Tse-tung's "cultural revolution" brought Chinese industry and agriculture under state control and closed schools and colleges, forcing teachers and students to work on the land. Any opposition was brutally put down by the Red Guards, the Communist Party police.*
EUROPE	**1961** Berlin Wall built. Russian cosmonaut Yuri Gagarin is first man in space. **1962** British pop group The Beatles release *Love Me Do*, their first hit record.	**1965** US troops start arriving in South Vietnam to help in the fight against communist North Vietnam. **1966** Chinese Cultural Revolution begins. **1964** Fighting between Greeks and Turks in Cyprus. **1967** Military coup in Greece.
AMERICAS	**1961** Election of John F. Kennedy, the youngest US president. **1962** Cuban Missile Crisis. **1963** President Kennedy assassinated.	**1965** Malcolm X, campaigner for black civil rights, assassinated. Riots break out in Chicago and Los Angeles.
OCEANIA	**1960** Aboriginals recognized as Australian citizens, gaining full voting rights two years later.	**1965** Ferdinand E. Marcos elected President of the Philippines.

Fidel Castro
In 1962, Cuban dictator Fidel Castro allowed the USSR to build missile bases on Cuban soil. The US Navy blockaded Cuba and the Russians withdrew.

Martin Luther King
During the 1960s, civil rights leaders such as Martin Luther King and Malcolm X campaigned for the rights of black Americans.

1968–1971

1970 Biafra region defeated by Federal Nigerian government in civil war.

1968 US soldiers kill hundreds of unarmed civilians in Vietnamese village of My Lai.
1971 East Pakistan gains independence from India, becoming Bangladesh.

Allied troops in Vietnam

1968 Riots in Paris as students call for educational and social reform and workers demand a new minimum wage. Anti-communist uprising in Prague, former Czechoslavkia.
1969 Britain sends troops to Northern Ireland.

1968 Assassination of Martin Luther King in Memphis.
1969 US astronauts Neil Armstrong and Edwin "Buzz" Aldrin walk on the moon.

Men on the Moon
The live television broadcast of Neil Armstrong taking humankind's first steps on the lunar surface was seen by around 600 million people.

1973 Sydney Opera House opens in Australia.

1972–1975

1975 Portuguese colonies in Africa win independence.

1972 Ceylon becomes Republic of Sri Lanka.
1973 US, Australian, and New Zealand allied troops withdraw from Vietnam. Arab states attack Israel in October War and raise oil prices, leading to a world economic crisis.

Arabian oil
Many countries dependent on Arabian oil faced economic disaster when the Arab states raised their oil prices in 1973.

1972 "Bloody Sunday" in Londonderry, Northern Ireland, as British troops fire on civil rights marchers.

1973 Elected Chilean president Allende killed in military coup led by General Pinochet.
1974 US President Richard Nixon resigns in disgrace after Watergate scandal.

1975 Australia grants Papua New Guinea independence.

	1976–1980	1981–1985
AFRICA	**1976** Riots in black townships across South Africa. **1979** Ugandan leader Idi Amin ousted by Tanzanian-backed rebels. **1980** Independent Zimbabwe formed under leadership of Robert Mugabe.	**1983** War and drought lead to famine in Ethiopia. **Ethiopian Famine**
ASIA	**1976** North and South Vietnam reunited as a communist country after 22 years of separation. **1979** Camp David peace treaty between Egypt and Israel. Islamic revolution in Iran.	**1982** Israeli troops invade southern Lebanon. Palestinians massacred in Beirut refugee camp. **1984** Siege at Amritsar, India, ends with Sikh extremists being forced out of Golden Temple. Indian Prime Minister Indira Gandhi assassinated by her Sikh bodyguards.
EUROPE	**1976** Adoption of Helsinki Convention on human rights. **1978** Margaret Thatcher becomes Britain's first woman Prime Minister. **1980** President Tito of Yugoslavia dies. Lech Walesa leads Solidarity trade union in Poland.	**Iranian Revolution** *Ayatollah Khomeini, a fundamentalist (strict) Muslim hostile to the West, led the Islamic revolution that overthrew the Shah (King) of Iran in 1979. The exiled Shah's entry into the USA led to Iranian students taking 53 Americans hostage in the US embassy in Tehran.*
AMERICAS	**1977** Jimmy Carter elected US President. **1979** Sandinista guerillas defeat government forces and take power in Nicaragua.	**1981** Death of 11 Irish republican prisoners on hunger strike. **1984** French and US scientists independently identify the AIDS virus.
OCEANIA	**1978** The Solomon islands of Tuvalu and Dominica become independent nations.	**1980s** First personal computers developed in USA. **1981** Victory for Ronald Reagan in US Presidential elections. **1982** Britain defeats Argentine forces occupying British-held Falkland islands in Falklands War. Creation of Canadian constitution independent from UK. **1984** New Zealand declares itself a nuclear-free zone.

Personal computing
The first personal desk-top computer (PC) was developed by the American company IBM in 1981.

1986–1990	1991–1996
1990 Dismantling of apartheid begins in South Africa as Nelson Mandela is freed after 27 years in prison. Namibia gains independence from South Africa. **1990** Civil war begins in Liberia.	**1991** Collapse of government rule in Somalia. **1992** USA leads UN troops into Somalia. **1993** Eritrea gains independence from Ethiopia. **1994** ANC wins South Africa's first free elections. Civil war in Rwanda.

1988 Ceasefire in Iran-Iraq war ends eight years of conflict.
1989 Chinese security forces kill pro-democracy protestors in Beijing's Tiananmen Square.
1990 Iraq invades Kuwait.

Protestor at Tiananmen Square

1994 Palestinian self-rule over the Gaza Strip under 1993 peace treaty between Israel and the Palestinian Liberation Organization (PLO).

Yasser Arafat, leader of the PLO

1991 Gulf War ends with Iraq being driven from Kuwait by UN forces.
1992 Rioting between Muslims and Hindus spreads across India.

1986 New Soviet leader Mikhail Gorbachev introduces the policies of *glasnost* (openess) and *perestroika* (remodelling), eventually resulting in the break-up of the Soviet Union. **1989** Communist governments overthrown in Romania, Hungary, East Germany, and Czechoslovakia.	**1991** Dissolution of Soviet Union into Commonwealth of Independent States. **1992–95** Civil war begins in former Yugoslavia. **1994–96** Temporary Irish Republican Army (IRA) ceasefire as Anglo-Irish peace talks begin.

Fall of USSR

1986 "Irangate" revelations as US President Reagan admits to secret arms deals with Iran. **1989** George Bush becomes US President.	**1993** Canada creates Nunavut, its largest Native territory at 2.2 million sq km (850,000 sq miles). Election of Bill Clinton to US Presidency.
1986 Treaty of Rarotonga sets up South Pacific Nuclear-Free Zone.	**1996** John Hansard becomes Australian Prime Minister.

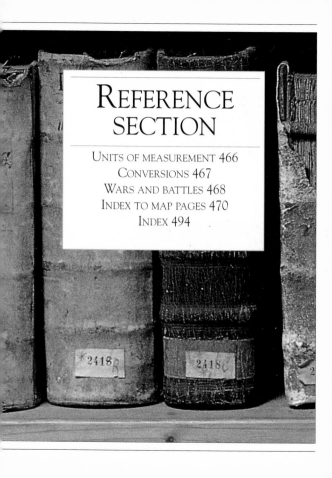

REFERENCE SECTION

2418

2418

Major wars

3100 BC First recorded war. Pharaoh
Narmer unites Upper and Lower Egypt.
c.1200 BC Trojan War War between
Greeks and Trojans, as in Homer's *Iliad*.
264–146 BC Punic Wars
Three wars between Rome and
Hannibal's Carthage, which is destroyed.
c. AD 1096–1291 Crusades
Series of religious wars in which
European Christians try to recapture
the Holy Land from Muslims.
1337–1453 Hundred Years War
English and French battle for control
of France. The French win.
1455–1485 Wars of the Roses
English war between Houses of York and
Lancaster for control of English throne.
1618–1648 Thirty Years War
Initially between German Catholics and
Protestants but later involves all Europe.
1756–1763 Seven Years War
Prussia and England fight against Austria
and France for control of Germany.
1775–1783 American Revolution
American colonists fight for
independence from British rule.
After they win, they form the USA.
1792–1815 Napoleonic Wars Fought
between Napoleon's France and Austria,
Britain, Russia, Prussia, and Sweden.
1821–1829 Greek War of
Independence Greeks fight Turkish rule.
1825–1830 Java War
Revolt of Indonesians against Dutch.
1839–1842 Opium War
Trade war between Britain and China.

1846–1848 Mexican-American War
Mexico and USA battle over Texas.
1853–1856 Crimean War
Turkey, allied with Britain, France, and
Sardinia, fights Russia in the Black Sea.
1861–1865 American Civil War
Civil war between Unionists of north
and Confederates of south.
1870–1871 Franco-Prussian War
Prussian war against France ends with
establishment of German Empire.
1894–1895 Chinese-Japanese War
Japanese defeat Chinese.
1899–1902 Boer War
Britain and the Commonwealth fight
Boers for control of South Africa.
1914–1918 World War I
Britain, France, Russia, USA and others
in global war against Germany, Austria-
Hungary, and Turkey.
1939–1945 World War II
Global war between Axis powers of
Germany, Italy, and Japan and Allied
powers of Britain, USA, and USSR.
1950–1953 Korean War
Communist North Korea fights against
South Korea and US allies.
1965–1975 Vietnam War
Communist North Vietnam fights
against South Vietnam and US allies.
1967 Six Day War Egypt against Israel.
1980–88 Iran-Iraq War
1991 Gulf War Saddam Hussein's Iraq
defeated by United Nations forces.
1991–1995 Bosnian war
Civil war in former Yugoslavia.

Famous battles

490 BC Marathon (Greece) Athenians defeat Persians and save Greece.

331 BC Gaugamela (Persia) Alexander the Great's greatest victory, defeating the Persian King Darius II.

31 BC Actium (Greece) Octavian defeats Mark Antony and Cleopatra of Egypt and becomes Emperor Augustus, ending the Roman civil wars.

AD 378 Adrianople (Turkey) Goths (Germanic tribes) defeat Romans.

636 Yarmuk (Israel) Arabs under Khalid ibn–al Walid defeat Byzantines in desert sandstorm.

732 Tours (France) Charles Martel leads Franks to victory over Moors to halt their advance in Europe.

1066 Hastings (Britain) Normans under William the Conqueror invade England and beat the Saxons.

1429 Orléans (France) French heroine Joan of Arc lifts English siege of Orléans.

1453 Constantinople (Turkey) Turks besiege and capture Constantinople (Istanbul), ending Byzantine Empire.

1526 Panipat (India) Babur conquers Delhi and establishes Mughal empire.

1571 Lepanto (Greece) End of Turkish seapower in the Mediterranean.

1588 Spanish Armada (Britain) English ships, and storms, defeat great Spanish invasion fleet of 130 ships.

1704 Blenheim (Germany) British-Austrian army led by Duke of Marlborough beats French, limiting French power in Europe.

1709 Poltava (Ukraine) Peter the Great of Russia defeats Swedes under Charles XII to control the Baltic Sea.

1759 Quebec (Canada) Britain gains control of Canada.

1777 Saratoga (USA) Decisive battle in American Revolution. British, led by Gen. Burgoyne, surrender to Americans.

1781 Yorktown (USA) George Washington leads Americans to final victory over British, ending American Revolution.

1805 Trafalgar (South of Spain) Nelson's British fleet destroys French and Spanish fleet.

1815 Waterloo End of Napoleonic wars. Allies under Wellington crush Napoleon.

1863 Gettysburg (USA) Decisive battle of American Civil War. Unionists defeat Confederates.

1914 Marne (France) Allies halt German advance on Paris.

1916 Somme (France) The deadliest battle of World War I. 1,265,000 men are killed in a few days.

1940 Battle of Britain Aircraft of British Royal Air Force (RAF) drive off German bombing raids.

1942 Midway (Pacific) Japanese aircraft fail to capture Midway Island from the USA.

1944 D–day (Normandy, France) Allies invade German-occupied France.

1991 Operation Desert Storm (Iraq) Airborne attack on Iraq by United Nations forces decides Gulf War.

Units of measurement

The metric system, based on the
number ten, is the most common
system of measurement and is used
by scientists worldwide. Certain
countries, such as the USA, use
the older imperial system.

TEMPERATURE CONVERSIONS

To convert
Fahrenheit (°F) into
centigrade (°C), use
the formula:
$$°C = (°F - 32) \div 1.8$$

To convert centigrade
(°C) into Fahrenheit
(°F), use the formula:
$$°F = (°C \times 1.8) + 32$$

VOLUME

1 cubic in (in³)	
1 cubic ft (ft³)	144 in³
1 cubic yd (yd³)	9 ft³
1 fluid oz (fl oz)	4,840 yd³
1 pint (pt)	20 fl oz
1 gallon (gal)	
1 cubic mm (mm³)	
1 cubic cm (cm³)	100 mm³
1 cubic metre (m³)	1,000,000 cm³
1 litre (l)	1,000 cm³

LENGTH

1 inch (in)	
1 foot (ft)	12 in
1 yard (yd)	3 ft
1 mile	1,760 yd
1 millimetre (mm)	
1 centimetre (cm)	10 mm
1 metre (m)	100 cm
1 kilometre (km)	1,000 m

AREA

1 square inch (in²)	
1 sq foot (ft²)	144 in²
1 sq yard (yd²)	9 ft²
1 acre	4,840 yd²
1 sq mile	640 acres
1 sq millimetre (mm²)	
1 sq centimetre (cm²)	100 mm²
1 sq metre (m²)	10,000 cm²
1 hectare	10,000 m²
1 sq kilometre (km²)	1,000,000 m²

MASS AND WEIGHT

1 ounce (oz)	
1 pound (lb)	16 oz
1 stone	14 lb
1 hundredweight (cwt)	8 stones
1 ton	20 cwt
1 gram (g)	
1 kilogram (kg)	1,000 g
1 tonne (t)	1,000 kg

Conversions

You can convert between the metric and imperial systems of measurement by using the following conversion tables.

LENGTH

To convert	Into	X by
in	cm	2.54
ft	m	0.3048
yd	m	0.9144
miles	km	1.6093
cm	in	0.3937
m	f	3.2808
m	yd	1.0936
km	miles	0.6214

AREA

To convert	Into	X by
sq in	sq cm	6.4516
sq ft	sq m	0.0929
sq yd	sq m	0.8361
acres	hectares	0.4047
sq miles	sq km	2.59
sq cm	sq in	0.155
sq m	sq ft	10.7639
sq m	sq yd	1.1960
hectares	acres	2.4711
sq km	sq miles	0.3861

MASS AND WEIGHT

To convert	Into	X by
oz	g	28.3495
lb	kg	0.4536
stones	kg	6.3503
cwt	kg	50.802
tons	tonnes	1.0161
g	oz	0.0352
kg	lb	2.2046
kg	stones	0.1575
kg	cwt	0.0197
tonnes	tons	0.9842

VOLUME

To convert	Into	X by
in³	cm³ (millilitres)	16.3871
ft³	litres	28.3169
yd³	m³	0.7646
fl oz	cm³	28.4131
pints	litres	0.5683
gallons	litres	4.5461
cm³	in³	0.0610
cm³	fl oz	0.0352
litres	ft³	0.0353
m³	yd³	1.3080
litres	pints	1.7598
litres	gallons	0.2200

PREFIXES

kilo	=	1000	centi	=	$\frac{1}{100}$
hecto	=	100	milli	=	$\frac{1}{1,000}$
deci	=	$\frac{1}{10}$	micro	=	$\frac{1}{1,000,000}$

Index to map pages

Grid references in the Index help find places on the map. If you look up Nairobi in the Index, you will see 302 F4. The first number, 302, is the page number on which the map of Nairobi appears. Next, find the letters and numbers which border the page and trace a line across from the letter and down from the number. This will direct you to the exact grid square in which the city of Nairobi is located.

Bafoussam Cameroon 305 C5

Baghdad Iraq 321 E3

Baguio Philippines 347 E2

Bahamas (Country) 231 E2

Bahrain (Country) 321 F5

Baia Mare Romania 276 C2

Baikal, Lake Rus. Fed. 327 F6

Baja California Mexico 222 C3

Baker City USA 220 D4

Bakersfield USA 221 D7

Bakhtarān Iran 321 F2

Baku Azerbaijan 287 H7

Balaton, Lake Hungary 266 D7

Balearic Is. Spain 259 H5

Bali (I.) Indonesia 346 D8

Balikesir Turkey 318 C4

Balikpapan Indonesia 346 D6

Balkan Mts. S.E. Europe 275 H6

Balkhash, Lake Kazakhstan 326 D7

Balsas (R.) Mexico 223 F6

Baltic Sea N. Europe 360 G3/249/266 D2/282 B4

Baltimore USA 213 H2

Bamako Mali 296 D5

Ban Me Thuot Vietnam 345 G6

Banda Sea Indonesia 347 F7

Bandar Seri Begawan Brunei 346 D5

Bandar-e Abbās Iran 321 G5

Bandundu Zaire 305 D6

Bandung Indonesia 346 C8

Bangalore India 333 E7

Bangkok Thailand 345 D5

Bangladesh (Country) 333 G4

Bangui Central African Republic 305 E5

Banja Luka Bosnia & Herzegovina 274 D4

Banjarmasin Indonesia 346 D7

Banjul Gambia 296 B5

Banská Bystrica Slovakia 267 E6

Baotou China 337 F4

Baranavichy Belorussia 283 D6

Barbados (Country) 231 H7

Barcelona Spain 259 G3

Bareilly India 325 F3

Barents Sea Arctic Ocean 365 H6/284 E3/326 D3

Bari Italy 263 G5

Barinas Venezuela 236 C3

Barnaul Rus. Fed. 327 E6

Barquisimeto Venezuela 236 D3

Barranquilla Colombia 236 B3

Barysaw Belorussia 283 F6

Basle Switzerland 270 B4

Basque Provinces Spain 259 E2

Bassein Burma 345 B5

Bata Equatorial Guinea 305 B5

Batangas Philippines 347 E2

Bătdâmbâng Cambodia 345 E6

Baton Rouge USA 212 D5

Bavaria Germany 269 F6

Bavarian Alps (Mts.) Germany 269 F7

Bayan Har Mts. China 336 D6

Beaufort Sea 206 D3/365 F3

Beaumont USA 219 H6

Béchar Algeria 294 D3

Beersheba Israel 317 C6

Beira Mozambique 311 G5/363 B6

Beirut Lebanon 316 C4

Beja Portugal 258 C6

Belém Brazil 240 F4

Belfast Northern Ireland UK 253 D5

Belgium (Country) 255

Belgrade Yugoslavia 274 F4

Belize (Country) 230 B4

Bellevue USA 220 B3

Bellingshausen Sea Antarctica 364 B4

Belmopan Belize 230 B4

Belo Horizonte Brazil 241 F4

Belorussia (Country) 283

Bengal, Bay of India/South Asia 362 F4/333 G5/344 A4

Benghazi Libya 295 G3

Benin (Country) 297 F6

Berbera Somalia 301 G6

Berbérati Central African Republic 305 D5

Bergen Norway 360 F3/249 A3

Bergen op Zoom Netherlands 254 C4

Bering Sea Pacific Ocean 206 B4/327 H2/353 E2

Bering Strait Arctic Ocean/Pacific Ocean 206 B3/327 H1/353 E1

Berlin Germany 268 G4

Bermuda (I.) UK 360 C4

Bern Switzerland 270 B4

Bernese Alps (Mts.) Switzerland 270 B6

Beskid Mts. Poland 267 F5

Bhopal India 333 E4

Bhutan (Country) 333 G3

Bielefeld Germany 268 D4

Bien Hoa Vietnam 345 G6

Bila Tserkva Ukraine 286 D3

Birmingham UK 253 F6

Birmingham USA 213 E4

Biscay, Bay of Spain 259 E1

Bishkek Kyrgyzstan 325 G2

Bissau Guinea-Bissau 296 C4

Bitola Macedonia 275 G7

Biysk Rus. Fed. 327 E6

Black (R.) China/Vietnam 344 E4

Black Forest Germany 269 D6

Black Sea 277 H6/285 A7/ 287 G6/318– 319

Blagoveshchensk Rus. Fed. 327 G6

Blanco, Cape USA 220 A4

Blantyre Malawi 303 F7

Bob-Dioulasso Burkina 297 E6

Bogor Indonesia 346 C7

Bogotà Colombia 236 B4

Bohemia Czech Republic 267 B5

Boise USA 216 C3

Bolivia (Country) 237 E7

Bologna Italy 262 D4

Bombay India 362 E4/ 333 E5

Bomu (R.) Central African Republic/Zaire 305 F5

Bonifacio, Strait of Sardinia 263 B5

Bonn Germany 269 C5

Borås Sweden 249 C7

Bordeaux France 260 D6

Borneo (I.) Indonesia 363 G5/346 D5

Bosnia & Herzegovina (Country) 274– 275

Bosporus Turkey 318 D3

Boston USA 211 G5

Bothnia, Gulf of Sweden/ Finland 249 E5

Botswana (Country) 311

Bouvet I. Norway 361 F7

Bradford UK 253 G5

Brahmaputra (var. Yarlung Zangbo) (R.) 333 H3/336 C7

Brăila Romania 276 G4

Brasília Brazil 241 F5

Braşov Romania 276 E4

Bratislava Slovakia 267 D6

Brazil (Country) 240– 241

Brazilian Highlands (Mts.) Brazil 241 G5

Brazzaville Congo 305 D6

Brecon Beacons (Mts.) UK 253 E7

Breda Netherlands 254 D4

Bregenz Austria 270 D4

Bremen Germany 268 D3

Brest Belorussia 283 C7

Brest France 260 C3

Bridgeport USA 211 F6

Brisbane Australia 355 G4

Bristol UK 253 F7

Bristol Bay Alaska USA 206 B5

British Columbia (Province) Canada 206 D7

British Indian Ocean Territory UK 363 H5

British Virgin Is. UK 231 H5

Brittany France 260 C3

Brno Czech Republic 267 D5

Bruges Belgium 255 B5

Brunei (Country) 346 D4

Brunswick Germany 268 E4

Brussels Belgium 255 D5

Bucharest Romania 277 E5

Budapest Hungary 267 E6

Buenaventura Colombia 236 B4

Buenos Aires Argentina 243 E5/361 C6

Buenos Aires, Lake Argentina 243 C7

Buffalo USA 210 D4

Bug (R.) Poland/Ukraine 266 G3

Bujumbura Burundi 302 D4

Bukavu Zaire 305 G6

Bukhara Uzbekistan 325 E4

Bulawayo Zimbabwe 311 E5

Bulgaria (Country) 277

Buraydah Saudi Arabia 321 E4

Burgas Bulgaria 277 G6

Burgundy France 261 F3

Burkina (Country) 297 E5

Burma (Country)344

Bursa Turkey 318 D4

Buru (I.) Indonesia 347 F6

Burundi (Country) 302 D4

Butuan Philippines 347 F3

Buzău Romania 276 F4

Bydgoszcz Poland 266 D3

C

Cabanatuan Philippines 347 E2

Cabinda Angola 310 A3

Cabora Bassa, Lake Mozambique 310 F4

Cadiz Philippines 347 E3

Caen France 260 D2

Caesarea Israel 317 C5

Cagayan de Oro Philippines 347 F4
Cagliari Sardinia 263 B6
Cairo Egypt 300 C3
Calabria Italy 263 G6
Calais France 261 E1
Calbayog Philippines 347 F3
Calcutta India 362 F3/333 G4
Calgary Canada 207 E8
Cali Colombia 236 B4
California (State) USA 221 C7
Callao Peru 237 B6/353 H5
Cambodia (Country) 345
Cambrian Mts. UK 253 E6
Cameroon (Country) 305 C5
Campeche Mexico 223 H6
Campinas Brazil 241 F6
Can Tho Vietnam 345 F6
Canaveral, Cape USA 215 F7
Canberra Australia 355 F6
Caniapiscau, Lake Canada 209 E4
Canton China 339 E5
Cape Town South Africa 361 G6/311 C7/363 B6
Capeenda Camulemba Angola 310 C3
Cappadocia Turkey 319 F5
Capri (I.) Italy 263 E6
Caracas Venezuela 236 D3
Cardiff UK 253 E7
Caribbean Sea 236 C2/361 B5
Carpathians (Mts.) E. Europe 267 E5/276
Carpentaria, Gulf of Australia 355 E2
Carson City USA 218 C2
Cartagena Colombia 236 B3

Casablanca Morocco 294 D3
Casper USA 217 E4
Caspian Sea Asia/Europe 285 C7/287 H7/321 G1/326 B4
Catalonia Spain 259 G3
Catania Sicily 263 F7
Catskill Mts. USA 211 E5
Caucasus (Mts.) 285 B7/287 F6
Cayenne French Guiana 236 H4
Cedar Rapids USA 217 H4
Celebes (I.) Indonesia 347 E6
Central African Republic (Country) 305 E5
Cephalonia (I.) Greece 278 D4
Cevennes (Mts.) France 261 F7
Chad (Country) 304 E3
Chad, Lake C. Africa 297 H5/304 D4
Chagai Hills Pakistan 332 C2
Chalbi Desert Kenya 302 G3
Changchun China 338 G2
Changsha China 339 E5
Channel Is. UK 253 F8/260 C2
Chardzhou Turkmenistan 325 E4
Charleroi Belgium 255 D6
Charleston (South Carolina) USA 213 F5
Charleston (West Virginia) USA 213 F2
Charlottetown Canada 209 F6
Chattanooga USA 213 E3
Cheju South Korea 338 G4

Chelyabinsk Rus. Fed. 326 D5
Chemnitz Germany 269 G5
Chengdu China 338 C4
Cherbourg France 260 D2
Chernihiv Ukraine 286 D2
Chernivtsi Ukraine 286 C4
Chernobyl Ukraine 286 D2
Chesapeake Bay USA 213 H2
Cheyenne USA 217 E4
Chiang Mai Thailand 344 D4
Chiba Japan 341 F5
Chicago USA 215 F5
Chiclayo Peru 237 A6
Chico USA 218 B2
Chidley, Cape Canada 209 F2
Chihuahua Mexico 223 E3
Chile (Country) 242–243
Chillán Chile 243 B5
Chimbote Peru 237 A6
China (Country) 336–339
Chingola Zambia 303 C6
Chios (I.) Greece 279 G3
Chirchik Uzbekistan 325 F3
Chisinau Moldavia 286 D4
Chittagong Bangladesh 333 G4
Chitungwiza Zimbabwe 311 F5
Ch'ŏngjin North Korea 338 H2
Chon Buri Thailand 345 D6
Christchurch NZ 357 D6
Christmas I. Australia 363 G5
Chukchi Sea Arctic Ocean 365 G2
Chungking China 338 C4
Churchill Canada 207 F6

Denmark Strait 365 F8
Denpasar Indonesia 346 D8
Denver USA 219 F2
Derby UK 253 G6
Des Moines USA 217 G4
Detroit USA 215 G5
Devon I. Canada 207 F3/
  365 F5
Dezfûl Iran 321 F3
Dhanbad India 333 G4
Dharwad India 333 E6
Dieppe France 261 E2
Dijon France 261 F4
Dinaric Alps (Mts.) Bosnia
  & Herzegovina/Croatia
  275 C5
Dire Dawa Ethiopia 301 F6
Diyarbakir Turkey 319 G5
Djibouti (Country) 301
Djibouti Djibouti 301 F6/
  362 C4
Dnieper (R.) E. Europe
  283 G7/285 B5/287 E4
Dniester (R.) Ukraine/
  Moldavia 286 C3
Dnipropetrovs'k Ukraine
  287 E4
Dobrich Bulgaria 277 G5
Dodecanese (Is.) Greece
  279 G6
Dodoma Tanzania 303 F5
Doha Qatar 321 F5
Dolomites (Mts.) Italy
  262 D3
Dominica (Country) 231 H6
Dominican Republic
  (Country) 231 F4
Don (R.) Rus. Fed. 285 B6
Donets (R.) Rus. Fed./
  Ukraine 287 E3
Donets'k Ukraine 287 F4
Dongguang China 339 E5
Dordogne (R.) France
  261 E6

Dordrecht Netherlands
  254 D4
Dortmund Germany
  268 C4
Douala Cameroon 305 B5
Dover USA 211 E7
Dover, Strait of France/
  UK 261 E1
Drakensberg (Mts.) South
  Africa 311 E7
Dresden Germany 269 H5
Drin (R.) Albania 275 F6
Drobeta-Turnu-Severin
  Romania 277 C5
Dubai United Arab
  Emirates 321 G5
Dublin Ireland 253 D5
Dubrovnik Croatia 275 D5
Duero (R.) Spain 259 E3
Duisberg Germany
  268 C4
Dunedin NZ 357 C8
Durance (R.) France 261 G7
Durban South Africa 311
  F7/363 B6
Durham USA 213 G3
Dushanbe Tajikistan
  325 F4
Düsseldorf Germany 269 C5
Dvina, Western (R.)
  Belorussia 285 F5
Dzhizak Uzbekistan 325 E3
Dzhugdzhur Range (Mts.)
  Rus. Fed. 327 G5

E
East China Sea 338 G4/
  341 A7
East London South Africa
  311 E7
East Siberian Sea Arctic
  Ocean 365 H3/327 G2
- Ebro (R.) Spain 259 F3
Ecuador (Country) 237 A5

Edinburgh UK 253 F4
Edmonton Canada 207 E7
Edward, Lake Uganda/
  Zaire 305–302
Edwards Plateau USA
  219 G6
Egypt (Country) 300 C4
Eindhoven Netherlands
  254 E4
Eisenstadt Austria 271 H3
El Aaiun Western Sahara
  294 C4
El Faiyûm Egypt 300 C3
El Mansûra Egypt 300 C3
El Minya Egypt 300 C3
El Obeid Sudan 301 C6
El Paso USA 219 E6
El Salvador (Country)
  230 B5
Elat Israel 317 C6
Elâziğ Turkey 319 G5
Elba (I.) Italy 263 C5
Elbe (R.) Germany 268 F3
Elburz Mts. Iran 321 G2
Ellesmere I. Canada
  207 F2/365 F5
Ellsworth Mts. Antarctica
  364 B5
Ems (R.) Germany 268 C4
En Gedi Israel 317 C5
Enderby Land Antarctica
  364 D4
England (Country) 252–253
English Channel France/
  UK 253/260
Enschede Netherlands
  254 G3
Ephesus Turkey 318 C5
Equatorial Guinea
  (Country) 305 C5
Erfurt Germany 269 F5
Erie, Lake Canada/USA
  208 D8/210 D5/215 H5
Eritrea (Country) 301

Erzurum Turkey 319 G3
Eşfahān Iran 321 G3
Eskişehir Turkey 318 D4
Essen Germany 268 C4
Estonia (Country) 282 D3
Ethiopia (Country) 301
Ethiopian Highlands
(Mts.) Ethiopia 301 E6
Eugene USA 220 B4
Euphrates (R.) S.W. Asia
319 F6/316 G3/321 E3
Eureka USA 221 A5
Evansville USA 215 F8
Everett USA 220 B2
Everglades, The USA
213 F8
Evvoia Greece 279 E4
Eyre, Lake Australia
355 E5

F

Faeroe Is. Denmark 360 E3
Fairbanks Alaska USA
206 C4
Faisalabad Pakistan 333 E2
Falkland Is. UK 361 C7
Famagusta Cyprus 319 E7
Farewell, Cape Greenland
360 D3
Fargo USA 217 G2
Faro Portugal 258 C7
Farvel, Cape Greenland
365 E8
Fergana Uzbekistan 325 F3
Fez Morocco 294 D3
Fiji (Country) 353 E5
Finland (Country)
248–249
Finland, Gulf of Baltic Sea
249 F6/282 D2
Flinders Ranges (Mts.)
Australia 355 E5
Flint USA 215 G5
Florence Italy 262 D4

Flores (I.) Indonesia 347 E8
Florida (State) USA 213 F6
Florida Keys USA 213 F8
Focşani Romania 276 F4
Formosa Paraguay 242 E3
Fort McMurray Canada
207 E7
Fort Wayne USA 215 G6
Fort Worth USA 219 G5
Fortaleza Brazil 240 H4
Forth (R.) UK 252 E4
France (Country) 260–261
Francistown Botswana
311 E5
Frankfort USA 215 F2
Frankfurt Germany 269 D5
Frankivs'k Ukraine 286 C3
Franz Josef Land (Is.) Rus.
Fed. 365 H6
Fredericton Canada 209 F7
Freetown Sierra Leone
296 C6
Fremantle Australia
363 G6
French Guiana France
236 H4
French Polynesia France
353 F5
Fresno USA 221 C7
Fukuoka Japan 341 B6
Fushun China 338 G3
Fuzhou China 339 F5

G

Gabon (Country) 305 C6
Gaborone Botswana 311
E6
Galápagos Is. Ecuador
353 G4
Galaţi Romania 276 G4
Galicia Poland 267 F5
Galicia Spain 258 D2
Galle Sri Lanka 333 F8
Gallipoli Turkey 318 C4

Galway Ireland 253 B5
Gambia (Country) 296 C5
Gäncä Azerbaijan 287 G7
Gangdise Range (Mts.)
China 336 C7
Ganges (R.) India 362 F3/
333 F3
Garda, Lake Italy 262 C3
Garonne (R.) France 260 D6
Garoua Cameroon 304 C4
Gary USA 215 F6
Gaza Gaza Strip 317 C5
Gaza Strip 317 C5
Gaziantep Turkey 319 F6
Gdańsk Poland 266 E2
Geelong Australia 355 F7
General Santos Philippines
347 F4
Geneva Switzerland 270 A7
Geneva, Lake France/
Switzerland 261 G4/
270 B6
Genoa Italy 262 B4
Genoa, Gulf of Italy 262 C4
Georgetown Cayman Is.
230 D4
Georgetown Guyana 236 F3
Georgia (Country) 287
Georgia (State) USA 213 F5
Germany (Country)
268–269
Ghana West Africa 297 E6
Ghāt Libya 295 F5
Ghent Netherlands 255 C5
Gibraltar Gibraltar 258 D8
Gibraltar UK 360 F4/258
D8
Gibraltar, Strait of
Morocco/Spain
258 D8/ 294 D2
Gibson Desert Australia
354 D4
Giza Egypt 300 C3
Glasgow UK 252 E4

Helwân Egypt 300 C3
Henzada Burma 344 B4
Herât Afghanistan 324 D6
Hermosillo Mexico 222 D2
Hidaka Mts. Japan 340 F2
Highlands (Mts.) UK
252 E3
Himalayas (Mts.) S. Asia
333 F2/336 C7
Ḥimṣ Syria 316 D4
Hindu Kush (Mts.)
Afghanistan 325 F5
Hiroshima Japan 341 B5
Ho Chi Minh City Vietnam
345 F6
Hobart Australia 355 F8
Hodeida Yemen 320 D8
Hohe Tauern (Mts.)
Austria 271 F4
Hohhot China 337 F4
Hokkaidō (I.) Japan 340 F2
Hollywood (Florida) USA
213 F8
Holon Israel 317 C5
Homyel' Belorussia
283 G7
Honduras (Country)
230 B4
Hong Gai Vietnam 344 G4
Hong Kong (UK) 339 E6/
352 C3
Hongshui He (R.) China
339 C5
Honolulu USA 353 E3
Honshú (I.) Japan 340 E4
Horlivka Ukraine 287 F4
Hormuz, Strait of Iran/
Oman 321 G5
Horn of Africa Somalia
301 H6
Horn, Cape Chile 243 D8/
361 C7/353 H7
Houston USA 219 H6
Hrodna Belorussia 283 C6

Huainan China 338 E4
Huambo Angola 310 B4
Huancayo Peru 237 B6
Hudson Bay Canada
208 D3/207 G5
Hudson Strait Canada
207 G4/209 E1
Hue Vietnam 345 G5
Hulun Nur (Lake) China
337 G2
Hungary (Country) 267
Huntsville USA 213 E3
Huron, Lake Canada/USA
208 C7/215 G3
Hyderabad India 333 E6
Hyderabad Pakistan
332 D3

I
Iaşi Romania 276 F3
Ibadan Nigeria 297 F7
Ibiza Balearic Is. Spain
259 G5
Ica Peru 237 B7
Iceland (Country) 360 E3
Idaho (State) USA 216 C3
Ilâm Iran 321 F3
Ilebo Zaire 305 E6
Iligan Philippines 347 F4
Illinois (R.) USA 215 E7
Illinois (State) USA 215 E6
Iloilo Philippines 347 E3
Ilorin Nigeria 297 F6
Imphal India 333 H4
Inch'ŏn South Korea 338 G3
India (Country) 352– 333
Indian Ocean 301 H7/
311– 363/346 C8
Indiana (State) USA F6
Indianapolis USA 215 F7
Indigirka (R.) Rus. Fed.
327 G3
Indonesia (Country)
346– 347

Indore India 333 E4
Indus (R.) Pakistan
332 D3
Inn (R.) Austria 271 E4
Inner Mongolia China
337 F3
Innsbruck Austria
271 E5
Insein Burma 345 C5
Invercargill NZ 357 B8
Ionian Is. Greece 278 C4
Ionian Sea Greece 263 H7/
278 C4
Ios (I.) Greece 279 F6
Iowa (State) USA 217 G4
Ipoh Malaysia 345 D8
Iquitos Peru 237 C5
Iraklion Greece 279 F8
Iran (Country) 321 G3
Iraq (Country) 321 E2
Irbid Jordan 317 D5
Irbil Iraq 321 F2
Ireland (Country)
252– 253
Irian Jaya Indonesia
347 H6
Irish Sea 253
Irkutsk Rus. Fed. 327 F6
Irrawaddy (R.) Burma
208 C3/362 F3
Ishikari Mts. Japan 340 F2
Islamabad Pakistan
333 E1
Ismâ'iliya Egypt 300 D3
Isparta Turkey 318 D5
Israel (Country) 317
Istanbul Turkey 318 D4
Italy (Country) 262– 263
Ivory Coast (Country)
296 D7
Izhevsk Rus. Fed. 285 E5/
326 C5
Izmir Turkey 318 C5
Izmit Turkey 318 D3

J

Jabalpur India 333 F4
Jackson USA 212 D4
Jacksonville USA 213 F6
Jaffna Sri Lanka 333 F7
Jaipur India 333 E3
Jalandhar India 333 E2
Jamaica (Country) 231 E4
Jambi Indonesia 346 B6
James Bay Canada 208 D4
Jan Mayen I. Norway
   365 G8
Japan (Country) 340–341
Japan, Sea of E. Asia 327
   H6/340 D4/352 D2
Java (I.) Indonesia 363 G5/
   346 C8
Java Sea Indonesia 346 C7
Jayapura Indonesia 347 H6
Jedda Saudi Arabia 320 D5
Jefferson City USA 217 H5
Jember Indonesia 346 D8
Jersey (I.) UK 253 F8
Jerusalem Israel 317 C5
Jilin China 338 G2
Jinan China 338 E3
Jingdezhen China 338 F5
Jodhpur India 333 E3
Johannesburg South
   Africa 311 E6
Johor Baharu Malaysia
   345 E8
Jönköping Sweden 249 C7
Jordan (Country) 317
Juan de Fuca, Strait of
   USA/Canada 220 A2
Juneau Alaska 206 D6
Jutland Denmark 249 A7

K

Kabul Afghanistan 325 F6
Kabwe Kenya 303 C7
Kagoshima Japan 341 B6

Kahramanmaraş Turkey
   319 F5
Kalahari Desert Botswana
   311 D6
Kalemie Zaire 305 G7
Kaliningrad Rus. Fed.
   283 B5
Kamchatka Rus. Fed.
   327 H3
Kampala Uganda 302 E3
Kâmpóng Cham
   Cambodia 345 F6
Kananga Zaire 305 F7
Kano Nigeria 297 G5
Kanpur India 333 F3
Kansas (State) USA
   217 G5
Kansas City USA 217 G5
Kao-hsiung Taiwan 339 F5
Kara Sea Rus. Fed. 365 H5/
   284 G3/326 D3
Karachi Pakistan 362 E3/
   332 D3
Karaganda Kazakhstan
   326 D6
Karakorum Mts. China
   336 B5
Karakum Canal
   Turkmenistan 324 C4
Karbala Iraq 321 E3
Kariba, Lake Zambia/
   Zaire 305 C7/311 E5
Karlsruhe Germany 269 D6
Karpathos (I.) Greece
   279 G7
Karshi Uzbekistan 325 E4
Kasai (R.) Zaire 305 E6
Kathmandu Nepal 333 F3
Katowice Poland 267 E5
Kattegat Denmark 249 B7
Kaunas Lithuania 283 C5
Kawasaki Japan 341 F5
Kayseri Turkey 319 E5
Kazakhstan (Country) 326

Kazan' Rus. Fed. 285 D6/
   326 C5
Kediri Indonesia 346 D8
Kelang Malaysia 345 D8
Kendari Indonesia 347 E6
Kentucky (State) USA
   213 E2
Kenya (Country) 302
Kermān Iran 321 G4
Khabarovsk Rus. Fed.
   327 H6
Khadzhent Tajikistan
   325 F3
Kharkiv Ukraine 287 E3
Khartoum Sudan 301 D5
Khasab Oman 321 G5
Kherson Ukraine 287 E4
Khmel'nyts'kyy Ukraine
   286 D3
Khon Kaen Thailand
   345 E5
Khulna Bangladesh 333 G4
Khyber Pass Afghanistan/
   Pakistan 325 F6
Kiel Germany 268 E2
Kiev Ukraine 286 D3
Kigali Rwanda 302 D4
Kikwit Zaire 305 E7
Kimberley South Africa
   311 D7
King Leopold Range
   (Mts.) Australia 354 C3
Kingston Jamaica 231 E4
Kinshasa Zaire 305 D6
Kirghiz Range (Mts.)
   Kyrgyzstan 325 G2
Kiribati (Country) 353 E4
Kirkük Iraq 321 F2
Kirov Rus. Fed. 326 C4
Kisangani Zaire 305 F6
Kismaayo Somalia 301 F8
Kitakyūshū Japan 341 B6
Kithira (I.) Greece 279 E7
Kitwe Zambia 303 C6

Libreville Gabon 305 B6
Libya (Country) 295
Libyan Desert Egypt 300 B4
Liechtenstein (Country) 270 D5
Liège Belgium 255 E6
Liepāja Latvia 282 B4
Ligurian Sea Italy 262 B4
Likasi Zaire 305 G8
Lille France 261 E1
Lilongwe Malawi 305 E7
Lima Peru 237 B6
Limassol Cyprus 319 E7
Limnos (I.) Greece 279 F3
Limoges France 261 E5
Limpopo (R.) Mozambique/Southern Africa 311 E6/363 B6
Lincoln USA 217 G4
Linköping Sweden 249 D6
Linz Austria 271 F3
Lipari Is. Italy 263 F7
Lisbon Portugal 258 C5
Lithuania (Country) 283 C5
Little Rock USA 212 D3
Liverpool UK 253 F6
Ljubljana Slovenia 274 B3
Lobito Angola 310 A4
Loch Lomond UK 252 E4
Loch Ness UK 252 E3
Łódź Poland 266 E4
Lofoten Vesterålen (Is.) Norway 248 D3
Logrono Spain 259 F2
Loire (R.) France 260 D4
Lombardy Italy 262 C3
Lombok (I.) Indonesia 346 D8
Lomé Togo 297 E7
London Canada 208 D8
London UK 253 G7
Londonderry Northern Ireland UK 252 C4

Long Beach USA 221 D8/353 F3
Long I. USA 211 F6
Long Xuyen Vietnam 345 F6
Longyearbyen Svalbard Arctic Ocean 365 G7
Lopatka, Cape Rus. Fed. 327 H4
Los Àngeles Chile 243 B6
Los Angeles USA 221 D8
Louang Phrabang Laos 344 E4
Louisiana (State) USA 212 C5
Louisville USA 213 E2
Lower Tunguska Rus. Fed. 327 E5
Lualaba (R.) Zaire 305 G6
Luanda Angola 310 A3
Luanshya Zambia 305 C6
Lubbock USA 219 F5
Lübeck Germany 268 E3
Lublin Poland 266 G4
Lubumbashi Zaire 305 G8
Lucena Philippines 347 E2
Lucerne, Lake Switzerland 270 C5
Lucknow India 333 F3
Ludhiana India 333 E2
Luhans'k Ukraine 287 F4
Luoyang China 338 E4
Lusaka Zambia 305 C7
Luts'k Ukraine 286 C3
Luxembourg (Country) 255 F7
Luxor Egypt 300 D4
Luzon (I.) Philippines 347 E1
L'viv Ukraine 286 C3
Lyon France 261 F5

M
Maas (R.) W. Europe 254 F4
Maastricht Netherlands 255 E5
Macao Portugal 339 E6
Macdonnell Ranges (Mts.) Australia 354 D4
Macedonia (Country) 275
Maceió Brazil 241 H5
Mackenzie (R.) Canada 207 E5
Madagascar (Country) 363 C6
Madeira (Is.) Portugal 360 E4
Madeira (R.) Bolivia/Brazil 240 C4
Madison USA 215 E5
Madras India 362 E4/333 E7
Madrid Spain 259 E4
Madurai India 333 E7
Magadan Rus. Fed. 327 H4
Magdalena (R.) Colombia 236 B3
Magdeburg Germany 268 F4
Magellan, Strait of Chile 243 D8
Maggiore, Lake Italy 270 C6/262 B3
Mahilyow Belorussia 283 G6
Mai-Ndombe, Lake Zaire 305 E6
Maine (State) USA 211 G2
Mainz Germany 269 D5
Majorca Balearic Is. Spain 259 H5
Makassar Strait Indonesia 347 E6
Makiyivka Ukraine 287 F4
Malabo Equatorial Guinea 305 B5
Málaga Spain 259 E7

Mississippi (R.) USA
212 D3/214 D3
Mississippi (State) USA
212 D4
Missouri (R.) USA 217 E2
Missouri (State) USA 217 H5
Mitumba Mts. Zaire 305 G7
Mobile USA 212 D5
Mogadishu Somalia 301 G7
Mojave Desert USA 221 E7
Moldavia (Country) 286
Molucca Sea Indonesia
347 F5
Moluccas (Is.) Indonesia
347 F6
Mombasa Kenya 302 G4/
363 C5
Monaco (Country) 261 G7
Mongolia (Country)
336– 337
Monrovia Liberia 296 C7
Mons Belgium 255 C6
Montana (State) USA
216 D2
Monte Carlo Monaco
261 G7
Montenegro (Republic)
Yugoslavia 275
Monterrey Mexico 223 F4
Montevideo Uruguay
245 E5
Montgomery USA 213 E4
Montpelier USA 211 F4
Montpellier France
261 F7
Montréal Canada 209 E7
Montserrat UK 231 H6
Monywa Burma 344 B3
Morava (R.) Czech
Republic/Slovakia 267 D6
Moravia Czech Republic
267 D5
Morocco (Country) 294
Moroni Comoros 363 C5

Moscow Rus. Fed. 285 C5/
326 C4
Mosel (R.) Germany 269 C6
Moselle (R.) France 261 G3
Mostar Bosnia &
Herzegovina 275 D5
Mosul Iraq 321 E2
Moulmein Burma
345 C5
Moundou Chad 304 D4
Mozambique (Country)
310– 311
Muang Phitsanulok
Thailand 345 D5
Mufulira Zambia 305 C6
Mull (I.) UK 252 D3
Multan Pakistan 333 E2
Munich Germany 269 F7
Münster Germany 268 C4
Murcia Spain 259 F6
Murmansk Rus. Fed.
360 H3/284 D3/326 D3
Murray (R.) Australia
355 E6
Murrumbidgee (R.)
Australia 355 F6
Muscat Oman 321 G6
Mwanza Tanzania 302 E4
Mweru, Lake Zambia/
Zaire 305 C5
Mykolaïv Ukraine 286 D4

N
Naberezhnyye Chelny
Rus. Fed. 285 E6/
326 C5
Nacala Mozambique 310 H4
Naga Philippines 347 E2
Nagoya Japan 341 D5
Nagpur India 333 E4
Nain Canada 209 F3
Nairobi Kenya 302 F4
Nakhodka Rus. Fed.
327 E4

Nakhon Ratchasima
Thailand 345 E5
Nakhon Sawan Thailand
345 E5
Nakhon Si Thammarat
Thailand 345 D7
Nam Dinh Vietnam 344 F4
Namangan Uzbekistan
325 F3
Namibe Angola 310 A4
Namibia (Country) 311
Namp'o North Korea
338 G3
Nampula Mozambique
310 H4
Namur Belgium 255 D6
Nanchang China 339 E5
Nancy France 261 F2
Nanjing China 338 F4
Nanning China 339 D6
Nantes France 260 D4
Napier NZ 356 G4
Naples Italy 263 F6
Narsarsuaq Greenland
365 E8
Nashville USA 213 E3
Nasik India 333 E5
Nassau Bahamas 231 E2
Natal Brazil 240 H4
Nauru (Country) 352 D4
Navarin, Cape Rus. Fed.
327 H2
Navoi Uzbekistan 325 E3
Naxos (I.) Greece 279 F6
N'djamena Chad 304 D4
Ndola Zambia 305 C6
Nebit Dag Turkmenistan
324 C3
Nebraska (State) USA
217 F4
Negro (R.) Brazil 240 C4
Negros (I.) Philippines
347 E5
Nepal (Country) 333 F3

Ohrid, Lake Albania/
Macedonia 275 G7
Ohře (R.) Czech Republic/
Germany 267 B5
Okayama Japan 341 C5
Okhotsk, Sea of Japan
327 H4/340 F1/352 D2
Okinawa (I.) Japan 341 A8
Oklahoma (State) USA
217 G7
Oklahoma City USA 217 G7
Olenëk Bay Rus. Fed.
327 F3
Olympia USA 220 B3
Omaha USA 217 G4
Oman (Country) 321 G7
Oman, Gulf of 321 G6
Omdurman Sudan 301 D5
Omsk Rus. Fed. 326 D6
Onega (R.) Rus. Fed. 284 D4
Onega, Lake Rus. Fed.
284 C4
Onitsha Nigeria 297 F7
Ontario (Province) Canada
208 C5
Ontario, Lake Canada/
USA 208 D8/ 211 E4
Oran Algeria 295 E2
Orange (R.) Southern
Africa 311 C7
Ordos Desert China 337 F5
Örebro Sweden 249 D6
Oregon (State) USA
220 C4
Orenburg Rus. Fed.
285 E6/326 C5
Orinoco (R.) Venezuela
256 E3
Orkney Is. UK 252 F2
Orlando USA 213 F6
Orléans France 261 E3
Orsha Belorussia 283 G5
Oruro Bolivia 237 D7
Ōsaka Japan 341 D5

Osh Kyrgyzstan 325 G3
Oshogbo Nigeria 297 F7
Osijek Croatia 274 E3
Oslo Norway 249 B6
Osorno Chile 243 B6
Ostrava Czech Republic
267 E5
Otranto, Strait of 275 E7
Ottawa Canada 209 E7
Ou Mts. Japan 340 F3
Ouagadougou Burkina
297 E5
Ouargla Algeria 295 E3
Oujda Morocco 295 E2
Oulu Finland 248 F4
Outer Hebrides UK 252 D2
Oviedo Spain 258 D2
Oxnard USA 221 D8
Ozark Plateau USA 217 H6

P
Pacific Ocean 206/
340–341/347/352–353
Padang Indonesia 346 B6
Padua Italy 262 D3
Painted Desert USA
219 E4
Pakistan (Country)
332–333
Pakokku Burma 344 B4
Pakxé Laos 345 F5
Palau (I.) USA 352 D4
Palawan (I.) Philippines
347 E3
Palembang Indonesia
346 B7
Palermo Sicily Italy 263 E7
Palma de Mallorca
Majorca 259 H5
Palmer Land Antarctica
364 B4
Palu Indonesia 347 E6
Pamirs (Mts.) Tajikistan
325 G4

Pamplona Spain 259 F2
Pamukkale Turkey 318 D5
Pančevo Yugoslavia 274 F4
Panaji India 333 E6
Panama (Country) 230 D7
Panama Canal Panama
230 D7
Panama City Panama
230 D7/361 B5/353 H4
Panay (I.) Philippines
347 E3
Panevėžys Lithuania
283 D5
Papua New Guinea
(Country) 355 G2
Paraguay (Country) 242 D3
Paraguay (R.) Paraguay
242 E3
Paramaribo Surinam
256 G4
Paraná (R.) S. America 241
E6/243 D5
Paraná Argentina 242 D4
Paris France 261 E3
Paros (I.) Greece 279 F6
Pasadena USA 219 H6/
221 D8
Patagonia Argentina
243 C7
Paterson USA 211 F6
Patna India 333 F4
Patrai, Gulf of Greece
278 D5
Peč Yugoslavia 275 F5
Pécs Hungary 267 E7
Pegu Burma 345 C5
Peipus, Lake Estonia
282 E3
Peking China 338 E3
Pelagie Is. Italy 263 D8
Peloponne Greece 278 D5
Pennines UK 253 F5
Pennsylvania (State) USA
210 D6

Penza Rus. Fed. 285 C6/ 326 C5
Peoria USA 215 E6
Perm' Rus. Fed. 285 E5/ 326 D5
Persian Gulf 362 D3/ 321 F4
Perth Australia 354 B6
Peru (Country) 237 B6
Peshawar Pakistan 333 E1
Petra Jordan 317 C6
Petropavlovsk-Kamchatskiy Rus. Fed. 327 H4
Philadelphia USA 211 E7
Philae Egypt 300 D4
Philippines (Country) 347
Phnom Penh Cambodia 345 F6
Phoenix USA 218 D5
Phuket (I.) Thailand 345 C7
Piatra-Neamţ Romania 276 F3
Pierre USA 217 F3
Pietermaritzburg South Africa 311 F7
Pilcomayo (R.) Bolivia/ Paraguay 242 D3
Pinang Malaysia 345 D7
Pindus Mts. Greece 278 D3
Pinsk Belorussia 283 D7
Piraeus Greece 279 E5
Pitcairn Is. UK 353 F5
Piteşti Romania 276 E4
Pittsburgh USA 210 D6
Piura Peru 237 A5
Plate (R.) Argentina/ Uruguay 243 E5
Pleven Bulgaria 277 D5
Ploieşti Romania 276 E4
Plovdiv Bulgaria 277 D6
Plymouth UK 253 E7

Plzeō Czech Republic 267 B5
Po (R.) Italy 262 D3
Podgorica Yugoslavia 275 E6
Podlasie Poland 266 G3
Pointe-Noire Congo 305 C7
Poitiers France 260 D3
Poland (Country) 266–267
Polynesia Pacific Ocean 353 F3
Pontianak Indonesia 346 C6
Port Elizabeth South Africa 311 D7
Port Harcourt Nigeria 297 F7
Port Louis Mauritius 363 D6
Port Moresby Papua New Guinea 355 G2
Port of Spain Trinidad 231 H8
Port Said Egypt 360 H4/ 300 D3/362 B3
Port Sudan Sudan 301 E5
Port-au-Prince Haiti 231 F5
Port-Gentil Gabon 305 B6
Portland USA 220 B3
Pôrto Alegre Brazil 241 E7
Porto Portugal 258 C3
Porto-Novo Benin 297 F7
Portugal (Country) 258
Posadas Argentina 242 E4
Potsdam Germany 268 G4
Powell, Lake USA 219 E3
Poza Rica Mexico 223 F6
Poznań Poland 266 D4
Prague Czech Republic 267 B5
Prespa, Lake S.E. Europe 275 G7

Pretoria South Africa 311 E6
Priština Yugoslavia 275 G6
Prince Edward I. (Province) Canada 209 F6
Prince of Wales I. Canada 207 F3
Prome Burma 344 B4
Provence France 261 G7
Providence USA 211 F5
Prudhoe Bay Alaska USA 206 D3
Pskov Rus. Fed. 326 C3
Puebla Mexico 223 F6
Puerto Montt Chile 243 B6
Puerto Rico USA 231 G5
Puerto Santa Cruz Argentina 243 D8
Pune India 333 E5
Punta Arenas Chile 243 C8
Purus (R.) Brazil/Peru 240 C4
Pusan South Korea 338 H3
Putorana Mts. Rus. Fed. 327 E4
Pyinmana Burma 344 C4
Pyongyang North Korea 338 G3
Pyrénées (Mts.) S.W. Europe 259 G2/260 D8

Q
Qandahār Afghanistan 325 E7
Qatar (Country) 321 F5
Qena Egypt 300 D4
Qinghai China 337 E6
Qiqihar China 338 F2
Qondūz (R.) Afghanistan 325 F5

Québec (Province) Canada 209 E5
Queensland (State) Australia 355 F4
Qui Nhon Vietnam 345 G5
Quito Ecuador 237 A5

R

Rabat Morocco 294 D2
Rach Gia Vietnam 345 F6
Rajkot India 332 D4
Rajshahi Bangladesh 333 G4
Raleigh USA 213 G3
Ranchi India 333 F4
Rangoon Burma 362 F4/345 C5
Rasht Iran 321 F2
Rat Buri Thailand 345 D5
Rawalpindi Pakistan 333 E1
Recife Brazil 241 H5
Red (R.) China/Vietnam 344 E3
Red Sea 300 E4/362 C3/320 D5
Redding USA 221 B5
Regina Canada 207 F8
Reno USA 218 C2
Resistencia Argentina 242 E4
Reşiţa Romania 276 B4
Reykavik Iceland 360 E3
Rheims France 261 F2
Rhine (R.) W. Europe 254 F4/268 C7/270 C4
Rhode I. (State) USA 211 G5
Rhodes (I.) Greece 279 H7
Rhône (R.) W. Europe 261 F6/270 B6
Richmond USA 213 G2

Riga Latvia 282 D4
Riga, Gulf of Estonia/ Latvia 282 D4
Rîmnicu Vîlcea Romania 276 D4
Río Cuarto Argentina 245 C5
Rio de Janeiro Brazil 241 G6/360 D6
Río Grande (R.) Mexico 223 F3
Rio Grande USA 219 F6
Riverside USA 221 D8
Rivne Ukraine 286 C3
Riyadh Saudi Arabia 321 E5
Roanoke USA 215 G2
Rochester USA 211 E4
Rockford USA 215 E5
Rocky Mts. N. America 206 D6/219 E4
Romania (Country) 276
Rome Italy 263 D5
Rosario Argentina 243 D5
Rostock (Germany) 268 F3
Rostov-na-Donu Rus. Fed. 285 B6/326 B5
Rotterdam Netherlands 360 F4/254 D4
Rouen France 261 E2
Rovuma (R.) C. Africa 310 H4
Rub' al Khali Saudi Arabia 321 E7
Ruse Bulgaria 277 E5
Russian Federation (Country) 283 B5/ 284–285/ 326– 327
Rwanda (Country) 302 D4
Ryazan' Rus. Fed. 285 C5/ 326 C4

S

Saarbrücken Germany 269 C6
Sabah Malaysia 346 D5
Sabhã Libya 295 G4
Sacramento USA 221 B6
Sagaing Burma 344 C3
Sahara (Desert) N. Africa 294–295/296– 297
Sahel West Africa 297 E5
Sakhalin (I.) Rus. Fed. 326 H5
Salem USA 220 B4
Salt Lake City USA 218 D2
Salta Paraguay 242 C3
Salton Sea USA 221 E8
Salvador Brazil 241 H5
Salween (R.) Burma/ China 337 E7/339 B5/ 344 C4
Salzburg Austria 271 F3
Samar (I.) Philippines 347 F3
Samara Rus. Fed. 285 D6/ 326 C5
Samarinda Indonesia 346 D6
Samarkand Uzbekistan 325 E4
Sambre (R.) Belgium/ France 255 D6
Samos (I.) Greece 279 G5
Samsun Turkey 319 F3
San'a Yemen 321 E8
San Antonio USA 219 G7
San Bernardo Chile 243 B5
San Diego USA 221 D8
San Francisco USA 221 B6
San José Costa Rica 230 C7
San Jose USA 221 B7
San Juan Puerto Rico 231 G5
San Luis Potosí Mexico 223 F5

Smederevo Yugoslavia 274 G4

Smolensk Rus. Fed. 326 C4

Socotra (I.) Yemen 362 D4

Sofia Bulgaria 277 C6

Sohâg Egypt 300 C4

Solomon Is. (Country) 352 D5

Somalia (Country) 301

Songkhla Thailand 345 D7

Sosnowiec Poland 267 E5

South Africa (Country) 311

South Australia (State) Australia 355 E5

South Carolina (State) USA 213 F4

South China Sea S.E. Asia 362 G4/359 E6/ 345 G6/346 C4

South Dakota (State) USA 217 F3

South Georgia (I.) UK 361 D7

South I. NZ 357 D7

South Korea (Country) 338 H3

South Pole Antarctica 364 C5

South Sandwich Is. UK 361 E7

Southampton I. Canada 207 G5

Southern Alps (Mts.) NZ 357 C6

Southern Ocean 352–353

Soweto South Africa 311 E6

Spain (Country) 258–259

Spitsbergen (I.) Norway 365 G7

Split Croatia 275 C5

Sporades (Is.) Greece 279 E3

Springfield USA 211 F5/ 215 E7/217 H6

Sri Lanka (Country) 362 E4/353 F8

Srinagar India 333 E1

St. Étienne France 261 F5

St. Helena (I.) UK 361 E6

St. John's Canada 209 H5

St. Kitts and Nevis (Country) 231 H6

St. Lawrence (R.) Canada 209 F6

St. Lawrence Seaway Canada 209 E7/360 B4

St. Lawrence, Gulf of Canada 209 F5

St. Louis USA 217 H5

St. Lucia (Country) 231 H7

St. Paul USA 214 D4

St. Petersburg Rus. Fed. 284 B4/326 C3

St. Petersburg USA 213 F7

St. Pierre & Miquelon France 209 G6

St. Polten Austria 271 G2

St. Vincent and The Grenadines (Country) 231 H7

Stara Zagora Bulgaria 277 E6

Stewart I. NZ 357 B8

Stockholm Sweden 249 D6

Stockton USA 221 C6

Stony Tunguska Rus. Fed. 327 F5

Strasbourg France 261 G2

Stromboli (I.) Italy 265 F7

Stuttgart Germany 269 D6

Suceava Romania 276 E2

Sucre Bolivia 237 E8

Sudan (Country) 301

Sudbury Canada 208 D7

Sudeten Mts. Czech Republic/Poland 266 D5

Suez Canal Egypt 362 B3

Suez, Gulf of S.W. Asia 300 D3

Sula Is. Indonesia 347 F6

Sulu Archipelago (Is.) Philippines 347 E4

Sumatra (I.) Indonesia 363 G5/346 B6

Sumba (I.) Indonesia 347 E8

Sumbawa (I.) Indonesia 347 E8

Sumy Ukraine 287 E3

Superior, Lake Canada/ USA 208 C6/215 F2

Surabaya Indonesia 346 D8

Surat India 333 E5

Surinam (Country) 236 G4

Svalbard (Is.) Norway 365 G5

Swaziland (Country) 311 F6

Sweden (Country) 248–249

Switzerland (Country) 270

Sydney Australia 352 D6/ 355 F6

Syracuse USA 211 E4

Syria (Country) 316

Syrian Desert Middle East 317 E5/321 E3

T

Tabora Tanzania 303 E5

Tacloban Philippines 347 F3

Tacna Peru 237 C7

Tacoma USA 220 B3

Taegu South Korea 338 H3

Tagus (R.) Spain 258 D3

Tahiti (I.) France 353 F5

Tahoe, Lake USA 218 C2/ 221 C6

Taipei Taiwan 339 G5

Taiping Malaysia 345 D8
Taiwan (Country) 339 G5
Taiwan Strait 359 F5
Taiyuan China 338 E3
Talcahuano Chile 243 B6
Tallahassee USA 213 E5
Tallinn Estonia 282 D3
Tamanrasset Algeria 295 E6
Tampa USA 213 F7
Tampere Finland 249 F5
Tanganyika, Lake C. Africa 305 H7/303 D5
Tanggula Mts. China 336 D6
Tangier Morocco 294 D2
Tangshan China 338 F3
Tanjungkarang Indonesia 346 C7
Tanzania (Country) 302–303
Tapachula Mexico 223 G8
Tapajós (R.) Brazil 240 D4
Taranto Italy 265 G6
Tartu Estonia 282 E3
Tashauz Turkmenistan 324 D3
Tashkent Uzbekistan 325 F3
Tasman Sea 352 D6/ 355 F7/357 E4
Tasmania (State) Australia 355 E7
Taunggyi Burma 344 C4
Taupo, Lake NZ 356 F4
Taurus Mts. Turkey 319 E6
Tavoy Burma 345 C5
Tbilisi Georgia 287 G7
Tegucigalpa Honduras 230 B5
Tehran Iran 321 G2
Tel Aviv-Yafo Israel 317 C5
Temuco Chile 243 B6

Tennessee (R.) USA 213 E2
Tennessee (State) USA 213 E3
Teresina Brazil 240 G4
Ternopil' Ukraine 286 C3
Tetovo Macedonia 275 G6
Texas (State) USA 219 G6
Thai Nguyen Vietnam 344 F4
Thailand (Country) 344–345
Thames (R.) UK 253 F7
Thane India 333 E5
Thanh Hoa Vietnam 344 F4
Thaton Burma 345 C5
Thessaloniki Greece 279 E2
Thimphu Bhutan 333 G3
Thule Greenland 365 F6
Thunder Bay Canada 208 C6
Tibetan Autonomous Region China 336 C6
Tientsin China 338 E3
Tierra del Fuego (I.) Argentina/Chile 243 D8
Tigris (R.) S.W. Asia 319 G5/316 H2/321 E2
Tijuana Mexico 222 C1
Timbuktu Mali 297 E4
Timmins Canada 208 D6
Timor (I.) Indonesia 347 F8
Tirana Albania 275 G6
Tîrgovşte Romania 276 E4
Tîrgu Mureş 276 D3
Tobago (I.) 231 H8
Togo (Country) 297 E6
Tokelau (Is.) NZ 353 E5
Tokyo Japan 341 F5
Toledo Spain 259 E5
Toledo USA 215 G5

Tol'yatti Rus. Fed. 285 D6/ 326 C5
Tomsk Rus. Fed. 327 E6
Tonga (Country) 353 E5
Tongking, Gulf of China/ Vietnam 339 D6/ 344 G4
Topeka USA 217 G5
Toronto Canada 208 D7
Toulouse France 261 E7
Trabzon Turkey 319 G3
Transantarctic Mts. Antarctica 364 C5
Trenton USA 211 E6
Trieste Italy 262 E3
Trinidad (I.) 231 H8
Trinidad and Tobago (Country) 231 H8
Tripoli Lebanon 316 D4
Tripoli Libya 295 F3
Tristan da Cunha (I.) UK 361 F7
Trondheim Norway 249 C5
Trujillo Peru 237 A6
Tselinograd Kazakhstan 326 D6
Tuamotu Archipelago (Is.) France 353 F5
Tucson USA 218 D5
Tulsa USA 217 G6
Tunis Tunisia 295 F2
Tunisia (Country) 295 F3
Turin Italy 262 B3
Turk and Caicos Is. UK 231 F4
Turkana, Lake Ethiopia/ Kenya 301 E7/302 F3
Turkey (Country) 318–319
Turkmenistan (Country) 324–325
Turku Finland 249 F6
Tuvalu (Country) 353 E5
Tuzla Bosnia & Herzegovina 274 E4

U

Ubon Ratchathani
Thailand 345 F5

Udon Thani Thailand
345 E5

Ufa Rus. Fed. 285 E6/326 C5

Uganda (Country) 302

Ujung Pandang Indonesia
347 E7

Ukraine (Country) 286–287

Ulan Bator Mongolia
337 F3

Ulan-Ude Rus. Fed. 327 F6

United Arab Emirates
(Country) 321 F6

United Kingdom
(Country) 252– 253

United States of America
(Country) 206– 221

Uppsala Sweden 249 D6

Ural Mts. Rus. Fed.
285 F5/326

Ural'sk Rus. Fed. 326 C5

Urgench Uzbekistan
324 D3

Uroševac Yugoslavia 275 G6

Uruguay (Country)
242–243

Ürümqi China 336 D4

Utah (State) USA 218 D2

Utrecht Netherlands 254 E4

Uvira Zaire 305 G6

Uzbekistan (Country)
324– 325

V

Vaasa Finland 249 E5

Vadodara India 333 E4

Vaduz Liechtenstein
270 D5

Valdivia Chile 243 B6

Valencia Spain 259 F5

Valencia Venezuela 236 D3

Valladolid Spain 259 F3

Valletta Malta 263 F8

Valparáiso Chile 243 B5/
353 H6

Van Turkey 318 H5

Vanadzor Armenia 287 G7

Vancouver Canada 206 D8/
353 F2

Vancouver I. Canada
206 D8

Vaner, Lake Sweden
249 C6

Vanuatu (Country) 352 D5

Varanasi India 333 F4

Vardar (R.) Greece/
Macedonia 275 H6

Varna Bulgaria 277 G6

Västerås Sweden 249 D6

Vatican City (Vatican City
State) Italy 263 D5

Vatter, Lake Sweden
249 C6

Venezuela (Country)
236 D3

Venezuela, Gulf of 236 D3

Venice Italy 262 D3

Venice, Gulf of Italy 262 E3

Verkhoyansk Range
(Mts.) Rus. Fed.
327 G4

Vermont (State) USA
211 F4

Verona Italy 262 D3

Victoria Canada 206 D8

Victoria Seychelles 362 D5

Victoria Falls Zambia
303 B7

Victoria Falls Zambia/
Zimbabwe 311 E5

Victoria I. Canada 207 E4

Victoria, Lake E. Africa
302 E4

Vienna Austria 271 H2

Vientiane Laos 344 E4

Viet Tri Vietnam 344 F4

Vietnam (Country)
344– 345

Vijayawada India 333 F6

Villahermosa Mexico
225 G7

Villavicencio Colombia
236 B4

Vilnius Lithuania 283 D5

Viña del Mar Chile 243 B5

Vinh Vietnam 344 F4

Vinnytsya Ukraine 286 D3

Virgin Is. US 231 G5

Virginia (State) USA
213 G2

Vishakhapatnam India
333 F5

Vistula (R.) Poland 266 F4

Vitoria Spain 259 F2

Vitsyebsk N.E. Europe
283 G5

Vladivostok Rus. Fed.
327 H7

Vlorë Albania 275 E7

Volga (R.) Rus. Fed. 285 D6

Volgograd Rus. Fed.
285 C6/326 C5

Volta, Lake Ghana 297 E7

Vorkuta Russia 284 G4

Voronezh Rus. Fed. 285
B6/326 C5

W

Wabash (R.) USA 215 F6

Waco USA 219 G6

Wad Medani Sudan 301 D5

Waddenzee Netherlands
254 E2

Wairau (R.) NZ 357 E5

Wales UK 253

Walla Walla USA 220 D3

Wallis & Futuna (Is.)
France 353 E5

Index

Acknowledgements

PAGEOne and Dorling Kindersley would like to thank:

Christiane Gunzi for editorial assistance; Sarah Watson for general assistance; Thomas Keenes for design assistance; Hilary Bird for the index; Gordon Models, Peter Griffiths, and John Holmes for model making; Ashmolean Museum; Beaulieu Motor Museum; The British Library; Capotine Museum; Ermine Street Guard Museum; Louisiana State Museum; Musée du Louvre; Museum of London; Museum of Mankind; Museum of the Moving Image; Museum of Natural History; National Railway Museum; Pitt Rivers Museum; Royal Academy of Arts; The Science Museum, London; Uffizi, Florence; University Museum of Archaeology and Anthropology, Cambridge.

Photographs by:

Geoff Brightling, Jane Burton, P. Chadwell, Peter Chadwick, Andy Crawford, Geoff Dann, Philip Dowell, Mike Dunning, Neil Fletcher, Philip Gatward, Steve Gorton, Frank Greenaway, Colin Keates, Gary Kevin, Dave King, Nick Nicholls, Andrew McRobb, Ray Moller, Stephen Oliver, Roger Phillips, Tim Ridley, Karl Shone, James Stevenson, Clive Streeter, Kim Taylor, Andreas Von Einsiedel, Matthew Ward, Jerry Young, Christian Zuber.

Illustrations by:

Evi Antoniou, Rick Blakely, Peter Bull, Mike Courtney, John Crawford Fraser, Bill Donohoe, Simone End, Eugene Fleury, Giuliano Fornari, Ann George-Marsh, Jeremy Gower, Elizabeth Gray, Andrew Green, Ray Grinaway, Nick Hewetson, Dave Hopkins, Aziz Khan, Jason Lewis, Stuart Mackay, Judith Maguire, Janos Marffy, Kevin Marks, Angus Mcbride, Sean Milne, Sergio, Colin Salmon, Michael Saunders, Rodney Shackell, Rob Shone, Clive Spong, Roger Stewart, John Temperton, Pete Visscher, Richard Ward, John Woodcock, Dan Wright.

Picture credits:

a = above, b = below, l = left, t = top
The publisher would like to thank the following for their kind permission to reproduce the photographs:

Aardman Animations 403bl; Action Plus/Glyn Kirk 412ac; AKG, London, 349acl; AKG, Berlin, 442bcr; Ancient Art and Architecture 437tc; Directed and produced by Animation City/A.C. Live 402cl; Audi 185br; Austin Brown and The Aviation Picture Library 197br; Biology Media 142cl; Bettmann Archive 443br; Bridgeman Art Library/Glraudon 389acl; Museum of Mankind 370bc; Museum of Natural History, London, 99br; The British Museum 371tr, 371ac, 376ar, 376bl, 376br, 377acl, 377acr,

377br, 378al, 378acl, 378br, 379ac, 427ar, 428br, 430tc, 439cl; Camera Press/Ian Stone 460ac; Carolco 1991, courtesy of Kobal collection 402tr; J. Allan Cash 430cr; Christie's Colour Library 313br; Bruce Coleman Ltd/Jeff Foott Productions 224cl; Christian Zuber 307tr; Colorsport © Duono; David Madlen 404bl; Comstock 432ar; James Davis 375bl; et archive 427acl, 434tr, 436al, 437cr, 439br, 452ac; Mary Evans Picture Library 69ac, 370tr, 375bc, 375br, 380tr, 397bcl; The British Library 372cl, 446acl, 446acr, 449br, 454bc; Exeter Maritime Museum 190acr, 190bcl; Fiat 185bcl, Gilbert and George, courtesy of Anthony d'Offay Gallery, London, 389br; Ronald Grant Archive 396bl, 403cr; Sonia Halliday 371br; Robert Harding Picture Library 181tr, 423bcl, 436bl, 439tr, 444bc; Michael Holford 377ar, 429acl, 432br, 434bc; Hulton-Getty Picture Collection 380cr; Robert Hunt Library 454acl; Hutchison Library, 373br, 374bl; J.G. Fuller 235bl; Image Bank/Kaz Mori 66-67; Image Select 395tcl, 399tcl, 444tcl; Ann Ronan 394cr; Simon James 377bl; David King 380cl; Kobal Collection 403bc; Magnum/ Cagnoni 460cl; Mander & Mitcheson 397cr; Museum of the Moving Image/ © Academy of Motion Picture Arts and Sciences R 3br, 403br; Nasa 5al, 32bcl, 32bcr, 36acr, 36bcr, 37cl, 37tcr, 37br, 461bc; National Maritime Museum, 190bcr, 190b, 193br, 440acr; Peter Newark Pictures 435c, 451cr; Oxford Scientific Films/Root; Okapia 111cl; Ann and Bury Peerless, 372bc, 374acr; Photostage/Donald Cooper 397br; Popperfoto 456ac, 457bc, 459acr; Press Association 380bcl; Redferns 395br; Renault 185bl; Rex features 381tl; 461cl, 462ar; Cheryl Hatch, Sipa Press, 463acr; Coll. Privé, Sipa 457tl; Setbon, Sipa Press 462c; Royal Geographical Society/Paul Harris 288ac, jacket spine bcr; The Royal Ballet School 396bcl, 396acr; Scala 371bcl, 377tl; Biblioteca Nazionale Centrale, Florence 438bc; Science Photo Library/Biology Media 142cl; Chris Bjornberg 12-13; Jeremy Burgess 84tr; Cern 149tl; CNRI 79bcl; Tony Hallas 16tr; Adam Jones 38-39; James King-Holmes 171br; Thomas Ligon 198-99; Lawrence Migdale 171cr; Prof. P. Motta, Dept. of Anatomy, University Lasapienza, Rome 114-115; Professors P.M. Motta, K.R Porter & P.M Andrews 123tr; NOAO 32bc; Novostl 36cl, 329bl; Omikron 128tr; David Parker 171tr; John Sanford 32ar; David Sharfe 133cr; Simon Terrey 146tr; Sporting Pictures (UK) Ltd 156tr, 187tc, 189tc, 404bcr, 413tl, 413tr; Tony Stone Images/Tony Craddock 257tr; Sepp Dietrich 273br, Ian Murphy 396br; Hugh Sitton 306cl; Suzuki/Farquhar PR 185bcr; Warner Brothers/courtesy Kobal Collection 403cl; Werner Forman Archives 370acl, 396tl, 420-421, 428cl; Jerry Young 103br, Michael Zabé 441bc; Zefa Pictures 379bl, 464-465; Ian Bradshaw 368-369; Stockmarket 322c; Krebs 176-177.

Every effort has been made to trace the copyright holders and we apologise in advance for any unintentional omissions. We would be pleased to insert the appropriate acknowledgement in any subsequent edition of this publication.